MEDITATIONS ON THE INCARNATION, PASSION, AND DEATH OF JESUS CHRIST

A Series Edited by Margaret L. King and Albert Rabil Jr.

RECENT BOOKS IN THE SERIES

MADELEINE DE L'AUBESPINE
Selected Poems and Translations: A Bilingual Edition
Edited and Translated by Anna Kłosowska

PRINCESS ELISABETH OF BOHEMIA AND RENÉ DESCARTES
The Correspondence between Princess Elisabeth of Bohemia and René Descartes
Edited and Translated by Lisa Shapiro

MODERATA FONTE (MODESTA POZZO)
Floridoro: A Chivalric Romance
Edited with an Introduction by Valeria Finucci, Translated by Julia Kisacky, Annotated by Valeria Finucci and Julia Kisacky

MARÍA DE GUEVARA
Warnings to the Kings and Advice on Restoring Spain: A Bilingual Edition
Edited and Translated by Nieves Romero-Díaz

LOUISE LABÉ
Complete Poetry and Prose: A Bilingual Edition
Edited with Introductions and Prose Translations by Deborah Lesko Baker, with Poetry Translations by Annie Finch

HORTENSE MANCINI AND MARIE MANCINI
Memoirs
Edited and Translated by Sarah Nelson

MARGUERITE DE NAVARRE
Selected Writings: A Bilingual Edition
Edited and Translated by Rouben Cholakian and Mary Skemp

CHIARA MATRAINI
Selected Poetry and Prose: A Bilingual Edition
Edited and Translated by Elaine Maclachlan, with an Introduction by Giovanni Rabitti

ANA DE SAN BARTOLOMÉ
Autobiography and Other Writings
Edited and Translated by Darcy Donahue

MARGHERITA SARROCCHI
Scanderbeide: The Heroic Deeds of George Scanderbeg, King of Epirus
Edited and Translated by Rinaldina Russell

JUSTINE SIEGEMUND
The Court Midwife
Edited and Translated by Lynne Tatlock

MARÍA DE ZAYAS Y SOTOMAYOR
Exemplary Tales of Love and Tales of Disillusion
Edited and Translated by Margaret R. Greer and Elizabeth Rhodes

Catharina Regina von Greiffenberg

MEDITATIONS ON THE INCARNATION, PASSION, AND DEATH OF JESUS CHRIST

Edited and Translated by Lynne Tatlock

THE UNIVERSITY OF CHICAGO PRESS
Chicago & London

Catharina Regina von Greiffenberg, 1633–94

Lynne Tatlock is the Hortense and Tobias Lewin Distinguished Professor in the Humanities in the Department of Germanic Languages and Literatures at Washington University in St. Louis. Among her publications is a translation of Justine Siegemund's *The Court Midwife,* published in 2005 in the Other Voice in Early Modern Europe series by the University of Chicago Press.

The University of Chicago Press, Chicago 60637
The University of Chicago Press, Ltd., London

Printed in the United States of America
18 17 16 15 14 13 12 11 10 09 1 2 3 4 5
ISBN-13: 978-0-226-86487-7 (cloth)
ISBN-13: 978-0-226-86489-1 (paper)
ISBN-10: 0-226-86487-1 (cloth)
ISBN-10: 0-226-86489-8 (paper)

The University of Chicago Press gratefully acknowledges the generous support of James E. Rabil, in memory of Scottie W. Rabil, toward the publication of this book.

Library of Congress Cataloging-in-Publication Data
Greiffenberg, Catharina Regina von, 1633–1694.
[Andächtigen Betrachtungen. English]
Meditations on the incarnation, passion, and death of Jesus Christ /
Catharina Regina von Greiffenberg ; edited and translated by Lynne Tatlock.
p. cm. — (The Other voice in early modern Europe)
Includes bibliographical references and index.
ISBN-13: 978-0-226-86487-7 (cloth : alk. paper)
ISBN-13: 978-0-226-86489-1 (pbk. : alk. paper)
ISBN-10: 0-226-86487-1 (cloth : alk. paper)
ISBN-10: 0-226-86489-8 (pbk. : alk. paper) 1. Jesus Christ—Passions—Meditations. 2. Jesus Christ—Crucifixion—Meditations. 3. Incarnation—Meditations. I. Tatlock, Lynne, 1950– II. Title. III. Series: Other voice in early modern Europe.
BT430.G7413 2009
232—dc22 2008046573

♾ The paper used in this publication meets the minimum requirements of the American National Standard for Information Sciences—Permanence of Paper for Printed Library Materials, ANSI Z39.48-1992.

For Joe

CONTENTS

ACKNOWLEDGMENTS

To assert the difficulty of finding English words for a writer who believed so utterly in the redemptive power of her own voice is to indulge in understatement. I could not have found these words without help, and I have been fortunate in my friends and colleagues who have responded to my requests for assistance with patience and generosity.

I have pestered many people about obscure words and references and am indebted to them for their readiness to bring their expertise to bear on my questions. I especially thank Renate Schmidt and Gerhild Scholz Williams for their enduring willingness to discuss difficult passages with me. Alexander Schwarz, David Steinmetz, Robert Kolb, Mara Wade, Cornelia Moore, James F. Poag, and Emily Davis also responded readily and kindly to my requests for aid. Paula V. Mehmel, whom I have frequently cited in the notes, in particular deserves thanks for her unflagging engagement and eagerness to answer my many queries about Lutheran theology and biblical passages. Paula was once my student; while working on this translation, I felt that the tables had been neatly turned. I was lucky to be working in the age of the Internet and to have nearly instantaneous connection to her in far-off North Dakota where she ministers to her parishioners.

I recall with gratitude a delightful afternoon in March 2007 at Jesuit House in St. Louis when Carl Starkloff, SJ (1933–2008), cleared up some of my most nagging questions about Greiffenberg's theological vocabulary and brought into focus the theology of the cross. I am also much obliged to Karl F. Otto Jr. for perusing the original German of the poetry included in the translation and for answering my questions about the verse forms that Greiffenberg employs. Walton Schalick again proved willing to advise me concerning early modern medical vocabulary and to suggest avenues to explore for deciphering the language that Greiffenberg uses to describe the intrauterine Christ.

I would like to express special appreciation to the Herzog August Bibliothek in Wolfenbüttel, Germany, for making it so easy for me to work efficiently in repeated short-term study visits and for providing illustrations for this volume. I am beholden, too, to Jill Bepler, Head of Programs and Scholarships at the Herzog August Bibliothek, for her encouragement of my work on Greiffenberg and for seeing to it that I was—and am—always accommodated in Wolfenbüttel.

I thank Laurie Klein, Public Services Assistant of the Beinecke Rare Book and Manuscript Library at Yale University, as well for her expeditious assistance in procuring illustrations for this translation. The Rare Book and Manuscript Library of Nicholas Murray Butler Library at Columbia University kindly provided access to a unique edition in the United States of the Elector's Bible.

A collaborative research grant from the National Endowment for the Humanities that was awarded to several projects in the Other Voice series helped finance the cost of my travel to Germany as well as research and other expenses involved in producing the present volume. A significant portion of the work on this project took place during my semester at Rutgers University as the Charlotte M. Craig Distinguished Visiting Professor in the Department of Germanic, Russian, and East European Languages and Literatures. Charlotte M. Craig, Martha Helfer, Fatima Naqvi, Nicholas Rennie, and the undergraduate and graduate students at Rutgers made this time stimulating and fruitful for me.

I am indebted to the series editors, Margaret L. King and Albert Rabil Jr., for their decision to expand The Other Voice series to include German-speaking women and to Randolph Petilos for patiently and judiciously shepherding the project through the process of review and production. I also thank Susan Tarcov for her expert copy editing, and Randy's colleagues at the University of Chicago Press, Maia Rigas, Natalie Smith, Chezin Lee, Joan Ellen Davies, and Lindsay Dawson, for their hard work and their guidance through the publication process.

To translate is inevitably to make mistakes that are difficult for one to catch oneself. I therefore enlisted the aid of a number of graduate students in Germanic Languages and Literatures at Washington University in checking the translation against the original for inadvertent omissions and misreadings, and in otherwise proofreading the manuscript in progress. Mary LeGierse in particular deserves thanks for meticulously comparing large chunks of the translation in one of its earliest and very rough drafts to the original German. Necia Chronister, Nancy Richardson, Magdalen R. Stanley, and Faruk Pašić provided welcome editorial assistance in later stages of production. I am grateful to the Graduate School of Arts and Sciences and the Department of Germanic Languages and Literatures at Washington University for funding these student research assistants. I, furthermore, thank Albert Rabil for his discerning eye, and also the anonymous reader for the University of Chicago Press for useful suggestions in preparing the final version of the manuscript for copyediting.

In addition to the friends and colleagues mentioned above, I would like to express my gratitude to my friends and colleagues Michael Sherberg and Jana Mikota for patiently listening to my worries about the progress of the translation and for showing interest in this project even though it is a bit distant from their own scholarly passions. I am ever grateful to my teacher and dissertation director, Hugh Powell, who long ago introduced me to the meditations of Catharina Regina von Greiffenberg. Little did he or I suspect that I would ever spend extended time with them.

Finally, I would like to thank my husband, Joseph F. Loewenstein, who, with this project, as with nearly everything I do, had more confidence in me than I at times did in myself. In his own scholarly work, he reminds me repeatedly of the power of the imagination and study, and the need for humility to bridge the centuries that separate us from early modern writers. In appreciation and gratitude, I dedicate this volume to him.

Lynne Tatlock

THE OTHER VOICE IN EARLY MODERN EUROPE: INTRODUCTION TO THE SERIES

Margaret L. King and Albert Rabil Jr.

THE OLD VOICE AND THE OTHER VOICE

In western Europe and the United States, women are nearing equality in the professions, in business, and in politics. Most enjoy access to education, reproductive rights, and autonomy in financial affairs. Issues vital to women are on the public agenda: equal pay, child care, domestic abuse, breast cancer research, and curricular revision with an eye to the inclusion of women.

These recent achievements have their origins in things women (and some male supporters) said for the first time about six hundred years ago. Theirs is the "other voice," in contradistinction to the "first voice," the voice of the educated men who created Western culture. Coincident with a general reshaping of European culture in the period 1300–1700 (called the Renaissance or early modern period), questions of female equality and opportunity were raised that still resound and are still unresolved.

The other voice emerged against the backdrop of a three-thousand-year history of the derogation of women rooted in the civilizations related to Western culture: Hebrew, Greek, Roman, and Christian. Negative attitudes toward women inherited from these traditions pervaded the intellectual, medical, legal, religious, and social systems that developed during the European Middle Ages.

The following pages describe the traditional, overwhelmingly male views of women's nature inherited by early modern Europeans and the new tradition that the "other voice" called into being to begin to challenge reigning assumptions. This review should serve as a framework for understanding the texts published in the series the Other Voice in Early Modern Europe. Introductions specific to each text and author follow this essay in all the volumes of the series.

TRADITIONAL VIEWS OF WOMEN, 500 B.C.E.–1500 C.E.

Embedded in the philosophical and medical theories of the ancient Greeks were perceptions of the female as inferior to the male in both mind and body. Similarly, the structure of civil legislation inherited from the ancient Romans was biased against women, and the views on women developed by Christian thinkers out of the Hebrew Bible and the Christian New Testament were negative and disabling. Literary works composed in the vernacular of ordinary people, and widely recited or read, conveyed these negative assumptions. The social networks within which most women lived—those of the family and the institutions of the Roman Catholic Church—were shaped by this negative tradition and sharply limited the areas in which women might act in and upon the world.

GREEK PHILOSOPHY AND FEMALE NATURE. Greek biology assumed that women were inferior to men and defined them as merely childbearers and housekeepers. This view was authoritatively expressed in the works of the philosopher Aristotle.

Aristotle thought in dualities. He considered action superior to inaction, form (the inner design or structure of any object) superior to matter, completion to incompletion, possession to deprivation. In each of these dualities, he associated the male principle with the superior quality and the female with the inferior. "The male principle in nature," he argued, "is associated with active, formative and perfected characteristics, while the female is passive, material and deprived, desiring the male in order to become complete."[1] Men are always identified with virile qualities, such as judgment, courage, and stamina, and women with their opposites—irrationality, cowardice, and weakness.

The masculine principle was considered superior even in the womb. The man's semen, Aristotle believed, created the form of a new human creature, while the female body contributed only matter. (The existence of the ovum, and with it the other facts of human embryology, was not established until the seventeenth century.) Although the later Greek physician Galen believed there was a female component in generation, contributed by "female semen," the followers of both Aristotle and Galen saw the male role in human generation as more active and more important.

In the Aristotelian view, the male principle sought always to reproduce

1. Aristotle, *Physics* 1.9.192a20–24, in *The Complete Works of Aristotle,* ed. Jonathan Barnes, rev. Oxford trans., 2 vols. (Princeton, 1984), 1:328.

itself. The creation of a female was always a mistake, therefore, resulting from an imperfect act of generation. Every female born was considered a "defective" or "mutilated" male (as Aristotle's terminology has variously been translated), a "monstrosity" of nature.[2]

For Greek theorists, the biology of males and females was the key to their psychology. The female was softer and more docile, more apt to be despondent, querulous, and deceitful. Being incomplete, moreover, she craved sexual fulfillment in intercourse with a male. The male was intellectual, active, and in control of his passions.

These psychological polarities derived from the theory that the universe consisted of four elements (earth, fire, air, and water), expressed in human bodies as four "humors" (black bile, yellow bile, blood, and phlegm) considered, respectively, dry, hot, damp, and cold and corresponding to mental states ("melancholic," "choleric," "sanguine," "phlegmatic"). In this scheme the male, sharing the principles of earth and fire, was dry and hot; the female, sharing the principles of air and water, was cold and damp.

Female psychology was further affected by her dominant organ, the uterus (womb), *hystera* in Greek. The passions generated by the womb made women lustful, deceitful, talkative, irrational, indeed—when these affects were in excess—"hysterical."

Aristotle's biology also had social and political consequences. If the male principle was superior and the female inferior, then in the household, as in the state, men should rule and women must be subordinate. That hierarchy did not rule out the companionship of husband and wife, whose cooperation was necessary for the welfare of children and the preservation of property. Such mutuality supported male preeminence.

Aristotle's teacher Plato suggested a different possibility: that men and women might possess the same virtues. The setting for this proposal is the imaginary and ideal Republic that Plato sketches in a dialogue of that name. Here, for a privileged elite capable of leading wisely, all distinctions of class and wealth dissolve, as, consequently, do those of gender. Without households or property, as Plato constructs his ideal society, there is no need for the subordination of women. Women may therefore be educated to the same level as men to assume leadership. Plato's Republic remained imaginary, however. In real societies, the subordination of women remained the norm and the prescription.

The views of women inherited from the Greek philosophical tradition became the basis for medieval thought. In the thirteenth century, the su-

2. Aristotle, *Generation of Animals* 2.3.737a27–28, in *The Complete Works,* 1:1144.

preme Scholastic philosopher Thomas Aquinas, among others, still echoed Aristotle's views of human reproduction, of male and female personalities, and of the preeminent male role in the social hierarchy.

ROMAN LAW AND THE FEMALE CONDITION. Roman law, like Greek philosophy, underlay medieval thought and shaped medieval society. The ancient belief that adult property-owning men should administer households and make decisions affecting the community at large is the very fulcrum of Roman law.

About 450 B.C.E., during Rome's republican era, the community's customary law was recorded (legendarily) on twelve tablets erected in the city's central forum. It was later elaborated by professional jurists whose activity increased in the imperial era, when much new legislation was passed, especially on issues affecting family and inheritance. This growing, changing body of laws was eventually codified in the *Corpus of Civil Law* under the direction of the emperor Justinian, generations after the empire ceased to be ruled from Rome. That *Corpus*, read and commented on by medieval scholars from the eleventh century on, inspired the legal systems of most of the cities and kingdoms of Europe.

Laws regarding dowries, divorce, and inheritance pertain primarily to women. Since those laws aimed to maintain and preserve property, the women concerned were those from the property-owning minority. Their subordination to male family members points to the even greater subordination of lower-class and slave women, about whom the laws speak little.

In the early republic, the *paterfamilias*, or "father of the family," possessed *patria potestas*, "paternal power." The term *pater*, "father," in both these cases does not necessarily mean biological father but denotes the head of a household. The father was the person who owned the household's property and, indeed, its human members. The *paterfamilias* had absolute power—including the power, rarely exercised, of life or death—over his wife, his children, and his slaves, as much as his cattle.

Male children could be "emancipated," an act that granted legal autonomy and the right to own property. Those over fourteen could be emancipated by a special grant from the father or automatically by their father's death. But females could never be emancipated; instead, they passed from the authority of their father to that of a husband or, if widowed or orphaned while still unmarried, to a guardian or tutor.

Marriage in its traditional form placed the woman under her husband's authority, or *manus*. He could divorce her on grounds of adultery, drinking wine, or stealing from the household, but she could not divorce him. She could neither possess property in her own right nor bequeath any to her children upon her death. When her husband died, the household property passed not to her but to his male heirs. And when her father died, she had no claim to any family inheritance, which was directed to her brothers or more remote male relatives. The effect of these laws was to exclude women from civil society, itself based on property ownership.

In the later republican and imperial periods, these rules were significantly modified. Women rarely married according to the traditional form. The practice of "free" marriage allowed a woman to remain under her father's authority, to possess property given her by her father (most frequently the "dowry," recoverable from the husband's household on his death), and to inherit from her father. She could also bequeath property to her own children and divorce her husband, just as he could divorce her.

Despite this greater freedom, women still suffered enormous disability under Roman law. Heirs could belong only to the father's side, never the mother's. Moreover, although she could bequeath her property to her children, she could not establish a line of succession in doing so. A woman was "the beginning and end of her own family," said the jurist Ulpian. Moreover, women could play no public role. They could not hold public office, represent anyone in a legal case, or even witness a will. Women had only a private existence and no public personality.

The dowry system, the guardian, women's limited ability to transmit wealth, and total political disability are all features of Roman law adopted by the medieval communities of western Europe, although modified according to local customary laws.

CHRISTIAN DOCTRINE AND WOMEN'S PLACE. The Hebrew Bible and the Christian New Testament authorized later writers to limit women to the realm of the family and to burden them with the guilt of original sin. The passages most fruitful for this purpose were the creation narratives in Genesis and sentences from the Epistles defining women's role within the Christian family and community.

Each of the first two chapters of Genesis contains a creation narrative. In the first "God created man in his own image, in the image of God he created him; male and female he created them" (Gn 1:27). In the second, God created Eve from Adam's rib (2:21–23). Christian theologians relied principally on Genesis 2 for their understanding of the relation between man and woman, interpreting the creation of Eve from Adam as proof of her subordination to him.

The creation story in Genesis 2 leads to that of the temptations in Genesis 3: of Eve by the wily serpent and of Adam by Eve. As read by Christian theologians from Tertullian to Thomas Aquinas, the narrative made Eve responsible for the Fall and its consequences. She instigated the act; she deceived her husband; she suffered the greater punishment. Her disobedience made it necessary for Jesus to be incarnated and to die on the cross. From the pulpit, moralists and preachers for centuries conveyed to women the guilt that they bore for original sin.

The Epistles offered advice to early Christians on building communities of the faithful. Among the matters to be regulated was the place of women. Paul offered views favorable to women in Galatians 3:28: "There is neither Jew nor Greek, there is neither slave nor free, there is neither male nor female; for you are all one in Christ Jesus." Paul also referred to women as his coworkers and placed them on a par with himself and his male coworkers (Phlm 4:2–3; Rom 16:1–3; 1 Cor 16:19). Elsewhere, Paul limited women's possibilities: "But I want you to understand that the head of every man is Christ, the head of a woman is her husband, and the head of Christ is God" (1 Cor 11:3).

Biblical passages by later writers (although attributed to Paul) enjoined women to forgo jewels, expensive clothes, and elaborate coiffures; and they forbade women to "teach or have authority over men," telling them to "learn in silence with all submissiveness" as is proper for one responsible for sin, consoling them, however, with the thought that they will be saved through childbearing (1 Tm 2:9–15). Other texts among the later Epistles defined women as the weaker sex and emphasized their subordination to their husbands (1 Pt 3:7; Col 3:18; Eph 5:22–23).

These passages from the New Testament became the arsenal employed by theologians of the early church to transmit negative attitudes toward women to medieval Christian culture—above all, Tertullian (*On the Apparel of Women*), Jerome (*Against Jovinian*), and Augustine (*The Literal Meaning of Genesis*).

THE IMAGE OF WOMEN IN MEDIEVAL LITERATURE. The philosophical, legal, and religious traditions born in antiquity formed the basis of the medieval intellectual synthesis wrought by trained thinkers, mostly clerics, writing in Latin and based largely in universities. The vernacular literary tradition that developed alongside the learned tradition also spoke about female nature and women's roles. Medieval stories, poems, and epics also portrayed women negatively—as lustful and deceitful—while praising good housekeepers and loyal wives as replicas of the Virgin Mary or the female saints and martyrs.

There is an exception in the movement of "courtly love" that evolved in southern France from the twelfth century. Courtly love was the erotic love between a nobleman and noblewoman, the latter usually superior in social rank. It was always adulterous. From the conventions of courtly love derive modern Western notions of romantic love. The tradition has had an impact disproportionate to its size, for it affected only a tiny elite, and very few women. The exaltation of the female lover probably does not reflect a higher evaluation of women or a step toward their sexual liberation. More likely it gives expression to the social and sexual tensions besetting the knightly class at a specific historical juncture.

The literary fashion of courtly love was on the wane by the thirteenth century, when the widely read *Romance of the Rose* was composed in French by two authors of significantly different dispositions. Guillaume de Lorris composed the initial four thousand verses about 1235, and Jean de Meun added about seventeen thousand verses—more than four times the original—about 1265.

The fragment composed by Guillaume de Lorris stands squarely in the tradition of courtly love. Here the poet, in a dream, is admitted into a walled garden where he finds a magic fountain in which a rosebush is reflected. He longs to pick one rose, but the thorns prevent his doing so, even as he is wounded by arrows from the god of love, whose commands he agrees to obey. The rest of this part of the poem recounts the poet's unsuccessful efforts to pluck the rose.

The longer part of the *Romance* by Jean de Meun also describes a dream. But here allegorical characters give long didactic speeches, providing a social satire on a variety of themes, some pertaining to women. Love is an anxious and tormented state, the poem explains: women are greedy and manipulative, marriage is miserable, beautiful women are lustful, ugly ones cease to please, and a chaste woman is as rare as a black swan.

Shortly after Jean de Meun completed *The Romance of the Rose,* Mathéolus penned his *Lamentations,* a long Latin diatribe against marriage translated into French about a century later. The *Lamentations* sum up medieval attitudes toward women and provoked the important response by Christine de Pizan in her *Book of the City of Ladies.*

In 1355, Giovanni Boccaccio wrote *Il Corbaccio,* another antifeminist manifesto, although ironically by an author whose other works pioneered new directions in Renaissance thought. The former husband of his lover appears to Boccaccio, condemning his unmoderated lust and detailing the defects of women. Boccaccio concedes at the end "how much men naturally surpass women in nobility" and is cured of his desires.[3]

3. Giovanni Boccaccio, *The Corbaccio, or The Labyrinth of Love,* trans. and ed. Anthony K. Cassell, rev. ed. (Binghamton, NY, 1993), 71.

WOMEN'S ROLES: THE FAMILY. The negative perceptions of women expressed in the intellectual tradition are also implicit in the actual roles that women played in European society. Assigned to subordinate positions in the household and the church, they were barred from significant participation in public life.

Medieval European households, like those in antiquity and in non-Western civilizations, were headed by males. It was the male serf (or peasant), feudal lord, town merchant, or citizen who was polled or taxed or succeeded to an inheritance or had any acknowledged public role, although his wife or widow could stand as a temporary surrogate. From about 1100, the position of property-holding males was further enhanced: inheritance was confined to the male, or agnate, line—with depressing consequences for women.

A wife never fully belonged to her husband's family, nor was she a daughter to her father's family. She left her father's house young to marry whomever her parents chose. Her dowry was managed by her husband, and at her death it normally passed to her children by him.

A married woman's life was occupied nearly constantly with cycles of pregnancy, childbearing, and lactation. Women bore children through all the years of their fertility, and many died in childbirth. They were also responsible for raising young children up to six or seven. In the propertied classes that responsibility was shared, since it was common for a wet nurse to take over breast-feeding and for servants to perform other chores.

Women trained their daughters in the household duties appropriate to their status, nearly always tasks associated with textiles: spinning, weaving, sewing, embroidering. Their sons were sent out of the house as apprentices or students, or their training was assumed by fathers in later childhood and adolescence. On the death of her husband, a woman's children became the responsibility of his family. She generally did not take "his" children with her to a new marriage or back to her father's house, except sometimes in the artisan classes.

Women also worked. Rural peasants performed farm chores, merchant wives often practiced their husbands' trades, the unmarried daughters of the urban poor worked as servants or prostitutes. All wives produced or embellished textiles and did the housekeeping, while wealthy ones managed servants. These labors were unpaid or poorly paid but often contributed substantially to family wealth.

WOMEN'S ROLES: THE CHURCH. Membership in a household, whether a father's or a husband's, meant for women a lifelong subordination to others.

In western Europe, the Roman Catholic Church offered an alternative to the career of wife and mother. A woman could enter a convent, parallel in function to the monasteries for men that evolved in the early Christian centuries.

In the convent, a woman pledged herself to a celibate life, lived according to strict community rules, and worshiped daily. Often the convent offered training in Latin, allowing some women to become considerable scholars and authors as well as scribes, artists, and musicians. For women who chose the conventual life, the benefits could be enormous, but for numerous others placed in convents by paternal choice, the life could be restrictive and burdensome.

The conventual life declined as an alternative for women as the modern age approached. Reformed monastic institutions resisted responsibility for related female orders. The church increasingly restricted female institutional life by insisting on closer male supervision.

Women often sought other options. Some joined the communities of laywomen that sprang up spontaneously in the thirteenth century in the urban zones of western Europe, especially in Flanders and Italy. Some joined the heretical movements that flourished in late medieval Christendom, whose anticlerical and often antifamily positions particularly appealed to women. In these communities, some women were acclaimed as "holy women" or "saints," whereas others often were condemned as frauds or heretics.

In all, although the options offered to women by the church were sometimes less than satisfactory, they were sometimes richly rewarding. After 1520, the convent remained an option only in Roman Catholic territories. Protestantism engendered an ideal of marriage as a heroic endeavor and appeared to place husband and wife on a more equal footing. Sermons and treatises, however, still called for female subordination and obedience.

THE OTHER VOICE, 1300–1700

When the modern era opened, European culture was so firmly structured by a framework of negative attitudes toward women that to dismantle it was a monumental labor. The process began as part of a larger cultural movement that entailed the critical reexamination of ideas inherited from the ancient and medieval past. The humanists launched that critical reexamination.

THE HUMANIST FOUNDATION. Originating in Italy in the fourteenth century, humanism quickly became the dominant intellectual movement in

Europe. Spreading in the sixteenth century from Italy to the rest of Europe, it fueled the literary, scientific, and philosophical movements of the era and laid the basis for the eighteenth-century Enlightenment.

Humanists regarded the Scholastic philosophy of medieval universities as out of touch with the realities of urban life. They found in the rhetorical discourse of classical Rome a language adapted to civic life and public speech. They learned to read, speak, and write classical Latin and, eventually, classical Greek. They founded schools to teach others to do so, establishing the pattern for elementary and secondary education for the next three hundred years.

In the service of complex government bureaucracies, humanists employed their skills to write eloquent letters, deliver public orations, and formulate public policy. They developed new scripts for copying manuscripts and used the new printing press to disseminate texts, for which they created methods of critical editing.

Humanism was a movement led by males who accepted the evaluation of women in ancient texts and generally shared the misogynist perceptions of their culture. (Female humanists, as we will see, did not.) Yet humanism also opened the door to a reevaluation of the nature and capacity of women. By calling authors, texts, and ideas into question, it made possible the fundamental rereading of the whole intellectual tradition that was required in order to free women from cultural prejudice and social subordination.

A DIFFERENT CITY. The other voice first appeared when, after so many centuries, the accumulation of misogynist concepts evoked a response from a capable female defender: Christine de Pizan (1365–1431). Introducing her *Book of the City of Ladies* (1405), she described how she was affected by reading Mathéolus's *Lamentations*: "Just the sight of this book . . . made me wonder how it happened that so many different men . . . are so inclined to express both in speaking and in their treatises and writings so many wicked insults about women and their behavior."[4] These statements impelled her to detest herself "and the entire feminine sex, as though we were monstrosities in nature."[5]

The rest of *The Book of the City of Ladies* presents a justification of the female sex and a vision of an ideal community of women. A pioneer, she has received the message of female inferiority and rejected it. From the fourteenth to the seventeenth century, a huge body of literature accumulated that responded to the dominant tradition.

4. Christine de Pizan, *The Book of the City of Ladies*, trans. Earl Jeffrey Richards, foreword by Marina Warner (New York, 1982), 1.1.1, pp. 3–4.

5. Ibid., 1.1.1–2, p. 5.

The result was a literary explosion consisting of works by both men and women, in Latin and in the vernaculars: works enumerating the achievements of notable women; works rebutting the main accusations made against women; works arguing for the equal education of men and women; works defining and redefining women's proper role in the family, at court, in public; works describing women's lives and experiences. Recent monographs and articles have begun to hint at the great range of this movement, involving probably several thousand titles. The protofeminism of these "other voices" constitutes a significant fraction of the literary product of the early modern era.

THE CATALOGS. About 1365, the same Boccaccio whose *Corbaccio* rehearses the usual charges against female nature wrote another work, *Concerning Famous Women.* A humanist treatise drawing on classical texts, it praised 106 notable women: ninety-eight of them from pagan Greek and Roman antiquity, one (Eve) from the Bible, and seven from the medieval religious and cultural tradition; his book helped make all readers aware of a sex normally condemned or forgotten. Boccaccio's outlook nevertheless was unfriendly to women, for it singled out for praise those women who possessed the traditional virtues of chastity, silence, and obedience. Women who were active in the public realm—for example, rulers and warriors—were depicted as usually being lascivious and as suffering terrible punishments for entering the masculine sphere. Women were his subject, but Boccaccio's standard remained male.

Christine de Pizan's *Book of the City of Ladies* contains a second catalog, one responding specifically to Boccaccio's. Whereas Boccaccio portrays female virtue as exceptional, she depicts it as universal. Many women in history were leaders, or remained chaste despite the lascivious approaches of men, or were visionaries and brave martyrs.

The work of Boccaccio inspired a series of catalogs of illustrious women of the biblical, classical, Christian, and local pasts, among them Filippo da Bergamo's *Of Illustrious Women,* Pierre de Brantôme's *Lives of Illustrious Women,* Pierre Le Moyne's *Gallerie of Heroic Women,* and Pietro Paolo de Ribera's *Immortal Triumphs and Heroic Enterprises of 845 Women.* Whatever their embedded prejudices, these works drove home to the public the possibility of female excellence.

THE DEBATE. At the same time, many questions remained: Could a woman be virtuous? Could she perform noteworthy deeds? Was she even, strictly speaking, of the same human species as men? These questions were debated over four centuries, in French, German, Italian, Spanish, and English, by authors male and female, among Catholics, Protestants, and Jews, in ponderous volumes and breezy pamphlets. The whole literary genre has been called the *querelle des femmes,* the "woman question."

The opening volley of this battle occurred in the first years of the fifteenth century, in a literary debate sparked by Christine de Pizan. She exchanged letters critical of Jean de Meun's contribution to *The Romance of the Rose* with two French royal secretaries, Jean de Montreuil and Gontier Col. When the matter became public, Jean Gerson, one of Europe's leading theologians, supported de Pizan's arguments against de Meun, for the moment silencing the opposition.

The debate resurfaced repeatedly over the next two hundred years. *The Triumph of Women* (1438) by Juan Rodríguez de la Camara (or Juan Rodríguez del Padron) struck a new note by presenting arguments for the superiority of women to men. *The Champion of Women* (1440–42) by Martin Le Franc addresses once again the negative views of women presented in *The Romance of the Rose* and offers counterevidence of female virtue and achievement.

A cameo of the debate on women is included in *The Courtier,* one of the most widely read books of the era, published by the Italian Baldassare Castiglione in 1528 and immediately translated into other European vernaculars. *The Courtier* depicts a series of evenings at the court of the duke of Urbino in which many men and some women of the highest social stratum amuse themselves by discussing a range of literary and social issues. The "woman question" is a pervasive theme throughout, and the third of its four books is devoted entirely to that issue.

In a verbal duel, Gasparo Pallavicino and Giuliano de' Medici present the main claims of the two traditions. Gasparo argues the innate inferiority of women and their inclination to vice. Only in bearing children do they profit the world. Giuliano counters that women share the same spiritual and mental capacities as men and may excel in wisdom and action. Men and women are of the same essence: just as no stone can be more perfectly a stone than another, so no human being can be more perfectly human than others, whether male or female. It was an astonishing assertion, boldly made to an audience as large as all Europe.

THE TREATISES. Humanism provided the materials for a positive counterconcept to the misogyny embedded in Scholastic philosophy and law and inherited from the Greek, Roman, and Christian pasts. A series of humanist treatises on marriage and family, on education and deportment, and on the nature of women helped construct these new perspectives.

The works by Francesco Barbaro and Leon Battista Alberti—*On Mar-*

riage (1415) and *On the Family* (1434–37)—far from defending female equality, reasserted women's responsibility for rearing children and managing the housekeeping while being obedient, chaste, and silent. Nevertheless, they served the cause of reexamining the issue of women's nature by placing domestic issues at the center of scholarly concern and reopening the pertinent classical texts. In addition, Barbaro emphasized the companionate nature of marriage and the importance of a wife's spiritual and mental qualities for the well-being of the family.

These themes reappear in later humanist works on marriage and the education of women by Juan Luis Vives and Erasmus. Both were moderately sympathetic to the condition of women without reaching beyond the usual masculine prescriptions for female behavior.

An outlook more favorable to women characterizes the nearly unknown work *In Praise of Women* (ca. 1487) by the Italian humanist Bartolommeo Goggio. In addition to providing a catalog of illustrious women, Goggio argued that male and female are the same in essence, but that women (reworking the Adam and Eve narrative from quite a new angle) are actually superior. In the same vein, the Italian humanist Mario Equicola asserted the spiritual equality of men and women in *On Women* (1501). In 1525, Galeazzo Flavio Capra (or Capella) published his work *On the Excellence and Dignity of Women.* This humanist tradition of treatises defending the worthiness of women culminates in the work of Henricus Cornelius Agrippa *On the Nobility and Preeminence of the Female Sex.* No work by a male humanist more succinctly or explicitly presents the case for female dignity.

THE WITCH BOOKS. While humanists grappled with the issues pertaining to women and family, other learned men turned their attention to what they perceived as a very great problem: witches. Witch-hunting manuals, explorations of the witch phenomenon, and even defenses of witches are not at first glance pertinent to the tradition of the other voice. But they do relate in this way: most accused witches were women. The hostility aroused by supposed witch activity is comparable to the hostility aroused by women. The evil deeds the victims of the hunt were charged with were exaggerations of the vices to which, many believed, all women were prone.

The connection between the witch accusation and the hatred of women is explicit in the notorious witch-hunting manual *The Hammer of Witches* (1486) by two Dominican inquisitors, Heinrich Krämer and Jacob Sprenger. Here the inconstancy, deceitfulness, and lustfulness traditionally associated with women are depicted in exaggerated form as the core features of witch behavior. These traits inclined women to make a bargain with the devil—

sealed by sexual intercourse—by which they acquired unholy powers. Such bizarre claims, far from being rejected by rational men, were broadcast by intellectuals. The German Ulrich Molitur, the Frenchman Nicolas Rémy, and the Italian Stefano Guazzo all coolly informed the public of sinister orgies and midnight pacts with the devil. The celebrated French jurist, historian, and political philosopher Jean Bodin argued that because women were especially prone to diabolism, regular legal procedures could properly be suspended in order to try those accused of this "exceptional crime."

A few experts such as the physician Johann Weyer, a student of Agrippa's, raised their voices in protest. In 1563, he explained the witch phenomenon thus, without discarding belief in diabolism: the devil deluded foolish old women afflicted by melancholia, causing them to believe they had magical powers. Weyer's rational skepticism, which had good credibility in the community of the learned, worked to revise the conventional views of women and witchcraft.

WOMEN'S WORKS. To the many categories of works produced on the question of women's worth must be added nearly all works written by women. A woman writing was in herself a statement of women's claim to dignity.

Only a few women wrote anything before the dawn of the modern era, for three reasons. First, they rarely received the education that would enable them to write. Second, they were not admitted to the public roles—as administrator, bureaucrat, lawyer or notary, or university professor—in which they might gain knowledge of the kinds of things the literate public thought worth writing about. Third, the culture imposed silence on women, considering speaking out a form of unchastity. Given these conditions, it is remarkable that any women wrote. Those who did before the fourteenth century were almost always nuns or religious women whose isolation made their pronouncements more acceptable.

From the fourteenth century on, the volume of women's writings rose. Women continued to write devotional literature, although not always as cloistered nuns. They also wrote diaries, often intended as keepsakes for their children; books of advice to their sons and daughters; letters to family members and friends; and family memoirs, in a few cases elaborate enough to be considered histories.

A few women wrote works directly concerning the "woman question," and some of these, such as the humanists Isotta Nogarola, Cassandra Fedele, Laura Cereta, and Olympia Morata, were highly trained. A few were professional writers, living by the income of their pens; the very first among them was Christine de Pizan, noteworthy in this context as in so many others. In addition to *The Book of the City of Ladies* and her critiques of *The Romance of the Rose,* she wrote *The Treasure of the City of Ladies* (a guide to social decorum for women), an advice book for her son, much courtly verse, and a full-scale history of the reign of King Charles V of France.

WOMEN PATRONS. Women who did not themselves write but encouraged others to do so boosted the development of an alternative tradition. Highly placed women patrons supported authors, artists, musicians, poets, and learned men. Such patrons, drawn mostly from the Italian elites and the courts of northern Europe, figure disproportionately as the dedicatees of the important works of early feminism.

For a start, it might be noted that the catalogs of Boccaccio and Alvaro de Luna were dedicated to the Florentine noblewoman Andrea Acciaiuoli and to Doña María, first wife of King Juan II of Castile, while the French translation of Boccaccio's work was commissioned by Anne of Brittany, wife of King Charles VIII of France. The humanist treatises of Goggio, Equicola, Vives, and Agrippa were dedicated, respectively, to Eleanora of Aragon, wife of Ercole I d'Este, Duke of Ferrara; to Margherita Cantelma of Mantua; to Catherine of Aragon, wife of King Henry VIII of England; and to Margaret, Duchess of Austria and regent of the Netherlands. As late as 1696, Mary Astell's *Serious Proposal to the Ladies, for the Advancement of Their True and Greatest Interest* was dedicated to Princess Anne of Denmark.

These authors presumed that their efforts would be welcome to female patrons, or they may have written at the bidding of those patrons. Silent themselves, perhaps even unresponsive, these loftily placed women helped shape the tradition of the other voice.

THE ISSUES. The literary forms and patterns in which the tradition of the other voice presented itself have now been sketched. It remains to highlight the major issues around which this tradition crystallizes. In brief, there are four problems to which our authors return again and again, in plays and catalogs, in verse and letters, in treatises and dialogues, in every language: the problem of chastity, the problem of power, the problem of speech, and the problem of knowledge. Of these the greatest, preconditioning the others, is the problem of chastity.

THE PROBLEM OF CHASTITY. In traditional European culture, as in those of antiquity and others around the globe, chastity was perceived as woman's quintessential virtue—in contrast to courage, or generosity, or leadership, or rationality, seen as virtues characteristic of men. Opponents of women charged them with insatiable lust. Women themselves and their defenders—without disputing the validity of the standard—responded that women were capable of chastity.

The requirement of chastity kept women at home, silenced them, isolated them, left them in ignorance. It was the source of all other impediments. Why was it so important to the society of men, of whom chastity was not required, and who more often than not considered it their right to violate the chastity of any woman they encountered?

Female chastity ensured the continuity of the male-headed household. If a man's wife was not chaste, he could not be sure of the legitimacy of his offspring. If they were not his and they acquired his property, it was not his household, but some other man's, that had endured. If his daughter was not chaste, she could not be transferred to another man's household as his wife, and he was dishonored.

The whole system of the integrity of the household and the transmission of property was bound up in female chastity. Such a requirement pertained only to property-owning classes, of course. Poor women could not expect to maintain their chastity, least of all if they were in contact with high-status men to whom all women but those of their own household were prey.

In Catholic Europe, the requirement of chastity was further buttressed by moral and religious imperatives. Original sin was inextricably linked with the sexual act. Virginity was seen as heroic virtue, far more impressive than, say, the avoidance of idleness or greed. Monasticism, the cultural institution that dominated medieval Europe for centuries, was grounded in the renunciation of the flesh. The Catholic reform of the eleventh century imposed a similar standard on all the clergy and a heightened awareness of sexual requirements on all the laity. Although men were asked to be chaste, female unchastity was much worse: it led to the devil, as Eve had led mankind to sin.

To such requirements, women and their defenders protested their innocence. Furthermore, following the example of holy women who had escaped the requirements of family and sought the religious life, some women began to conceive of female communities as alternatives both to family and to the cloister. Christine de Pizan's city of ladies was such a community. Moderata Fonte and Mary Astell envisioned others. The luxurious salons of the French *précieuses* of the seventeenth century, or the comfortable English drawing rooms of the next, may have been born of the same impulse. Here women not only might escape, if briefly, the subordinate position that life in the family entailed but might also make claims to power, exercise their capacity for speech, and display their knowledge.

THE PROBLEM OF POWER. Women were excluded from power: the whole cultural tradition insisted on it. Only men were citizens, only men bore arms, only men could be chiefs or lords or kings. There were exceptions that did not disprove the rule, when wives or widows or mothers took the place of men, awaiting their return or the maturation of a male heir. A woman who attempted to rule in her own right was perceived as an anomaly, a monster, at once a deformed woman and an insufficient male, sexually confused and consequently unsafe.

The association of such images with women who held or sought power explains some otherwise odd features of early modern culture. Queen Elizabeth I of England, one of the few women to hold full regal authority in European history, played with such male/female images—positive ones, of course—in representing herself to her subjects. She was a prince, and manly, even though she was female. She was also (she claimed) virginal, a condition absolutely essential if she was to avoid the attacks of her opponents. Catherine de' Medici, who ruled France as widow and regent for her sons, also adopted such imagery in defining her position. She chose as one symbol the figure of Artemisia, an androgynous ancient warrior-heroine who combined a female persona with masculine powers.

Power in a woman, without such sexual imagery, seems to have been indigestible by the culture. A rare note was struck by the Englishman Sir Thomas Elyot in his *Defence of Good Women* (1540), justifying both women's participation in civic life and their prowess in arms. The old tune was sung by the Scots reformer John Knox in his *First Blast of the Trumpet against the Monstrous Regiment of Women* (1558); for him rule by women, defects in nature, was a hideous contradiction in terms.

The confused sexuality of the imagery of female potency was not reserved for rulers. Any woman who excelled was likely to be called an Amazon, recalling the self-mutilated warrior women of antiquity who repudiated all men, gave up their sons, and raised only their daughters. She was often said to have "exceeded her sex" or to have possessed "masculine virtue"—as the very fact of conspicuous excellence conferred masculinity even on the female subject. The catalogs of notable women often showed those female heroes dressed in armor, armed to the teeth, like men. Amazonian heroines romp through the epics of the age—Ariosto's *Orlando Furioso* (1532) and Spenser's *Faerie Queene* (1590–1609). Excellence in a woman was perceived as a claim for power, and power was reserved for the masculine realm. A woman who possessed either one was masculinized and lost title to her own female identity.

THE PROBLEM OF SPEECH. Just as power had a sexual dimension when it was claimed by women, so did speech. A good woman spoke little. Excessive speech was an indication of unchastity. By speech, women seduced men. Eve had lured Adam into sin by her speech. Accused witches were commonly accused of having spoken abusively, or irrationally, or simply too much. As enlightened a figure as Francesco Barbaro insisted on silence in a woman, which he linked to her perfect unanimity with her husband's will and her unblemished virtue (her chastity). Another Italian humanist, Leonardo Bruni, in advising a noblewoman on her studies, barred her not from speech but from public speaking. That was reserved for men.

Related to the problem of speech was that of costume—another, if silent, form of self-expression. Assigned the task of pleasing men as their primary occupation, elite women often tended toward elaborate costume, hairdressing, and the use of cosmetics. Clergy and secular moralists alike condemned these practices. The appropriate function of costume and adornment was to announce the status of a woman's husband or father. Any further indulgence in adornment was akin to unchastity.

THE PROBLEM OF KNOWLEDGE. When the Italian noblewoman Isotta Nogarola had begun to attain a reputation as a humanist, she was accused of incest—a telling instance of the association of learning in women with unchastity. That chilling association inclined any woman who was educated to deny that she was or to make exaggerated claims of heroic chastity.

If educated women were pursued with suspicions of sexual misconduct, women seeking an education faced an even more daunting obstacle: the assumption that women were by nature incapable of learning, that reasoning was a particularly masculine ability. Just as they proclaimed their chastity, women and their defenders insisted on their capacity for learning. The major work by a male writer on female education—that by Juan Luis Vives, *On the Education of a Christian Woman* (1523)—granted female capacity for intellection but still argued that a woman's whole education was to be shaped around the requirement of chastity and a future within the household. Female writers of the following generations—Marie de Gournay in France, Anna Maria van Schurman in Holland, and Mary Astell in England—began to envision other possibilities.

The pioneers of female education were the Italian women humanists who managed to attain a literacy in Latin and a knowledge of classical and Christian literature equivalent to that of prominent men. Their works implicitly and explicitly raise questions about women's social roles, defining problems that beset women attempting to break out of the cultural limits that had bound them. Like Christine de Pizan, who achieved an advanced education through her father's tutoring and her own devices, their bold questioning makes clear the importance of training. Only when women were educated to the same standard as male leaders would they be able to raise that other voice and insist on their dignity as human beings morally, intellectually, and legally equal to men.

THE OTHER VOICE. The other voice, a voice of protest, was mostly female, but it was also male. It spoke in the vernaculars and in Latin, in treatises and dialogues, in plays and poetry, in letters and diaries, and in pamphlets. It battered at the wall of prejudice that encircled women and raised a banner announcing its claims. The female was equal (or even superior) to the male in essential nature—moral, spiritual, and intellectual. Women were capable of higher education, of holding positions of power and influence in the public realm, and of speaking and writing persuasively. The last bastion of masculine supremacy, centered on the notions of a woman's primary domestic responsibility and the requirement of female chastity, was not as yet assaulted—although visions of productive female communities as alternatives to the family indicated an awareness of the problem.

During the period 1300–1700, the other voice remained only a voice, and one only dimly heard. It did not result—yet—in an alteration of social patterns. Indeed, to this day they have not entirely been altered. Yet the call for justice issued as long as six centuries ago by those writing in the tradition of the other voice must be recognized as the source and origin of the mature feminist tradition and of the realignment of social institutions accomplished in the modern age.

We thank the volume editors in this series, who responded with many suggestions to an earlier draft of this introduction, making it a collaborative enterprise. Many of their suggestions and criticisms have resulted in revisions of this introduction, although we remain responsible for the final product.

Figure 1. Unknown artist, *Catharina Regina von Greiffenberg* (seventeenth century). Herzog August Bibliothek, Wolfenbüttel: Portrait Collection (A-8142).

VOLUME EDITOR'S INTRODUCTION

> He possessed her as it were and said through her to those women that they had been created by God in the image of God for the highest good, for the most sublime virtue, with a heart just like the men—yes!—that they were made of the man's rib and bones so that they would remain strong, firm, and immovable in all agony for the sake of God's glory.
>
> —Catharina Regina von Greiffenberg,
> "On the Pregnancy of the Holy Mother of Jesus"

THE OTHER VOICE

Catharina Regina von Greiffenberg, labeled by an effusive male contemporary a "miracle of our times,"[1] constituted an anomaly in the seventeenth-century German-speaking world. Privileged by her social station and education, uncommonly gifted, and imbued with religious zeal, she turned out an oeuvre, published under her own name, of largely devotional writing that spans ten volumes in its twentieth-century reprint edition. No other German woman received as much acclaim in the seventeenth century for her writing, and few women had the access to print culture and supportive contacts with male writers that Greiffenberg ultimately enjoyed. Greiffenberg has thus by no means been ignored in German Studies—her poetry has been anthologized, and literary histories include her.[2] Yet she was a

1. Sigmund von Birken to Casper von Lilien, January 1666, in vol. 1 of Catharina Regina von Greiffenberg, *Sämtliche Werke,* ed. Martin Bircher and Friedhelm Kemp, 10 vols. (Millwood, NY: Kraus Reprint, 1983), 1: 469.

2. See, e.g., Harald Steinhagen and Benno von Wiese, *Deutsche Dichter des 17. Jahrhunderts* (Berlin: Erich Schmidt, 1984). Greiffenberg is one of only two woman writers treated in Steinhagen and von Wiese's *Deutsche Dichter,* a work that includes thirty-five authors in all. Similarly, of the 197 works cited by the author's name and included in Albrecht Schöne's anthology of baroque

peculiar figure, and her meditations, selections of which are translated here, went largely unread once their initial popularity as devotional writings had waned; after the seventeenth century they were not republished in full until the twentieth-century reprint of 1983.[3] Thus while Greiffenberg's poetic talent has been recognized, the meditations as a whole have until recently received surprisingly little attention from literary, religious, and cultural historians. Yet these meditations are now held to be her most ambitious and important works and to constitute both a carefully composed literary life work and a fascinating and powerful documentation of religious belief and practice in the late seventeenth-century German-speaking world.[4]

When in the 1970s feminists began the recovery work of forgotten women's voices, Greiffenberg was also certainly acknowledged. Yet at first glance her meditations did not lend themselves easily to that project. Her piety and zeal, her religious sensibility, the idiosyncrasy and opacity of her language, and her elaborate wordplay did not speak readily to those who in a secular age were seeking a voice in the past that heralded modern times. Nevertheless, during the last decade and a half, a handful of scholars of early modern German literature, informed by feminism and gender studies, have begun to take a closer look at this densely written life work and have begun to discover not only that Greiffenberg offered, in the words of Kathleen Foley-Beining, "a benevolent affront" to the gender codes of her times, but that her devotional writing is intimately and consciously, sometimes even stridently, concerned with what we now term gender, that is, with gender as it dictates social roles and access to language and authority, as well as gender as it figures religious capacities and practices.[5]

A skilled rhetorician, Greiffenberg overtly concerns herself with women's spiritual authority, even suggesting that it can surpass that of men. She begins each of her works with the apologies customary in the seventeenth century, especially compelled to beg for the reader's indulgence since

---

literature, six works are by women and three of these are by Greiffenberg. Schöne devotes to Greiffenberg's work two and a half times the small space devoted to all three additional women anthologized. Albrecht Schöne, ed., *Das Zeitalter des Barock: Texte und Zeugnisse,* 2nd ed., vol. 3 of *Texte und Zeugnisse* (Munich: C. H. Beck, 1968).

3. Friedhelm Kemp, afterword, in Greiffenberg, *Sämtliche Werke,* 1: 512.

4. In her study of the meditations on the birth of Jesus Christ, Cristina Pumplun convincingly refutes the view of the meditations as devotional literature written without a view to literary aesthetic considerations. Cristina M. Pumplun, *"Begriff des Unbegreiflichen": Funktion und Bedeutung der Metaphorik in den Geburtsbetrachtungen der Catharina Regina von Greiffenberg (1633–1694),* Amsterdamer Publikationen zur Sprache und Literatur 120 (Amsterdam: Rodopi, 1995).

5. Kathleen Foley-Beining, *The Body and Eucharistic Devotion in Catharina Regina von Greiffenberg's "Meditations"* (Columbia, SC: Camden House, 1997), 15.

she dares to write as a woman. Yet her writing exhibits boldness in its assertion of religious authority and quickly abandons the initial meek stance that attempts to gain a favorable hearing. Greiffenberg's meditations of 1672 on Christ's passion, for example, open with an apology that a simple, weak, and untutored woman, who is not qualified to speak, makes bold to publish. It concludes, however, as we shall see, with the author's presentation of herself as the consort of Christ and an aggressive address to the potentates of Europe—and implicitly to the Holy Roman Emperor himself—to lead their subjects to join the armies in praise of Jesus. Indeed, Greiffenberg hoped to convert the Holy Roman Emperor and Habsburg monarch Leopold I to Protestantism, the very monarch who was aggressively promoting the Counter-Reformation in Habsburg lands; over a ten-year period (1666–76), she made six trips to Vienna to gain an audience with him for that very purpose.[6] Her sense of religious mission and authority and her self-confidence are nothing if not startling, what the literary historian Burkhard Dohm characterizes as an inclination to a "Promethean self-understanding" of what she as author can accomplish with words.[7]

To engage with Greiffenberg's oeuvre is to encounter protean female bodies that effect transformation through empathic suffering, to witness Christ as an anatomically elaborated fetus in the womb and Mary as an inspired and articulate celebrant, to be introduced to alchemical images that figure religious experience as well as to a plethora of classical allusions, to be confronted with baroque wordplay and startling word combinations and images that explode and careen before the mind's eye. It is also to come to appreciate these meditations for their dense and meticulous interweaving of biblical allusions that bear witness to participation in biblical exegesis and promulgation of Lutheran theology.[8] Most of all, one hears a distinct voice that pointedly asserts itself as female, a voice that passionately takes on the task as writer to praise, commemorate, and mourn the being that she believes to be God incarnate.

6. Bircher and Kemp list six trips to Vienna in their chronology of Greiffenberg's life ("Lebenstafel," in Greiffenberg, *Sämtliche Werke*, 1: 536–46).

7. Burkhard Dohm, "Die Auferstehung des Leibes in der Poesie. Zu einem Passionsgedicht Catharina Regina von Greiffenbergs," *Daphnis* 21 (1992): 690.

8. The theologian Vanessa Lohse confirms that Greiffenberg exhibits thorough knowledge of central tenets of the Lutheran faith in her meditations on the passion of Christ. Vanessa Lohse, "Poetische Passionstheologie: Beobachtungen zu Catharina Regina von Greiffenbergs Betrachtungen des Leidens Christi," in *Passion, Affekt, und Leidenschaft in der Frühen Neuzeit*, ed. Johann Anselm Steiger (Wiesbaden: Harrassowitz, 2005), 1: 289–99.

HISTORICAL CONTEXT

Religious division and persecution tied to cynical and opportunistic territorial designs constituted the seventeenth-century context of Catharina Regina von Greiffenberg. These historical conditions caused her acute personal suffering and loss and undoubtedly strengthened her religious beliefs and fueled her sense of literary religious mission. She was born in 1633 to Lutheran landed gentry at Castle Seisenegg in Lower Austria near the town of Amstetten, an area that to the east borders the present-day Czech Republic and Slovakia. The social milieu of her birth was a doomed world;[9] by 1678, when Greiffenberg, widowed and beleaguered from all sides, lost the family estate and finally made the decision to move permanently to Protestant Nuremberg, she numbered among the last of the Protestant nobility in Lower Austria. By the end of the decade this Protestant nobility had virtually vanished, their disappearance marking yet another milestone in the Habsburg monarchy's policy of re-Catholicization.

At the time of Greiffenberg's birth, the Thirty Years' War, which had raged in Europe for fifteen years, was at its midpoint. The immediate cause of the war, the Second Defenestration of Prague of 1618, stemmed from the Habsburg monarchy's religious persecution of Protestant nobility in Bohemia and the subsequent rebellion of Bohemia. Three decades of armed conflict that involved most of Europe, particularly Central Europe, ravaged the economies, decimated the civilian population of the German-speaking territories, and rendered the Holy Roman Empire even less viable as a political entity. The war ended in 1648 with the Peace of Westphalia, a pair of treaties that left the German-speaking world carved up into sixty-one imperial cities and around three hundred states with territorial sovereignty. Confronted with the need to put an end to a war ostensibly fought on confessional grounds, the fashioners of the peace reaffirmed the pragmatic solution to religious conflict in the German territories formulated nearly one hundred years previously by the Peace of Augsburg (1555), namely, *cuius religio eius religio*, that is, the religion of the sovereign ruler of each territory determined the religion of his subjects, a principle promulgated in the previous century in the Confession of Augsburg (1530). In the lands ruled by the Habsburg dynasty that religion remained Catholicism; thus the Peace of Westphalia in effect assured the triumph of the Counter-Reformation in the very lands that in the previous century had been open to the Reformation.

9. Urs Herzog, "Literatur in Isolation und Einsamkeit. Catharina Regina von Greiffenberg und ihr literarischer Freundeskreis," *DVjS* 45 (1971): 519.

How then did things stand in the seventeenth century in the areas of Habsburg dominion that had embraced Protestantism in the previous century?

As R. J. W. Evans asserts in his study of the Habsburg monarchy, "by the middle of the sixteenth century the ethos of the Austrian Habsburg lands was Protestant."[10] "Protestant" here comprises a range of religious opinion, including Calvinism and Lutheranism, the confession that predominated in Lower Austria. Even as both town and country embraced Protestantism of various stripes in the sixteenth century in Austria, Catholic monasteries lost their inhabitants and vitality. The loss of influence by the church profited both the towns and the landed estates, giving them new strength and confidence in their negotiations with the monarch who remained Catholic.[11] At the same time the variety of religious practice produced a de facto toleration of religious difference.[12]

In the second half of the sixteenth century, the Habsburg monarchs Maximilian II (reigned 1564–76) and Rudolph II (reigned 1576–1612), influenced by humanism and cosmopolitanism, practiced a certain spirit of toleration, with Maximilian outright favoring Lutherans. More important, the need to win the loyalty of their subjects and their support against the Turks made it expedient for the monarchs to leave their subjects to their chosen religious practices.[13] Nevertheless, the seeds of Counter-Reformation were sown mid-sixteenth century when Peter Canisius led a band of Jesuits, mainly foreigners, into Austria and founded a college in Vienna.[14] Over the next fifty years the various Austrian princes began to pursue an aggressive course of re-Catholicization in their individual territories.

This aggressive re-Catholicization gained renewed impetus in Habsburg dominions with the support of the monarch himself after the Peace of Zsitvatorok in 1606, which ended armed conflict between the Habsburg monarchy and the Ottoman Empire for twenty years. Matthias I (reigned 1612–19) thus felt free to pursue a course of religious persecution centered especially in Bohemia, and Ferdinand II (reigned 1619–37), who had all but eradicated Protestantism in the general population of his own Inner Austrian lands (Styria, Carinthia, and Carniola) before ascending to the throne,

10. R. J. W. Evans, *The Making of the Habsburg Monarchy, 1550–1700: An Interpretation* (Oxford: Clarendon Press, 1979), 4.

11. Ibid., 5.

12. Ibid., 13.

13. Charles Ingrao, *The Habsburg Monarchy, 1618–1815*, New Approaches to European History, 3 (Cambridge: Cambridge University Press, 1994), 28.

14. Evans, *Making of the Habsburg Monarchy*, 41.

aggressively pursued re-Catholicization on through the Thirty Years' War. Indeed, after the decisive defeat of rebellious Bohemian Protestant forces at the Battle of White Mountain near Prague on 8 November 1620, the Austrian government executed twenty-seven rebel leaders; their mutilated corpses were then displayed on the Charles Bridge in Prague.[15] In 1625 Ferdinand II forbade all Protestant church services and in 1628 commanded the nobility as well to return to the Catholic faith.

As a result of the measures taken by the Habsburg monarchy, the majority of the nobility in Habsburg-ruled lands had been re-Catholicized by the time of the Peace of Westphalia in the mid-seventeenth century. Nevertheless, many nobles remained Protestant in Silesia, Lower Austria, and Hungary. In the ensuing years, the Habsburg monarchy, which now turned its sights away from the Holy Roman Empire toward internal affairs, vigorously set about addressing these pockets of resistance. At the same time the monarchy strove to secure the loyalty to state and church of the landed nobility by guaranteeing their continued economic, social, and local political privileges.[16]

The situation of the Protestant nobility in Greiffenberg's homeland, Lower Austria, after 1648 was dire, although special concessions had been made to them under pressure from Sweden in the Treaty of Westphalia. These concessions granted them the right to remain in Lower Austria, despite their religious beliefs, and thus personal liberty of confession.[17] Yet this was an empty freedom, for they were not allowed actually to practice their religion. No Protestant clergy were allowed in the land, the nobility could not take Communion even in the privacy of their country castles, and they were not allowed to hire teachers to give their children religious instruction.[18] While the nobility could travel abroad to take Communion, their retainers were effectively prevented from doing so: retainers were not allowed to make such trips independently and were forbidden from accompanying their employers abroad in significant numbers.[19] In 1652 the government ultimately forbade the Lutheran nobility to employ non-Catholics.[20] They therefore found themselves in a situation in which they were raising their

15. Ingrao, *Habsburg Monarchy*, 34.

16. Ibid., 51.

17. Martin Bircher, *Johann Wilhelm von Stubenberg (1619–1663) und sein Freundeskreis: Studien zur österreichischen Barockliteratur protestantischer Edelleute* (Berlin: Walter de Gruyter, 1968), 3.

18. Ibid., 4.

19. Ibid.

20. Evans, *Making of the Habsburg Monarchy*, 119.

children in the absence of a Protestant grounding in the surrounding culture. Given the restrictions on the practice of religion, the nobility made arduous journeys to such cities in neighboring territories as Pressburg (Bratislava) in Hungary to worship and take Communion. In effect, the Protestant landed estates had three choices—to convert to Catholicism, to rent their lands and live elsewhere, or to sell their lands and emigrate. Under this pressure the families emigrated one by one until eventually none remained who were openly Protestant.

As Martin Bircher has pointed out in his study of Johann Wilhelm von Stubenberg, a member of the Protestant nobility and important teacher of and friend to Greiffenberg, through all this persecution the nobility remained staunchly loyal to the Habsburg monarch, even traveling to Vienna to celebrate the Habsburgs on festive occasions. Greiffenberg herself patriotically declared her loyalty to Leopold I in the introduction to her *Victory Column of Repentance and Faith* (begun 1663, published 1675), written in reaction to the Turkish threat of 1663, where she describes her fatherland as incorporated in the monarch.[21] As Bircher asserts, the nobility tended to believe that bad advisers had led the monarch astray, a monarch who, after all, in the commonly held and largely unquestioned belief of the time ruled by the will of God.[22] A badly counseled monarch potentially could change his ways with better advisers. As we shall see, Greiffenberg thought that with God's help, she herself would be able to convert the monarch to Lutheranism. The hope and loyalty of Greiffenberg and her fellow Protestant nobles were misplaced. Leopold I pursued his father's policies of converting Protestants to Catholicism in Habsburg territories. In staunchly Protestant Silesia, for example, which even at mid-century maintained a Protestant majority, of 1,500 Protestant places of worship in 1648, only 220 remained by 1700.[23]

Even as the Habsburg monarchy sought to secure its power internally, it found itself threatened again militarily, from both the east and the west; the Peace of Westphalia had by no means brought an end to military conflict in seventeenth-century Europe. In the west, France, under the rule of the Sun King, Louis XIV, posed the most serious threat to the status of the Habsburg monarchy as an international power. Secondarily Sweden, with which the Lutheran nobility of Lower Austria maintained cultural ties,[24] constituted an

21. Catharina Regina von Greiffenberg, *Sieges-Seule der Buße und Glaubens / wider den Erbfeind Christliches Namens,* in vol. 2 of Greiffenberg, *Sämtliche Werke,* , sig.):(vi^{r}–vi^{v}.

22. Bircher, *Johann Wilhelm von Stubenberg,* 13.

23. Ingrao, *Habsburg Monarchy,* 63.

24. Bircher, *Johann Wilhelm von Stubenberg,* 5.

ongoing menace to Habsburg political designs. In the east, troubled relations with the Protestant nobility of Hungary culminated in the Kuruc revolt (1678–85) that was supported by the Turks; still more troubling to the monarchy, the Ottoman Empire began to reassert its territorial ambitions.

If Protestants were viewed as the religious menace from within, the Muslim Turks were seen as the religious menace from without. In 1683 during the Turkish advance toward Vienna, the seat of the Habsburg monarchy, court preacher Abraham a Santa Clara, in his flamboyant sermons, chastised his flock for their sins that, he told them, had empowered the Turkish menace, for "in the ABC's *S* is followed by *T*, after sin comes the Turk."[25] In fact, the series of conflicts with the Turks, beginning in 1663 with the declaration of war by Sultan Mehmed IV (reigned 1648–87) and finally ceasing over a century later in 1791, concerned Turkish domination in Hungary and Transylvania. The threat of strengthened and expanded Turkish power enabled the Habsburg monarchy to muster support from other European powers, in particular Bavaria, Brandenburg-Prussia, and Saxony; thus in August 1664, their combined forces were able to repel Turkish attempts to cross the Rába River from Hungary into the duchy of Styria, a Habsburg Hereditary Land that included territory in present-day southeast Austria and Slovenia.[26] In the summer of 1683, the Turks returned with a vengeance, reaching the gates of Vienna where they were again repelled. Three years later in 1886 Habsburg armies advanced into central Hungary and thereafter in 1688 imperial forces, commanded by the elector of Bavaria, captured Belgrade, the symbol of the Turkish menace to Europe.[27] Despite the religious propaganda of the era, the Habsburg monarchy's conflict with the Turks was ultimately not so much one of Christians against "infidels" as a struggle for political power between Near and Middle East and Western and Central Europe.[28] When, however, Greiffenberg offered a literary response to the so-called Turkish threat, she saw it largely in religious terms.

A second venue outside Austria played a critical role in the lives of the Protestant nobility of Lower Austria. Approximately 230 miles west of Greiffenberg's home in Lower Austria lay the once powerful and affluent Free Imperial City of Nuremberg on the Pegnitz River. In the seven-

25. Abraham a Santa Clara, "Arise, Arise, You Christians," trans. Lynne Tatlock, in *Seventeenth Century German Prose*, ed. Lynne Tatlock, German Library 7 (New York: Continuum, 1993), 90.

26. Ingrao, *Habsburg Monarchy*, 66.

27. Robert A. Kann, *A History of the Habsburg Empire, 1526–1919* (Berkeley: University of California Press, 1974), 66.

28. Ibid., 65.

teenth century, after the devastation of the Thirty Years' War, Nuremberg was gradually reclaiming its economic and cultural importance.[29] A haven of Protestantism just to the north of Catholic Bavaria, it was also the locus of a remarkable flowering of German letters. In both respects Nuremberg loomed large for the Protestant nobility of Lower Austria; indeed, in the end, Nuremberg provided asylum for many of them. Greiffenberg herself eventually numbered among those who sought a home there when it became impossible to maintain a footing in Habsburg lands. But even before emigration to Nuremberg, Greiffenberg and many in her circle maintained a lively cultural exchange via letters with important Nuremberg literati, in particular, with the creative, versatile, and enterprising poet, educator, and cultural and political agent Sigmund von Birken (1626–81).

Nuremberg additionally provided fertile ground for a lively culture of publication and printing. Those members of the Lower Austrian nobility who, like Greiffenberg, were engaged in literary production most often found their publishers in Nuremberg. The prolific Nuremberg printer Michael Endter, for example, published not only Greiffenberg and some of her Lower Austrian friends, but also Bibles, devotional books, schoolbooks, and almanacs.[30]

The "republic of letters" in Nuremberg exhibited openness, rare for the seventeenth-century German territories, to the participation of women. That same Sigmund von Birken who figured so prominently in the lives of the Lower Austrian nobility furthered this openness by, among other things, recruiting women to the local language and literature society, the Pegnitzsche Hirten- und Blumenorden (Pegnitz Order of Shepherds and Flowers, founded 1644), of which he was the longtime president (1658–81). Birken's *Fürtrefflichkeit des Lieblöblichen Frauenzimmers* (1669; The Excellence of the Praiseworthy Female Sex) outlines the attitude of the order toward women in the second half of the seventeenth century. The gifted female members of the order exhibit not merely external beauty but wisdom and virtue, he writes; their speech and manners, furthermore, indicate their excellence.[31] The

29. See Klaus Garber, "Nuremberg, Arcadia on the Pegnitz," in *Imperiled Heritage: Tradition, History, and Utopia in Early Modern German Literature. Selected Essays by Klaus Garber,* ed. and introd. Max Reinhart, Studies in European Cultural Transition 5 (Aldershot: Ashgate, 2000), 117–208.

30. Josef Benzing, *Die Buchdrucker des 16. und 17. Jahrhunderts im deutschen Sprachgebiet,* 2nd ed., Beiträge zum Buch- und Bibliothekswesen 12 (Wiesbaden: Harrassowitz, 1982), 365. Benzing's catalogue of the Nuremberg printers of the sixteenth and seventeenth centuries, which lists eighty-seven printers, gives a sense of the liveliness of the city's print culture (350–69).

31. Klaus Garber, "Utopia and the Green World: Critique and Anticipation in Pastoral Poetry," in *Imperiled Heritage,* 98.

work reinterprets the Judeo-Christian creation myth, insisting that women were in fact created the same as men, except for their sex, and that society has wrongly limited women's potential. The shepherdess Dorilis laments, "Many a woman is forced to become Martha when she would prefer to be Mary. Indeed, we are condemned to such barbarity and ignorance that not only men, but even most other women, having so degenerated in vanity and ignorance, despise and deride the few of us who engage ourselves with learning."[32] Birken was, however, by no means the first man of letters in Nuremberg to reconsider the status of women during this cultural renaissance. Georg Philipp Harsdörffer's eight-volume *Frauenzimmer Gesprächspiele* (Women's Conversation Games; 1641–49), which had appeared twenty years earlier, depicts women participating in lively conversation with men on literature and the other arts and sciences. While closer analysis quickly reveals that the female interlocutors occupy a position subordinate to that of their male counterparts, the work nevertheless depicts literate women who are curious about and ready to converse on matters that were shaping European high culture; they are not merely present as a silent implied audience for cultural production by men.[33]

Political fragmentation and prolonged warfare had made it difficult in the seventeenth century for German letters to keep pace with their Italian and French counterparts. While various German territories had played a significant role in the burgeoning European publishing industry, developments in literature lagged. Societies of language and literature, modeled after the Florentine Accademia della Crusca (founded 1582), offered one remedy for this cultural stagnation. Over the course of the century, indeed, in the midst of the Thirty Years' War, language societies arose that aimed both to promote German virtue and to cultivate German as a literary language: in addition to the aforementioned Pegnitz Order of Shepherds and Flowers, the Fruchtbringende Gesellschaft (Fruit-Bearing Society; founded in Weimar in 1617), which was also known as the Palmenorden (Order of the Palm); the Deutschgesinnte Genossenschaft (German-Minded Association; founded in Hamburg in 1643); the Aufrichtige Gesellschaft von der Tannen (Up-

32. Quoted by Garber, ibid., 100.

33. Christl Griesshaber-Weninger and Karin A. Wurst, among others, caution against an undifferentiated understanding of Harsdörffer's *Frauenzimmergesprächspiele* as promoting women. Karin A. Wurst, "Die Frau als Mitspielerin und Leserin in Georg Philipp Harsdörffers Frauenzimmer Gesprächspielen, *Daphnis* 21, no. 4 (1992): 615–39; Christl Griesshaber-Weninger, "Harsdörffers 'Frauenzimmer Gesprächsspiele' als geschlechtsspezifische Verhaltensfiebel: Ein Vergleich mit heutigen Kommunikationsstrukturen," *Women in German Yearbook: Feminist Studies in German Literature and Culture* 9 (1993): 49–70.

right Society of the Pine Tree; founded in Strasbourg in 1633); and the Elbschwanenorden (Order of the Elbe Swans; founded in Lübeck in 1658).

The members of these societies, a mix of the nobility and the literary elite of the middle class, not only engaged in literary production but undertook activities designed to standardize the language (its lexicon and orthography) and, moreover, to "purify" it. The heavy influence of Italian and French, especially the latter, had in the view of the members led to an aesthetically unpleasing spurious language. Inherent in the exercise of purification was not merely an incipient cultural chauvinism but also the idea of a return to an ancient original language; indeed, many German intellectuals thought that the German language was one of the oldest languages. The attempt to restore German to a pure language thus bore a resemblance to some of the archeological work of the Renaissance with regard to the literature of classical antiquity. At the radical end of this movement, the Hamburg-based writer Philipp von Zesen (1619–89) even proposed German substitutions for loan words from Latin and Greek that had long been in use in the German language. His efforts produced such oddities as *Tageleuchter* (day lighter) for *Fenster* (window; Latin *fenestra*), *Jungferzwinger*(virgin-keep) for *Nonnenkloster* (convent, cloister; Latin *nonna* and *claustrum*)—two frequently cited examples—or *Wort-Stümpler* (word-bungler) for "bad poet" and *Gesichtsendiger* (sight-ender) for "horizon" (derived from Greek).[34] Zesen's own contemporaries did not, however, hesitate to deride such preposterous and provocative proposals.[35]

As a significant part of a program of cultivating the German language, the members of the language societies, furthermore, engaged in translation. Translation not only made high European culture in the vernacular—particularly that of Italy, France, and Spain—available in German but also helped Germans to school themselves in European genres and to begin to mold German itself into a literary language. Greiffenberg too tried her hand at translation.

Change and instability marked the seventeenth-century social and political context. While the nobility insisted on and clung to its privileges, monarchs asserted their power over them as never before. Moreover, even as

34. Herbert Blume, "Die Morphologie von Zesens Wortneubildungen" (Ph.D. diss., University of Gießen, 1967), 10–11, 91, and 92.

35. See, e.g., Christian Weise (1642–1708), *Die drei ärgsten Erznarren in der ganzen Welt* (1672; The Most Awful Archfools in the Entire World). Two excerpts from this novel that address the misguided attempts at language reform, translated by Linda Feldman, appear in Tatlock, *Seventeenth Century German Prose*, 148–56.

the real power of the aristocracy waned, ambitious middle-class men sought the prestige of the title of nobility. Life was uncertain as a result of high mortality rates, the ravages of war, changing patterns of professions, and bankruptcies and reversals of complex and obscure economies. Contemporaries depict a world in which lawsuits abound, in part because people must struggle at every turn to establish their precedence and to maintain some kind of existential ground.

Controversy, contradiction, and paradox shaped intellectual life as well. Even as religious zeal fueled Habsburg policies, some intellectuals practiced studied skepticism, and interest in the occult and in alchemy grew. The theme of vanity, moreover, stood at the center of many of the most important literary works from the period. The poet Andreas Gryphius (1616–64) lamented in 1637, in one among many such sonnets, "Where'er you look on earth, you see only vanity."[36] Likewise Hans Christoph von Grimmelshausen (1621–76) depicted in his *Simplicius Simplicissimus* (1668), the most important German novel of the seventeenth century, a world in which the only certainty was the certainty of change. For Greiffenberg, in the midst of the afflictions of this mutable, corrupt, and unreliable world, religious belief provided both a compass and the certainty of eternal salvation.

LIFE AND WORKS

Catharina Regina von Greiffenberg was the granddaughter of an enterprising lawyer, Johann Baptist Linsmayr (1540–1609), whose talent and energy had afforded him social mobility.[37] A not uncommon type of his era, he acquired the castle and seigniorial rights to the estate Seisenegg as a result of his service as imperial and archducal councilor and attorney for finances (*Kammerprokurator*). In 1603 Johann Baptist was ennobled, and five years later in 1608 Rudolph II conferred the rank of baron on him. The name Greiffenberg derived from that of the former owner of Seisenegg.

Born twenty-five years later, Greiffenberg partook of the advantages and privileges due the baronial rank attained by her grandfather, and she maintained throughout her personal and economic setbacks a firm sense of

36. Andreas Gryphius, "Es ist alles eitell," in *Sonette,* ed. Marian Szyrocki, vol. 1 of *Gesamtausgabe der deutschsprachigen Werke,* ed. Marian Szyrocki and Hugh Powell (Tübingen: Max Niemeyer, 1963), 33.

37. The following biographical summary benefits from my previous publication "Catharina Regina von Greiffenberg (1633–94)," in *Deutsche Frauen der Frühen Neuzeit: Dichterinnen, Malerinnen, Mäzeninnen,* ed. Kerstin Merkel and Heide Wunder, (Darmstadt: Wissenschaftliche Buchgesellschaft, 2000), 93–106.

her place in the Estates of Austria.[38] Indeed such a sense of aristocratic entitlement and obligation comes through quite clearly in 1672 in her meditation on the cruel treatment of Jesus on the cross, when her textual persona declares repeatedly that it is better to die than to live without honor (9: 238–39).[39] Honor is important to her even if she is merely a woman: "I was born of noble parents who valued honor, who possessed all of these ideas about and principles of honor that the nobility share," she declares. "I myself have the most delicate sense of honor, and even though I am a woman, I feel the greatest disgust toward all unworthiness and timidity" (9: 239). Even after she had lost Seisenegg and had immigrated to Nuremberg, she conformed in style to the rank to which she had been born, among other things, by living in the most elegant quarter of the city.[40]

Greiffenberg's father, Johann Gottfried von Greiffenberg (1575–1641), who had married late, died suddenly at age sixty-six of a stroke when Greiffenberg was seven, leaving his widow in a precarious financial situation. Even as she was pressed from all sides by her creditors, Johann Gottfried's much younger half brother, Hans Rudolf (1608–77), took possession of the inheritance, sold off part of the estate to pay debts, and offered the widow and her children his help, succeeding in ameliorating the family's finances to such a degree that they could live in a manner appropriate to their rank.[41]

Hans Rudolf assumed the responsibility not only for managing the family's finances but also for personally educating his gifted niece, who proved an eager pupil. Under her uncle's tutelage, Greiffenberg was introduced to the literature of antiquity, humanism, and the vernacular literature of France, Italy, and Spain. She thus not only studied the ancient languages (Latin and Greek) but also learned French, Italian, and Spanish. As was customary, she learned to translate and to imitate the authors she read. The family library,

38. Horst-Joachim Frank, *Catharina Regina von Greiffenberg: Leben und Welt der barocken Dichterin,* Schriften zur Literatur 8 (Göttingen: Sachse and Pohl, 1967), 11–12.

39. Whenever possible, Greiffenberg's meditations will be cited from the present translation. Otherwise, citations from the meditations appear in the body of the text with volume and page number corresponding to *Der Allerheiligsten Menschwerdung / Geburt und Jugend Jesu Christi* and *Des Allerheiligst- und Allerheilsamsten Leidens und Sterbens Jesu Christi,* vols. 3 and 4 and 9 and 10 of Greiffenberg, *Sämtliche Werke.*

40. Heimo Cerny, "Neues zur Biographie der Catharina Regina von Greiffenberg," *Literatur in Bayern* 38 (1994): 49.

41. The above-cited biographical dates correspond to those cited by Hartmut Laufhütte, in *Der Briefwechsel zwischen Sigmund von Birken und Catharina Regina von Greiffenberg,* ed. Laufhütte with Dietrich Jöns und Ralf Schuster, vol. 12 of Sigmund von Birken, *Werke und Korrespondenz* (Tübingen: Max Niemeyer, 2005), pt. 1, p. xvi; they deviate slightly from those cited by Kemp (Afterword, 536).

furthermore, enabled her to acquire the basics of law appropriate to her rank and knowledge of natural philosophy, science, alchemy, medicine, and mathematics. She appears also to have read widely in the area of theology including Luther, Augustine, Bernard de Clairvaux, Thomas à Kempis, the widely circulating *Wahres Christentum* (True Christianity) by Johann Arndt, and devotional literature by Harsdörffer, Birken, and Johann Michael Dilherr.[42]

The death of her father was only the first of many losses. In 1651 Greiffenberg's beloved younger sister, Anna Regina, died. Shortly after her sister's death, Greiffenberg experienced something akin to a pietistic awakening in the Lutheran church at Pressburg (Bratislava), where she and her mother had gone to take Communion.[43] She afterward claimed to have seen what she called her "Deoglori-Licht" (Deoglori-light), her "Seelen-Göttin" (goddess of the soul). She understood this vision as an admonishment to spread the glory of God in word and deed during the last days of the world, and she would later cite the obligations placed on her by this Deoglori-light as her motivation for writing and publishing her religious works.[44] She resolved, furthermore, to devote her life solely to God and never to marry.

The ground for this awakening had in fact been well prepared by her mother, Eva Maria, Baroness von Pranck zu Reinthal und Frondsberg. When Eva Maria, pregnant with Catharina, feared a miscarriage, she vowed to dedicate the child to God if she should be born alive. Responsible for her daughter's religious instruction in the absence of clergy and religious teachers, she raised Greiffenberg with the knowledge of this promise. As we shall see, Greiffenberg would later cite it as a reason for writing.

Greiffenberg shared a home with her mother until the latter's death in 1675. This relationship appears to have been very close, and the two most certainly bonded through their struggle to remain true to the Lutheran faith. When Eva Maria died, Greiffenberg wrote Birken of her sorrow with the same sort of gesture that she had employed in her meditations on Christ's suffering three years earlier, that is, a blazon of anguish:

> Oh! It is miserable knowing that that woman is ceasing to be from whom one received one's being through God, to see the woman give up the spirit before one's very eyes from whom one received one's

42. Frank, *Leben und Welt der barocken Dichterin,* 17–18; Kemp, Afterword, 496–97.

43. Frank, *Leben und Welt der barocken Dichterin,* 20.

44. Ibid., 20. See also Laufhütte, *Der Briefwechsel zwischen Sigmund von Birken und Catharina Regina von Greiffenberg,* pt. 1, p. xvii.

> own, to hear the most faithful mother's heart break beneath which one lay for so many days and hours. O heartfelt sorrow! To see the caring eyes pressed shut that so faithfully watched over my childhood and youth! To hear the pious mouth praying the prayer of one's dying hour, the mouth that so early on and so eagerly taught me to pray.[45]

This stylization of grief, designed no doubt in part, even if unconsciously so, to impress Birken, suggests that Greiffenberg on this occasion sought comfort in a tried and true mode of dealing with suffering, that is, she experimented with writing. In this same letter, she stylizes the death of her mother, describing its peacefulness and insisting that her mother lay as if still living and remained so up to the ninth day without emitting an odor of any kind.[46] Greiffenberg concludes this familiar scenario of the good death with the wish for a joyful resurrection for both mother and daughter and a reunion in heaven.[47]

In the meantime, Greiffenberg's wish to remain celibate had not been granted. A few years after her religious awakening, her half uncle, guardian, and teacher Hans Rudolf, twenty-five years her senior, openly expressed his affection for her, claiming to have been in love with her for years, and pressed her to marry him. Did her uncle really love her? Their contemporaries thought so. Indeed, it does not require a large stretch of the imagination to suppose that Hans Rudolf might have become very fond of the woman whose intellectual development and literary talent he had fostered. Stubenberg, who had at Hans Rudolf's request also served as young Catharina's tutor, wrote to Sigmund von Birken in 1659 that Hans Rudolf was head over heels in love with her ("sterblich in sie verlibt").[48] Yet in aristocratic circles, material considerations and not affection typically constituted the decisive factor in marriage choices. In this case, marriage of niece and uncle prevented a division of the Greiffenberg property and promised a bit of financial stability for the entire family.[49] Hans Rudolf no doubt had multiple reasons for loving Catharina so ardently.

Catholic law prohibited marriage between uncle and niece and thus

45. Greiffenberg to Sigmund von Birken, 15 October 1675 (my translation), in Heimo Cerny, *Catharina Regina von Greiffenberg geb. Freiherrin von Seisenegg (1633–1694): Herkunft, Leben und Werk der größten deutschen Barockdichterin,* Amstettner Beiträge 1983 (Amstett: Stadtgemeinde, 1983), 81.

46. Ibid., 82.

47. Ibid.

48. Bircher, *Johann Wilhelm von Stubenberg,* 200.

49. Cerny, *Catharina Regina von Greiffenberg,* 44.

presented a serious obstacle to the union. Furthermore, Greiffenberg herself resisted her uncle's suit on the grounds of both the impropriety of consanguinity and her own wish to remain celibate. When, however, Hans Rudolf fell ill, allegedly out of love for her, and furthermore flirted with the idea of converting to Catholicism in return for a special dispensation for the marriage, she capitulated. The couple married on 12 October 1664 in Frauenaurach near Nuremberg in Protestant territory with special dispensation from Protestant authorities and beyond the reach of the Catholic church and Austrian authorities.

In the following summer of 1665, the couple returned to their estate, whereupon Hans Rudolf was arrested by the local authorities. Although once a reluctant bride, Greiffenberg now stood by her husband and wrote three separate petitions to the emperor asking for Hans Rudolf's release. In these petitions she outlines her husband's great love for her and begs in the name of Jesus Christ for clemency. Greiffenberg's trust in the power of her words paid off. In 1666 Hans Rudolf was set free, and the marriage was recognized as legal in Habsburg lands.[50]

While the circumstances leading to this marriage are cruel by modern standards, it is worth noting that women from the nobility were raised with the expectation of arranged marriages and thus did not expect to have a choice in such matters. Although Greiffenberg later mentions pangs of conscience on account of the consanguinity, it appears that she reconciled herself to her new married estate. In a private letter to her husband from 1666, for example, she affectionately alludes to his sexual obligations to her after their long separation.[51] The couple did not, however, have children. Upon Hans Rudolf's death in 1677 after thirteen years of marriage, she fell ill and wrote a friend that her heart had been torn into a million pieces and that she now wished only for death.[52] Certainly these lamentations are stylized, yet they do suggest that Greiffenberg had become attached to her husband.

She had, however, also reason beyond that of emotional loss to mourn her husband's death. As a widow, she found herself, like her mother upon her father's death, besieged by creditors. One such creditor went so far as to attack her physically in 1678.[53] In that same year she lost her estate to her longtime nemesis, Franz von Riesenfels. At this point she had no choice but

50. Cerny, "Neues zur Biographie," 47–48.

51. Ibid., 48.

52. Greiffenberg to Siegmund von Birken, 3 May 1677, in Cerny, *Catharina Regina von Greiffenberg*, 90–91.

53. Cerny, *Catharina Regina von Greiffenberg*, 56.

to emigrate. Like many in her circle, she chose Nuremberg, where she had previously stayed for short periods of time. Here she could live relatively comfortably thanks to her inheritance from her mother. This final reversal of fortune can, however, only have been devastating for her. Indeed, in her third set of meditations published thirteen years later, one year before her death, she writes of the wretchedness of widows: "The widow . . . is the target toward which all the arrows of persecution fly, the mark of all the shots of misfortune. . . . If there is a lightning bolt in the sky, it rolls around until it strikes a poor widow."[54] It would appear that thirteen years in relative comfort and among friends who admired her had not dispelled the memory of the bitter end of life as she had known it upon the death of her husband.

Greiffenberg's letters and religious works testify to close friendships—particularly with women—that were cemented in literary and religious sociability. Greiffenberg, along with her closest friend, Susanna Popp, née Priefer (d. 1683), was a member of the so-called Ister-Gesellschaft (Ister Society, referring to the ancient name for the Lower Danube, which runs through Lower Austria), a club for poets founded by the landed gentry in Lower Austria.[55] Greiffenberg, known as Clio (the muse of history) in the Ister Society, conducted a lively correspondence with Popp, known as Isis, even after Popp emigrated to Nuremberg in 1667. When Greiffenberg herself finally emigrated and settled in Nuremberg in 1680, she was able to resume regular contact with Popp for the remaining years of Popp's life.

Within the Ister Society, a subdivision of female members called themselves the Ister Nymphs. A subgroup of this subdivision, consisting of around seven women, in turn affiliated with one another largely for religious purposes and met at Seisenegg for the sake of edifying discussion. They gathered in an idyllic grove with gardens, paths, a pond, and a grotto covered with broom and jasmine in the background. Greiffenberg dedicated an allegorical "Tugend-Übung" (Exercise in Virtue) to these "shepherdesses," which appeared in 1675 as an appendix to her *Victory Column of Repentance and Faith*. Eventually, like Popp, all of the Ister Nymphs emigrated under pressure from the Habsburg re-Catholicization.

The best documented of Greiffenberg's friendships is that with the aforementioned Birken. A rich letter exchange between Greiffenberg and

54. Catharina Regina von Greiffenberg, *Des Allerheiligsten Lebens JESU Christi*, vols. 4–8 of *Sämtliche Werke*, 6: 119.

55. Karl F. Otto Jr. differentiates between language societies and poets' clubs, assigning the *Ister-Society* to the latter category. *Die Sprachgesellschaften des 17. Jahrhunderts* (Stuttgart: Metzler, 1972), 2–3.

Birken—from 1662 until Birken's death in 1681—bears witness to shared religious views, literary interests, broad reading, social connections, and habits of daily life. Birken, recognizing the superior talent of his correspondent, not only supported her literary work but helped her to find a publisher, offered her constructive criticism, served as her editor, and as outlined below, even contributed to it. The language of the letter exchange remains formal throughout. Birken, who was from the middle class, addresses Greiffenberg as "Your Grace" or "Highborn Gracious Lady," while Greiffenberg salutes him as "Esteemed Sir." They also refer to one another and themselves by their literary names, as Urania (muse of astronomy), Coris (a type of flower), and Silvanus (Roman god of the forest). The content of the correspondence bears witness to an intense emotional and spiritual affinity and to Greiffenberg's sense of Birken as a willing audience for her linguistic virtuosity and religious convictions.

From a modern perspective, Greiffenberg is perhaps at her most startling in political matters. Even as the Habsburgs pursued their domestic policy of re-Catholicization, Greiffenberg conceived of a plan to convert the emperor to Lutheranism, firmly believing that with God's help she could accomplish this, in her view, heroic deed through the power of persuasion. Once converted, the emperor would, she thought, guide all his subjects to the true faith. To this end, Greiffenberg repeatedly journeyed to Vienna (1666–76) in an attempt to gain an audience. When the sixth journey proved, like the previous ones, unsuccessful, she finally abandoned her plan, believing that God must have intended the glorious event to occur not in her lifetime but at some moment in the future. The final pages of *Des Allerheiligst- und Allerheilsamsten Leidens und Sterbens Jesu Christi* (1672; On the Supremely Holy and Supremely Salvific Suffering and Dying of Jesus Christ), written during this period, reflect her sense of religious mission, for here she addresses the "potentates of Europe" and specific matters of Lutheran doctrine. As Hartmut Laufhütte asserts, her letters indicate that she had one particular potentate especially in mind: Leopold I.[56]

In 1678 Philipp von Zesen included Greiffenberg as "The Brave Woman" in his German-Minded Association as one of only two female members, making her the head of one of four subdivisions, the Liljenzunft

56. Laufhütte, *Der Briefwechsel zwischen Sigmund von Birken und Catharina Regina von Greiffenberg*, pt. 1, p. xxiii. See also pt. 2, p. 667, where Laufhütte points out that Greiffenberg transparently aims her text at the emperor in these final pages in passages that are aggressively Lutheran in outlook.

(Lily Guild). In his encomium of 1678 for her, he wrote, "Whenever our Brave Woman fortifies her spirits / she far surpasses most of poetry's male masters."[57] Indeed, by the mid-1670s, Greiffenberg had proved herself in the public arena of print culture.

Greiffenberg entered print culture in 1662 with her *Geistliche Sonnette / Lieder und Gedichte* (Spiritual Sonnets, Songs, and Poems), the work that established her reputation as a poet. The title page states explicitly, however, that Hans Rudolf von Greiffenberg published the work without her knowledge. Divided into two parts and provided with a subject index and an index of first lines, the work claims to offer pious entertainment. The indices make clear, however, that it can serve additionally to edify; with the aid of these indices, readers seeking edification on specific subjects can quickly locate the pertinent poems. While Greiffenberg's deep piety shapes the tenor of the work as a whole, the poems are by no means limited to overtly religious themes; Greiffenberg writes here of, among other things, nature, the seasons, and poetry and provides her own poetic treatment of themes and stories from classical mythology.

Evidence of sensitivity to her precarious position as female writer surfaces in this first work, as does an interest in women's roles in spiritual matters. Referring to the presence of women at Jesus' tomb, as recorded in all four Gospels, one poem remarks that Christ appeared not to the lofty male rulers of the world but to "weak women."[58] Another poem specifically addresses her life mission as woman writer to praise Jesus. Her soul was chosen by God for this purpose, the poem asserts. Just as Jesus favorably regarded the halfpenny of the poor woman, the lyrical subject exults, so too does he like the sound of her simple little poem (1: 6).[59]

Not long after the publication of the *Spiritual Sonnets,* Greiffenberg began a second formidable project, inspired by the so-called Turkish threat of 1663 that had led her and her mother to flee to Nuremberg for a short

57. [Philipp von Zesen], *Lobklingende Ruhm- und Nahmen-Reime / damit Der Hoch-Wohlgebohrnen / zum Zierraht und Preise der Deutschgesinneten Welt auserkohrnen Frauen / Frauen Katharinen Reginen / Frauen von Greiffenberg* etc. (Hamburg, 1678), sig. π4[v]. Heinz Engels lists 1678 as the date of the founding of the Lily Guild. *Die Sprachgesellschaften des 17. Jahrhunderts.* Beiträge zur deutschen Philologie 54 (Gießen: Wilhelm Schmitz, 1983), 139.

58. Catharina Regina von Greiffenberg, *Geistliche Sonnette / Lieder und Gedichte / zu Gottseligem Zeitvertreib,* vol. 1 of *Sämtliche Werke,* 1: 171. Further references to this work are cited parenthetically within the body of the text with volume and page number.

59. Greiffenberg refers here to the widow of Mk 12: 42–44 and Lk 21: 1–4, who offers two halfpennies in the temple. Jesus points out that she has given more than anyone else because she has given from her poverty while others have given from abundance.

time. This work, entitled *Die Sieges-Seule der Buße und Glaubens / wider den Erbfeind Christliches Namens* (The Victory Column of Repentance and Faith against the Archenemy of the Christian Name), did not actually appear until 1675 and then allegedly only at the insistence of Hans Rudolf, who by then was Greiffenberg's husband.

In electing to address world-historical events in a religious context, Greiffenberg most certainly overstepped the then common understanding of woman's place. Hans Rudolf's insistence on the publication served as a convenient excuse to write. The introductory pages furthermore provided "Lines of Evaluation" by Greiffenberg's old friend and mentor Johann Wilhem von Stubenberg, who stresses here that men too would be pleased to call this work their own and that it is a miracle that a woman wrote it.[60] To defend it, Greiffenberg herself offered a new twist to the perennial argument about the relative power of the sword and the pen: weapons of war, she allows, are for men; weak women can write.[61]

In keeping with its title, *Victory Column of Repentance and Faith,* which consists of seven thousand lines of alexandrine verse in rhymed couplets, has both a patriotic and a religious didactic mission. It calls on the emperor and the people to join forces in opposing the Turks who, as "infidels," menace Austria. The Turks, the text asserts, have achieved power as a result of the Austrians' own sins, and thus repentance and prayer are critical to driving them out. Moreover, in keeping with her wish to see the emperor and his subjects converted to Protestantism, Greiffenberg insists that victory over the Turks will not be assured until all people are united in faith. A bold (if unrealistic) political and religious work, *Victory Column of Repentance and Faith* is, as Cristina Pumplun has demonstrated, also a carefully composed work with aesthetic and rhetorical aspiration. Indeed, it displays architectonic features, its line lengths reproducing the shape of the commemorative column of its title, that is, a monument consisting of a wide pedestal surmounted by a column crowned with a capital.[62] This literary victory column, like architectural ones, is thus to serve as a sign of both the triumph of faith and of state power. The work's appendix consists, furthermore, of Greiffenberg's translation of Guillaume du Bartas's (1544–90) *Triomphe de la Foy* (Triumph of Faith) and the above-mentioned *Tugend-Übung* (Exercise in Virtue). Besides the op-

60. Greiffenberg, *Die Sieges-Seule der Buße und Glaubens*, 2: sig.):(xii^{v}.

61. Ibid., 2: sig.):(iii^{v}–iiii^{v}.

62. Cristina Pumplun, "Die *Sieges-Seule* der Catharina Regina von Greiffenberg: Ein poetisch-politisches Denkmal für Gott und Vaterland," in *Literatur und politische Aktualität,* ed. Elrud Ibsch and Ferdinand van Ingen, Amsterdamer Beiträge zur neueren Germanistik 36 (Amsterdam: Rodopi, 1993), 355.

portunity to display her skill as translator, *Triumph of Faith* offered her the opportunity to show off her learnedness with an extensive commentary.

In 1672 Greiffenberg with the help of Birken published *Des Allerheiligst- und Allerheilsamsten Leidens und Sterbens Jesu Christi, Zwölf andächtige Betrachtungen* (Twelve Devout Meditations on the Supremely Holy and Supremely Salvific Suffering and Dying of Jesus Christ), the first part of a still greater undertaking that became her life work.[63] In commencing with the passion, Greiffenberg went to the heart of Luther's "theology of the cross," according to which Christ's passion is the central moment of the hidden God's revelation of himself; the selections chosen for the present anthology highlight Greiffenberg's insistence on women's special relationship to this suffering Christ.[64] The second set of meditations, *Der Allerheiligsten Menschwerdung, Geburt und Jugend Jesu Christi, Zwölf andächtige Betrachtungen* (Twelve Devout Meditations on the Supremely Holy Incarnation, Birth, and Youth of Jesus Christ), followed six years later in 1678, and in 1683 the *Supremely Holy and Supremely Salvific Suffering and Dying* appeared in a second edition. In 1793, one year before her death, the third and longest installment was published in two volumes: *Des Allerheiligsten Lebens JESU Christi* (On the Supremely Holy Life of Jesus Christ). Greiffenberg planned to undertake a fourth work on the ascension, resurrection, and the trinity but died before she could realize this ambition.

Greiffenberg's three sets of meditations on the life of Christ amount to thirty-six meditations in all and compose eight volumes totaling over four thousand pages in the reprint edition of 1983, quite visibly constituting the bulk of her published work. With these meditations, Greiffenberg claimed, she hoped to accomplish the course set long ago for her in her mother's womb, to commemorate and spread God's glory. Although the three sets vary in length, they share a common structure. As will be explained in further detail below, each meditation is introduced by an image that embodies its central themes, along with an introductory poem. The body of the meditation consists in turn of a series of bolded quotations from Scripture that serve both to narrate and to provide the basis or rather impetus for contemplation. Each of these quotations is followed by meditative commentary—in both prose and verse—that ranges from ecstatic praising to consideration

63. Hartmut Laufhütte, "Passion Christi bei Sigmund von Birken und Catharina Regina von Greiffenberg," in Steiger, *Passion, Affekt, und Leidenschaft in der Frühen Neuzeit*, 1: 271–87. Laufhütte succinctly outlines the considerable aid that Birken provided Greiffenberg—from offering encouragement to finding a publisher for her.

64. On the theology of the cross, see Walther von Loewenich, *Luther's Theology of the Cross*, trans. Herbert J. A. Bouman (Belfast: Christian Journals, 1976).

of lofty theological matters to preaching on personal habits of worship. As has been painstakingly demonstrated in the case of the meditations on the incarnation and birth and as can be generalized to the others, ostensibly unstudied outpourings are in fact carefully composed texts that demonstrate literary aspiration on the part of their author.[65] To separate religious zeal and literary pretension is to misunderstand Greiffenberg's oeuvre.

As with the *Victory Column of Repentance,* Greiffenberg hoped that her meditations would serve to commemorate and celebrate as well as to confirm readers in their faith or to convert them to what she saw as the true faith. She prided herself on the fact that both Protestants and Catholics read her meditations and showed herself particularly eager for Catholics to read them, ever hoping that they would be persuaded of Lutheran truth.[66] As mentioned above, her ideal reader was none other than the Holy Roman Emperor and Austrian monarch himself, a reader whom she never reached.

Greiffenberg by no means published all of her literary and religious writing.[67] Yet even if most of the efforts that remained unpublished during her lifetime have been lost, her published work still surpasses in quantity that of all of her German-speaking women contemporaries and that of many male writers as well, thus serving as a weighty testimony to her religious faith, ambition, and literary talent.

Greiffenberg died peacefully in Nuremberg on 8 April 1694 on the Monday after Easter, having taken Communion for the last time on Good Friday. As Georg Albrecht Hagendorn pointedly noted in his eulogy for her, this was the day on which Christ had first appeared to his disciples.[68] Thus Greiffenberg met her maker, as it were, on the very day that perhaps best expressed her literary religious mission—the revelation of him whom she believed to be the true god.

65. See Pumplun, "*Begriff des Unbegreiflichen.*"

66. See Greiffenberg to Sigmund von Birken, 6 February 1673, quoted by Frank, *Leben und Welt der barocken Dichterin,* 85.

67. According to Frank, Greiffenberg refers to unpublished work in her letters (*Leben und Welt der barocken Dichterin,* 125–26). Greiffenberg's recently published correspondence with Birken, for example, includes undated and unpublished poetry. See *Der Briefwechsel zwischen Sigmund von Birken und Catharina Regina von Greiffenberg,* pt. 1, pp. 375–410. See also Greiffenberg, *Gelegenheit und Geständnis: Unveröffentlichte Gelegenheitsgedichte als verschleierter Spiegel des Lebens und Wirkens der Catharina Regina von Greiffenberg. Faksimiledruck nach Handschriften im Archiv des Pegnischen Blumenordens,* ed. Ingrid Black and Peter M. Daly, Kanadische Studien zur deutschen Literatur 3 (Bern: H. Lang, 1971).

68. Georg Albrecht Hagendorn, "Leichenpredict auf Catharina Regina von Greiffenberg," in Greiffenberg, *Sämtliche Werke,* 1: 489.

ANALYSIS OF THE *MEDITATIONS*

The present anthology includes excerpts from the first two sets of meditations, *Supremely Holy and Supremely Salvific Suffering and Dying of Jesus Christ* (1672, 1683) and *Supremely Holy Incarnation, Birth, and Youth of Jesus Christ* (1678). These selections aim to give a sense of the structure and nature of Greiffenberg's meditations, to show them at their most interesting and distinct, and to fulfill the aspiration of the Other Voice, namely, to give early modern women's writing a hearing that highlights the alternative that it presents to the received view of early modern cultural production and women's place in it. I have thus translated the introductory material of both works and three meditations in their entirety as well as parts of four additional meditations that focus largely on the role of women in the Christian story of salvation.

According to Friedhelm Kemp, the Gospel of Matthew, as it was rendered in the annotated Kurfürstenbibel (Elector's Bible), an edition of the Bible completed and first published in 1641 under the reign of Duke Ernst I of Saxe-Gotha (1601–75, reigned 1640–75), provided the source text for Greiffenberg's meditations on the life of Christ.[69] The Matthew of the Elector's Bible is furnished with parenthetical explanations of verse and cross-references to the three other Gospels; sometimes the cross-referenced verses are reproduced in their entirety. Greiffenberg does not, however, proceed through Matthew verse by verse in her recapitulation of the life of Christ; her text shifts among Gospels, by no means taking up every verse from Matthew.[70] Occasionally she includes seamlessly blended verses from two different Gospels, creating, unlike her source text, an unremarked hybrid version of Scripture. While she may have been aided by the Elector's Bible in her compilation, as Kemp claims, her text exhibits some independence of selection and presentation of Scripture. Whereas some of these deviations

69. Friedhelm Kemp, "Nachwort," in vol. 1 of Greiffenberg, *Sämtliche Werke*, 510.

70. See, e.g., *Biblia, Das ist, Die gantze H. Schrifft, Altes und Neues Testament, Teutsch D. Martin Luthers: Auf gnädige Verordnung deß . . . Herrn Ernsts, Herzogen zu Sachsen* [5th ed.] (Nuremberg: Christoph and Paul Endter, 1662). A later edition of 1700 (call no. BS239 1700), which I was able to examine at Columbia University, conforms in format to the earlier edition of 1662, which I consulted at the Herzog August Bibliothek in Wolfenbüttel, Germany, leading me to conclude that the edition of 1662 can reasonably be taken as indicative of the format in which Greiffenberg knew this work, whichever edition she might have consulted. For an overview of the editions of this so-called Elector's Bible, see Veronika Albrecht-Birkner, *Reformation des Lebens. Die Reformen Herzog Ernsts des Frommen von Sachsen-Gotha und ihre Auswirkungen auf Frömmigkeit, Schule und Alltag im ländlichen Raum (1640–1675)*, Leucorea-Studien zur Geschichte der Reformation und der Lutherischen Orthodoxie 1 (Leipzig: Evangelische Verlagsanstalt, 2002), 462–67.

may initially seem minor, they in the end result in a text that has a different character from its source—not Scripture as object of scholarly study, but Scripture as the foundation of belief and object of meditation. Furthermore, as the current anthology should help to make clear, her choice to include in the *Suffering and Dying of Jesus Christ* every scriptural mention of women in the account of the last days of Jesus Christ in all four Gospels indicates a preoccupation with women's role in spiritual matters and specifically with her own role as religious writer.

Greiffenberg's meditations number among many such devotional works published throughout Europe in the seventeenth century. They share with many of these works practices of meditation formulated by Jesuits and adopted and adapted by other confessions.

The meditational exercise consists of three parts, in Louis Martz's words, "composition," "analysis," and "colloquy," each of which is seen as a function of the three powers of the soul—memory, understanding, and will.[71] According to Greiffenberg's older contemporary English bishop Joseph Hall, meditation "begins in the understanding, endeth in the affection; It begins in the braine, descends to the heart; Begins on earth, ascends to Heaven."[72] In the meditational exercise, one is supposed to concentrate one's imagination, senses, and thought fully on a particular object, word, or theme. First, one is to perceive the object with all one's senses, that is, experience it, in order to be able to understand it emotionally and intellectually; thereafter, one is to ponder its full meaning.

A concise description of the mental exercise of meditation in fact precedes the first published set of Greiffenberg's meditations and serves as an introduction to this work and the thirty-six meditations as a whole. This description consists of a frontispiece depicting a figure in flowing robes that is standing before a slate with a sponge, with which all but a picture of the crucifixion has been erased, and an accompanying poem that evokes the meditational exercise as well. The person meditating is, according to the poem, to clear his mind of everything so that it retains nothing but a mental image of Christ on the cross. When one does so, one will, according to the explanation, find peace in the infinity of God.

Even as she writes in the tradition of Jesuit exercises, Greiffenberg is

71. Louis L. Martz, *The Poetry of Meditation: A Study in English Religious Literature* (New Haven: Yale University Press, 1954), 34–35, cited by Peter M. Daly, *Dichtung und Emblematik bei Catharina Regina von Greiffenberg,* Studien zur Germanistik, Anglistik und Komparatistik 36 (Bonn: Bouvier Verlag Herbert Grundmann, 1976), 116.

72. Martz, *Poetry of Meditation,* 25, cited by Daly, *Dichtung und Emblematik,* 115.

given, as Peter Daly points out, to occasional meditation. In such practice one briefly describes objects or occurrences from the everyday world and interprets them in a spiritual vein. In 1668 Greiffenberg wrote in a letter to Birken of the difficulty of finding time for religious devotion in a life fraught with social obligations, household responsibilities, and many personal difficulties. Her way of preventing herself from becoming mired in earthly things was to make these mundane things into "Geistlichen Gedächtnus Öhrteren" (locations of spiritual mindfulness), that is, to transform them into occasions to be mindful of God.[73] One finds this practice in the meditations translated for this volume when, for example, the text speaks of working flax as an occasion for devotion and contemplation of the passion, since Jesus was wrapped in a linen shroud.

A much remarked aspect of Greiffenberg's art is her use of the emblem to figure religious experience. Indeed, all thirty-six of the meditations are preceded by an emblem, and seven of these emblems appear in the present anthology. The emblem, which expresses a key idea contemplated in the respective meditation, serves as an introduction of sorts to the meditation it precedes.

In choosing this form for her devotional work, Greiffenberg selected a symbolic mode ubiquitous in seventeenth-century high culture. Daly offers the following "minimal description" of the emblem: "emblems are composed of symbolic pictures and words; a meaningful relationship between the two is intended; the manner of communication is connotative rather than denotative."[74] The emblem is thus at once representation and interpretation. Typically it exhibits a tripartite structure: *pictura, inscriptio,* and *subscriptio,* that is, image, motto (usually printed above the image), and subscription (a prose or verse quotation beneath the picture). Sometimes it is accompanied by an expanded explanation on a separate page. The emblems that punctuate Greiffenberg's text exhibit a motto within the engraved image itself but omit the quotation beneath the images. They, however, generally include an explanatory poem on a separate page. Emblems, Greiffenberg explained in a letter to Birken, ought to be at once clear and obscure, comprehensible and incomprehensible.[75] Daly proposes that we can understand her description as articulating her pedagogical intention, that is, the emblem should address

73. Daly, *Dichtung und Emblematik,* 130–32.

74. Peter M. Daly. *Literature in the Light of the Emblem: Structural Parallels between the Emblem and Literature in the Sixteenth and Seventeenth Centuries,* 2nd ed. (Toronto: University of Toronto Press, 1998), 8.

75. "Klaar und dunkel . . . Verständlich und unverständig," quoted by Daly, *Dichtung und Emblematik,* 119–20.

the intellect in such a way as to stimulate the spirit; the effort necessary to comprehend the emblem should ensure that the religious belief expressed by the emblem is more easily remembered.[76]

The picture or image of the emblem "may depict one or several objects, persons, events or actions, in some instances set against an imaginary or real background. . . . These objects are found in organic and inorganic combinations, or real and unreal combinations."[77] The images included in the present translation exhibit a range of combinations. The picture preceding the meditation on the conception of Christ, for example, appears with the motto "The Most in the Least" (das Mehrste im Minsten). It depicts a sea flowing between two rocky cliffs into a tiny fountain. The image makes visible the pun in the root of the German word for "most" (*mehr,* "more"), which is pronounced the same as *Meer* (sea). The explanation makes clear, furthermore, that the picture alludes to the miracle of clothing infinite divinity in human flesh within a finite woman's body, an idea that Greiffenberg then ponders at length over the course of the meditation. "On Mary's Pregnancy" is, as a further example, preceded by the image of a man looking into a dark image in a pool of water beneath the *inscriptio* "Overshadowed but Unblemished" (Überschattet aber unbefleckt). The accompanying poem makes clear that the picture refers to Joseph, who is confronted with the fact of his bride's pregnancy before he has had sexual intercourse with her and who must through faith in God accept that appearances are not what they seem. The image thus anticipates the section of the following meditation when Greiffenberg ponders Mt 1: 18–25.

Although they constitute an integral part of her meditations, Greiffenberg did not in fact execute these emblems herself.[78] Rather, her mentor and friend Birken designed the pictures and wrote the accompanying poems in accordance with her instructions.[79] The unattributed inclusion of these emblems thus constitutes a rare reversal of the common practice of the age, that is, of lack of attribution of *women's* contribution to *male*-authored works. In this case male collaboration is not identified. While the text of the meditations proper does not refer specifically to the emblems, each emblem quite deftly adumbrates principal ideas treated in the meditation that it in effect

76. Daly, *Dichtung und Emblematik,* 121.

77. Daly, *Literature in the Light of the Emblem,* 7.

78. The only emblems completely of her own design are those in her final set of meditations, which was published after Birken's death.

79. Daly, *Dichtung und Emblematik,* 119.

introduces. Thus the emblems can be seen as structurally and thematically integrated into the work as a whole.

The effusiveness of Greiffenberg's meditations may give the impression of spontaneity, yet they are meticulously crafted and stylized in accordance with contemporary spiritual and literary practice; they are not mere emotional effusions. Even when they take up real, everyday objects, these are quickly incorporated into a spiritual program of worshiping and memorializing Jesus Christ in which these same everyday objects and experiences are transformed. Kathleen Foley-Beining's contention that the mention of everyday activities bears witness to Greiffenberg's "keen interest in the life experience of women" could therefore bear some adjustment, for these everyday experiences provide the occasion and tools but are not the object or final result of these meditations.[80] Yet as the excerpts included in the present anthology indicate, the meditations do make a strong claim for women's spiritual authority and for women's role in the story of salvation. Moreover, as we shall see, the text acknowledges historical conditions of women but ultimately lifts them out of precisely the limitations of biology and circumscribed social roles.

It was not uncommon for authors to publish anonymously or under a pseudonym or anagram in the seventeenth century. Furthermore, as mentioned above, women frequently were simply not credited for their contributions to works written by men. Greiffenberg's name by contrast appears on the title pages of all her works, and her introductions are signed as well. In 1672, as she prepared for the publication of the *Suffering and Dying of Jesus Christ,* her husband expressed reservations about the advisability of her putting her name to the work, for he feared political consequences. In two letters to Birken, written 1 August 1672 and 4 October 1672, Greiffenberg insists, however, that the meditations must appear under her name even if it might be dangerous for her. For one thing, she asserts, she has a reputation and people are used to hearing such things from her. Styling herself in both letters as something of a martyr, she claims, furthermore, to be eager to take full responsibility for what she writes. She is, moreover, prepared to defend herself in public: "I feel capable of defending what I have written with the help of God."[81]

Alert readers new to Greiffenberg's meditations may be struck not only

80. Foley-Beining, *Body and Eucharistic Devotion,* 14.

81. Greiffenberg to Sigmund von Birken, 1 August 1672 and 4 October 1972, *Der Briefwechsel zwischen Sigmund von Birken und Catharina Regina von Greiffenberg,* pt. 1, pp. 215–16.

by the prominence of the author's name but by the text's use of the first person, by a voice that frequently reminds the reader that it emerges from a woman. The liveliness and forcefulness of this narrative female voice may, furthermore, tempt readers to read the text autobiographically, a reading that can lead them to miss the rhetorical deftness of the author. While the text certainly offers insight into the author's life, it by no means operates principally in an autobiographical mode. To equate the textual persona with the real person can in turn result in a narrow understanding of the author's life circumstances, which by no means revolved solely around religious matters. Finally, such unconsidered equation of textual persona and author can result in a misapprehension of the linguistic achievement and the aims of the text itself. Greiffenberg's self-presentation is stylized and geared toward appropriating spiritual and literary authority particularly to herself as woman religious writer and generally to women in the religious sphere.

From her earliest published work, Greiffenberg reveals interest in women's active participation in religious matters and in particular in Gospel accounts of the salvation of humankind. This preoccupation bears fruit in the meditations selected for the present anthology, in which not only such named biblical figures as Mary, Elizabeth, Mary Magdalene, and Mary of Clopas receive extended attention, indeed, even speak, but where Jesus' unnamed female disciples—the anonymous women who accompanied Jesus to Golgotha (Lk 23: 27), those who followed him from Galilee (Lk 23: 49), and the women at the tomb (unnamed women from Galilee in Lk 23: 55–56 and Lk 24: 1–5)—receive consideration, as does even mundane labor performed by women that might figure in salvation. Greiffenberg's textual persona insists that "the Holy Spirit dignifies women with His fulfillment and excludes from His grace neither sex, nor estate, nor age. . . . He does not show partiality toward one sex or the other, and even if weak women are otherwise despised, He does not despise them. He works, sings, plays, shouts for joy, and jubilates in their hearts as in men's" (205, in this volume). Meditating on the unnamed women from Galilee, Greiffenberg's textual persona insists, furthermore, that in addition to these women, many more played a role in salvation, not just those mentioned in the Bible: "many others whose names are written in heaven although not in this book. The Holy Spirit would not have omitted them," she reasons, "if it did not suffice for them to be recognized there to greater glory" (115, in this volume). Greiffenberg steers a course among various possibilities for women in her oeuvre: she assents to women's lowly status and plays that status to advantage; in an essentializing turn, she asserts women's greater spiritual capacities; and, as we shall examine in greater detail below, she pursues a spirituality that transcends the constraints of material bodies and their gendered cultural and social positioning.

The selections from Greiffenberg's life work included in the present anthology ponder central mysteries of Christian faith, namely, the incarnation and the passion; at the same time, these very mysteries, with their emphasis on the body, perforce raise questions about sex and gender for Greiffenberg as a female religious writer, that is, gender as it is imposed on sexed bodies and as it regulates access to spiritual authority.

The body stands at the center of Christian theology, for Jesus Christ is believed to be uniquely God incarnate. His martyrdom redeemed the world because he suffered it in a mortal human body capable of experiencing pain. Thus according to Christian belief, his resurrection holds out the promise that all human beings will be not only cleansed of their sins but restored, body and soul, at the end of time. Greiffenberg is at her most eloquent when she contemplates incarnation, pregnancy, and gestation; Jesus as fetus in the womb; the corporeal experience of pain and sorrow; martyrdom; and burial.

Even as Greiffenberg contemplates mysteries that according to Christian theology took place in real, historical time, she seizes the opportunity for textual play, the opportunity to create fictions of transformative female bodies that give birth to, worship, praise, and suffer alongside the embodied Christ; she thus suggests a profound destabilization of seventeenth-century hierarchical gender arrangements, a destabilization that grants women—and particularly Greiffenberg as woman writer—authority in religious matters both by virtue of their sex and by virtue of their ability ultimately to transcend the limitations of that material, historical sexed body.

The meditations translated for this anthology are arranged in the order in which they were published, not in the order in which the events are narrated in the Gospels. Reading the texts in this sequence enables a sense of the author's development as a writer and makes clear how importantly the woman with nard oil, the object of the first meditation, figures Greiffenberg's life project and the understanding of religious mission that informs the thirty-six meditations as a whole.

SUFFERING AND DYING OF JESUS CHRIST (1672/1683)

Greiffenberg opens her meditations on Christ's suffering and sacrifice by dedicating them to Jesus, the bridegroom of her soul. Demonstrating her sophisticated knowledge of the dynamics and conventions of publication, she proceeds to review the reasons that drive authors to dedicate their books to certain people—adulation, tribute, love, friendship, gratitude, protection, patronage, and profit. All of these motivations, she asserts, apply to her relationship to Jesus. Even as she expresses deep piety with this lofty dedication, she thereby also deftly circumvents customary preliminaries such as those that characterize her *Spiritual Songs* published ten years earlier. This new work is thus not framed by the voices of her male contemporaries recommending or apologizing for the book or publishing it without her knowledge. While in the "Prefatory Remarks to the Noble Reader" that follow the dedication she herself assumes the expected apologetic stance and expresses humility, humility is not, as we shall see, the attitude that she will maintain throughout the meditations.

The first meditation in this set takes up the biblical verses that narrate the episode involving the woman who anoints Christ with nard oil in the house of Simon the Leper in Bethany. According to Mt 26: 12, to which Greiffenberg alludes but which she does not quote, this anointment prepares Jesus for burial. Greiffenberg's rendering of this episode at the outset of a 950-page work sets the tone and encapsulates salient aspects of the treatment of gender in the meditations that follow.

By opening with the woman with nard oil, Greiffenberg places Jesus' female disciples in the foreground of the meditations that constitute her life's work; these are women who in the Gospels remain for the most part nameless and in the background.[82] After this first meditation, Greiffenberg seizes every opportunity presented by the Gospels to return to the women who followed Christ. Many, but not all, of these passages have been included in this anthology.

The episode of the woman with nard oil foregrounds Jesus' defense of a well-meaning woman before his twelve male disciples. By standing up for this woman, the text asserts, Jesus defended the honor of all women. Christ repeatedly appears in the eleven subsequent meditations as the vindicator of women, and the text asserts that women deserve his support because of

82. Only the Gospel according to John names the woman with nard oil. Here (Jn 12: 3) she is called Mary and identified as the sister of Lazarus. She is implicitly contrasted with her worldly sister, Martha, who worries about dinner while she, the more contemplative of the siblings, anoints Jesus. In Lk 10: 38–42 by contrast, Jesus' meeting with Mary and Martha is distinct from an unnamed woman's anointing of Christ's feet in Lk 7: 36–50. See also Jn 11: 2, where Mary, one of the sisters of Lazarus, is identified as "the woman who anointed the Lord with ointment and wiped his feet with her hair," an episode that is not actually related until the following chapter. Combined readings of John and Luke, where the woman who anoints Jesus' feet and wipes them with her hair is identified as a sinner, gave rise to the tradition that conflates the woman with nard oil with Mary Magdalene, out of whom seven demons were cast and who was numbered among the women present at the tomb.

their profound faith and, moreover, their capacity to empathize with his suffering.[83]

In the eleventh meditation Greiffenberg touts women's greater faith, claiming that women, as opposed to men who are cunning and deceitful, have ever been more willing to fear God and that they, moreover, have always followed Christ in greater numbers, like the women from Galilee in Mt 27: 55–56. Women surpass even the male disciples in their readiness openly to mourn Jesus. Furthermore, while men are inclined to violence, Greiffenberg maintains, women are disposed to empathize and to relieve suffering (84, in this volume). Women, she asserts over the course of her meditations, possess special qualities that make them more steadfast and ready to believe in the first place. Even as Greiffenberg reminds her readers of social prejudice against women in this first meditation and elsewhere, even as she stresses women's weakness, humility, and lowliness, she elevates them within the story of redemption by virtue of these and other qualities having largely to do with their subordination qua women; indeed, she proposes that the women who followed Jesus were especially chosen by virtue of their sex. With the use of paradox, a common rhetorical device of the period, that is, with assertions like "the lowest is the highest," Greiffenberg adroitly asserts that women who are despised in temporal existence possess greater spiritual authority.

The woman with the jar of nard oil becomes in the theology of this text "a true prophet," for, Greiffenberg writes, she foretold the death of Christ by breaking the jar with nard oil when she anointed him. This woman, moreover, reflects the female framing that Greiffenberg gives her writing overall, as most explicitly outlined in the introduction to precisely the *Suffering and Dying of Jesus Christ.* Here the author characterizes her book as resulting from a woman's lived life, that is, she claims that she wrote the book as a result of her mother's promise: she owes Jesus love and devotion, she declares, "on account of the vow of my mother who, when I still lay in her womb (during a dangerous illness, when she despaired of the possibility of keeping me), offered me up and promised me to Thy service and glory, should I be born alive. She kept this vow too, instructing me in piety in a Christian fashion" (54–55, in this volume).

83. For a fuller treatment of Greiffenberg's foregrounding of women's roles in the Christian story of salvation in the *Suffering and Dying of Jesus Christ* and its implications for Greiffenberg as woman writer, see Lynne Tatlock, "Empathic Suffering: The Inscription and Transmutation of Gender in Catharina Regina von Greiffenberg's *Leiden und Sterben Jesu Christi*," *Wolfenbüttler Barock-Nachrichten* 34, no. 1 (2007): 27–50. Much of the current discussion of this set of meditations is based on the insights of this earlier essay.

While, as scholars have claimed, this passage does help to explain the author's zealous sense of religious mission, the passage can also be understood as stylized writing.[84] In its situating of the book within a female spirituality anchored in the body, this carefully planted detail ties the author's own life to the feminized passion fashioned in the *Suffering and Dying of Jesus Christ.* The daughter's fate is determined in the mother's womb, and the mother's promise is fulfilled through the daughter's writing.

Greiffenberg in fact does not let her readers forget her mother's vow and the part it played in determining her destiny. Having invoked the vow on the opening page of her dedication to Jesus, the bridegroom of her soul, she returns to it on the penultimate page of the book after she has audaciously concluded her meditations by addressing the potentates of Europe—indeed, by addressing the Holy Roman Emperor himself in veiled fashion: "I was promised to this while still in my mother's womb and have since then myself devoted and offered up all my life and doings to it. I knew of no better way of attending to this offering and vow than with this public eulogy and expression of gratitude for my Savior's holy suffering and dying" (153, in this volume). In effect, her mother's vow obliged her to transcend the constraints of the given. This given, as characterized in the meditations themselves, discourages women from speaking even in religious matters. As author, however, Greiffenberg has undertaken an ascendant journey framed and sustained by her mother's promise: she has traveled from the dedication where she speaks apologetically of her simple work to the final pages where, transgressing women's circumscribed roles, she boldly addresses the potentates of Europe, preaching Lutheran doctrine.[85]

In the first of these twelve meditations, Greiffenberg imagined her heart as bursting with love of Jesus, a love that caused her pain like breasts full of milk. Alluding to the process of distillation used in alchemy, she figured her brain as the shattering glass retort of an overheated still; she called upon the Holy Spirit to burn drops of praise (i.e., her writing) from her brain as alcoholic spirits are distilled from mash. In the last pages of the final meditation in this set of twelve, however, she reaches for still more extravagant

84. See, e.g., Cerny, *Catharina Regina von Greiffenberg,* 29. Foley-Beining speculates that knowledge of her mother's vow—as described in the *Suffering and Dying of Jesus Christ*—could have "influenced the author to consider the impact of the spirit on the unborn and on mother-child symbiosis, thus awakening a keener sensibility toward the initial stages of the Incarnation" (*Body and Eucharistic Devotion,* 138).

85. See above, note 56. In these final pages Greiffenberg in effect preaches against, among other things, the intercession of saints, the intermediary role of priests, doctrine that is not based on Scripture, and Catholic Eucharistic practices.

conceits, making startling claims for her body as site of devotion and for her intimacy with Christ in her praise, worship, and commemoration of him. Here she invokes the manner in which a queen of antiquity, Artemisia, expressed her sorrow over the death of her husband, Mausolus. Just as Artemisia mourned Mausolus by commissioning the construction of the mausoleum of Halicarnassus, one of the seven wonders of antiquity, Greiffenberg intends to create a glorious mausoleum for Christ with her book. As if this claim for her writing were not bold enough, she refers to yet another affinity to this queen. According to legend, while waiting for the mausoleum to be completed, Artemisia ingested her husband's ashes in order to serve as his living reliquary. Greiffenberg conflates Artemisia's method of mourning with Eucharistic devotion, expressing her wish to scatter the "holy relics of my darling (His body and blood)" (152, in this volume) in her food and drink until her temple of glory is completed and then to be buried with him.[86] Greiffenberg's textual persona has thus become both the reliquary and the mourning consort of Christ.

The public monumentalism of Greiffenberg's closing stance contrasts sharply with the tentativeness and humility of the opening remarks about the decision to publish. Greiffenberg's textual persona has discarded the pose of the untutored woman, who wrote her praise of Jesus in isolation without the aid of learned men, and assumed instead the authority of a queen of antiquity and inventor of the most magnificent monument of all time. In imagining a role for herself as royal consort of Christ, she has, moreover, effectively deployed her gender to posit an intimacy with and authority vis-à-vis Christ available to her most particularly as a woman.

INCARNATION, BIRTH, AND YOUTH OF JESUS CHRIST (1678)

After dedicating her meditations *On the Supremely Holy Incarnation, Birth, and Youth of Jesus Christ* to God the father (in keeping with the dedication of the *Suffering and Dying* to Jesus), Greiffenberg again assumes a pose of humility in the foreword to the noble reader. Even though she knew full well that she by this time enjoyed a reputation as an accomplished writer, in the text she pushes this renewed apology to an extreme, claiming not only to know nothing and to babble like a child but to have made it her business "to be abased, small, and childish with [baby Jesus]" (159, in this volume). She claims only to offer the "lullaby" of a "poor shepherdess" (161, in this vol-

86. Greiffenberg pursues the idea of her writing as mausoleum three years later in the introduction to her *Sieges-Seule der Buße und Glaubens*, 2: sig.):(5^{r}.

ume). Even in a print culture in which apologies are customary and expected in the introductions to books, this one is strikingly exaggerated; indeed, the meditations that follow evidence a sophisticated knowledge of theology and an erudition that belie the naiveté of the lullaby of a poor shepherdess. In fact, the author tells her readers directly in this same apologetic introduction that she is acquainted with patristic writing and textual evidence, and she suggests, furthermore, that she has also widely consulted writing in other fields of knowledge including natural philosophy and anatomy.

Incarnation, the subject of the two meditations from this work that are included in the present anthology, required the author to ponder what it means for spirit to be united with matter, for the divinity to take on a tangible body that lives in the world like any other human being, that feels pain and hunger, that grows and changes, that digests food and breathes the air. This body, according to Christian theology, was made from the matter of Jesus' mother, Mary, and conceived of the Holy Spirit. But how did Jesus' body, this historical body, emerge and live in the world? Greiffenberg wonders too in these meditations about Mary's subjective experience, the experience of being overshadowed by the Holy Spirit and carrying Christ in her womb for nine months.

The contemplation of Christ's nascent body results in twenty-three of the most startling pages of the over four thousand pages that constitute the thirty-six meditations on Christ, for in these pages Greiffenberg offers an anatomical blazon of the fetus in the womb. This blazon addresses not only the exterior of the fetus but the interior as well, that is, the narrative eye not only inspects Christ in the womb but penetrates beneath the skin of Christ the fetus. While images of the fetus in the womb do exist in Christian art, Greiffenberg's rendering of the fetus *beneath the skin* is to my knowledge unique.[87]

To some extent, Greiffenberg produces Christ's historical body as a uni-

87. Greiffenberg was certainly not, however, alone in her interest in Mary's pregnancy and in the intrauterine Christ. Gregor Martin Lechner points to specific Catholic customs, common in the seventeenth and eighteenth centuries, that centered on the celebration of the pregnant Mary: the Visitation and Seeking Shelter. Lechner also reports that two works by Catholic authors appeared in German almost simultaneously with Greiffenberg's second set of meditations, namely, *Os trabalhos de Jesus* by Thomas of Jesus (1529–82), which was published in German translation in Munich in 1678 (trans. P. W. Eder), and the *Großes Leben Christi oder: Außführliche andächtige und bewögliche Beschreibung deß Lebens und Leydens unseres Herrn Jesu Christi und seiner Glorwürdigsten Mutter Mariae,* by Martin von Cochem (1634–1712), which first appeared in 1677. Both of these works show lively interest in the intrauterine Christ. Gregor Martin Lechner, *Maria gravida. Zum Schwangerschaftsmotiv in der bildenden Kunst* (Munich: Schnell and Steiner, 1981), esp. 155–62.

versal body, one concretized and standardized according to the beliefs and authorities of her time.[88] However, even as she draws a verbal anatomy of Christ, she, in keeping with her meditative practice, also seizes on each concrete body part as the point of departure for meditation on spiritual mysteries. Thus the three bones of the ear that she accurately and explicitly identifies provide the occasion to think of the Christian trinity. The developing hands of the fetus provide the occasion for pondering the paradox of the creator now being created within the confines of a human womb. Other body parts lead Greiffenberg to ponder what happens to them when Christ is crucified—for example, she supposes that the uvula will practically fall down into the throat from sighing. Still other parts of Christ's anatomy, although graphically rendered, foreshadow redemption: the backbone, for example, is a tower reaching to heaven that will enable humanity to climb out of its debtor's prison.

The meditations on conception and pregnancy, however, in the end devote more space to Mary than to Jesus. Such extended attention to the Virgin is striking in the writing of a woman who understood herself as a staunch Lutheran. While Greiffenberg's writing carefully retreats from Catholic belief and practices regarding the veneration of Mary—as I point out where pertinent in the notes to the translation—the text nevertheless displays an interest in and sympathy for Mary that bring to mind precisely these beliefs and practices. Beth Kreitzer, in her study of images of the Virgin, has meticulously traced the general waning of interest in Mary in Lutheran sermons by men over the course of the sixteenth century, alongside the reconfiguration of the meanings of Mary to conform with Lutheran tenets.[89] This reconfiguration acknowledged and praised Mary's virtues, Kreitzer explains, but downplayed her traditional roles, for example, as intermediary.[90] Given such trends within Lutheranism, the extended engagement with Mary in the two

88. Thomas Laqueur makes the important point that the anatomies were themselves subjective renditions of what researchers thought they saw when surveying the interior of the body. *Making Sex: Body and Gender from the Greeks to Freud* (Cambridge; Harvard University Press, 1990). For a detailing of the anatomical information contained in this blazon and for a fuller treatment of Greiffenberg's rendering of Christ's and Mary's bodies, see Lynne Tatlock, "*Scientia divinorum:* Anatomy, Transmutation, and Incorporation in Catharina Regina von Greiffenberg's Meditations on Incarnation the Gestation of Christ," *German History* 17, no. 1 (1999): 9–24. Some of the insights of this earlier essay are reworked in the current discussion.

89. Beth Kreitzer, *Reforming Mary: Changing Images of the Virgin Mary in Lutheran Sermons of the Sixteenth Century* (New York: Oxford University Press, 2004), esp. 135–41.

90. See, e.g., Kreitzer's discussion of the Lutheran critique of the Ave Maria as a rejection of the idea of the intercession of saints and Mary's mediation between believers and Christ. Kreitzer, *Reforming Mary,* 32–36.

meditations included in this anthology suggests that the Catholic-saturated environment of Lower Austria had an impact on Greiffenberg, even if she separates herself in her writing from Catholicism on specific doctrinal matters; it, furthermore, supports the contention that Greiffenberg was acutely sensitive to the special meanings that Mary could have for a woman religious writer. Her interest in and devotional meditations on Mary and the annunciation and the visitation and her textual inventions on Mary's pregnancy may have, furthermore, constituted one of the attractions—if we can lend credence to Greiffenberg's own account of her ecumenical appeal—of her religious writings for Catholics.

Mary is the source of the matter that makes the divinity also human and capable of suffering and thus able to redeem humankind. Greiffenberg's conception of the incarnation adheres to a tradition of religious writing that employs Aristotelian notions of human reproduction to speculate on the operation of the Holy Spirit in Mary's womb. Like the sperma in the Aristotelian model, the Holy Spirit is understood to do "its work by intellection" on the material provided by Mary's body.[91] Thus in keeping with this tradition Mary provides the workshop, the tool, and the medium, yet Mary's body becomes more than mere medium in Greiffenberg's writing; ultimately it transmutes and transcends material constraints.

In contrast to Christ the fetus's articulated body, Mary's body lacks definition and is textually rendered as liquid, e.g., blood, boiling water, or a sea. While Greiffenberg assembles Christ's body so that her readers can visualize it and meditate on it, she erases the contours of Mary's. Indeed the text explicitly demonstrates that the operation of the Holy Spirit transmutes Mary's body, pointedly figuring incarnation as an alchemical process: "In this virgin-retort the quint-essence of the body is prepared" (263, in this volume). Christ as quintessence is the product of this process; Mary is the retort and the medium. In yet another expressive transformation, the text describes the changing of Mary's flesh and blood into praise of the Lord: "no blood vessel is in me but it praises the Lord; they are not as full of blood as they are full of His praise. My legs have less marrow than divine praise in them; I have not so much hair on my head as I have heavenly desire for glory, and my inner being is completely filled with it" (217, in this volume). Furthermore, Greiffenberg writes, the incarnation transforms Mary's entire body into blazing love: "Shall [such great deeds] not drive love forth from the mouth and eyes in a hundred thousand flames? Shall they not transform all the blood that is left into heat and cinders?" (226, in this volume).

91. Laqueur, *Making Sex*, 54.

Although she dearticulates Mary's body, Greiffenberg does not decorporealize Mary herself. Physical sensation leads Mary as well as Greiffenberg and her readers to knowledge of God, just as empathic suffering, physically manifested, granted women a special relationship to Christ in Greiffenberg's rendering of the passion six years earlier. Phyllis Mack's description of spirituality in seventeenth-century England reminds us of the significance of such corporeal feeling for religious practice: "Far from posing a clear dichotomy between mind and body, seventeenth-century men and women *felt* certain kinds of knowledge. They described their own spirituality not as an ethereal, disembodied state but as polymorphous, subterranean energy."[92] Mary's body occupies a privileged place in such a sensuous epistemology; it is exalted by its apprehension of the embodied Christ within. Greiffenberg therefore savors the visitation, the meeting of the two pregnant women Mary and Elizabeth. Neither woman experiences pregnancy as a physical burden or as punishment for Eve's disobedience, as it was commonly seen in the seventeenth century.[93] Rather, their astonishingly light, though pregnant, bodies resonate with the power of the Holy Spirit.

Throughout these two meditations Greiffenberg plays with the idea of the word (Christ) becoming flesh (Jn 1: 14) and the notion of the words arising from corporeal sensations or indeed of the body transforming into words, an idea that she introduced in her meditation on the woman with nard oil in the *Suffering and Dying of Jesus Christ.* Mary's entire body sounds the Lord's praise in Greiffenberg's amplified rendering of the Magnificat (216–42, in this volume). Likewise, Greiffenberg's text relishes the speech of Elizabeth upon having sensed the power of the Holy Spirit within her. In her textual play with Christ as the word and women as transforming into words, Greiffenberg, however, has something more in mind. Having described Elizabeth's joyful shout, Greiffenberg calls on God to fill her, the author, as he has filled Elizabeth.

Greiffenberg repeatedly draws parallels between women's speech in the Gospels—Mary's Fiat (let it be done, Lk 1: 38), the Magnificat (Lk 1: 46–55), and Elizabeth's greeting (Lk 1: 42–43)—and her own work. "When God's glory does not have a doubled and multiplied echo, it believes that it has not resounded sufficiently," she writes of the Magnificat and thus simul-

92. Phyllis Mack, *Visionary Women: Ecstatic Prophecy in Seventeenth-Century England* (Berkeley: University of California Press, 1992), 23.

93. Martin Luther, "Eine Predigt vom Ehestand (1525)," in vol. 17, pt. 1 of *Werke. Kritische Gesamtausgabe* (Weimar: H. Böhlau, 1907), 24. See also Johann Heinrich Zedler, *Großes vollständiges Universal-Lexicon aller Wissenschaften und Künste* (1732–54; photographic reprint, Graz: Akademische Druck- und Verlagsanstalt, 1993–99), s.v. "Weib."

taneously names the doubling and repetition that mark her own style (202, in this volume). She asks the Holy Spirit to perform a miracle in her body as well as in Mary's, one that will result in praise of Jesus. If Greiffenberg imagines Christ as the quintessence of Mary's body, produced by the operation of the spirit, she imagines hymns of praise as the "thank-essence" of their authors' corporeal beings (195, in this volume). The transmutation of matter by the Holy Spirit thus yields not only the word made flesh but also words—Greiffenberg's words—made printed text, and in this case a text created by a writer who actively presents herself as female.

VOLUME EDITOR'S BIBLIOGRAPHY

PRIMARY SOURCES

Abraham a Santa Clara. "Arise, Arise, You Christians." Trans. Lynne Tatlock. In *Seventeenth Century German Prose*, ed. Tatlock, 86–91. German Library, 7. New York: Continuum, 1993.

Angelus Silesius (pseud. Johann Scheffler). "Die Psyche sehnet sich nach Jesu alleine." In *Heilige Seelen-Lust oder Geistliche Hirtenlieder der in ihren Jesum verliebten Psyche, 1657 (1668)*, ed. Georg Ellinger, 12–13. Halle a. S.: Max Niemeyer, 1901.

Augustine of Hippo. Sermon 215. In *Sermons*. Translation and notes by Edmund Hill, OP. Ed. John E. Rotelle, OSA. Vol. 3.6 of *The Works of Saint Augustine: A Translation for the Twenty-first Century*, 160–66. New Rochelle, NY: New City Press, 1993.

Babington, John. *Pyrotechnia; or, Artificiall fire works [1635]*. Amsterdam: Theatrum Orbis Terrarum; New York: Da Capo Press, 1971.

Bible, The. King James Version. http://www.hti.umich.edu/k/kjv.

Bible, The. Revised Standard Version. http://etext.virginia.edu/rsv.browse.html.

Biblia, Das ist, Die gantze H. Schrifft, Altes und Neues Testament, Teutsch D. Martin Luthers: Auf gnädige Verordnung deß . . . Herrn Ernsts, Herzogen zu Sachsen. [5th ed.] Nuremberg: Christoph and Paul Endter, 1662.

Biblia, Das ist, Die gantze H. Schrifft, Altes und Neues Testament, Teutsch D. Martin Luthers: Auf gnädige Verordnung deß . . . Herrn Ernsts, Herzogen zu Sachsen. Nuremberg: Christoph and Paul Endter, 1700.

Birken, Sigmund von. *Der Briefwechsel zwischen Sigmund von Birken und Catharina Regina von Greiffenberg*. Ed. Hartmut Laufhütte, with Dietrich Jöns and Ralf Schuster. 2 vols. Vol. 12.1–2 of Sigmund von Birken, *Werke und Korrespondenz*. Tübingen: Max Niemeyer, 2005.

———. Sigmund von Birken to Casper von Lilien, January 1666. In vol. 1 of Catharina Regina von Greiffenberg, *Sämtliche Werke*, ed. Martin Bircher and Friedhelm Kemp, 469. Millwood, NY: Kraus Reprint, 1983.

———. Vor-Ansprache zum edlen Leser. In Catharina Regina von Greiffenberg, *Geistliche Sonnette / Lieder und Gedichte*, vol. 1 of *Sämtliche Werke*, ed. Martin Bircher and Friedhelm Kemp, sig. 7^r–9^v. Millwood, NY: Kraus Reprint, 1983.

Book of Common Prayer (1559). Ed. John E. Booty. Charlottesville: University of Virginia Press, 1976.

Fleming, Paul. *Gedichte Auff des Ehrnvesten und Wolgelahrten Herrn Reineri Brockmans / Der Griechischen Sprache Professorn am Gymnasio zu Revall / Und der Erbarn / Viel-Ehren und Tugendreichen Jungfrawen Dorotheen Temme / Hochzeit* (Leipzig 1635). Faber du Faur 316. New Haven: Research Publications, 1969.

———. "Tugend ist mein Leben." In *Gedichte von Paul Fleming*, ed. Julius Tittman, 85–86. Leipzig: F. A. Brockhaus, 1870.

Greiffenberg, Catharina Regina von. *Des Allerheiligst- und Allerheilsamsten Leidens und Sterbens Jesu Christi, Zwölf andächtige Betrachtungen*. Nuremberg: Johann Hofmann, 1672.

———. *Des Allerheiligst- und Allerheilsamsten Leidens und Sterbens Jesu Christi, Zwölf andächtige Betrachtungen*. 2nd ed. 1683. Reprint, vols. 9–10 of *Sämtliche Werke*, ed. Martin Bircher and Friedhelm Kemp. Millwood, NY: Kraus Reprint, 1983.

———. *Des Allerheiligsten Lebens JESU Christi*. 1693. Reprint, vols. 4–8 of *Sämtliche Werke*, ed. Martin Bircher and Friedhelm Kemp. Millwood, NY: Kraus Reprint, 1983.

———. *Der Allerheiligsten Menschwerdung, Geburt und Jugend JEsu Christi, Zwölf Andächtige Betrachtungen*. 1678. Reprint, vols. 3 and 4 of Catharina Regina von Greiffenberg. *Sämtliche Werke*, ed. Martin Bircher and Friedhelm Kemp. Millwood, NY: Kraus Reprint, 1983.

———. *Geistliche Sonnette / Lieder und Gedichte / zu Gottseligem Zeitvertreib*. 1662. Reprint, vol. 1 of Catharina Regina von Greiffenberg, *Sämtliche Werke*, ed. Martin Bircher and Friedhelm Kemp. Millwood, NY: Kraus Reprint, 1983.

———. *Gelegenheit und Geständnis: Unveröffentlichte Gelegenheitsgedichte als verschleierter Spiegel des Lebens und Wirkens der Catharina Regina von Greiffenberg. Faksimiledruck nach Handschriften im Archiv des Pegnischen Blumenordens*. Ed. Ingrid Black and Peter M. Daly. Kanadische Studien zur deutschen Literatur 3. Bern: H. Lang, 1971.

Greiffenberg, Catharina Regina von, trans. *Der Glaubens-Triumf oder die Siegprachtende Zuversicht*, by Guillaume du Bartas. 1675. Reprint. In vol. 2 of *Sämtliche Werke*, ed. Martin Bircher and Friedhelm Kemp, 250-328. Millwood, NY: Kraus Reprint, 1983.

———. "The Most Holy and Most Healing Passion and Death of Jesus Christ," in *Seventeenth-Century German Prose*, ed. Lynne Tatlock. New York: Continuum, 1993.

———. *Sieges-Seule der Buße und Glaubens/ wider den Erbfeind Christliches Namens*. 1675. Reprint, in vol. 2 of Catharina Regina von Greiffenberg. *Sämtliche Werke*, ed. Martin Bircher and Friedhelm Kemp, sigs. π^r–L 5^v. Millwood, NY: Kraus Reprint, 1983.

———. "'Trost im eüssersten Unglükk!': einige bislang unentdeckte handschriftlich überlieferte Gedichte der Catharina Regina von Greiffenberg." Ed. Hartmut Laufhütte. In *Brückenschläge: eine barocke Festgabe für Ferdinand van Ingen*, ed. Martin Bircher and Guillaume van Gemert, 177–209. Amsterdam: Rodopi, 1995.

———. *Tugend-übung / Sieben Lustwehlender Schäferinnen*. 1675. Reprint, in vol. 2 of *Sämtliche Werke*, ed. Martin Bircher and Friedhelm Kemp, 329–48. Millwood, NY: Kraus Reprint, 1983.

Gryphius, Andreas. "Es ist alles eitell." In *Sonette*, ed. Marian Szyrocki. Vol. 1 of *Gesamtausgabe der deutschsprachigen Werke*, ed. Marian Szyrocki and Hugh Powell, 33. Tübingen: Max Niemeyer, 1963.

Hagendorn, Georg Albrecht. "Leichenpredigt auf Catharina Regina von Greiffenberg." In vol. 1 of Catharina Regina von Greiffenberg, *Sämtliche Werke*, ed. Martin Bircher and Friedhelm Kemp, 482–91. Millwood, NY: Kraus Reprint, 1983.

Herodotus. *Herodotus*. Trans. A. D. Godley. 3 vols. Loeb Classical Library. Cambridge: Harvard University Press, 1990.

Luther, Martin. "Eine Predigt vom Ehestand" (1525). In vol. 17, pt. 1 of *Werke: Kritische Gesamtausgabe*, 12–101. Weimar: H. Böhlau, 1907.

———. "The Small Catechism." In *The Book of Concord: The Confessions of the Evangelical Lutheran Church*, ed. Robert Kolb and Timothy J. Wengert, 347–75. Minneapolis: Fortress Press, 2000.

Navarre Bible, The: Gospels and Acts. Text and Commentaries. Trans. Michael Adams. Dublin: Four Courts Press, 2000.

New American Bible. Http://www.catholic.org/phpframedirect/out.php?url=http://www.nccbuscc.org/nab/bible/index.htm.

Ovid. *Metamorphoses*. Trans. Frank Justus Miller. 2 vols. Loeb Classical Library. Cambridge: Harvard University Press, 1976.

Pliny the Elder. *Natural History*. Trans. H. Rackham. 10 vols. Loeb Classical Library. Cambridge: Harvard University Press, 1950.

Suetonius. *Lives of the Caesars*. In vol. 1 of *Suetonius*, trans. J. C. Rolfe. Loeb Classical Library, 1–385. Cambridge: Harvard University Press, 1914.

Synopsis of the Four Gospels. English edition. Ed. Kurt Aland. New York: American Bible Society, 1982.

Tacitus, Cornelius. *Tacitus*. 5 vols. Loeb Classical Library. Cambridge: Harvard University Press, 1968–69.

Voigts, Linda E., and Michael R. McVaugh. "A Latin Technical Phlebotomy and Its Middle English Translation." *Transactions of the American Philosophical Society* 74, no. 2 (1984): 1–69.

Weise, Christian. Excerpts from *The Three Most Awful Arch-Fools in the Entire World*. Trans. Linda Feldman. In *Seventeenth Century German Prose*, ed. Lynne Tatlock, 148–55. German Library 7. New York: Continuum, 1993.

Zedler, Johann Heinrich. *Großes vollständiges Universal-Lexicon aller Wissenschaften und Künste*. 64 vols. Halle, 1731–50. Also accessed at http://www.zedler-lexicon.delindex.html.

Zesen, Philipp von. *Lobklingende Ruhm- und Nahmen-Reime / damit Der Hoch-Wohlgebohrnen / zum Zierraht und Preise der Deutschgesinneten Welt auserkohrnen Frauen / Frauen Katharinen Reginen/ Frauen von Greiffenberg etc.* Hamburg, 1678.

SECONDARY SOURCES

Abraham, Lyndy. *A Dictionary of Alchemical Imagery*. Cambridge: Cambridge University Press, 1998.

Albrecht-Birkner, Veronika. *Reformation des Lebens. Die Reformen Herzog Ernsts des Frommen von Sachsen-Gotha und ihre Auswirkungen auf Frömmigkeit, Schule und Alltag im ländlichen Raum (1640–1675)*. Leucorea-Studien zur Geschichte der Reformation und der Lutherischen Orthodoxie, 1. Leipzig: Evangelische Verlagsanstalt, 2002.

Baum, Wilhelm. *Shirin. Christian—Queen—Myth of Love: A Woman of Late Antiquity; Historical Reality and Literary Effect*. Piscataway, NJ: Gorgias Press, 2004.

Becker-Cantarino, Barbara. *Der lange Weg zur Mündigkeit: Frau und Literatur (1500–1800)*. Stuttgart: J. B. Metzler, 1987.

Benzing, Josef. *Die Buchdrucker des 16. und 17. Jahrhunderts im deutschen Sprachgebiet*. 2nd ed. Beiträge zum Buch- und Bibliothekswesen, 12. Wiesbaden: Harrassowitz, 1982.

Bircher, Martin. *Johann Wilhelm von Stubenberg (1619–1663) und sein Freundeskreis. Studien zur österreichischen Barockliteratur protestantischer Edelleute*. Berlin: Walter de Gruyter, 1968.

Blume, Herbert. "Die Morphologie von Zesens Wortneubildungen." Ph.D. diss., University of Gießen, 1967.

Brandes, Uta. "Catharina Regina von Greiffenberg (1633–1694) Austria / German." In *Women Writers in German-Speaking Countries: A Bio-bibliographic Critical Sourcebook*, ed. Elke P. Frederiksen and Elizabeth G. Ametsbichler, 171–80. Westport, CT: Greenwood Press, 1998.

Brock, Alan St. H. *A History of Fireworks*. London: George G. Harrap, 1949.

———. *Pyrotechnics: The History and Art of Firework Making*. London: Daniel O'Connor, 1922.

Brown, A. D. Fitton. "Muses on Pindos." *Greece and Rome*, 2nd ser., 8, no.1 (1961): 22–26.

Bynum, Caroline Walker. *Jesus as Mother: Studies in the Spirituality of the High Middle Ages*. Berkeley: University of California Press, 1982.

Cerny, Heimo. "Die Barockdichterin Catharina Regina von Greiffenberg (1633–94)." *Mitteilungen des Vereins für Geschichte der Stadt Nürnberg* 69 (1982): 264–82.

———. *Catharina Regina von Greiffenberg, geb. Freiherrin von Seisenegg (1633–94). Herkunft, Leben und Werk der größten deutschen Barockdichterin*. Amstettner Beiträge 1983. Amstetten: Stadtgemeinde, 1983.

———. "Ister-Clio und Silvano. Catharina Regina von Greiffenbergs und Sigmund von Birkens 'Innigfreundschaft.'" In *Pegnesischer Blumenorden in Nürnberg. Festschrift zum 350jährigen Jubiläum*, 17–21. Nuremberg: Tümmels, 1994.

———. "Neues zur Biographie der Catharina Regina von Greiffenberg." *Literatur in Bayern* 38 (1994): 44–49.

Daly, Peter M. "Catharina Regina von Greiffenberg." In *Deutsche Dichter des 17. Jahrhunderts. Ihr Leben und Werk*, ed. Harald Steinhagen and Benno von Wiese, 615–39. Berlin: E. Schmidt, 1984.

———. *Dichtung und Emblematik bei Catharina Regina von Greiffenberg*. Studien zur Germanistik. Anglistik und Komparatistik, 36. Bonn: Bouvier Verlag Herbert Grundmann, 1976.

———. *Literature in the Light of the Emblem: Structural Parallels between the Emblem and Literature in the Sixteenth and Seventeenth Centuries*. 2nd ed. Toronto: University of Toronto Press, 1998.

Dohm, Burkhard. "Die Auferstehung des Leibes in der Poesie. Zu einem Passionsgedicht Catharina Regina von Greiffenbergs." *Daphnis* 21 (1992): 673–94.

Engels, Heinz. *Die Sprachgesellschaften des 17. Jahrhunderts*. Beiträge zur deutschen Philologie, 54. Gießen: Wilhelm Schmitz, 1983.

Evans, R. J. W. *The Making of the Habsburg Monarchy, 1550–1700: An Interpretation*. Oxford: Clarendon Press, 1979.

Falkner, Silke. "Rhetorical Tropes and Realities—A Double Strategy Confronts a Double Standard: Catharina Regina von Greiffenberg Negotiates a Solution in the Seventeenth Century." *Women in German Yearbook: Feminist Studies in German Literature and Culture* 17 (2001): 31–56.

Fichtner, Paula Sutter. *The Habsburg Monarchy, 1490-1848: Attributes of Empire*. Houndsmill, Basingstoke, Hampshire: Palgrove Macmillan, 2003.

Foley-Beining, Kathleen. *The Body and Eucharistic Devotion in Catharina Regina von Greiffenberg's "Meditations."* Columbia, SC: Camden House, 1997.

———. "Physicality and Women's Eucharistic Devotion in Catharina Regina von Greiffenberg's *Andächtige Betrachtungen*: 'Von Marien Schwanger-gehen' and the 'Abendmahls-Andachten.'" Ph.D. diss., University of California–Los Angeles, 1992.

Fontanier, Pierre. *Les figures du discours*. Paris: Flammarion, 1977.

Frank, Horst-Joachim. *Catharina Regina von Greiffenberg. Leben und Welt der barocken Dichterin*. Schriften zur Literatur, 8. Göttingen: Sachse and Pohl, 1967.

Gambero, Luigi, SM. *Mary and the Fathers of the Church*. Trans. Thomas Buffer. San Francisco: Ignatius Press, 1999.

Garber, Klaus. "Nuremberg, Arcadia on the Pegnitz." In *Imperiled Heritage: Tradition, History, and Utopia in Early Modern German Literature. Selected Essays by Klaus Garber*, ed. Max Reinhart, 117–208. Studies in European Cultural Transition, 5. Aldershot: Ashgate, 2000.

———. "Utopia and the Green World: Critique and Anticipation in Pastoral Poetry." In *Imperiled Heritage: Tradition, History, and Utopia in Early Modern German Literature. Selected Essays by Klaus Garber*, ed. Max Reinhart, 73–166. Studies in European Cultural Transition, 5. Aldershot: Ashgate, 2000.

Gnädinger, Louise. "Ister-Clio, Teutsche Uranie, Coris die Tapfere. Catharina von Greiffenberg (1633–94). Ein Porträt." In *Vom Mittelalter bis zum Ende des 18. Jahrhunderts*. Vol. 1 of *Deutsche Literatur von Frauen*, ed. Gisela Brinker-Gabler, 248–64. Munich: Beck, 1988.

Gössmann, Elisabeth. "'Ipsa enim quasi domus sapientiae.' Die Frau ist gleichsam das Haus der Weisheit: Zur frauenbezogenen Spiritualität Hildegards von Bingen." Chap. 5 in *Hildegard von Bingen. Versuche einer Annäherung*, 93–113. Munich: Iudicium, 1995.

Griesshaber-Weninger, Christl. "Harsdörffers 'Frauenzimmer Gesprächsspiele' als geschlechtsspezifische Verhaltensfibel: Ein Vergleich mit heutigen Kommunikationsstrukturen." *Women in German Yearbook: Feminist Studies in German Literature and Culture* 9 (1993): 49–70.

Grimm, Jacob, and Wilhelm Grimm. *Deutsches Wörterbuch*. Revised by Gustav Rosenhagen and the Arbeitsstelle des Deutschen Wörterbuchs zu Berlin. 33 vols. Leipzig: S. Hirzel, 1854–1954.

Große Brockhaus, Der. Handbuch des Wissens in zwanzig Bänden. 15th ed. Leipzig: F. A. Brockhaus, 1928–35.

Halton, Thomas. *The Church*. Message of the Fathers of the Church, 4. Wilmington, DE: Michael Glazier, 1985.

Herzog, Urs. "Literatur in Isolation und Einsamkeit. Catharina Regina von Greiffenberg und ihr literarischer Freundeskreis." *DVjS* 45 (1971): 515–46.

Ingrao, Charles. *The Habsburg Monarch, 1618–1815*. New Approaches to European History, 3. Cambridge: Cambridge University Press, 1994.

Johnson, Elizabeth A. "Wisdom Was Made Flesh and Pitched Her Tent among Us." In *Reconstructing the Christ Symbol: Essays in Feminist Christology*, ed. Maryanne Stevens, 95–117. New York: Paulist Press, 1993.

Kann, Robert A. *A History of the Habsburg Empire, 1526–1919*. Berkeley: University of California Press, 1974.

Kemp, Friedhelm. Nachwort. In vol. 1 of Catharina Regina von Greiffenberg, *Sämt-*

liche Werke, ed. Martin Bircher and Friedhelm Kemp, 495–535. Millwood, NY: Kraus Reprint, 1983.

Kreitzer, Beth. *Reforming Mary: Changing Images of the Virgin Mary in Lutheran Sermons of the Sixteenth Century*. New York: Oxford University Press, 2004.

Laqueur, Thomas. *Making Sex: Body and Gender from the Greeks to Freud*. Cambridge: Harvard University Press, 1990.

Laufhütte, Hartmut. "Der oedenburgische Drach. Spuren einer theologischen Kontroverse um die Ehe der Catharina Regina von Greiffenberg." *Daphnis* 20 (1991): 355–402.

———. "Passion Christi bei Sigmund von Birken und Catharina Regina von Greiffenberg." In vol. 1 of *Passion, Affekt, und Leidenschaft in der Frühen Neuzeit*, ed. Johann Anselm Steiger, 271–87. Wiesbaden: Harrassowitz, 2005.

———. "Der Plan Catharina Regina von Greiffenberg, Kaiser Leopold I. zum Protestantismus zu bekehren." *Literatur in Bayern* 38 (1994): 58–63.

———. "Die religiöse Dimension der Freundschaft zu Sigmund von Birken und Catharina Regina von Greiffenberg." In vol. 2 of *Religion und Religiosität im Zeitalter des Barocks*, ed. Dieter Breuer, 455–66. Wiesbaden: Harrassowitz, 1995.

Lechner, Gregor Martin. *Maria gravida. Zum Schwangerschaftsmotiv in der bildenden Kunst*. Munich: Schnell and Steiner, 1981.

Lexikon der Symbole. Ed. Udo Becker. Spectrum 4698. Freiburg: Herder, 1998.

Loewenich, Walther von. *Luther's Theology of the Cross*. Trans. Herbert J. A. Bouman. Belfast: Christian Journals, 1976.

Lohse, Vanessa. "Poetische Passionstheologie. Beobachtungen zu Catharina Regina von Greiffenbergs Betrachtungen des Leidens Christi." In vol. 1 of *Passion, Affekt, und Leidenschaft in der Frühen Neuzeit*, ed. Johann Anselm Steiger, 289–99. Wiesbaden: Harrassowitz, 2005.

Mack, Phyllis. *Visionary Women: Ecstatic Prophecy in Seventeenth-Century England*. Berkeley: University of California Press, 1992.

Martz, Louis L. *The Poetry of Meditation: A Study in English Religious Literature of the Seventeenth Century*. New Haven: Yale University Press, 1954.

Mehl, Jane M. "Catharina Regina von Greiffenberg: Modern Traits in a Baroque Poet." *South Atlantic Bulletin: A Quarterly Journal Devoted to Research and Teaching in the Modern Languages and Literatures* 45, no. 1 (1980): 54–63.

Moser, Dietz-Rüdiger. "Judas, die Lippen-Viper; Jesus, das auserlesenste Küsse-Ziel: Zu den Passionsbetrachtungen der Catharina Regina von Greiffenberg." *Literatur in Bayern* 38 (1994): 50–57.

Needham, Joseph. *A History of Embryology*. Cambridge: Cambridge University Press, 1934.

New Catholic Encyclopedia, The. New York: McGraw-Hill, 1967.

Otto, Karl F., Jr. *Die Sprachgesellschaften des 17. Jahrhunderts*. Stuttgart: Metzler, 1972.

Posset, Franz. "The Sweetness of God's Grace according to Bernard of Clairvaux—The Bridge between Augustine and Luther." Animabit Multimedia Editions (WWW) Nr. 3 (1998). Http://www.animabit.de/quarterly/bernhard.htm (accessed January 20, 2006).

Princeton Encyclopedia of Poetry and Poetics. Enlarged Edition. Princeton, NJ: Princeton University Press, 1974.

Pumplun, Christina M. *"Begriff des Unbegreiflichen." Funktion und Bedeutung der Metaphorik in den Geburtsbetrachtungen der Catharina Regina von Greiffenberg (1633–1694)*. Amsterdamer Publikationen zur Sprache und Literatur 120. Amsterdam: Rodopi, 1995.

———. "Die gottliebende Seele und ihr Wegbereiter. Catharina Regina von Greiffenbergs *Geburtsbetrachtungen* (1678) und der Einfluß der Embleme der *Pia Desideria* Herman Hugos S. J. (1624)." In *Brückenschläge. Eine barocke Festgabe für Ferdinand van Ingen*, ed. Martin Bircher and Guillaume van Gemert, 211–31. Chloe. Beihefte zum Daphnis, 23. Amsterdam: Rodopi, 1995.

———. "Die *Sieges-Seule* der Catharina Regina von Greiffenberg. Ein poetisch-politisches Denkmal für Gott und Vaterland." In *Literatur und politische Aktualität*, ed. Elrud Ibsch and Ferdinand van Ingen, 347–60. Amsterdamer Beiträge zur neueren Germanistik, 36. Amsterdam: Rodopi, 1993.

Riley, Helene M. Kastinger. "Protestant Clarion in the Habsburg Empire: Catharina von Greiffenberg." In *Women Writers of the Seventeenth Century*, ed. Katharina M. Wilson and Frank J. Warnke, 464–70. Athens: University of Georgia Press, 1998.

Schnabel, Werner Wilhelm. "Ein ruhig Schäferhüttlein an der Pegnitz? Zu den Lebensumständen der Catharina Regina von Greiffenberg in Nürnberg 1680–1694." *Jahrbuch für fränkische Landesforschung* 53 (1992): 159–87.

Schöne, Albrecht, ed. *Das Zeitalter des Barock*. Vol. 3 of *Texte und Zeugnisse*. 2nd ed. Munich: C. H. Beck, 1968

Schürk, Ingrid. "Sey dennoch unverzagt! Paul Fleming und Catharina Regina von Greiffenberg." In *Aus der Welt des Barock*, ed. Richard Alewyn, 56–68. Stuttgart: J. B. Metzler, 1957.

Siekhaus, Elisabeth Bartsch. *Die lyrischen Sonette der Catharina Regina von Greiffenberg*. Berner Beiträge zur Barockgermanistik, 4. Bern: Lang, 1983.

Tatlock, Lynne. "Catharina Regina von Greiffenberg (1633–1694)." In *Deutsche Frauen der Frühen Neuzeit: Dichterinnen, Malerinnen, Mäzeninnen*, ed. Kerstin Merkel and Heide Wunder, 93–106. Darmstadt: Wissenschaftliche Buchgesellschaft, 2000.

———. "Empathic Suffering: The Inscription and Transmutation of Gender in Catharina Regina von Greiffenberg's *Leiden und Sterben Jesu Christi*." *Wolfenbüttler Barock-Nachrichten* 34, no. 1 (2007): 27–50.

———. Introduction. In *Seventeenth-Century German Prose*, ed. Tatlock, xvii–xxxii. German Library 7. New York: Continuum, 1993.

———. "*Scientia divinorum*: Anatomy, Transmutation, and Incorporation in Catharina Regina von Greiffenberg's Meditations on Incarnation and the Gestation of Christ." *German History* 17, no.1 (1999): 9–24.

Tatlock, Lynne, Mary Lindemann, and Robert Scribner. "Sinnliche Erfahrung und spirituelle Autorität: Aspekte von Geschlecht in Catharina Regina von Greiffenbergs Meditationen über die Empfängnis Christi und Marias Schwangerschaft." In *Geschlechterperspektiven. Forschungen zur Frühen Neuzeit*, ed. Heide Wunder and Gisela Engel, 177–90. Königstein/Taunus: Ulrike Helmer, 1998.

Wandel, Lee Palmer. *The Eucharist in the Reformation: Incarnation and Liturgy*. Cambridge: Cambridge University Press, 2006.

Wilpert, Gero von. *Sachwörterbuch der Literatur*. Stuttgart: Alfred Kröner, 1969.

Wurst, Karin A. "Die Frau als Mitspielerin und Leserin in Georg Philipp Harsdörffers Frauenzimmer Gesprächspielen." *Daphnis: Zeitschrift für Mittlere Deutsche Literatur* 21, no. 4 (1992): 615–39.

NOTE ON TRANSLATION

To translate is to compromise, and I have made many compromises in rendering Greiffenberg's seventeenth-century prose and poetry into English in the twenty-first century. These meditations are not easy to read in German; today even well-educated native speakers have difficulty with them. The language has changed in the over three hundred ensuing years, and seventeenth-century German itself was not standardized to begin with. What is more, Greiffenberg is known for her idiosyncratic and extravagant language, to use her own neologism, for her "Wort-Carthaunen" (word-cannons, 1: 194). Even in the prose sections of the meditations, her language is characterized by wordplay and formal experimentation. Greiffenberg makes use of such devices as rhyming pairs of words, alliteration, assonance, repetition, and doubling and of such rhetorical figures as oxymoron and paradox. She is, furthermore, fond of neologisms and startling word combinations. Her images are sometimes obscure, or they are keyed to such contemporary phenomena as the art of fireworks so as to be difficult to decipher in the twenty-first century. In addition to pyrotechnics, she takes inspiration from such fields as optics, painting, medicine, and alchemy. At one moment her prose sounds colloquial and in the next elevated and learned; the contrast can be grating. I have tried to suggest all of these qualities but have not always been able to reproduce the precise formal aspects. I have therefore sometimes rhymed where she alliterates and vice versa, or when I could do neither at the point in the text where they appeared without distorting the meaning, I seized the opportunity to reproduce similar formal aspects elsewhere in the text.

Greiffenberg is known for invented compounds, and they abound in the meditations. Nevertheless, I have reproduced such compounds selectively and circumspectly in this translation, as in the examples Deoglori-light,

Jesus-heart, Jesus-paradise-flower, heart-grave, Icarus-army, and virgin-retort. An English translation that reproduced these hyphenated compounds in every case in which they occur would run the risk of sounding more like the practical and laconic language of the twenty-first century, the age of advertising and computers, which uses nouns as adjectives, rather than like the artistic and extravagant wordplay of the seventeenth century and thus would have belied Greiffenberg's era and sensibility.

Readers will note that Greiffenberg's use of verb tense is unstable in these meditations. While even in later historical periods German narrative prose sometimes switches mid-paragraph from the past to the present tense in the recounting of particularly important moments, Greiffenberg's use of verb tenses is even more striking and at times disorienting to the modern reader. These shifts in verb tense derive at least in part from the author's twofold project of retelling the events of the passion—events that according to Christian theology are historical and thus real (i.e., not merely metaphorical)—and making the passion present in the exercise of meditation. In this translation I have reproduced the shifts in tense when I deemed it possible to do so without unduly obscuring the meaning or rendering the English more jarring and distracting than the original German. I have thus tried to be true to the original in spirit, even if I have not literally reproduced every shift in tense that occurs in the original.

Since I have striven for a lightly archaic sound to enable readers to experience Greiffenberg as other in time, place, and mindset, I have tried to avoid obviously contemporary locutions and have instead deliberately used some old-fashioned ones. I was aided in part by the language of evangelical preaching in the United States, which employs the slightly archaic English of Scripture. I also turned to the Book of Common Prayer (1662) and the King James Bible for inspiration, but I by no means tried to reproduce seventeenth-century English.

For the quotations of Scripture themselves, I have generally used the Revised Standard Version (RSV) as the closest English version to Luther's translation of the Bible that Greiffenberg reproduced. While I would have preferred to quote the beautiful and moving seventeenth-century English of the King James Bible, knowledgeable colleagues convinced me that it deviates too widely from Luther's translation, and I myself recognized that it would not have meshed well with the more modern language that I was using to translate Greiffenberg's text. The RSV in turn also does not always correspond well to Luther's translation. Where the RSV deviates from the German so as to cause confusion in the meditation that follows the biblical verse, I either turn to the King James Bible or simply rephrase. All deviations from the RSV are indicated in the notes.

Readers who compare my translation with the German original will likely quickly note that I have often translated as "glory" the word *Ehre*, whose first present-day meaning is "honor." I based my choice on a comparison of the German Lutheran Bible with the RSV, where "Ehre" in the German Bible equates to "glory" in the English translation when "Ehre" relates to the qualities of God or the Godhead. It should be recalled that Greiffenberg's guiding light and the source of her sense of religious mission is what she called the "Deoglori-Licht" (Deoglori-light) and that she dedicated her life and her writing to increasing it. Here her use of Latin makes clear that she has in mind what we in English call glory. At other points in the text, it is clear that she makes analogies and puns with reference to the more profane and human idea of honor. Here too a comparison of biblical translations was helpful to acquiring a sense of the semantic field. "Ehre" in this sense is generally translated as "honor" in the RSV. For the sake of retaining the wordplay, however, I have sometimes translated "Ehre" as "honor" where the force of the word, with reference to God, is in fact "glory."

The German expression for which contemporary speakers of English still often use the word "mankind" is *Menschheit*, a word that is in effect more gender neutral than the English equivalent. First of all, *Menschheit* is a feminine noun. Second, although grammatically masculine, a *Mensch* is a person, as opposed to a *Mann* (man). I have therefore most often translated *Menschheit* as "humankind," even though the substitution of "humankind" for "mankind" has a more modern flavor. The grammatical gender of nouns in German likewise presents a quandary to the translator of a text like this one. The father, the son, and the Holy Spirit are all masculine in gender in German, but abstractions like the Godhead (*Gottheit*), the Almighty (*Allmacht*), and the totality or sum of the universe (*Allheit*) are feminine in gender. Thus Greiffenberg can comfortably write of divine persons using the feminine pronoun *sie* (literally, she), which in English must be translated as "it." Not only is it difficult to reproduce this play of grammatical gender in English without making the language forced, it is also uncertain how Greiffenberg actually perceived grammatical gender, that is, whether or not she actually connected it to male and female beings. In the end one hesitates to attribute to her an anachronistic feminist consciousness. Nevertheless, it should be noted that the gender attributes of Jesus are slightly unstable in her meditations. In a passage not included in this anthology, for example, Greiffenberg imagines herself sheltered in Jesus' abdomen as though he had a womb (10: 659). In a meditation on the last supper and Communion, Jesus urges his disciples to drink, declaring that the breast of his wounds is overflowing (10: 40). Thereafter Greiffenberg imagines the tongue ardently thirsting for a drop of Jesus' blood. The thirsting tongue is then palliated (Greiffenberg here uses the verb *stillen*, which means both "to quench" and "to nurse") by Jesus' breast (10: 47–48). When meditating on the Sabbath, Greiffenberg's textual persona cries out for Jesus' breast of which the world wishes to wean her (133, in this volume). In such imaginings she touches on an old tradition of Jesus as mother.[1] Nevertheless, I decided in the end to let standard English practice dictate how I handled the translation of pronouns. With few exceptions, all of which are either explained within the translation itself or obvious from context, abstractions are gender neutral in this translation. I refer to the Holy Spirit with the masculine pronoun in keeping with the idea that he is one of the persons of the trinity.

In rendering the poems too I was forced to compromise. I had initially planned simply to offer prose translations of the poems in ordinary paragraphs but upon reflection determined to reproduce at least the appearance of poetry on the page, inasmuch as Greiffenberg had so carefully composed her book. In the end, I opted at least to suggest the effect of language placed under tension by the requirements of verse forms, even as I continued to privilege meaning over form. Greiffenberg, as did many of her contemporaries, wrote much of her poetry in a German adaptation of the alexandrine, the twelve-syllable line favored in seventeenth-century French poetry. Taking Greiffenberg's strict adherence to the count of syllables as my cue, I therefore reproduced the syllabic meter (number of syllables per line) employed in each of the poems. While I occasionally was able also to reproduce the rhyme or the accentual meter (number and pattern of stress accents), I did so opportunistically and not as part of a grand design.

Greiffenberg's use of the intimate thou form also presents a dilemma to the translator. The thou form is used in German largely to express intimacy, and thus family members, close friends, and children, as well as God, are addressed as "thou" (*du*). Although Greiffenberg frequently uses the thou form in her meditations, to use it in an English rendering would be to give the text an overly quaint, indeed odd, sound that it would not have had in the seventeenth century and that with respect to the form of address it still does not have. As a compromise and in an attempt to capture the religious ardor expressed by the use of the intimate form, I have, in keeping with the use of thou in Psalms in the RSV, used the thou form only when Greiffenberg's textual persona addresses Jesus, God the father, or the Holy Spirit.

1. For an examination of this tradition, see, e.g., Caroline Walker Bynum, *Jesus as Mother: Studies in the Spirituality of the High Middle Ages* (Berkeley: University of California Press, 1982).

TWELVE DEVOUT MEDITATIONS ON THE SUPREMELY HOLY AND SUPREMELY SALVIFIC SUFFERING AND DYING OF JESUS CHRIST

by His most ardent lover and most zealous admirer Catharina Regina,
lady of Greiffenberg, Baroness at Seisenegg

FOR INCREASING THE GLORY OF GOD AND AWAKENING TRUE DEVOTION

Drawn up and Fitted out
With Twelve Copper Engravings of Emblems.

Nuremberg
PUBLISHED BY JOHANN HOFMANN, DEALER IN BOOKS AND ART
NEUSTADT AN DER AYSCH / PRINTED BY JOHANN CHRISTOFF DRECHSLER
1683

Figure 2. J. C. Baur, "Nothing but Jesus" from *Des Allerheiligst- und Allerheilsamsten ;. . . Christi* (1672). The Beinecke Rare Book and Manuscript Library.

MEDITATIONS ON THE PASSION AND DEATH OF JESUS CHRIST

Explanation of the Frontispiece

Blot out the entire world.[1] The tablet of my thoughts
be wiped clean. Let nothing remain but Jesus Christ.
I will stand for nothing else. There shall be no thing
within remembrance's bounds but Him who is all.
Lust for knowledge may inspire many lovely things;
Jesus alone restores me, more than can vast knowledge.
However the world may lust for money, art, wisdom,
I want and know nothing but the strength of His cross.
May gall and vinegar's sponge blot out all vanity:
Let the crucified one alone stay in my mind.
How far Totality, when alone, can outspread
and change everything we clearly see herein.
I want this sum of all things alone in my mind:

1. According to Peter M. Daly, the explanatory poems accompanying all of the copper engravings as well as the engravings themselves were composed by Sigmund von Birken in keeping with Greiffenberg's instructions (see the volume editor's introduction above, 26). The sixteen-line poem that serves as the explanation of the frontispiece is composed of alexandrines (twelve or thirteen syllables, depending on whether the line ends with a stressed or unstressed syllable, respectively) in iambic hexameter. Each of the four lines is cross-rhymed, that is, according to the scheme *abab,* etc. I have adhered to the syllabic meter (syllable count) of the alexandrine to suggest the effects of language under tension as a result of the constraints of the verse form but have otherwise not attempted to reproduce the accentual meter (iambic hexameter) or rhyme; similarly, I have not reproduced the caesura (break within the poetic line) after the third stress accent that typifies the alexandrine in German as seen, for example, in the first line of the poem. See *Princeton Encyclopedia of Poetry and Poetics. Enlarged Edition* (Princeton: Princeton University Press, 1974), s.v. "alexandrine," "caesura," "meter," and Gero von Wilpert, *Sachwörterbuch der Literatur* (Stuttgart: Alfred Kröner, 1969), s.v. "Alexandriner." The requirements of the alexandrine line led me here and in some of the following translations of poetry to strain English word order, as

Thus I have all of it und crucified as well.[2]
But its gifts of grace are all the more unreachable
the more they are affixed. In Him is my repose.

To the most ardently beloved Bridegroom of my Soul, Jesus Christ, Son of God and Mary, my most supremely praised Savior and Redeemer.[3]

MOST HUMBLE DEDICATION

Dearest Lord Jesus! Sole ruler of my heart and treasure of my soul! Thou knowest with what infinite obligation my love and devotion belong to Thee. Not only because of the creation and the redemption (which all human beings, if they somehow hope for it, have in common with me) but also on account of other mercies shown especially to me, and no less on account of the vow of my mother who, when I still lay in her womb (during a danger-

---

in fact Birken and Greiffenberg strain German syntax in the German original. I have followed this same procedure for all of the poetry translated in this volume.

Lesch aus/ die ganze Welt. Die Tafel der Gedanken
rein werd gewischet ab. Nichts bleib / als JEsus Christ.
Nichts will ich dulten sonst. Es soll nichts in den schranken
der Angedächtnis seyn / als der / der Alles ist.
Es mag die wiß-begier viel schönes wesen reitzen:
mich labt mein JESUS nur / vor tausend-wissenschaft.
Die Welt mag / wie nach Geld / nach Kunst und Weißheit geitzen:
ich will und weiß sonst nichts / als seine Creuzeskraft.
Der Gall- und Essig-Schwamm lesch' aus all' Eitelkeiten:
nur der Gekreutzigte bleib stehn in meinem Sinn.
Wie weit / wann sie allein / die Allheit sich ausbreiten
und alles wenden kan / das siht man klar hierinn.
Die Allheit ich allein will im Gedächtnis haben:
so hab ich alls / und sie gekreutzigt noch darzu.
Nur unerreichlicher sind ihre Gnaden-Gaben /
je mehr sie angehäfft. In ihm / ist meine Ruh.

2. In addition to modeling a method of meditation, this introductory poem and especially this line point to the central role of the crucified God in the Lutheran "theology of the cross" as opposed to the "theology of glory." According to Luther, the theology of glory tried to know God's invisible nature by the works of creation. As Walter von Loewenich explains, according to Luther "knowledge of God comes into being at the cross of Christ," that is, the theology of the cross is "a theology of revelation" and "God's revelation is recognized not in works but in suffering" (*Luther's Theology of the Cross*, 20, 22).

3. The first edition of Greiffenberg's meditations on the passion of Christ appeared in 1672. This translation follows the second edition, which was published during Greiffenberg's lifetime and which is also the edition used in the twentieth-century reprint of the works. Catharina Regina von Greiffenberg, *Des Allerheiligst- und Allerheilsamsten Leidens und Sterbens Jesu Christi, Zwölf andächtige Betrachtungen*, vols. 9 and 10 *Sämtliche Werk*, ed. Martin Bircher and Friedhelm Kemp (Millwood, NY: Kraus Reprint, 1983).

ous illness, when she despaired of the possibility of keeping me), offered me up and promised me to Thy service and glory, should I be born alive. She kept this vow too, instructing me in piety in a Christian fashion. And since then I have had Thee in my heart, served Thee most eagerly in silence, and ardently loved Thee, insofar as it was possible for me in my weakness. However, it did not satisfy my conscience, but instead it seemed too little merely to love Thee quietly with my heart, if I did not at the same time publicly embrace and praise Thee with my mouth and hand, and thus praising Thee, induce others to do so as well. For this reason I wanted to draw up these ardent heart-meditations on Thy holy passion and to make them see the light of day as a public confession before all the world that I desire to love, laud, honor, and serve Thee alone, supremely holy Lord Jesus, one and only, above all and in all. Oh! Accept it then as a clear sign and a testimony with mouth and quill of the love that overflows my heart. O Thou who art most pleasing to the angels, let please Thee what Thou canst perceive with the penetrating beams of Thy heart to be meant for Thee out of ardent love of Thine utmost glory. If it is neither capable nor powerful enough to accomplish what I desire—namely, to increase Thy glory and spread it throughout the world—oh! then lend it soundness and importance, Thou granter of all—even impossible—good wishes that come from the heart. Thou who hast created everything from nothing canst still create from a tiny spark not just a great torch but an entire Etna that would serve Thy divine glory.[4] My boldness in dedicating to Thee, Supreme Lord, this most paltry little book stems for the largest part from all the reasons that anybody might think of for dedicating something to someone. For if one dedicates one's books to the person whom one honors the most, then I rightly dedicate it to Thee, Thou Lord Jesus, most honored above all the heavens! If it is done, however, for them who are loved the most dearly and are the most closely related, then it is again due Thee as the most beloved bridegroom of my soul and most faithful brother of my heart. If it is a sign of friendship to dedicate one's writings to them whom one has chosen as friends, then it is once again fitting for Thee, because Thou hast chosen me before all the world and I chose Thee as my friend as soon as I could reason. If one dedicates one's works to the great potentates in order to recommend one's works to the world under the protection of their lofty names, to whom else should I come but to Thee, who, along with Thy heavenly father and the Holy Spirit, art the true monarch in heaven and on earth and the master of all the potentates. Should not a book venture confidently into the world under the protection of the

4. Mount Etna, a live volcano on the island of Sicily, had erupted violently in 1669, resulting in the collapse of the summit cone.

name before which all knees in heaven and on and beneath the earth must bend? Some honor with their books those from whom they have received great mercy and kindness. To whom am I again more greatly indebted for such things than to Thee, O Lord Jesus, who hast flooded and filled me with kindnesses and mercy to overflowing so that I can hardly find the breath that I need to praise Thee and so that I therefore and herewith do it with the pen? One probably also comes to dedicate books to some people because they provide the content, material, and occasion for these books with their heroic deeds, wondrous stories, and lineage; thus one sends books back to their origins as their own. Indeed, I have this reason too, dearest Lord Jesus! The most highly praiseworthy deeds and most unheard-of wondrous stories of Thy suffering and dying give me sufficient substance and content; indeed, Thine unfathomable love of humankind gives me material as deep as the sea and the most praiseworthy occasion for laudation. Since not merely the content but also the manner of writing and the gracious choice of this holiest of materials originate with Thee, thus I should properly pour it back into its source with millions of words of praise. The last and most unworthy manner of presentation (which only the ignoble and common people undertake) is carried out with an eye to profit, which for all that nevertheless finds a place here in a noble and innocent manner. Thou, omniscient Jesus, knowest that my heart is otherwise incapable of seeking profit of any kind except the profit of Thy heavenly heart, and it aims at this alone. Thus all the kinds of motivation for dedication come together in Thee:

> I find what there could be,
> Lord Jesus Christ, in Thee![5]

Oh! Then let me too experience the goal of my words and pen, namely, to inspire for Thee in others a host of infinite thoughts of laudation and praise that the entire world may be filled with Thy glory and the heavens tell of Thy miracles. Thus I most obediently bow down to the feet of Thy divine majesty, most humbly asking Thee to grant me the crown of all glories and glory of all crowns that I may call myself before all the world, Almighty Lord Jesus,

Thy most loyal and most obedient servant
Catharina
Dedicated at Castle Seisenegg
4 October 1672

5. Dann was nur zuersinnen ist / find' ich in dir / HErr JEsu Christ!

PREFATORY REMARKS TO THE NOBLE READER

The devout and generous reader will, I hope, take up this humble little book in the spirit in which it was written, namely, to increase the glory of God and the love of Jesus as well as to awaken true devotion. This was my purpose for writing; may the reader make it his purpose for reading. May he not seek herein lofty intellect, sharp intelligence, and great eloquence; for they are not present in humble and tender-hearted people and cannot be sought among those not able to speak for themselves.[6] If he is to find what he seeks, then let him seek nothing herein but simple devotion, ardent love of Jesus, and supreme desire to augment His praise alongside faithful contemplation of all the circumstances of His passion. I promise this, and no one can demand more of me. I have my reasons for being so bold as to let this humble, artless little work see the light of day. Many good men and women friends and other godly people have entreated me to do so. I finally let it be done, swearing up and down and indeed stipulating that it did not happen out of bare and base ambition, which thing I swore off long ago and to which I am, as it were, dead, and I have my life and sensibility in the love and glory of Christ alone. Thus I will not fret and fuss about the momus[7] either, as is otherwise customary, but in patient simplicity submit myself willingly to the judgment of all reasonable people, gladly confessing that countless mistakes are to be found herein and that I shall rightly earn all kinds of punishment and displeasure, if high-minded people do not exercise forbearance and lenience with me. I request only this: may the kind reader consider that I wrote it not only as a simple, weak, and untutored woman but, beyond that, in such isolation, where I was removed from contact with and the advice and assistance of wise and learned men—and robbed not only of that but also even of the opportunity to consult stimulating and spiritual books useful for my purpose. There was none of the peaceful solitude that one desires and that seems meant for such meditations, but instead a restless glut of all kinds of domestic matters mixed with thousands of aversions;

6. Greiffenberg uses the plural adjectival noun "Unmündigen" here. *Unmündig* often refers to minors and dependents, those who have not reached their majority and thus are not legally able to speak for themselves. It can also mean generally those who are immature, without power, incapable, mentally disabled, or not responsible for what they do (see also n. 11 below). Since Greiffenberg speaks of her writing here, I have translated the word as "those not able to speak for themselves" to evoke her status as woman and thus her alleged incapacities as a writer. Greiffenberg may have thought that the word derived from *Mund* (mouth) and thus have chosen the word speak with particular care for this opening apology for her work.

7. Critic; according to Greek mythology, the god Momus was eventually banned from Mt. Olympus because of his mocking and caviling.

I was also sometimes interrupted (causing various and sundry delays) with paying little calls and going on trips and to parties so that often over many weeks I hardly had a day, and over many days, hardly an hour to work on [the meditations]. So I will let the wise man judge for himself how a person could write anything good in such a way. However, since I have eyes only for the glory of Jesus and not for my own, I am allowing my mistakes to see the light of day and to appear before the eyes of the world, even if they are indeed capable of bringing me shame and disgrace. I am happy as long as my God be thereby honored, the love of Jesus increased, and the world inflamed with true devotion, even if I am shot with the arrows of calumny over it, like a poor Phaeton.[8] My goal is to exalt the wounds of Jesus through praise, even if my own reputation is thereby wounded and brought down. In the end I esteem nothing but Jesus whom I herewith desire to honor and worship. May the clever reader not reject the pearls of blood thus served up to him on account of the wretched dishes made of bark, and may he enjoy the sweet fruits of ardent love of Jesus, even if they be placed before him on a wretched cabbage leaf of my words. May he be forbearing with these graceless lines and in the meantime excuse my deficiencies until he hears me praising God in eternity, fully and completely, and until he himself joins in most gloriously. May he meanwhile fare well and consider her who wishes to lead him to God through devotion as his

Bosom friend in dutiful Christian loyalty.
C. R. F. V. G.

CALL TO WORSHIP

1

O Jesus![9] My delight, ecstasy of my soul!
My heart's heavenly kingdom, my innermost throne,
where the spirit's joy reigns! O quiet but loud throne!
Let the stream of Thy spirit well up in my soul.

8. According to Greek mythology, when Phaeton tried to drive the chariot of his father, the sun god, he lost control of it. When his wild ride began to wreak havoc, Zeus struck him down with a thunderbolt.

9. The Call to Worship consists of three sonnets, each composed of alexandrines that rhyme according to the scheme *abbaaddacddcee* (including some impure rhymes).

I. O JEsu! meine Lust / Verzuckung meiner Seelen /
Mein Hertzen-Himmelreich / mein innerlicher Thron /
Wo Geistes-Freude herrscht! O Still-doch lauter Thon!

Deign Thou to light up my gloom with the gleam of grace!
Place the ruby diadem of blood on my heart.
Be Thou my Mount Pindos, be Thou my Helicon.[10]
Inspire spirit and mind; animate soul and throat.
May Thy blood, my arts' fountain, sate me with delight,
that my heart and mouth as well overflow with sweetness.

Laß deinen Geistes-Strom in meiner Seele quellen.
Wolst meine Düsterheit mit Gnaden-Glantz erhellen.
Setz meinem Hertzen auf / die Blut-Rubinen-Kron.
Sey du mein Pindus-Berg / sey du mein Helikon.
Begeistre Geist und Sinn / beseele Seel und Kehlen.
Dein Blut/ mein Künste-Brunn / mich träncke Wollust-voll:
Das auch mein Hertz und Mund von Süßheit übergehen.
Laß lauter Flammen-Strahl aus meinen Lippen wehen:
Daß ich Welt-sichtbar mach / das inner Hertzens Wohl.
O JEsu! Wunder-Held! durch deine Gnade gib /
Daß ich die Andacht führ in deines Geistes Trieb.

II. Ach! Lobe / lobe / lob / ohn End / und Odem heben /
Den Schatz der Göttlichkeit / das unausdencklich Gut.
Ach! daß ein Lobes-Brunn würd all mein Safft und Blut!
Ach! daß mein Marck doch möcht ein Ehren-Oel abgeben /
sich Lieb-und Lob verzehrt! Ach! daß mein gantzes Leben /
Von GOttes Ehr und Preiß / würd eine Spiegel-Fluth.
Ach! daß mein Hertz und Sinn wird JEsu Lobes-Glut /
Mein Odem sollte stets ihm aufzudienen streben.
In reinem Ruhmes-Rauch! O Printz der Ewigkeit!
Du Wunden-Wunder-Held! Entdeckter GOttheit-Strahl!
Mit Ertz-Aussprechlichkeit / auf Mund und Zunge fall.
O Wesen-Wort! die Wort in meine Lippen leit.
Der Allheit Himmel-lob / durch mich / den Erden-Staub /
Zu preisen / unermüdt im Glauben / mir erlaub.

III. O Wort! dem alle Wort zu wenig / es zu preisen!
O Wort! durch welches ward / das man mit Worten nennt.
Durch dich / O Wesen-Wort! man dessen Selbstheit kennt /
Der seinen Allheit-Glantz / dich zeugend / wollte weisen.
O Wort! das / auf das Wort des Engels wollte reisen /
In keuschen Tugend-Thron! das bleibet ungetrennt /
Von seinem Ausspruch-Mund / doch alle Welt durchrennt.
Wort! das mit Worten kan / die voll der Wercke speisen/
Worte! das eh / als / sein Mund und Zunge / war geboren!
Ja / Wort! das seinen Mund und Zunge selbst erschuff!
Wort! das zu reden ihm durch Schweigen hat erkoren!
Wort! des Unmündigkeit die gantze Welt ausruff /
O Wort das Gott beredt / zum Schaffen und Erlösen!
Wolst Worte / dir zu Lob / in mir jetzt auserlesen.

10. According to ancient Greek tradition, the muses were to be found on the mountain Helicon. Later on, Pindos too is written of as the home of the muses. See A. D. Fitton Brown, "Muses on Pindos," *Greece and Rome,* 2nd ser., 8, no. 1 (1961): 22–26.

Figure 3. Cornelius Nicolas Schurtz(?), "Out of Love and Design" from *Des Allerheiligst- und Allerheilsamsten . . . Christi* (1672). The Beinecke Rare Book and Manuscript Library.

Let nothing but flashes of flame shoot from my lips,
that I show the world my innermost heart's well-being,
O Jesus Christ! Wondrous hero! Grant with Thy grace
that I worship within Thy spirit's driving force.

2

Oh! Praise, praise, commence praising without end or pause
Divinity's treasure, inconceivable good.
Oh! That all my sap and blood were a fount of praise!
Oh! That my marrow would but yield an oil of glory,
consumed in love and laud! Oh! That my entire life
became a crystal-clear flood of God's praise and glory.
Oh! That my heart and mind were fiery praise of Jesus,
that to serve Him my breath should eternally strive.
In glory's pure incense! Prince of Eternity!
The Godhead's disclosed beam! Hero of wounds and wonders!
Fall on mouth and tongue with utmost expressiveness.
O Substantial Word! Guide Thou the words to my lips.
Let me praise to the heavens in unflagging faith
the Sum of all Things, praise Him with myself, earth's dust.

3

O Word! Which all the words do not suffice to praise!
O Word, through which what one names with words came
to be.
Through Thee, Substantial Word, His very selfhood is known,
who in begetting Thee His allness-luster showed.
O Word that meant to travel on the angel's word
to the chaste throne of virtue! May it still adhere
to the mouth that spoke it, yet run through all the world.
Word that with words can feed those who are full of works.
Word that was begotten before its mouth and tongue!
Yes! Word that created its very mouth and tongue!
Word that itself elected through silence to speak!
Word! whose infancy the entire world does proclaim![11]

11. Greiffenberg here once again employs the word "Unmündigkeit," which can refer to someone who has not reached his or her majority either in a legal sense or in the sense of being physically or mentally incapable (see above, note 6). Greiffenberg is interested in the fact that in being born as a human Christ allowed himself to pass through a stage in which he was physically helpless—like all human beings—and yet was always and forever the world's salvation.

O Word that persuades God to create and redeem!
May Thou select in me the words to sing Thy praise!

Oh, yes, Thou Eternal Word of the Eternal Father! Grant spirit and words to love Thy laud and to laud Thy love. Grant, most praiseworthy Savior, to Thine infinite glory, that Thy laud be my life and my life Thine everlasting laud. Oh! Speaking the most ardent thoughts of my heart—where are worthy words to be found other than with the substantial Word? So speak in me, Thou heavenly speaker of all things, so that I can speak quite spiritually of and before Thee. Loosen my tongue, Thou Redeemer of the World, so that it can give the profound thanks owed Thee for Thy redemption. Begin, Thou beginning of all things without beginning, to make Thine infinite praise sound forth from my mouth. Thou, without whom we can do nothing, help me to a good beginning and ending of this undertaking—to Thy glory.

EXPLANATION OF THE COPPER ENGRAVING

Jesus speaks.

Love, let me not remain in the sweet repose of heaven.[12]
The throne resounding with joy can keep me on it no longer.

12. See figure 3. This emblem introduces the first meditation. The sixteen lines of the explanatory poem rhyme according to the following scheme: *ababcdcdefefghgh*, including the imperfect rhyme of lines 6 and 8. In the translation I have preserved the regular count of fifteen syllables per line in accordance with the original but have not attempted to reproduce the rhyme or accentual meter. In this poem Jesus explains why he must depart heaven even though he knows what suffering awaits him on earth.

JESUS redet.
Liebe lässet mich nicht bleiben in der süssen Himmel-Ruh.
Der von Freud beschallte Thron kan mich nicht mehr an sich halten.
Die verkehrte Art der Flammen flieget diesem Abgrund zu.
Keine Noth-Gefahr man scheut / wann man läst die Liebe walten.
Löw und Drach / als Laut' und Harffe / locken in die Höll hinein;
Tyger sind ein Lieb-Magnet / Schlangen eine Reitzung-Ruthe;
Ja die selbste Heule-Höle / muß ein Jubel-Himmel seyn:
Nur / daß seiner Lieben Qual / durch die eigne / man vernichte.
Nicht in unvermeinte Schmertzen Unvorsichtigkeit mich stürtzt.
In den tieffsten Abscheu-Pfuhl / den er recht hat vorerkennet /
Durch den klärsten Ferne-Spiegel / der die Ewigkeit verkürzt.
Und als gegenwärtig weist / mein entschloßner wille rennet.
Vorsatz kan mich also setzen in ein hertz-entsetzlichs Ort.
Ich sih' alle Mord-Gefahr: bin doch blind sie zu betrachten.
Ein ertz-Abgrund höchster Liebe reisset mich in diesen Fort.
Meiner Gottheit Schlusses-Fels keine Wellen pflegt zu achten.

The inverted manner of the flames flies toward this abyss.
One shies away from no sort of peril, when one makes love
reign.
Lion and dragon, like lute and harp, entice one into hell;
tigers are a love-magnet, serpents a stimulating prod;
indeed, howling hell itself must be a jubilant heaven:
if only one may end the torment of loved ones through one's
own.
Imprudence does not plunge me into unforeseen agony.
My resolute will runs into the deepest slough of disgust,
rightly seeing it in advance through the clearest telescope,
which, compressing eternity, shows it present here and now.
Thus design can put me in a place that terrifies the heart.
I see all the murderous danger, but observe it blindly.
A deep abyss of highest love pulls me down into this one.
The cliff of my divine resolve is not wont to heed the waves.

ON THE SUPREMELY HOLY AND SUPREMELY SALVIFIC SUFFERING OF JESUS: FIRST MEDITATION

Jesus, who initiated and achieved our salvation, fulfilled the prophecies of the last days of the world when He chose to initiate the fulfillment of the prophecies of His suffering. He fixed on the prophecy of eternal life, which He meant to gain through death. His loving thoughts were to gain for us joy through His suffering, pleasure through His pain, and the crown through His cross. He distributed the jewels before He commenced the struggle. So certain was He of victory, so eager for our redemption, that He thought of our entry into life during His journey toward death, our welcome in heaven during His departure from the world. He spoke of how He would convey the joy of heaven to us even before He was consigned to the enemy—this last event nevertheless had to take place before [the other one could]: His misery thus meant less to Him than our joy.

The Infinite Omniscience saw an unfathomable sea of pain before Him that we flooded prodigiously with our sins. Still He promised eternal reward for a miserable drink of water. He saw, as in a mirror, the bitter bread of His affliction. His love still made Him promise the heavenly manna of joy to those who with a few crumbs prove themselves to be charitable to the poor. He piles love upon love on us who overload Him with anguish and torment. Oh, unimaginable love! Even as He sees rejection and repudiation before His very eyes and has no place to lay His head, He promises to reward the sheltering of a miserable beggar. He was aware then that He would hang naked and exposed on the cross and that He would die; still He insisted on praising and taking the clothing of the naked as a kindness done Him. Indeed, the unfathomable epitome of kindness was so magnanimous that even when hellish agony was about to assault Him, He, with inconceivable loving kindness, offered heavenly reward for comforting the most lowly person. When He was about to step into the shackles and bonds of the hellish prison, He, the supremely innocent one, grieved over the imprisonment of the guilty, and He promised them that they should enter eternal life that would come to them in their prisons, when He of course knew that He would soon be abandoned by God, the angels, and humankind. In short, His love was longer than eternity, deeper than the abyss, hotter than hell, and higher than heaven!

> O quintessence of love! Whose breath is purest tinder[13]
> and a kindling ember; whose words are nothing but arrows

13. The following poem is written in alexandrines and consists of two sonnets that are separated by two sentences in prose. The first of these follows the rhyme scheme *abbaabbaccddee* (including the imperfect rhyme of lines 3 and 8); the second follows the rhyme scheme *abbaabbacdcdee* (with *d* designating the impure rhyme *Schall/Strahl*).

> O Ausbund aller Lieb! des Odem lauter Zunder/
> Und eine ansteck-Glut; des Worte lauter Pfeil
> Und Hertz-durchdringung sind; des Leib ein Flammen-Seul.
> Voll Liebes-Feurwerck ist; des Welt-gepreiste Wunder /
> Sind Lieb erzeugte Frücht / durch die auch ein gesunder
> Gantz sterblich Lieb [*sic*] erkranckt / zu ewiglichem Heil.
> O Unzertrennlichkeit! ach werd auch mir zu Theil!
> Druck alle Eitelkeit in meiner Seele unter.
> Du All-erstrecklichkeit / doch gantz bey mir allein!
> pflegst überall / und doch vollkommen hier zu seyn.
> Ich kan / Welt-unverwehrt / dich in dem Hertzen hertzen.
> Du bringst in Unruh Ruh / du giebest Lust in Schmertzen.
> Aus mir du bringest mich / und bleibest doch in mir.
> Du Haupt-Vergnügung! machst mich hungern doch nach dir.
> Ach ja / süssester JESU! was kan / was soll ich mehr von dir sagen? Ach daß ich es recht sagen könnte! du bist und giebst.
> Die Wollust sonder Schmertz / im Hunger Ueberfluß /
> Und in der Sättigung inbrünstiges Verlangen;
> Die Glut / aus der doch nie Angst-Funcken sind gegangen.
> Das Ende / daß doch nur den Anfang schliessen muß;
> Ein in der Nichtigkeit / recht / wesender Genuß /
> Des reinen GOttheit-seyns; wazhafftiges [*sic*] empfangen /
> Des All-umpfangenden; untrennliches Anhangen /
> Des äusserst-guten Guts. O gantzer Schuß und Guß /
> Des Tugend-Allbegriffs! Du schöner GOttes-Spiegel /

and heart-transfixing; whose body a flaming column
filled with love's fireworks; whose wonders praised by the
world
are fruits begotten of love from which even a sane
mortal body[14] sickens for eternal salvation.
O Indivisibility! Oh, be mine too!
Suppress all vanity down under in my soul.
Thou, all-extending yet wholly alone with me,
art wont to be everywhere and yet fully here.
I press Thee to my heart, unfettered by the world.
Thou bringest unrest rest; givest delight in pain.
Thou removest me from me and yet stayest in me.
Thou delights' delight makest me hunger for Thee.

Oh, yes, sweetest Jesus! What can I, what more shall I say of Thee? Oh, that I could say it right! Thou art and givest:

Pleasure without pain; in hunger superabundance;
and amidst satiation, passionate desire;
the fire from which sparks of fear never have emerged.
The end that needs only to conclude the beginning,
a delight of the pure being of the divine,
quite substantial in nothingness; a true receiving
of the all-encompassing; firm and fast attachment
of the utmost Good. O complete shot and cast,
virtue's epitome! Beauteous mirror of God,
The heavenly echo of love and love returned,
thou art for us the best-attested seal of bliss.
The soul sees enough by the invisible beam.
It loves and feels driven by silent power, wishing
to depart the body for Jesus, its beloved.

Der Lieb und Gegen-Lieb / der himmlisch Echo-Schall /
Bist uns der Seeligkeit ein bäst-beglaubtes Siegel.
Die Seel sieht ihr genug / bey dem unsichtbarn Strahl.
Sie liebt und fühlet sich von stummer Krafft getrieben /
Und wünscht sich aus dem Leib / zu JESU ihrem Lieben.

14. The text reads "Lieb," (i.e., apparently a shortened form of the feminine noun *Liebe* [love]), but the modifiers all indicate that this word is a masculine noun. The spelling "Lieb" must therefore be incorrect. The text should instead read "Leib," a masculine noun meaning "body."

But what needs it many words to portray the Word? The works speak the proofs of His love. His obedience was not less perfect than the omniscience by whose power He knew everything in advance, and the knowledge of [His own] sensitivity [to pain] was not less than the desire to achieve our salvation. His divine nature, which gave Him the strength to suffer, took from His human nature none of the sensation of pain that is peculiar to it, but instead increased the anticipatory fear of this pain through foreknowledge of it.

"You know (he said) that after two days the Passover is coming."[15]

An otherwise joyous time, but a distressing one for me, because I shall eat not the sweet breads but the bitter ones of gall. In the time of remembering the deliverance I shall be imprisoned; I shall be spurned in the commemoration of the preservation. I who led them safely through the Red Sea shall be drowned by them in the sea of my blood. The storm clouds of affliction will come over me, the true pillar of a cloud.[16] I who redeem my people from all crosses shall be crucified by them. And to be sure I shall wither in the loveliest season when the sap runs and everything turns green. When everything is blooming, I must wilt; amid the sweetest delight of nature, I must languish. When the sun lengthens the day, they will shorten my days. When the little birds sing on the branches, I must wail on the tree of the cross. When heaven's eyes glimmer, the light of my eyes must fade. I, the source of all restoration, must die unrestored to restore you in all eternity.

I prophesy my crucifixion to you to crucify within you the desire for earthly splendor. It is far too little for my love, my beloved ones, to bless you with temporal well-being. That which is to gratify my ardor must be eternal. So expand your hearts and imagine nothing less than heavenly delights that I intend to gain for you through hellish torture. God is crucified by humankind so that humankind can be crowned by God. The Eternal Word meant to say this with these few words.

While substantial faithfulness poured out all its loving ardor, falsehood held a secret blood council to destroy that faithfulness. To ensnare Him, they filled their mouths with deceit and trickery over Him in whose mouth no deceit was found. He intended to save humankind; they intend to cap-

15. Mt 26: 2. The word employed in the original German for Passover is *Ostern* (Easter). English religious texts contemporary with Greiffenberg's writing such as the Book of Common Prayer and Acts 12: 4 in the King James Bible likewise use the word *Easter* for Passover.

16. According to Ex 13: 21–22, 14: 19, God led the Israelites out of Egypt in a pillar of a cloud by day.

ture God. The spiritually empty authorities on Scripture mean to annihilate the purpose and core of Scripture that they, in so doing and unbeknownst to them, are compelled to fulfill. They mean to remove from the world Him who encompasses and fills the entire world. They mean to play a secret, spiteful trick on Him who knows all hearts, to darken the sun with a little cloud, whereas the eye of the world cannot be darkened and the Creator cannot be deceived and Wisdom does not suffer herself to be obscured by a ruse.[17]

Are they concerned only about the people? Indeed, it is a childish way of thinking on the part of the elders of Israel! They fear the flies and not the lion. They mean to deceive the Omniscient One and they suspect simple people. They persecute the Almighty and fear the rabble. Certainly they have cause to fear a rebellion of the people since they themselves have perpetrated the greatest one against God. A bad conscience is never without fear: the right of retaliation always dogs its heels, if not in the substance of deed, then in the shadow of fear. O Archwonder of the divine art of reversal! They thought to destroy salvation and thereby gave cause for it to be preserved. One can properly say to them, as once to the great father of Cyrus:[18]

> You think to prevent heaven's end with your deceit.[19]
> Oh, far from it. You have called it to life with raving.
> Your attempt has kindled the anger of the Highest,

17. On the gender of "wisdom," see below, note 37.

18. Greiffenberg probably has Cyrus the Great's grandfather, Astyages, in mind instead of his father, Cambyses. According to Herodotus, the vain and superstitious King Astyages had a dream in which it was foretold that his grandson would overthrow him. He therefore arranged his daughter's marriage with the meek Cambyses thinking that they could produce no such audacious offspring. When Cyrus was born, Astyages ordered that he be killed. The courtier charged with the task of murdering him, however, left him to be raised by a shepherd. When Astyages discovered the deception, he tricked the courtier into eating his own son. *Herodotus*, trans. A. D. Godley, 3 vols., Loeb Classical Edition [Cambridge: Harvard University Press, 1990], 1: 139–57 (1.107–19). Cyrus II deposed Astyages in 550 BCE.

19. The following sonnet, written in alexandrines, follows the rhyme scheme *abbaabbacdcdcd*, lines 8 and 11 being impure rhymes.

> Ihr meint / des Himmels Schluß mit Räncken zu verhüten.
> O weit gefählt! ihr habt mit Toben ihn erweckt.
> Eu'r Anschlag hat den Zorn des Höchsten angesteckt /
> Und nehrt desselben Feu'r mit seinem gegen-wüten.
> GOtt läst sich nur mit Bus / mit Morten [*sic*] nicht begüten.
> Ach! wider seinen Rath kein Menschen-List erkleckt.
> Sein Vorsehn sich weit weit / auch über künfftigs streckt.
> Er kan des Schicksels Kunst / zu seinem Schluß auffbieten.
> Dersa [*sic*] den / der euch solt aus euren Irrgang führen /

and in raging against it, feeds that very fire.
Repentance only—not killing—appeases God.[20]
Oh! No human ruse suffices against His purpose.
His Providence extends far—o'er future things too.
He can summon destiny's art to reach His end.
The thread that will lead you out of your erring maze
becomes a net in which your knavish trick is hanged.[21]
He who fights against God can do nothing but lose.
Intervening, you provide the means that enable
the fulfillment of Scripture. Here one can well sense
that through opposition one oft achieves one's end.

They wanted to prevent the heavenly bowing of the sun before this Joseph and yet they themselves paved the way for it.[22] The betrayal was the precursor of this glory. Their deceitfulness had to serve the pious wisdom of God as a tool to carry out the design of eternity.

A woman came with an alabaster jar of ointment of pure nard, very costly.[23]

It was precious [ointment] because it served, as a sign of His incorruptibility, to embalm the Most Precious One in heaven and to anoint the Immortal

---

wird selbst ein Netz / darin eu'r Bubenstück erhanckt.
Wer GOtt bekämpft / der kan nicht anders als verliehren.
Vermittlend gebet ihr die Mittel / das gelangt /
Die Schrifft zu ihrem Ziel. Hier kan mann wohl verspühren.
Daß man oft seinen Zweck durch Wiederstand empfangt.

20. The second edition reads "Morten," whereas the first edition of 1672 reads "morden" (killing). See Catharina Regina von Greiffenberg, *Des Allerheiligst- und Allerheilsamsten Leidens und Sterbens Jesu Christi* (Nuremberg: Johann Hofmann, 1672), 12.

21. The text alludes here to the myth of Theseus and Ariadne, according to which Ariadne gave Theseus a ball of yarn to enable him to find his way out of the labyrinth on the island of Crete after he had killed the Minotaur who was housed therein. Greiffenberg frequently refers to this myth in her meditations.

22. Gn 37: 9–36. Joseph has a dream in which the sun and the moon and the eleven stars pay obeisance to him. Joseph's father, Jacob, understands this dream to mean that he and Joseph's mother and eleven brothers will bow down to Joseph and be ruled over by him. This interpretation causes the brothers to envy him and subsequently to betray him. Their selling him into slavery, however, in the end only leads to his ascent to influence under Pharaoh in Egypt.

23. Mk 14: 3 (compare Mt 26: 7, Lk 7: 37, Jn 12: 3). Greiffenberg refers to "Nardenwasser" (nard water), which in German sounds less like an ointment than a cologne. The four Gospels offer varying accounts of the anointment of Jesus by a woman. As a result of the conflation of these versions, this woman has traditionally been understood to be Mary Magdalene, the same woman who was later present at the crucifixion and at the opening of the empty tomb; while

One since His death drew nigh. The panacean seed of woman did not reject women, refusing to be served by them. Since He dignified them by His own being made flesh of a woman, He therefore also found them worthy to witness His death. He wanted to begin His life emerging from this sex and to end it in their company. He knew that He had caressed and pressed the ardor of love into them and granted fidelity to them in particular. Thus He meant to enjoy the noble fruit of this tree that His right hand had planted and to receive the sweet perfume of the love of this true-hearted refresher before His suffering, bitter as gall. Thus He testified that He respected not strength but gentleness and that He cared more for the inward ardor of love than the outward pretense of holiness from good works. What can soften His heart is ardor that melts the heart together with the desire to do good, however feebly their manifestations reflect them .

She broke the jar.[24]

Over Him who founded the feasts of heaven and for the sake of Him who for her and for all of us breaks the temple of His holy body. To erect the heavenly Jerusalem is this jar broken. She pours out the spirits of the balm over Him who has poured out the spirit of God over her. She refreshes the bearer of heavenly refreshment. O blissful woman! You who can truly prove your holy desire upon the principal object of love! It would have been no surprise if your heart and insides had melted when you saw this fountain of flames before you and had the chance to serve Him! Oh! That this blissful anointing had been granted to me! For love I would have spilled out my life along with the balm. But because I shall not be so fortunate as to live during the time of Thy dying, then grant, O sweetest Lord Jesus, that in my life I am mindful of Thy death and prepared to let the jar of my life be broken for Thy sake at whatever moment it may please Thee so that Thy glory—the costly balm of paradise—may be poured throughout the body of Thy church. O Thou heavenly maker of bliss, let me smash the jar of all earthly

---

in Mt 26: 7 and Mk 14: 3 the woman pours ointment on Jesus' head, in the version in Lk 7: 37–39, the woman is an unnamed repentant sinner (probably a prostitute) who washes Jesus' feet with her tears, wipes them with her hair, and anoints them with the ointment. In the version of the episode in the Gospel of John, the woman who anoints Jesus' feet with nard is actually called Mary, but there she is understood to be the sister of Lazarus whom Jesus raised from the dead. The section of this translation beginning with the quotation of Mk 14: 3 and concluding with the line "that Thou also mightst say of me: She has done a beautiful thing to me!" is a revised version of my previously published translation of these passages. See Catharina Regina von Greiffenberg, "The Most Holy and Most Healing Passion and Death of Jesus Christ," in Tatlock, *Seventeenth-Century German Prose,* 6–10.

24. Mk 14: 3.

vanity that I may smell the balm of Thy wounds. Get you behind me, you bitter worldly pleasure, you ashen-empty honor, you stone-laden lust for money, for you are the materials from which the jar of vanity was blown! I renounce you so that on that day I cannot be rejected and in the here and now am capable of smelling the poured-out balm of the holy passion. O Thou adorable adorer! Behold how my heart throbs, how my blood churns, how my spirits leap, how my insides seethe when I contemplate Thy sweet, fiery passion. How gladly (oh! were it in my power and Thy will!) would I burst my heart's jar to pour out my sap of love and praise! It hurts me, as does milk a mother, and it pains me that I must hold it in. O eternal, marvelous Wisdom! Anoint my spirit with heavenly influx and angelic effusions so that, with the power of imagination, I can seize the desire to praise that was conceived in my heart and draw it upward and [then], with reason and memory, purify, distill, and resolve it in glorious words of praise. Oh! Stoutly heat up the spirit with spirit and power so that it becomes fiery and flaming. Even if the fragile glass jar of my brain should burst from it, I will heed it not, if only a single glorious droplet of praise were burned out of me.

But, righteous God, how shall praise from the mouth of a sinner please Thee? For I belong among their number and yet am desirous of Thy glory. Oh! Then cleanse me of all my sins through Thy blood whose spilling I long to glorify. O Thou Savior of the entire world! Heal my frailties. May Thine innocent lamb's patience blot out my impatience! May Thy gentle forbearance curb my precipitous haste! May Thine unparalleled amicable love conquer my bitterness and irritability! In short, may all Thy virtues swallow all my vices and my secret faults! Oh! Let me shed the angelic balm of tears of repentance before Thee, like Mary, and cast off the adamantine jar of my heart so that I am not eternally cast out.[25]

Since, however, repentance is a fountain into eternal life, then let me pour out the balm of mercy for my poor fellow creatures. O Jesus! With Thy gently flowing blood make the little wellspring of my good deeds flow, along with mine eyes and heart: for Thou didst not spare Thy tears for me. You beloved poverty, you incarnate body of my Redeemer! Should one not gladly do you good, since He, to whom one ought, with greatest joy, to make all declarations of love, accepts what is done for Him? Get all hindrances behind me, heavenly transfixer, that keep me from this duty. Let my hands do that to which they pledge themselves, namely, to do every good deed for the Highest Good by doing good for the poor.

25. I.e., Mary Magdalene, who is understood to be the repentant sinner who anointed Jesus' feet (see above, note 23).

There is, however, nothing so good that people do not find fault with it on earth. Here the wisest message of God is called mess—and by those who were disciples of Christ and under His tutelage. Oh! How often are the doings of the Holy Spirit held to be rubbish out of ignorance even by those who are otherwise God-fearing? Just as Hannah's heartfelt prayer was deemed drunkenness by the priest Eli.[26] The Lord works in mysterious ways. Good need not always appear to be good. Virtue must sometimes don the mask of vice so that it may become more perfect. It is a right, noble disgrace to be despised for the sake of hidden virtue. And a magnanimous thing indeed to increase God's honor by letting one's own be decreased. All is well with the person subjected to such evil.

Oh, foolish calculation of reason! How could the [nard]water be sold more dearly and given to a more worthy poor man than the Dearest One who suffered Himself to be sold so cheaply for our good and who was transformed from the richest to the poorest man in the world?

Let the woman be completely silent so that the Eternal Word can say a word on her behalf. He who allowed the many injustices committed against Him to go unchallenged could not refrain from defending this woman. His endless goodness enabled Him to bear the ignominious insults to His own honor. But He cannot allow the slightest slight against His holy ones to go uncontested. When Judas betrayed Him, Peter denied Him, and the Jews wished to hang and kill Him, he did not say, "Do not trouble me!"[27] But when this godly woman was assailed, He spoke—

"Do not trouble the woman!"[28]

—to show that He cared more for those He loved than for Himself.

"She has done a beautiful thing to me."[29]

26. 1 Sm 1: 9–17. These verses recount the story of Hannah who was praying silently and fervently in the Temple. When the priest Eli saw her silently moving her lips, because she "was speaking in her heart," he wrongly accused her of being drunk. When Eli recognized his error, he told her that she should go in peace and that her petition would be granted.

27. The verses Jn 18: 28–19: 12 recount Jesus' refusal to defend himself before Pontius Pilate against the accusations of the Jews. Jesus explains in Jn 18: 36–37 that his kingdom "is not of this world" and that if it were, his servants would defend him. He does not defend himself since he was born for the express purpose of being martyred. Furthermore, in Jn 19: 9–11, Jesus does not respond to Pontius Pilate's assertion that he has the power to determine whether Jesus is crucified or not. Jesus explains that Pontius Pilate would not have power over him unless God had given him such power. Jesus' betrayal by Judas and by Peter is recounted in Jn 18: 1–18.

28. Mt 26: 10. The text reads "Lasset diß Weib unbekümmert!" Greiffenberg has changed the question in Matthew ("Why do you trouble the woman?" "Was bekümmert ihr das Weib?") to a forceful command by combining language from Mt 26: 10 and Mk 14: 6 ("Let her alone" "Lasset sie mit Frieden"). See the Kurfürstenbibel, 561.

29. Mt 26: 10.

O glorious advocate! Speak for me too when the world assails me! Say the same for me too, my Omniscient Guardian: Let her alone! Why do you trouble her?[30] Yes, Lord Jesus! Thou didst say it, when I was troubled on account of Thine inscrutable, wondrous ways. Thou didst say it, my sweetest Savior, whenever I was attacked and persecuted for the sake of heavenly things. Thou didst say it there in that holy place when on account of Thy wondrous ways I was again violently alarmed. Thou, most faithful dear heart, hadst not the heart to leave me, innocent one, unsatisfied. They had to bless against their will; they could not curse because I had Thy blessing in my heart. O Jesus, blessed fruit of my heart! Stay forever on my side and say to all of mine enemies and adversaries: Let her alone! Why do you trouble her? How comforted shall I wander, when Thou lightest my every way with this torch and followest me. But also grant me, O gentlest dispenser of virtue, that I do nothing but what this word of grace draws in its wake. Let all that I think and do be done in and from Thee to Thy service and infinite glory. Oh! That I could serve Thee alone with all human faculties and capacity. Indeed, that I might beg of Thee the power of all the angels in order to adore Thee sweetly like the archangels. O Almighty Jesus, who hast given me such great yearning, give me but the slightest power to realize some of it. Oh! That all my thoughts, deeds, and poetry might empty themselves into Thy love and glory, like the rivers into the sea! That I could think of nothing but Thy love and Thy passion; speak of nothing but of Thy wounds and wonders; write nothing but to Thy glory and its exaltation; do nothing but what would be the most pleasing and the sweetest to Thee, O dearest treasure of my soul. Oh, yes! I pledge my aspirations and actions to strive for the highest purpose of [increasing] Thy glory, so that Thou mightst also say of me: She has done a beautiful thing to me!

O Jesus, my love, Thou blazing fount of the soul,[31]
thou source of delight! Propagator of desire,

30. Here and further down in the paragraph, Greiffenberg quotes Mk 14: 6 (But Jesus said, "Let her alone; why do you trouble her? She has done a beautiful thing to me") in place of Mt 26: 10 (But Jesus, aware of this, said to them, "Why do you trouble the woman? For she has done a beautiful thing to me").

31. The following sonnet is written in alexandrines with the rhyme scheme *abbacbbcdedeff* (with line 7 as an imperfect rhyme).

O JEsu meine Lieb / du Flammen-Brunn der Seelen /
Du Quell der Lieblichkeit! Vermehrer der Begier /
Im höchsten Uberfluß / du höchste Wunder-Zier!
Leg deinen Geist-Geschmak in meiner Seele kehlen.
Laß den Lieb-Nectar-Thau / in meine Seele quellen:

in supreme abundance, Thou supreme wondrous jewel!
Put in the throat of my soul the taste of Thy spirit.
Let love's nectarous dew well up into my soul,
that I, dead to the earth, live heavenly in Thee,
move only from the spirit's force, honoring Thee.
Oh! May Thou brighten understanding with Thy light!
O ardent bliss of mankind! How Thy favor boils!
How love's sea seethes with the desire for doing good!
How the wise design works to bring us so much joy
that, through Thy pain, we too receive an entire sea
of heaven's sweetness. Forever is overlong:
thus from time to time Thou makest Thy grace cross o'er.

This crossing is so enrapturing that it is ineffable, so delightful that it is inconceivable. But inasmuch as it is the principal pleasure on earth, it leaves in its wake such a hunger and thirst to praise and glorify that one must sigh and scream all atremble with desire:

Heart, fill up with ardor! Desire, sit burning hot![32]
Boil and burst, you arteries; melt, power and spirit,

Daß ich / der Erden todt / ganz himmlisch leb in dir /
Vor starkem Geistes-Trieb / dich ehrend nur mich rühr.
Ach! wollest den Verstand / mit deinem Licht erhellen.
O brünstigs Menschen-Heil! wie wallet deine Gunst!
Wie siedt das Liebe-Meer / von Wolthuns-Lust verlangen!
Wie übt sich / uns zur Freud / die weise Ordnungs-Kunst /
Daß wir durch deine Pein / auch ganze See empfangen /
Von Himmels-Süssigkeit. Das Ewig wird dir lang:
Drum läst du/ deine Gnad / thun manchen Ubergang.

32. The following sonnet is likewise written in alexandrines with the rhyme scheme *abbaabbacddcee.* Line 8 is an imperfect rhyme.

Herz / werde voller Glut! Begierde / sitz entglühet!
Ihr Adern wallt und springt / zerschmelzet Krafft und Geist /
Fliest in die Lob-Wort aus! daß Jesus werd gepreist.
Ihr Glieder allzumal seyd mit dem Dank bemühet.
Ach! daß der Mund mit Lob / wie eine Rose blühet!
O meine Lippen / euch auf seinen Preiß befleist /
Belebten Balsam-Strich voll Ruhmes-Ruch erweist.
Der Seel entworfnes Bild / die Dankes-Pflicht / vollziehet!
Du Schöpfer-Preißerin! rühr keinen Bissen an /
Kost keinen Labung-Saft: du hast dann Lob gesaget /
Der Lobs-Unendlichkeit. Ihr Füße! mich nicht traget /
Macht fallen auf die Knieh / wie ich Gelübd gethan.
Vor alles geh sein Preiß / den du / O Hand! erkiest /
Zu schreiben / daß sein Ehr in aller Welt man list.

flow out into words of praise! May Jesus be praised.
You limbs, be ever eager to express your thanks!
Oh! That the mouth would, like a rose, blossom with praise!
O my lips, take pains to sing out His praise and laud,
prove balsam's animated streak filled with glory-scent.
Fulfill the soul's projection, the duty to thank!
You who laud the Creator shall not touch one bite,
taste no panacean liquid, ['til] you have praised
praise's eternity. You feet! Carry me not,
make [me] fall to my knees as once I swore I would.
Write, above all, O hand, praise of Him, whom you chose,
that over all the earth His glory shall be read.

"For you always have the poor with you, but you will not always have me."[33]

Thus spoke He who became the poorest of the poor for our sake. One can always carry out the usual exercises in devotion, but one cannot always attain that special power of the spirit. Thus one must not let go of such an occasion and must often do something that by all appearances seems undoable. He who follows God's singular lead must often suffer the world's singular judgments. But why would one pay heed to the world when one has God on one's side? To be scorned for the sake of Christ is the sweetest privilege of all. There is something so delightful in it that one must ever desire it. Even if there were no secret delight and compensation, but rather it remained ever concealed in deepest secrecy, suffering and working in Him would be such a sweet thing that one would not relinquish it for all the goods of the world. He resembles herein the good field that yields a hundredfold from one little seed; for He is really too faithful and kind not to reciprocate the honor sacrificed for Him.[34] For her being despised by an entire table [of men], He will make her famous in the eyes of the entire world. Her deed will be a flower in the wreath of His holy suffering and will perfume the wide world along with it.[35]

Thou superabundant recompenser! She fills a chamber with the precious scent of her ointment; thou, the entire earth with the report of her

33. Mt 26: 11.

34. Greiffenberg here refers to Christ's parable of the sower of grain. The yield of his sowing is different depending on the ground into which the seeds fall. Those that yield a hundredfold are those that hear and rejoice in Christ's message (Mt 13: 3–23).

35. "Truly, I say to you, wherever this gospel is preached in the whole world, what she has done will be told in memory of her" (Mt 26: 13).

good deed. Why should it astound that this scent should spread?[36] Since she anointed Him who is everything in everything, this scent fittingly spread out in all directions. It became known everywhere that she was a true prophet who indicated the death of Christ by breaking the jar and who indicated the incorruptibility of Christ by anointing Him. She herself knew not the loftiness of what she did. She did it out of simple love wrought within her by Supreme Wisdom herself who did not despise feminine weakness but frequently used it as the vessel of her omnipotence.[37] Since the annunciation of the conception of His holy body had been to a woman, thus His death and the immortality of this same body were to be announced through a woman as well. The Most High is accustomed to carry out and end His works as He began them; therefore the Resurrection also had to be proclaimed first through a woman so that we would see that the Almighty intended to use womenfolk at the beginning, middle, and end as the most faithful servants of the heart. And by no means did He exclude them from the most important business of the Kingdom of Heaven.

For this and for all other undeserved grace, I thank Thee, Thou Almighty Savior! I praise Thee eternally, Eternal Redeemer, for revealing to us the time of Thy crucifixion and our coronation. I laud Thee, Thou Supremely Wise Counsel of God, that Thou for our sakes didst suffer the wicked to gather and hold counsel over Thee, Most Pious Innocence, and to take Thee prisoner with trickery so that Thou couldst redeem us. Glory be to Thee, Thou Anointed One of the Lord and the true Messiah, for not scorning that

36. Greiffenberg here plays with the word for scent, *Geruch*, and that for rumor or report, *Gerücht*.

37. The text here refers to "die höchste Weisheit" (literally, the highest wisdom), meaning God. In German *Weisheit* is a feminine noun (as are many abstract nouns in German), and thus the text temporarily speaks of God as (grammatically) feminine. Inasmuch as Greiffenberg here makes a special point about women, I have by way of exception elected to use the feminine pronoun "her" in reference to supreme wisdom and to add the reflexive pronoun "herself" to make clear that wisdom is feminine, even though the play of gender is much more egregious and forced in English than it is in German. Precisely because English lacks the flexibility of delicate play with grammatical gender, I have elsewhere elected not to render grammatically feminine gender with reference to substitute names for God—e.g., totality (*Allheit*), divinity or Godhead (*Gottheit*)—so as not to give the impression that Greiffenberg stridently employs feminine-gendered personifications to speak of God. It should be noted that in the following sentence, God is referred to once again as a being with masculine gender. There is of course also a biblical precedent for personifying wisdom as a feminine entity. See Elizabeth A. Johnson, "Wisdom Was Made Flesh and Pitched Her Tent among Us," *Reconstructing the Christ Symbol: Essays in Feminist Christology*, ed. Maryanne Stevens (New York: Paulist Press, 1993), 95–117, and Elisabeth Gössmann, "'Ipsa enim quasi domus sapientiae.'" Die Frau ist gleichsam das Haus der Weisheit. Zur frauenbezogenen Spiritualität Hildegards von Bingen," chap. 5 of *Hildegard von Bingen. Versuche einer Annäherung* (Munich: Iudicium, 1995), 93–113.

wretched woman's anointing of Thee for burial and for instead defending her so gloriously to the honor of all women. Oh! What glory, praise, honor, laud, and gratitude we do owe Thee for this voluntary preparation for Thy suffering and our redemption! For this, may all gratitude that a grateful heart can ever conceive be Thine, all the effusions of which millions of heavens full of angels are capable; for I cannot, as I desire, accomplish the slightest thing with words. But Thou Holy One who knowest the heart, Thou pasturest in the meadow of desire as wouldst Thou with the sweetest pasture.

With [the security of] Thy true knowledge [of my intentions], I thus aver that I have not only the desire to praise but also the most ardent and zealous desire to do good works, to glorify Thee now and in all eternity with deeds that make the angels exult. Thou immutable being! Help me to bring all this into being so that Thou shalt be ever and ever extolled and exalted in my thoughts on earth as in heaven. Amen! Thou Eternal Amen, speak the amen Thyself! Amen.

1
Jesus! What shall I Thee give,[38]
who didst give Thyself to death,
thyself for myself, death life,
who restorest with Thy blood?
Jesus! This I can't conceive,
all my senses fade away.
This I simply cannot grasp:
that Life should be meant to die.

38. The nine numbered verses that follow (largely in trochaic tetrameter) consist of eight lines, each of seven or eight syllables (depending on whether they end with a stressed or unstressed syllable), rhymed according to the scheme *ababccdd*, etc.

1.JEsu! was soll ich dir geben /
Der du in den tod dich gabst /
dich vor mich den tod / das Leben /
mich mit deinem Blute labst?
JEsu! ich kans nicht ersinnen /
meine sinne mir zerrinnen.
Ich kan nicht begreiffen wol /
daß das Leben sterben soll.

2. Auserwehlter Weibes-saamen /
zugesagt im Paradeiß!
Du warst der verlangen flamme /
auf dem ersten Erden-kreiß.
Du woltst auch / in Noah hertzen /
jene grosse Sündflut schertzen /
bliebest unauslöschlich hell /
in des Welt-Erhalters seel.

2
Elect-select seed of woman
promised us in paradise!
Inextinguishably bright
in the World-Preserver's soul,
Thou wast the flame of desire
upon the first earthly globe,
didst mean to give Noah courage
to laugh at that mighty flood.

3
Thou wast shown to him anew
by means of the rainbow's gleam:
when henceforth through Thee was God
disposed to favoring us.
God, with the drops of Thy blood,
would plug the springs of the pit:

---

3. Du wardst durch den Regenbogen /
auf das neu ihm angezeigt:
Wie uns GOtt durch dich bewogen /
künfftig wollte seyn geneigt.
GOtt/ durch deine Blutes-tropffen /
wollt all' abgrunds-Brunnen stopffen:
Das noch flamm noch wasserfluth /
nimmermehr uns schaden thut.

4. Du warst auch des Abrams Segen /
und sein übergrosser Lohn /
als du redst / den grund zu legen
deinen werthen Menschheit-Thron.
Du versprachst ihm grosse Sachen /
die du aus ihm wolltest machen /
fürtest ihn offt in Gefahr /
O du rechter Wunderbar!

5. Isaac du / der ward geschlachtet /
den kein Engel nicht errett /
der das Creutz-holtz halb verschmachtet /
selber trug zur Schedelstätt!
Segen-Sohn und Segen-geber!
aller Lust und freud Urheber!
Meine Sonne bist nur du /
Meines hertzens freud und ruh.

6. Jacobs stein und Himmels-leiter /
sein blut-bunter Schäfer-stab /
du sein Englischer begleiter
und Erwerber aller haab /
GOtt und Mensch mit dem er runge /

so that neither flame nor flood
could harm us ever again.[39]

4
Thou wast Abram's blessing too
and his enormous reward
when Thou didst tell him to found
the worthy throne of mankind.
Thou didst promise him great things
that Thou wouldst make out of him.
Thou didst oft imperil him,
O Thou truly Wondrous One!

5
Thou Isaac, who wast cut down
and whom no angel delivered,

---

sieg und segen ihm abdrunge!
Du mein Schilo / held und heil /
bist auch meiner seele theil.

7. Wahrer Joseph! den sich sencket /
in die schwartze Höllen-grub /
den man zu verkauffen denket /
in der Heiden hände schub /
der recht fälschlich angegeben.
Doch kontst du das haupt erheben
aus der angst / daß du der welt /
würst zum Herrscher vorgestellt.

8. Sonne / die von fernen stralet!
Bild-bezielter wunder-zweck /
der den Vätern vorgemahlet /
in des schattens vorhang-deck!
ihrer aller Heil und Segen /
den zum grund und punct sie legen!
Dir sey lob / daß alle welt
Zu erlösen / dir gefällt.

9. Dir sey lob / aus allen Kräfften!
Lob / aus aller hertzen-macht /
Lob / aus aller adern säfften /
Lob / aus allem Geist bedacht.
Lob / aus gantzer seel und sinnen /
Lob / aus innerstem beginnen!
Lob / aus allem / was in mir /
sey / O JEsu! ewig dir!

39. Here Greiffenberg draws parallels between the sacrifice of Jesus and the covenant signified by the rainbow after the flood. God tells Noah that the rainbow will be a reminder that he has promised never again to send a flood to destroy the inhabitants of the earth (Gn 9: 13–17).

didst, half dead, bear the wood cross
there to the Place of the Skull![40]
Blessing's son, blessing's bestower!
Source of all delight and joy!
My sun art Thou and Thou only,
my heart's peace and jubilation.

6

Jacob's stone, celestial ladder,
and shepherd's crook, bright with blood,[41]
Thou his angelic companion
and acquirer of all goods.
God and man with whom he wrestled
forcing victory and blessing![42]
My Shiloh, hero, and Savior,
Thou art privy to my soul.[43]

40. The place of the skull is Golgotha where Jesus was crucified. In this verse Greiffenberg compares Jesus to Isaac who was nearly sacrificed by his father, Abraham. According to Genesis, God commanded Abraham to sacrifice his son Isaac as a burnt offering and Abraham obeyed with a heavy heart. Just as he prepared to sacrifice him, an angel of the Lord intervened and told Abraham not to lay a hand on his son and to sacrifice a ram instead. God thereafter told Abraham that he would be rewarded for his obedience and readiness to sacrifice even his son (Gn 22: 1–17).

41. Greiffenberg writes here of a "blut-bunter Schäfer-stab" (shepherd's crook or staff colored or bright with blood). Her meaning is not entirely clear. Jacob's staff is mentioned in Gn 32: 10. In this and the following verse, Jacob prays to God, speaking of having "passed over this Jordan" with his staff upon returning to the land of his father. He expresses his fear that his brother, Esau, might kill him and his wives and children. The "blood" mentioned by Greiffenberg might be an oblique reference to the fate of his favorite son, Joseph, who will be sold into slavery by his brothers and whose bloody coat will be shown to Jacob as proof that Joseph has died. The "shepherd's crook, bright with blood" also draws a parallel to Jesus, the Good Shepherd, who will be bloodied.

42. Gn 28: 11–22. Jacob goes forth from his father's house to Haran and stops for the night, where he takes a stone for his pillow and dreams that he sees angels ascending and descending a ladder that reaches to heaven. God speaks to him in his dream telling him of his prosperous future. Thereafter Jacob takes the stone that served as his pillow and sets it up as a pillar and pours oil on it, vowing that if the Lord takes care of him and enables him to return to his father's house, he will accept him as his God. Gn 32: 24–32 recounts how Jacob returns years later as a wealthy man and wrestles all night with a man who tells him that he has God's blessing and shall henceforth be called Israel.

43. "The scepter shall not depart from Judah, nor the ruler's staff from between his feet, until he comes to whom it belongs; and to him shall be the obedience of the peoples" (Gn 49: 10). The King James Version translates the verse as "until Shiloh come." The Hebrew word *Shiloh* is understood to refer to the Messiah. In chapter 49, Jacob addresses his twelve sons, telling them what will be in the last days. This line, addressed to his son Judah, is understood in the Christian context to refer to the coming of Jesus Christ.

7
True Joseph, who did descend
into the black pit of hell,
whom they intended to sell
and put in the hands of heathens,
who was falsely vilified.
But Thou couldst lift up Thy head
out of the fear, so as ruler
thou wouldst be shown to the world.[44]

8
Sun that shines from far away!
Wondrous end, fixed with images,
adumbrated for the fathers
in the shadow's curtained cover![45]
Bliss and blessing of them all,
foundation and center point!
Be Thou lauded that it please
thee to save the entire world.

9
Be Thou praised with all my might!
Praised with the strength of my heart,

44. The text here identifies the parallels between Joseph and Jesus. According to Genesis Joseph's envious brothers first put him in a pit without water and then for twenty pieces of silver sold him to Ishmaelites who took him to Egypt. Joseph's brothers told their father that Joseph had been devoured by wild animals and showed him as proof Joseph's coat, which they had dipped in animal blood (Gn 37: 23–33). Joseph later ascended to power in Egypt. Jesus was betrayed by Judas to the Romans for thirty pieces of silver. During the trial, when Pilate asked Jesus whether he was the king of the Jews, he declared that his kingship was not of this world (Jn 18: 36). Later he was mocked and scourged as "King of the Jews."

45. The text presumably refers here to the many prophecies of the Old Testament that Christians believe foretold the coming of Jesus. These include such prophecies as Is 7: 14 ("Therefore the Lord himself will give you a sign. Behold, a young woman shall conceive and bear a son, and shall call his name Immanuel"); Is 40: 3–5 ("A voice cries: 'In the wilderness prepare the way of the Lord, make straight in the desert a highway for our God. Every valley shall be lifted up, and every mountain and hill be made low; the uneven ground shall become level, and the rough places a plain. And the glory of the Lord shall be revealed, and all flesh shall see it together, for the mouth of the Lord has spoken'"); Mi 5: 2 ("But you, O Bethlehem Ephrathah, who are little to be among the clans of Judah, from you shall come forth for me one who is to be ruler in Israel, whose origin is from of old, from ancient days"); and Zec 9: 9 ("Rejoice greatly, O daughter of Zion! Shout aloud, O daughter of Jerusalem! Lo, your king comes to you; triumphant and victorious is he, humble and riding on an ass, on a colt, the foal of an ass").

praised with the sap of my veins,
praised with my spirit's pondering.
Praised with all my soul and senses,
praised with inmost enterprise!
Praised with all that is in me!
Be Thou evermore, O Jesus!

Figure 4. Unattributed, "For Slaying the Slayer" from *Des Allerheiligst- und Allerheilsamsten . . . Christi* (1672). The Beinecke Rare Book and Manuscript Library.

Explanation of the Copper Engraving

In Eden, the first garden, a snake and a tree
deprived us of our life.[46]
The serpent, armed with the might of venomous sin,
to slay us left the tree.
The sins, its brood, they glitter, bright from fiery hell:
to torment and to bite
the Christian company, the camp of Israel,
their souls grimly to smite.
What then would God's Son set out to do? From this tree
He thus a cross does fashion.
Like a worm, he hangs on this wood for all to see:
just think! 'Tis no illusion.
In the heat of God's anger He was cast like ore
to make the purple worm.
The nature of the serpent, all our sins, flowed o'er
Him in His martyr's storm.

46. See figure 4. This engraving introduces the ninth meditation. The poem explicating the copper engraving consists of alternating alexandrines and half lines with an alternating rhyme scheme (*abab*, etc.) throughout. In the case of this translation, by way of exception I have approximated the rhyme scheme and reproduced the syllabic meter. I have not, however, consistently reproduced the accentual meter.

Ein Baum / und eine Schlang / im ersten Garten Eden
uns üm das Leben bracht.
Die Schlange von dem Baum loßfuhre / uns zu töden
durch Sünd-vergiffte Macht.
Die Sünden / ihre Brut / von Höllenfeuer gleissen:
das Lager Israel /
Das volk der Christ-gemein / zu plagen und zu beissen /
zu morden an der Seel.
Was thäte GOttes Sohn? Er lässet ihme hauen
ein Creutz / aus diesen [*sic*] Baum.
Er läst / an diesem Holz / als einen Wurm sich sehen:
bedenk's / es ist kein Traum.
In GOttes Zornes-glut / ward er / wie Erz / gegossen
zum rothen Purpur-Wurm.
Ihn unsre Sünde hat / die schlangen-art / ümflossen /
in seinem Martersturm.
Da hängt er in der Luft: des Todes Tod zu werden /
des Giftes Gegengift.
Ja! diese todte Schlang den Tod nimt von der Erden:
den jene lebend stift.
Also die Schlang' am Baum uns konte wiedergeben /
Was Schlang und Baum verscherzt.
Schau jene glaubig an: so wirstu seelig leben.
Für dich / ward sie geerzt.

Suspended there, He thus becomes the death of death,
its venom's antidote.
Yes! This dead serpent removes from the earth the death
that the living one wrought.
The serpent on the tree could restore to us this:
What they lost, snake and wood.
Behold that one in faith, and you will live in bliss.
For you was cast this good.

ON THE SUPREMELY HOLY AND SUPREMELY SALVIFIC SUFFERING OF JESUS: NINTH MEDITATION

[The ninth meditation opens with a condensed paraphrase of Mt 27: 27–31 where Jesus is stripped of the robe that the soldiers have put on him, dressed again in his own clothes, and led away to be crucified. Greiffenberg then quotes Jn 19: 17, which emphasizes that Jesus is made to carry his own cross, and thereafter switches to Lk 23: 26, which describes how Simon of Cyrene is then compelled to carry the cross for Jesus, Beginning with Lk 23: 27, the following excerpt ponders the presence and feelings of the women who were at the crucifixion. Furthermore, it contemplates the excruciating agony that Jesus suffered on the cross to appease God's wrath and gain redemption for sinful humanity.]

And there followed him a great multitude of the people, and of women, who bewailed and lamented him.[47]

Common people are wont to accompany poor sinners [to the place of execution]. This is an evil practice (though certainly not a forbidden one) and [a matter of] cruel curiosity; for their tumult only increases the agony of these poor sinners, which is, moreover, completely unnecessary. People are supposed to rejoice in the carrying out of justice, but many a person (who should see himself reflected in the mirror there and mend his ways) derides it, since he finds in himself many greater crimes than in the condemned person and secretly triumphs that he himself gets off scot free. There is a thirst for blood in the hastening to the execution of these miserable people: their punishment alone is [agonizing] enough without all those eyes witnessing it. It is inhumane to relish the sight of another person's agony. It is more Christian meanwhile to bestir our lips at home to pray for his soul than to open our eyes wide to view his torment. It is much better to help the angels

47. Lk 23: 27.

bring his soul to heaven than to help the executioner with our eyes to torture his body, since the crowd of bystanders must increase his pain by no small amount. This accompanying of the condemned person is therefore an excruciating cruelty, because it tortures his feelings as the executioner tortures his body.

When, however, it is done (as with these women) out of love and sympathy, the circumstances change the matter, and what was otherwise reprehensible becomes praiseworthy. Love, like the philosopher's stone, makes everything it touches golden and good. It brings about the deftest changes of form: from evil, it makes goodness; from cruelty, sympathy; from inhumanity, ardor. What those people do out of evil curiosity, it does out of loving care. Even if both do the same thing [outwardly], [the latter] stems from different origins and aims at a completely different goal. The rabble follows in its fury; the sympathetic women in their ardor: they were much more ardent and constant in their love of and loyalty to Jesus, because they did not hesitate, despite the strict prohibition of their high priests, to bewail Him publicly. In contrast, almost none of His disciples, not to mention others from the rabble, bestirred themselves to open their mouths.

It becomes clear then that whereas men do surpass us when it is a matter of the courage to attack and when it comes to throttling and killing, we undeniably surpass them when it is a matter of the courage to avow unflinchingly and when it comes to suffering or dying with or for our friends. We do not find it as laudable to deflect danger forcibly from ourselves as to suffer this danger. But we find ourselves able to plunge into the greatest dangers in the world rather than fail to display even the slightest sign of resoluteness that can in some manner delight our friends in need.[48] As long as we can follow them, we fear neither death nor the grave. True love has no more joyous way than to rise up to her beloved over all the mountains of fire, swords, and needles. We hate the bliss that we enjoy while our dearest friends experience misfortune. We toss a Polycrates ring into the sea on purpose to gain the delight of being unhappy with them.[49] Women from India are often envied more for their good fortune to be allowed to jump into the fire to join their dead husbands than for their gold. Whoever understands

48. The second edition incorrectly reads "Feinden" (enemies), whereas the first edition correctly reads "Freunden" (friends). See Greiffenberg, *Des Allerheiligst- und Allerheilsamsten Leidens und Sterbens Jesu Christi* (1672), 582. *Freund* (friend) can also encompass the meaning "relative."

49. Polycrates, the tyrant of Samos, had such great good fortune that even when he attempted to make a sacrifice by throwing a valuable ring into the sea, a fisherman caught the fish, and the ring was found in the maw of the fish.

the true effect of righteous love and loyalty will not doubt my words but instead will know that this noble impulse can effect even more than I am able to express. Thus it is no wonder that these women had the courage to bewail Him loudly, Him who was so harshly indicted by the elders. They followed Him because they carried Him in their hearts; and they bewailed Him because they loved Him ardently. The fire of love made the moisture rise up into the distillation kettle of the brain and trickle down again through the glass tubes of the eyes.[50] They weep the white blood of their hearts when they see the red blood of His weals and cuts.

Oh! Who is more worthy of lamentation and bewailing than our dearest Lord Jesus? He who walks beneath the wooden cross so covered with weals and cuts, with wounds and bruises, with tears and drops [of blood] that He could probably move tigers and tyrants to pity, not to mention soft-hearted women. How should they not have bewailed Him? Did He not weep with them over the death of Lazarus?[51] Since He was sensitive to their pain, should they not have felt His? They who have removed the cause for wailing must be bewailed the most. The memory of His consoling words "Weep not!" was the greatest inducement to weep for Him.[52] He who dries the tears of sorrowful eyes is a magnet for them when things are going badly for Him. Should not their eyes become moist over Him who restored light to many eyes? Should not the agony of Him who helped to relieve the agony of many be lamented? Oh, yes! It is most right to sorrow over Him who relieved the sorrow of so many. It is right to bemoan the weakness of Him who provided everyone with strength. In short, there can be none more worthy of lamentation and bewailing than He who transformed all lamentation and wailing into jubilation and rejoicing. Thus these women very rightly and ardently bewailed Him, crying the most passionate tears.

50. The brain is imagined here as a still that liberates the alcohol from the raw material (fruits, grains, etc.) that is heated up. In distillation, the vapors rise in the kettle and pass through a narrow pipe and then through a coil; a cold-water bath then condenses the vapors in the coils, converting them to liquid form.

51. The text refers here to Jn 11: 1–44 and Jn 12: 1–10. At Bethany Jesus raises Lazarus from the dead. Later Lazarus's sister Mary anoints Jesus in preparation for Jesus' own burial. See above, note 23.

52. The text anticipates Lk 23: 28–30, which will be quoted just a few pages later. Jesus tells the women at the cross to weep not for him but rather for themselves when he makes the dire prediction here of future suffering. In the immediate passage, however, the text also evokes the words of comfort that Jesus speaks in Lk 7: 13 and Lk 8: 52 when he prepares to raise a young man and young girl, respectively, from the dead.

But Jesus turning to them.[53]

The sweetest of all hearts soon turned to them who loved Him, to them who bewailed and lamented Him. Even in His most excruciating suffering, He cannot leave His beloved ones without a sign of love or the sad ones without comfort. He was setting about doing the deed most freely done in the world, indeed, in heaven. All the same, He turned to the women who loved and lamented Him. Love is stronger than death. With all its cruelty, the latter cannot make Him turn around as can the former with its stirring of the heart. Its heat is fierier than hell. Hellfire could not harm a hair on His head, since love had twined around His entire body, or rather His heart. The sea of the tenderest fervor tore open the dam of salvation. The cloud is burst by the peal of their lamentation. He could not see their sympathy without sympathy. His omniscience showed Him the most pitiable spectacle, one that filled His heart and imagination to overflowing so that His mouth spoke.[54]

Said, "Daughters of Jerusalem, do not weep for me, but weep for yourselves and for your children. For behold, the days are coming when they will say, 'Blessed are the barren, and the wombs that never bore, and the breasts that never gave suck!' Then they will begin to say to the mountains, 'Fall on us'; and to the hills, 'Cover us.'"[55]

You unfortunate daughters of an evil mother! You who must bear her guilt into the third and fourth generations! Weep not so much for me as for yourselves; you have abundant reason for doing so. A hero is not to be bewailed; rather, to be hailed. His misfortune is the thread of triumph with which he will wind others out of their misfortune.[56] The hero's misfortunes will become ecstasies of jubilation when they are overcome. That which is to be rejoiced in is not to be bewailed. Now there is nothing to be more rejoiced in than the victories of heaven that I go forth to win. Therefore I am by no means to be bewailed, because the eternal fruits of joy and the delight of laughter will come from my suffering. Therefore weep not for me but for yourselves, with whom it will end with nothing but tears and sad tales when, on the contrary, nothing but glory and triumph will flourish with me. You,

53. Lk 23: 28.

54. Paraphrase of Lk 6: 45: "for out of the abundance of the heart his mouth speaks."

55. Lk 23: 28–30.

56. The text refers once again to the Greek myth of Theseus and the Minotaur. Armed with a sword and a spool of thread, Theseus entered the maze of the Minotaur on the island of Crete. As he walked deeper into the labyrinth, he unwound the thread, which enabled him to find his way out again once he had killed the monster.

you and your children are to be wept over. If you wept as many tears as that Indian rain tree, as the dampest spring clouds, indeed, as many drops as has the sea, you would hardly be able to bewail your misfortune sufficiently.[57]

For behold, the time will come (oh, the painful, miserable time that saddens me more than all my sorrows) when one will consider unhappy the happiness of the name mother, which has heretofore been treasured, and when one will think a blessing that which was thought an unlucky star. One will consider shame good fortune, and a curse mercy. The blessing will be lamented, and the gifts of God bewailed. Blessed are the barren, one will say (when previously these women were considered the accursed), because they bore no fruit with which our enemy could slake his inhumanity. Blessed are the breasts of them who have not given suck that they need not see the suckling drown in their tears and in his own blood and need not say, "Oh, hide us, you merciful mountains, from the merciless bloodthirsty tyrants! Your violent trembling and shaking will be a comfort to us, your quaking a waking because it shortens our lives, thus ending the cruel agony." The infertile chasms will become for you beloved places of refuge and will be a desirable shield against the enemy's cruel fire and sword. Oh! So weep if you at least might cry down from heaven the shortening of this agony. I will weep with you, more over your unlucky star than over my own agony. I would gladly suffer even more if I could thereby avert this misfortune from you. But God's righteousness must be satisfied; it has been provoked by obstinacy far too long. Still I shall in the end try to lighten the punishment with the salvation of your souls.

"For if they do this when the wood is green, what will happen when it is dry?"[58]

Just consider it yourselves: when God's righteousness imposes so much suffering on me who am innocent, what will come over the guilty? If the righteous one must suffer, how much more so the sinner? If this first revenge of God comes to pass on the green branch of virtue, what will happen on the accursed dry wood of hell? Thus spoke our dear Lord Jesus not only to these women, but thus He still speaks today to all impenitent sinners. Rouse your sense of caution, you stubborn ones! Take to heart the danger of your falling. Think on it! If infinite substantial love did not spare the core of its very own body and heart, it will spare you still less. If it made the floods of righteous anger rush at the most ardent child of love—and specifically for the

57. "Rain tree" (*Regenbaum*) refers in German generally to species of tropical trees from which rainlike drops fall, e.g., *Samanea samen*, sometimes called rain tree in English.

58. Lk 23: 31.

sake of the sins of others—it will make these same floods empty out over you for the sake of your own sins. If the immortal cedar tree and the uncrushable palm tree had to be crushed from the burden of sin and the holy ghostly olive tree itself had to suffer pain, how much more so will the same thing await the accursed fig tree, the thorn hedges, and the thistles? If this happens in the green tree, whose marrow is the divinity, what will happen in the dry one, which the flame of sinful desire has made ripe for hell!

Oh, yes! Dearest Lord Jesus! One has reason to draw such conclusions. If this is done in the Jesus-tree, which is laden with virtue and fruitful with piety, what will be done in the heinously and hellishly dry evil tree? If the Most Holy could not be freed, what hope does the sinner have who does not recognize himself as such and does not desire to repent? Arise, arise, you people slumbering in sin! Awaken, you stubborn hearts, and behold this cautionary mirror of divine punishment of sins that through optical devices makes you see into God's judgment, indeed, even into the far distant future![59] Oh! Take precautions so as to anticipate the danger that makes you build your house on sand that is undermined by the torrent of hell and plunges it into its fire. Let the honeyed words of Jesus make your eyes alert so that they can perceive the peril of being engulfed and thus escape it. Beware of sitting on the rickety seat over the bottomless pit so that you do not fall in or so that the strand of hair above your head, on which the sword hangs, does not break and wound you.[60]

How can you be impenitent when the wind of warning blows the hellish fire and flames to your heart that it should melt! Are you then more obdurate than the steel and iron that the fire can make molten, than the diamond that can be cut, and the marble that can be carved? Have you ingested an opiate of hell that the short sleep lowers you into the long sleep before you have awakened to your own salvation! Oh, wake up! It is already the sixtieth minute of the last hour of the world. Seize the lamp with oil and light before sulfur and pitch, fire and darkness, catch you unaware in hell. The door of grace is still open for just one more moment. Therefore jump up and go in before it is closed, closed—to be sure—forever. Hasten, for the flicker

59. The text reads *Beyspiegel,* a contraction of the word for mirror *(Spiegel)* and the word for example *(Beispiel).*

60. The text refers here to the sword of Damocles. According to legend, Damocles, a courtier, excessively flattered Dionysius I of Syracuse. Dionysius offered him the opportunity of seeing what it was like to be in his place. Thus, while he was feasting, Damocles discovered a sword suspended immediately above him by a single horse hair. The logic of Greiffenberg's sentence is faulty, since of course the sword wounds, not the hair. The throne over the bottomless pit may refer to Rv 20: 1–4, where thrones and a bottomless pit appear in John's vision.

and flash will likewise not be chastened, the flicker and flash that will bring eternity and the end of the time when you still have time to repent. Thereafter it will be said: they were judged as they were found to be and there will be no further appeal to a higher court because the highest court has already gone into effect.[61] There is no time to lose here, and each moment is worth more than a hundred thousand pounds. For if you mean now at the last moment to blow on the lamp and you already have your hand on the little jug to pour oil into it and the door opens while you are doing it, it is dangerous and you are done for. Therefore, now, now, when you hear His voice, do not harden your hearts! "'Tis time to hasten now! / Whosoever shall delay / Who is deficient now / Shall want in every way"—thus sings that eminent poet.[62]

I do not admonish you to repentance as if I were not in need of doing so myself. Oh, no! I am, like all people, a sinner. I speak only to those who are still far from doing so: I, however, believing, am already enclosed in the wounds and the heart of my Redeemer, and I have wrapped myself in the cloak of His righteousness so that no hell, world, sin, death, or judgment can tear me out of it. The oil of my lamp and the fuel of my faith are in the heart of Jesus and thus inexhaustible and perpetual.

Two others also, who were criminals, were led away to be put to death with him.[63]

The most incomparable virtue had to share the same fate as the perpetrators of vice! The most special holiness had to be mixed in with the godless so that the Prince of Life Himself was the companion of murderers! He is condemned with them to the same death, even when He has led a life completely unlike theirs. The end was to be one and the same, although the beginning and the middle were as far apart as the Ganges and the Nile. He means, however, to die with the evildoers so that the sinners can live with Him. He means to be led out with them to death so that they can be ushered into eternal life with Him. Because the unlike conduct of His life does not free Him from the like ending, thus the unlikeness of their lives to

61. The idea of a last judgment occurs, for example, in Acts 17: 30–31: "The Times of ignorance God overlooked, but now he commands all men everywhere to repent, because he has fixed a day on which he will judge the world in righteousness by a man whom he has appointed." In a vision of the last judgment, Rv 20: 12 asserts: "And the dead were judged by what was written in the books, by what they had done."

62. The text quotes Paul Fleming (1609–40), "Tugend ist mein Leben" (Virtue Is My Life): "Itzt ist Zeit, zu eilen; / Dem wird alles feilen, / Der sich wird verweilen / Und itzt verbricht." See *Gedichte von Paul Fleming*, ed. Julius Tittman (Leipzig: F. A. Brockhaus, 1870), 86. Greiffenberg replaces the word "gebricht" with "verbricht." This substitution does not change the meaning.

63. Lk 23: 32.

His will not prevent them from the like endless ending either, the ending of eternal bliss. Because He is to be executed at the same time as sinners, they too are to be resurrected with Him. The innocent one suffers with the guilty so that the guilty can one day prevail with the innocent Lamb of God.

And when they came to a place called in Hebrew Golgotha (which means in German the place of a skull).[64]

O Jesus! Thou head of all living creatures, indeed, of life itself, Thou art brought to the dead place of a skull. Thou head of all virtues art led to the place where vice costs one's head and where its gruesome monuments, the death heads, lie. Thou lord of incorruptibility must enter the place of corruptibility because, secured against it, Thou goest there to magnify the incorruptibility of Thy glory.

They offered him vinegar and wine to drink, mingled with myrrh and gall; but when he tasted it, he would not drink it.[65]

Although the wisest king of all commands that wretched people who have been condemned to die be given wine to drink so that they can forget their misery—as is customary in all municipal and regional courts, so that poor sinners are comforted with food and drink before their deaths—our dear Jesus did not experience this kindness. Rather He had to forgo that which even the worst evildoer receives. To be sure they pretended to observe this custom by giving Him wine, but their evil gall mixed it with gall. They embittered His refreshment too—so great is their poison that it makes even comfort terrible. In the midst of refreshment, they desire to suffocate Him and to suppress the life spirits that are to be thereby revived. Oh, unspeakable cruelty—it is as despicable as it is incomparable to weaken and embitter the life forces when one should support and revive them so that they can endure the bitterest pain. If it had been meant to dull the experience of pain by enfeebling the life spirits, one could still excuse it. But there was no such thought in the minds of these bloodthirsty villains. All-knowing Jesus realized, however, from the start that this poisonous gall would enfeeble him and that He would thus endure His entire martyrdom without being so sensitive [to pain], and so for this very reason He did not want to drink it.

He refused to take something that could have relieved His sensitivity

64. Mt 27: 33. Greiffenberg adds "in Hebrew" and "in German."

65. Myrrh appears in Mk 15: 23 and gall in Mt 27: 34. Furthermore, "vinegar" is here added to "wine," and thus this text anticipates a second such incident described in Mt 27: 48, Mk 15: 36, Lk 23: 36, and Jn 19: 28–30.

[to pain] somewhat. Not in order to spare Himself agony but instead to be robbed of none of it, He refused this drink of gall that with its sharp taste was to rob him of the sharpness of His pain. There is, moreover, yet another mystery hidden here, namely, that Christ refused no torment but this drink of gall. Nothing is as repugnant to Him as anger and the poison of gall, and He does not want us to mix our tears of repentance or still less His sacrosanct Communion wine with it. Instead without gall, like doves, we shall come before Him and thus be pleasing to Him in a different manner. Oh! Let us then not embitter these tears but spew all gall into the face of the hellish mischief maker and pasture our gentle little lamb with love and tenderness and have gentleness and sweetness in our mouths, eyes, hands, and hearts. Thus shall we be pleasing to Him.

And they crucified him at the place Golgotha.[66]

Now, dearest Lord Jesus, wilt Thou experience terrible agony, and I will agonize in my heart. Oh! It is a cross for me to bear to name Thy crucifixion and agony for me to imagine it. How can my hands describe the pain of Thine without trembling and shaking with pain? How can I recall the stripping of Thee without dying of sheer horror? O Jesus! Thou who surroundest all of creation and Creator of all the surroundings except for Thyself! Why must Thy noble body be robbed of even the smallest part of it? Thou who art beautifully and magnificently adorned with immortal glory and splendor sufferest Thyself to be most miserably and lamentably stripped. Thou, whose raiment is the blinding radiance of God and the most divine beam of light, standest now completely naked, covered with bloody welts and cuts. Thou who spreadest out heaven like a carpet hast on earth not a scrap in which to wrap Thyself. The raw, sharp air of the wind that is yet cold must cut through Thy body, which is covered with wounds, blood, and bruises? Oh, what agony must this alone have caused Thee? What lesions, wound-fever, and horror of nature must have arisen from this?

But what is all that compared with the violent hurling of Thy holy body onto the unplaned, rough, and splintery wooden cross? There they must have renewed and broken open and made bloody the wounds of lashing, torn open the cuts again, and pulled the weals wide apart so that a mortal pain arose. O Thou who embracest the entire globe, Thou who stretchest out heaven! How wilt Thou be stretched out on the cross! Oh! All of Thy

66. Scripture is supplemented here with the phrase "at the place Golgotha," which does not appear in the corresponding verse in any of the Gospels (see Mt 27: 27, Mk 15: 24, Lk 23: 33, Jn 19: 18).

veins crack, every sinew crunches, all the marrow in Thy bones trembles. Thy blood boils and flows to the heart, which trembles and hammers in pure pain as if it would burst into a thousand pieces. Thy parched tongue groans and moans, and there is hardly any air in that mouth from whose breath, after all, all living souls came to be. The Eternal Word who pronounced that Let There Be of the entire world cannot have enough words or strength to speak His own agony. The Word goes mute like the lamb that does not open its mouth before its sheerer, the innocent most perfect Lamb of God, and suffers the wolves to rave and rage over it.

Oh! Libyan-leonine, Tartar-leopardine, and more-than-tigerish tyrannical hands that bore through the hands of my dearest one (oh, and with them my heart too)! Oh! What unimaginable agony must our dearest Lord Jesus have suffered when they smashed through His most sensitive nerves and the little bones so that the sinews and veins snapped back even as the torturous iron and hellish nails of anguish stuck in the most painful wounds. How must the "oh"-echo have reverberated and how must one reflected ray of pain have kindled the next!

To keep His pain from having time to run its course of raving and raging a little, they went on and pierced the holy feet of my most ardently beloved Jesus (Oh! My insides [contract] in sympathy). Oh, torture! How must it have hurt when the rough hard iron was driven with torturous force through the delicate little veins, sinews, and tiny bones, mercilessly and painfully smashing and splintering them!

Oh! Inconceivable torture when creation thus martyred the Creator, when God thus suffers like a human being. Indeed, He suffered not merely like a human being but like a worm, and what is most wretched of all, He suffered more than a worm; for a worm may still twist and writhe with pain, but it was not granted to our supremely wretched Jesus to be capable of moving His feet, which were racked with pain but also nailed fast. The sacrosanct blood united with the divine gushed in incredible excess from His holy wounds. Weakness reigned most powerfully within the most powerful one and all the more painfully because Omnipotence prevented Weakness from prematurely removing His sensitivity [to pain]. Thus Divinity itself increased His agony by preventing the prevention of His having to endure the whole thing [to the bitter end]. Divinity, which is itself of course incapable of suffering, fortified the weakness of humanity [in Him], not to revive [Him] but to make [Him] more sensitive to the sensation of pain. It relieved the loss of strength to make Him feel more keenly the power of sin, and it prevented fainting so that the torments of torture would be all the more difficult for Him. It regulated lassitude so that torture's arrow might prick Him all the more sharply and keenly.

Oh, yes! (To be said in all piety), Divinity, [Thou art] unmerciful toward Thine own heart so as to lavish mercy upon us, Thine enemies! Thou dost not spare Thy most ardently beloved one so as to spare Thy faithless and disobedient serfs. The most virtuous and holy throne of innocence must do penance for what we, horribly depraved as we are, have committed. He feels in His pious heart what sprang forth from our godless hearts. His holy body, the purest temple of divinity, must be demolished on account of the evil and defects of ours. His heavenly hands must pay for what they did not steal and specifically for those hands that they themselves made and built of clay, that, however, beneath His hands (as a result of the devil's envy) came out badly. They must give up their red blood for the red apple that the disobedient hand of Eve picked. For this stretching out toward the forbidden tree, [these hands] must suffer themselves to be stretched out on the accursed wood. Penitence for striving to be like God has to be done by the very image of God in the guise of a worm. The rejecting and neglecting of God's commanding words caused the substantial Word to be abandoned by God.[67] The confirmation of the words of the serpent had to be replaced by the belief in the one prefigured by the brazen serpent.[68]

Divine Wisdom arranged everything so amazingly and precisely that not the slightest circumstance that had gone astray was left without amelioration. The pride of woman was replaced by the humility of the seed of woman. The agony of God-humanity refuted the debauchery of presuming to be like God, and Eve, the mother of us all, could not sin enough for the Son of God and Mary not to be able to do still more that was righteous. Her sin could not damn so powerfully that Jesus would not more powerfully redeem. Her curse was rapturously swallowed by the blessing of Abraham and thus of all nations and by Him who made of Himself a curse on the cross.[69] For the former pertained only to the people of this world, whereas

67. The text erroneously reads "morden" (murder); it should read "worden" (been) as an element of the passive construction used here. The first edition correctly reads "worden" (Greiffenberg, *Des Allerheiligst- und Allerheilsamsten Leidens und Sterbens Jesu Christi* [1672], 601).

68. Christ is understood to be prefigured by the serpent, because in bringing sin into the world, the serpent made Christ's coming necessary for the salvation of humankind.

69. In Gal 1: 8–17, Jesus is said to bring to the Gentiles the blessing of Abraham, just as Abraham was told in Gn 22: 18: "and by your descendants shall all the nations of the earth bless themselves." Here God blesses Abraham after Abraham has shown himself willing to sacrifice Isaac at God's command.

the blessing in Christ could redeem many hundreds of thousands of worlds, were there that many of them. The win of the Divinity is so much more important [for humankind] than [was] the loss of innocence, so much more perfect in the sight of God than was Adam.

Oh, rapture! A penny is paid for with a million, a droplet with a sea, and a speck of dust with a hundred thousand hundredweights. Who would demand further payment on a debt that is thus overpaid, indeed, not just paid but sunk into a bottomless pit by the overweight [of payment] so that it can no longer be found? Four whole rivers flow out of Thy Jesus-Paradise when a single little drop would have been enough to wash away the sins of the entire world.[70] This superabundance, however, produces the abundance of His love, which is completely unrestrained, gushing forth from the heart and blazing up. It makes wings for His blood so that all of it must fly to our redemption and our salvation must strive toward heaven. No drop will remain behind in this army of redemption. Each one aims to fire off its cannon of love and bare its fiery weapon to serve our everlasting bliss. These arrows of salvation will not be stopped from shooting to the goal of our happiness. The bullets of love travel with the speed of lightning into the center of the blissful target of eternity. Love cannot give less than it has. Therefore since divine love is superabundant, it must pay not according to necessity but according to its infinity.

Entire abysses of dismay and praise open up for me so that I know not to which one I ought to proceed, at which one I ought to begin, or which one I ought to push to the highest and most extreme. Imagining them, I become poor from wealth, mute from desire to praise, and weak from an abundant flood of ideas. How can I express the dismay I feel at the suffering of the one unified with divine majesty, at the degradation of the Highest One, at the creaturely misery of the splendor of heaven itself? Contemplating this is like that prophet's fathoming of the sea that becomes deeper and deeper and finally bottomless.[71] How can I escape the dismaying stirrings of sympathy so as not to plunge into a sea of tears that dissolves all my words when I contemplate His pain? This emotion alone would be enough to fill up all my faculties and to employ all my spirits and powers in its service; it also will hardly leave anything for those other abysses. All of those things that set it

70. The text refers here to the four rivers that according to Genesis were in Eden: Hiddekel (Tigris), Euphrates, Pison, and Gihon (Gn 2: 10–14).

71. The text may refer here to Jb 11: 7–9: "Can you find out the deep things of God? Can you find out the limit of the Almighty? It is higher than heaven—what can you do? Deeper than Sheol—what can you know? Its measure is longer than the earth, and broader than the sea."

into motion are found in abundance here—the highest, most extreme virtue and dignity, [His] most ardent love for and loyalty to me, and the most painful suffering and misfortune of an utterly perfect heavenly and bosom friend. Thus let [this emotion] make the streams of its impulses flow and flood the flat plain of eloquence that it be engulfed. Indeed, [this flood of emotion] grows so high that the hills of reason are flooded over and nothing visible remains but the single water of love that swells up to the clouds.

Gloomy sighs are the clearest expression of my feelings. A heartrending "oh" is here the best turn of phrase and the most beautiful oratorical figure. The heart dissolves out of sympathy and winds itself around the nails. This produces the mercurial caduceus; when one is touched with it, one sinks into the sleep of bliss that comes from the consigned power of mercy.[72] Now I want to push my heart into the wounds out of gentlest ardor, now push these out of utmost sympathy into my heart. Indeed, I wish I had as many hearts as there are nail punctures, so that I could push one into each heart. I wish, moreover, that they were full of balm that eases pain and might do my sweetest Jesus good. Oh, could I, lying in the wounds, but transform my heart into a Byblis who dissolved in a fountain of pure tears of balm![73] How I would cool and soothe the dear wounds, kissing His heart!

Oh! My chosen Savior! No refreshment and comfort at all are given Thee! Thou must lie there without any staying of blood so that Thy soul would depart from Thee with this bleeding. Oh! Why is not my heart the wound wood or my mouth the hematite to stay [the bleeding]?[74] Or if it is indeed to flow as the most precious balm of the soul to redeem the entire world, why is it not permitted to me (like Seneca's wife) to open and burst my veins out of love and sympathy so that I can keep Thee loyal company

72. The wand of Mercury has two intertwined serpents whose crossings form three circles; it is a central symbol of alchemy, representing the three principal separations and unions of male and female that take place during the so-called "chemical wedding," in which the union of opposites produces the philosopher's stone. Lyndy Abraham, *A Dictionary of Alchemical Imagery* (Cambridge: Cambridge University Press, 1998), s.v. "caduceus"; s.v. "chemical wedding." Here as elsewhere in her meditations Greiffenberg uses symbols and language borrowed from alchemy.

73. As described in Ovid's *Metamorphoses,* Byblis fell in love with her brother Caunus, whom she followed through various countries as he fled from her. By the time she reached Phoenicia, her tears had dissolved her, and a wood nymph turned her into a spring. Ovid, *Metamorphoses,* trans. Frank Justus Miller, 2 vols., Loeb Classical Library (Cambridge: Harvard University Press, 1976], 2: 35–51 (9.454–665).

74. It was thought that certain wood (particularly ash) could heal wounds. Wood cut from ash trees at a certain time was said to cure a fresh wound if it was rubbed on the wound while it was still bleeding. Zedler, *Grosses Vollständiges Universal-Lexikon,* s.v. "Wundholtz." Hematite, which derives from the Greek word for blood, was thought to stop bleeding.

in the hour of Thy dying?[75] Thou well knowest that loyally enamored blood does not rest quietly in its veins when the blood of the beloved spurts and rages in agony, which Sympathia or natural affinity soon makes known to it. But no! Thy love, O Jesus, means to be a phoenix; it means only to consume Thee in pain; it means only to indicate Thy supreme incomparability; it means only to generate extreme sympathy and not to suffer any sympathy to stem the amount of pain. But presumably it is granted to me to press Thee in faith, along with Thy cross, to my heart and bosom and with Bernard to greet and kiss Thy holy wounds so that my imagination would be Veronica's (alleged) sudarium on which Thy now-mourned heavenly form would be clearly imprinted, that I would suck up Thy blood with my mouth and on the other hand would breathe my soul into Thy hands, that I would hide myself in these crags where I am more secure than in heaven itself, because no one was ever thrown out of there as Lucifer was out of heaven.[76]

O Thou hell filled with heaven! How good is it to live in Thee? Thou paradise of nails! How gently does a devout soul rest in Thee? Oh Thou divine fruit bearer and heavenly head of the Fruit-Bearing Society![77] Thou most delicious one, not through the sting of wasps but through the sting of nails! Thou infinitely great known goodness! Through these wounds, I taste and perceive with Saint Bernard how sweet Thou art, Thou sweetest juicy one![78] It is worthless if not sucked out. For this reason I suck from Thy sweetest wounds the vim and vigor of my salvation. Thou truly sweet one

75. Seneca (4 BCE–65 CE). According to Tacitus, when Seneca was accused by Nero of plotting his murder and ordered to commit suicide, his wife, Pompeia Paulina, slit her wrists as well. Tacitus, *Annals*, , Loeb Classical Library (Cambridge: Harvard University Press, 1969), 311–19 (15.60–64).

76. Saint Bernard of Clairvaux (1090–1153) was the founding abbot of Clairvaux Abbey in Burgundy and the most powerful propagator of the Cistercian reform. According to Catholic tradition, Saint Veronica was among the women who accompanied Christ during the passion. She is alleged to have given him a cloth to wipe his face, on which an image of his face was thereafter imprinted. Greiffenberg, as a Lutheran, adds the word "alleged" *(vermeintlich)* in parenthesis here to distance herself from Catholicism and the veneration of saints. Lucifer is the name given in Christian tradition to the fallen angel who revolted against God. The image of hiding in the crags probably stems from Bernard's understanding based on Sg 2: 13 that Christ's wounds are the clefts in the rock ("My dove is in the clefts of the rock"). Bernard was a key influence on Luther, who quotes him frequently. Franz Posset, "The Sweetness of God's Grace according to Bernard of Clairvaux—The Bridge between Augustine and Luther," Animabit Multimedia Editions (WWW) Nr. 3 (1998) http://www.animabit.de/quarterly/bernhard.htm (accessed January 20, 2006).

77. The text refers here to the Fruit-Bearing Society (Fruchtbringende Gesellschaft), a language society that was founded in 1617 and was the largest such society of the age in the German-speaking territories. The text itself contains the following footnote: "The intention here is [to cite] several names, paintings, and words of the Fruit-Bearing Society."

78. Bernard of Clairvaux stresses the sweetness of Christ variously in his works and particularly in his sermons on the Song of Solomon (Posset, "Sweetness of God's Grace").

in the sucking out! If only I have Thee, then I shall not ask after heaven or earth.

[Greiffenberg continues with a mixture of prose and verse, meditating on the crucifixion and its fulfillment of Scripture. She concludes this meditation with a treatment of Mk 15: 25, "It was the third hour, when they crucified him."]

Explanation of the Emblem

When in old heathen Rome an imperial corpse
was cremated,[79] from the fun'ral pyre's peak, an eagle,
its wings beating mightily, was to soar on high.
And this was the apotheosis of His soul.[80]
Augustus of heaven, Caesar of all the earth,[81]
Jesus, Thou too didst rise from the bier of Thy cross
once Thy corpse was roasted, O Thou signpost to heaven,
like a noble eagle, it flew upward in love.
What was the man who had done evil doing there,
that robber who suffered crucifixion with Thee?
Converted, he then became like the tiny warbler.
Make it so (he begged) that I can fly up with Thee.
Faith gets what it will. Thou didst take him on Thy wings

79. See figure 5. This emblem introduces the tenth meditation. This explanation of the emblem is written in alexandrines according to the rhyme scheme *abbacddceffeghhgijji*.

WAnn/ seiner Käyser-Leich / die Brandbegängnis hielt
das alte heiden-Rom: Es must / mit flügel-wügen /
vom Gipfel des Gerüsts empor ein Adler fliegen.
Und diß / für seine Seel / war das Vergöttungs-Bild.
Du himmlischer August / des ganzen Erdrunds Käyser /
O JEsu! flogst auch so / von deiner Creutzes-baar /
als edler Adler / auf / da nun gebraten war
in Liebe deine Leich / du Himmelswege weiser!
Was hatte da zu thun / der übels hat gethan /
der Schächer / der mit dir den Kreutzes-Tod erlitten?
Er nahm bekehrt an sich der kleinen Glasmück Sitten.
Schaff / (bat' er) daß mit dir ich auch auffliegen kan.
Der Glaub hat / was er will. Du namst ihn auf die flügel /
und trugest / ihn mit dir / zu ihr / der Seeligkeit:
Sey heute (sprachest du) mein erste Leidensbeut /
mit mir im Paradeis: nun schieb ich weg / den Rigel.
Ja / JEsu! deine Leich ist meiner Leiche Trost.
Laß mich / auf deinen Tod / auch also seelig sterben.
Mit dir ich leiden will / mit dir das Leben erben.
Mein Glaub / von deinem ja / mir bringt die Freuden-Post.

80. A footnote provided in the text itself references the emblem book *Hieroglyphica, sive de sacris Aegyptiorum literis commentarii* (1556) compiled by Giovanni Pierio Valeriano (1477–1560)

81. Augustus (69 BCE–14 CE), first Roman emperor.

and carry him along with Thee up to salvation:
be today (thou didst say) the first spoil of my passion,
with me in paradise: now I unbolt the door.
Yes, Jesus! Thy corpse is the comfort of my corpse.
Suffer me as well to die blest upon Thy death.
I want to suffer with Thee, inherit life too.
My faith brings me the joyful news, indeed, of Thine.

Figure 5. Unattributed, "With You to It" from *Des Allerheiligst- und Allerheilsamsten . . . Christi* (1672). The Beinecke Rare Book and Manuscript Library.

ON THE SUPREMELY HOLY AND SUPREMELY SALVIFIC SUFFERING OF JESUS: TENTH MEDITATION

[Greiffenberg commences the tenth meditation with Lk 23: 34,"Father, forgive them; for they know not what they do" and then turns to Jn 19: 19–24 to ponder the inscription "Jesus of Nazareth, the King of the Jews" and the parting of the garments among the soldiers in fulfillment of Scripture, before reaching the excerpt that follows.]

And the people stood by, watching.[82]

Here again Holy Scripture was fulfilled that says, "I can count all my bones—they stare and gloat over me."[83] Oh! The godless rabble is permitted to behold with their curious eyes the torture that saved many among them from debilities of the eye and other things. They regard Him without feeling sympathy, Him who, filled with compassion, turned around their suffering and transformed it into joy. They nurse their cruel curiosity in beholding the agony of Him who so faithfully alleviated their agony and who made it so Satan's cruelty ceased with them. Oh, ingratitude that seeks delight in the torment of the Savior.

But standing by the cross of Jesus were his mother, and his mother's sister, Mary the wife of Clopas, and Mary Magdalene.[84]

These lovers of Jesus are to be sure also standing there but for a completely different reason—to satisfy not their curiosity but their love; out of love and not out of a desire for vengeance. They feel His wounds and nails in their hearts and His fear in their souls. Their eyes fastened on His transfixed hands and feet, and their sighs flew forth by the thousands. Their hearts overflowed through their eyes and began to weep as much white blood as He could spill red blood. His thorns cut them to the quick. They endlessly embraced the wooden cross spattered with His blood. They felt more blows to the heart than they spoke words.

Oh! The chastest mother, who without a doubt had the softest and most ardent heart—what piercing anguish of the soul must she have felt, when she saw the child who was hers alone (which no other mother in the whole world can say), saw Him hanging and suffering like that? I firmly believe that if the divinity that lay in her body had not left behind a power, she would have perished in fits of fainting. What unimaginable pain must

82. Lk 23: 35.

83. Ps 22: 17. Jn 19: 36–37 recalls the words of the psalm with reference to the crucifixion.

84. Jn 19: 25.

it have brought her when she saw Him wasting away on the wooden cross, Him whom she had carried with melting ardor in her womb, and when she could neither help nor touch him, when she had to watch the tender hands and feet that she had wrapped with most loving care (although in simple swaddling on account of her poverty), watch them be pierced with nails and see them racked with pain. She is forced to see the dearest mouth starving and thirsting or being given gall and vinegar to drink, the mouth that she fed with the honey of her heart and with the sugar of her breasts. She is forced with profoundest anguish to see Him writhing on the cross in extreme agony, Him whom she so gently rocked in His little crib and whom she cradled still more, however, in her lap and in her heart.[85] She must see Him nailed to the hard wood now—Him whom she so often pressed to her mother's heart. She must see scratched up with thorns the most worthy head on which there were more of her kisses than there was hair, which thing she could hardly look at for suffering, but which for love she could not refrain from looking at. It hurts her above all that He had received the body that was capable of suffering from her and that she thus (although innocently) contributed to His suffering. She must have wished that she could suffer in His stead. But because He is the only person in heaven and on earth who can do this thing for us—meritorious and salutary—she had to submit her will to the will of the Most High and watch the one suffer whom she loved more than herself and in whom she was more sensitive than in herself.

Her sister, Mary Clopas, the illustrious woman, kept her truehearted sad-hearted company. It is an illuminated gloominess to mourn and lament Christ. The holy souls illuminated with spirit feel it the most, and this is an affliction that befalls only the most loyal. Mary Magdalene, who was completely enamored, also had her part here. It is nothing rare for those who love Jesus to be sad about Him and on His account. Sorrow is their daily bread. Oh! What starving for joy! The devil does not refrain from attacking them, and the world does not let them be. They do not remain free from torment even by those closest to them and their best friends or by their own frailties and weaknesses. Their conscience too points out to them a thousand faults and mistakes that they have made. That very Beloved One Himself sometimes hides. God the father covers up His fatherly heart, and the Holy Spirit His beams of comfort. The earth in contrast displays its full

85. The text here employs the word "Schoß," which I have translated as "lap." *Schoß* can also be used to refer to women's interior anatomy in the region of the lap and thus can also mean "womb" or even vaguely "vagina." I have chosen "lap" as the overriding meaning of the word, but it is possible that Greiffenberg means to refer here particularly to Mary's having carried Christ in her womb.

bitterness and loathsomeness, everything that makes it appear to us completely unbearable, and makes us long for death as it were. No stag or feverish person can thus thirst for water as such a person longs for death. One finds the world as unbearable and dismaying as does a sick person meat that he can stand neither to look at nor to smell; one finds life as unbearable as does a child a hundredweight burden.

Weight does not plummet as readily to the earth, fire so shoot upward, fish plunge into the water, and birds so soar upward into freedom as such a body hurries to the grave, the soul to heaven, and the spirit to God and out of the earthly body into the freedom of the children of God. This is the bitterest state beneath Christ's cross: when one is tired of life and cannot manage to die, when one finds the world repugnant and yet must remain in it, when one finds that the chains and bonds of sin have become heavy and yet the complete release of death is not in sight, when one finds vanity repugnant and yet one must continue to drink there. It is as if one would very gladly sleep and yet one's eyelids, without which one cannot sleep, were cut away. There is no more impatient desire than the yearning for death when one is quite sick of the sin and vanity of this life and the love of God is quite embittered.

When Jesus saw his mother, and the disciple whom he loved standing near.[86]

Even on the cross, the most gracious eyes of Jesus look at His dearest ones and indeed with most ardent love and mercy. The agony that would soon take His life could not keep Him from satisfying His love. In Him there toils and boils not merely a general love of humanity but also a child's natural love for the person who bore him and the special love for friends that He bestowed on John above all the disciples and above all people (in that time). The noblest human nature in Him desired to show its power and to prove that it is virtuous and praiseworthy and proper to have the most tender and loving feelings toward one's parents. His lovely eyes beheld with pain that woman crying who had watched over His childhood so faithfully, the hands wringing with lamentation that had wrapped Him as a child in swaddling clothes, the mouth sighing that had sung to Him in such a lovely fashion, the heart shuddering, the breasts trembling and covered with tears from which the white sap of the veins, the lovely lily-white milk and child-honey, had flowed to Him. The Most Compassionate One could not, without providing comfort and refreshment, bear to see her body writhing and nearly bursting with pain, the body in and from which He assumed His own body.

86. Jn 19: 26.

He suffered insufferable pain not only in His but also in her body by means of extremely ardent compassion, which is sometimes more painful than one's own suffering, especially in noble natures. The sword that pierced her soul on His account must have raged miserably in His soul too. Like a burning mirror, she must have reflected the beams of pain that she received from Him back into His heart and have given rise to the most extreme ardor of pain.[87] This agony would have been neither the greatest nor the most extreme and perfect one if compassion had not been part of it too, compassion that surpasses all forms of suffering and indeed is the most painful and unbearable one of all. He had to feel this piece too and therein to become like us so that He could have compassion with our suffering and could gain help and comfort for us in it, especially in impossible cases when it appears that there is no comfort to be found on earth, indeed hardly in heaven either, and yet this comfort ultimately flows from His mercy—to which I can testify from experience. He looked at her, however, not only with compassionate eyes but also with providential ones and was in His extreme abandonment intent on her care.

He saw His beloved disciple standing there. He who leaned on His bosom at the Last Supper rightly stands with Christ beneath the cross.[88] One could say that Christ, through His foreknowledge of all that would come to pass, had seen John's steadfast perseverance ahead of time and therefore loved him so specially. But I say in a much more Christian manner that precisely that special love of Jesus was a cause of such perseverance and transmitted to him the grace of constancy, because all ability and capability of being loved by Jesus spring from Him alone. And precisely this is the greatest sign of His love that He makes His beloved capable of such and attuned to reciprocity. He Himself kindles the fire of love in them that neither hell nor earth with all their torrents and Belial's brooks can extinguish.[89] He makes them stand firm beneath the cross like John, even if the rocks flee and the whole world stands against them.[90] He makes them laugh among

87. A burning mirror is a convex lens that concentrates solar rays to produce high temperatures. Archimedes was said to have created a weapon consisting of a large burning mirror that set the Roman fleet afire during the siege of Syracuse in 213 BCE.

88. Jn 13: 23: "One of his disciples, whom Jesus loved, was lying close to the breast of Jesus."

89. Belial is a synonym for Satan.

90. Although she uses the plural, Greiffenberg may allude here to Peter, whom Christ called the rock on which he would build his church (Mt 16: 18). Yet Peter flees with the rest of the disciples when Christ is arrested. Later when he attends the trial, he winds up denying Christ three times as foretold (Mt 26: 56–75).

the lions, sing in the fiery oven, preach on the cross, and triumph in all martyrdom.[91] One hardly knows what the greater grace is—to love one person above all others or to make oneself loved by one person above all others and in everything. In this way it can be called holy: to love and be loved is the greatest joy on earth.

In this man whom Jesus loved, we can see all the special merits of the love of Jesus. He wanted to have him around and with Him always, both in the display of glory on Mount Tabor and in His hour of sorrow on the Mount of Olives.[92] The profound emotion of love knows no joy without its close friend and feels no deep comfort in sorrow, except with that tenderhearted and compassionate friend. Afterward He zealously defended him, [asking] what business it was of others if He wanted him to remain until He came.[93] And [Jesus] could not allow him to be envied or subject to ordinary conditions. This singular gracious liking and happy singling out is no ordinary sign of love. The clearest sign was, however, his leaning on the bosom of Jesus and Jesus pressing him to His heart: He thereby gave an open sign and made everyone see that He loved him especially. This is the greatest happiness and honor in heaven and on earth—the reason why all the angels and thrones (if they were capable of this) might have envied him, because there is nothing written of a single cherub or seraph and of no angel or archangel like that which is written of John, that he was loved by Christ especially and before others.

On Jesus' breast he extracted the secret of the traitor because Jesus

91. In Dn 6: 16–24 King Darius orders that Daniel be placed into a den of lions, but God closes their mouths, and Daniel remains unharmed. In Dn 3: 19–30, King Nebuchadnezzar casts Shadrach, Meshach, and Abednego into a fiery furnace when they refuse to worship an idol, but God keeps them from harm.

92. The text refers here to the transfiguration on the mountain, understood to be Mount Tabor (Mt 17: 1–8, Mk 9: 2–8, Lk 9: 28–36), the hour of glory that John witnessed. The Mount of Olives refers to Jesus' anguish in the Garden of Gethsemane. According to Lk 22: 39, Jesus retreated after the last supper with his disciples to the Mount of Olives to pray, and according to Mt. 26: 36 and Mk 14: 32–42, specifically to a place called Gethsemane. Here Jesus tells Peter, James, and John, "My soul is very sorrowful even to death: remain here, and watch" (Mk 14: 34, also Mt 26: 38) and calls on his faith in prayer, wrestling with the thoughts of his upcoming martyrdom and his wish not to have to die.

93. The text alludes here to Jn 21: 22–23: "Jesus said to him, 'If it is my will that he remain until I come, what is that to you? Follow me!' The saying spread abroad among the brethren that this disciple was not to die; yet Jesus did not say to him that he was not to die, but, 'If it is my will that he remain until I come, what is that to you?'" Thus Jesus responds to Peter when asked what will become of John. There is a suggestion here that the other disciples were envious of John.

could hide nothing from him, and it was said: whoever loves me (or rather whomever I love), I will reveal myself to him.[94] Oh! Certainly a great love shines forth from this revelation, of which Christ gave another proof that it was the greatest sign of His love by making the most splendid revelations to this disciple even after His ascension to heaven. He almost always paired love and revelation. How should He hide what is in His heart from him to whom He gives His heart? Should He not make him to whom He communicates His spirit see what is otherwise hidden in it? The secret of the Lord is with them who fear Him. Where is there more fear of God than in those who love God? This too is one of the advantages of being loved by God—to endure danger for the sake of Jesus and yet always to be saved from it—as happened with John whom no death brutally done to him could make die. Domitian's cruel vat of oil, into which he was thrown, must have been cooled with the oil of the Holy Spirit so that it could not hurt him. The love and the Word of God rendered salutary the deadly drink of poison of the Ephesian priest of Diana so that it might not harm him. He did not have to taste death but rather in that very place awaken a person from the dead as a testimony to the fact that the love of Jesus made His loved ones prevail over death not only in His own body but also in those of others.[95]

The love of Christ also gave him the advantage that his persecution and banishment to the island of Patmos ended up serving him as a school of heavenly wisdom and as the occasion for the revelation of divine mysteries. Thus God is wont to arrange things so that the ones He loves usually live obscurely in the loneliest spots in the world in order to be able to ponder His miracles all the more deeply. Blissful solitude that is filled with the totality, where the angels keep [us] company, that is used for meditating and

94. Jn 14: 21: "He who has my commandments and keeps them, he it is who loves me; and he who loves me will be loved by my Father, and I will love him and manifest myself to him." In a previous chapter, Peter asks John to find out which disciple will betray Jesus, and when John asks, Jesus tells him to identify him by a symbolic gesture that Jesus will make. Jn 13: 26–27: "Jesus answered, 'It is he to whom I shall give this morsel when I have dipped it.' So when he had dipped the morsel, he gave it to Judas, the son of Simon Iscariot. Then after the morsel, Satan entered into him."

95. The Emperor Domitian is said to have brought John the disciple to Rome where he had him thrown into a cauldron of boiling oil from which he emerged unharmed. Ephesus, where John spent many years exercising his apostolic office, was located in Asia Minor and known for its temple of Diana. One of the symbols of John came to be the chalice, referring both to the last supper and to the poison drink given him by the priests, from which, according to legend, a serpent emerged when he blessed it. John is also said to have raised a man from the dead at Ephesus. Finally, he is thought to be the author of the Gospel according to John as well as of the Book of Revelation, hence the references in this paragraph to revelations.

describing divine miracles and revelations, in which the heavenly Jerusalem comes down to us from heaven and eternity opens up its hidden treasures! O Jesus! Make my solitude so blissful that the seals of Thy mysteries are broken and I become worthy of seeing Thy splendor.[96] Let one angel of comfort after another open up to me Thy secret grace and let me above all hear the voice of Thy laudation and praise. In this manner even the desert can become a paradise and the cave of a wild animal a heaven. I would gladly, were it Thy will, be separated from all reasonable and charming people and spend my time with dumb animals and dim people, if only I could thereby enjoy Thy heavenly sustenance.

The greatest of all the advantages of the love of Jesus that John experienced is that he saw the portal of salvation, the door of the divine temple, and the gate of grace—Jesus' side—open up. He is the sole one among all the disciples and friends of Jesus who saw the stage opening up for the spectacle of love and grace and saw the best orators in heaven and on earth make their entrance; [he is the one] who looked into the holiest of holies, into the heart of all hearts, and saw this inestimable treasure.[97] I consider this one of the greatest proofs of love that Jesus found him worthy—out of immense trust [in him]—to stand in for Him and charged him with caring for His dearest mother, introducing him to her, as it were, as a second self.

He said to his mother, "Woman, behold your son!"[98]

"Woman!" He says, not to disdain calling her His mother, but to show that on the cross He is now the true seed of woman that was to crush the head of the serpent and that just as sin came into the world through a woman, He who will take sin away on the wood of the cross also came into the world through this woman.[99] He also did not want to plunge the sword of pain even deeper into her soul by calling her mother now. Behold your son (He

96. Greiffenberg alludes here to the book with seven seals that are broken open by the lamb of God in the Book of Revelation (Rv 5: 1–8).

97. Greiffenberg refers here to the piercing of Christ's side with a spear by the soldiers after they have taken Christ down from the cross. Scripture emphasizes that John saw it and then recorded it as testimony (Jn 19: 34–35). The "orators" are the drops of blood of the martyred Christ that according to Christian belief redeem humankind.

98. Jn 19: 26.

99. Allusion to Gn 3: 15: "I will put enmity between you and the woman, and between your seed and her seed; he shall bruise your head, and you shall bruise his heel." According to Christian tradition, the coming of Christ is prophesied immediately following Eve's succumbing to temptation in the Garden of Eden.

says), whom I, who see into hearts, chose to care for you. He will not be your friend who takes care of you out of good will, but your son who does it out of natural inclination, obligation, and obedience. I poured these things into him, planted them in him, and imposed them on him from my heart, which lay beneath yours; indeed, in doing this, I transformed him completely into my desire and incorporated my child's sensibility in him. He does not stand in for your son, but he is your son—to be sure not substantially, yet truly; not properly, yet with all the properties [thereof]; not the one born of you from the body, but the one born of me from the spirit, who replaces your begotten son on earth, who is to be a comfort in your old age, the staff of your years, the support of your life, and the strength of your weakness. In my life on earth he has been the one I have loved most; he should now be that for you and for my sake. You will be taken care of with him. Indeed, I have searched not only his inclinations but yours too and found that they completely harmonize together—child and mother.

Then he said to the disciple, "Behold your mother!"[100]

Behold how marvelously I have provided for the mother of your Creator (according to [God's] provision) to be your mother. I say that is your mother! Even though she has otherwise borne no one but me, the begotten son of God, she is still your mother because I charge you with her care, as it were, putting you in my place, inclining your heart to her, and hers to you, so that a proper love between mother and child comes to be. I can be as powerful in bearing from the spirit as is nature, which was created by me, in bearing from the body, and I can imprint precisely those inclinations that are implanted through the ordinary course of nature. Thus love her as if she had begotten you. She has borne for you more than you, namely, your Savior. Instead of carrying you under her heart she carried for you the one who carried you in His heart and whom you in turn carry in yours. Even if she did not nurse you with her breasts, her milk flowed into Him from whom all your salvation and bliss flows. If the body and the breasts that carried and nursed me are sanctified, then you can be called sanctified who are now to take care of her. Great trust flows out of great love. If I did not love you most particularly, I would not entrust to you the greatest jewel that I leave behind in this world. Thus show yourself worthy of me and give me cause to entrust you with the greatest things of the world.

100. Jn 19: 27.

And from that hour the disciple took her to his own home.[101]

Jesus' commands are to be fulfilled forthwith. From this hour on, one should put His holy words into practice. Obedience must have wings as well as ears. Thus in the Old Testament He so often commanded the sacrifice of doves and birds. Should we not hasten to do the will of Him who hastened to do the will of God to redeem us? Here hesitation has to be taken as omission and delaying as nay-saying. John answered with the deed. He did not waste time saying yes, or the pain did not let him speak. Rather in that [very] moment (when he, furthermore, had been standing there more than an hour) he took her into his care. He certainly must have comforted her over the death of her life and have sweetened the bitter mortality of her immortal son by reminding her of His incorruptibility. He must have opened to her his aquiline thoughts of the Eternal Word and the divinity of Christ and have calmed and satisfied her heart with that.[102] The lofty gifts of wisdom are given, next to glorifying God, mainly to comfort the afflicted, for which thing one should principally employ them and not for vainglory and fame.

[The meditation continues with the mockery of Christ on the cross by the priests, scribes, elders, and passersby; his promise to the convicts crucified with him that they will be with him in paradise; his crying out that he is thirsty; and his receiving vinegar to drink. It concludes with a blending of Lk 23: 46 and Jn 19: 30, "And having said this he bowed his head and gave up his spirit."]

Explanation of the Emblem

At Salem, where Zion's fortress arises,[103]
a hollow rock lies in the valleys' lap.

101. Jn 19: 27.

102. In Christian iconography John is symbolized by the eagle. The eternal Word refers to John's theology, according to which Christ is the Word. The Gospel according to John opens with the well-known verse "In the beginning was the word" (Jn 1: 1).

103. See figure 6. This emblem introduces the eleventh meditation. Salem refers to Jerusalem. Zion is the section of Jerusalem known as the City of David and sometimes refers to the hill on which the Temple stood or to the Temple itself. This explication of the emblem is written in iambic pentameter with rhymed couplets. Although the translation does not reproduce the rhyme or consistently reproduce the accentual meter, it does adhere to the syllabic meter of ten or eleven syllables depending on whether the line ends with a stressed or unstressed syllable.

Bey Salem dort / wo Sions Burg sich spitzet /
ein holer Fels im Schoß der Thäler sitzet /

Figure 6. Unattributed, "Found in the Wounds" from *Des Allerheiligst- und Allerheilsamsten. . . Christi* (1672). The Beinecke Rare Book and Manuscript Library.

---

trug einen Thurn [*sic*] / von Tauben zugenamt:
weil sie daselbst geheckt und sich besamt.
Unfern davon der Brunn Siloha floße
vom Sions-fels / ein klares Wasser gosse.
Ach Ort! ach! du bist meines JEsu Bild /
dem dort ein Speer die Seite hölt und spilt.

There was a tower there named after doves
because they brooded there and propagated.
Not far away, the spring Siloha flowed,
pouring a clear water from Zion's rock.
Spot! Oh! You are the image of my Jesus,
whose side a spear gouged and split open there.[104]
The rock of the doves is this dear sweet cavern
that I choose as my only dwelling place.
O Jesus, my rock! Call me in to Thee.
I fly, I come, I will be Thy wee dove.
The bird has found its domicile with Thee.
Within this cleft, within Thy noble wounds,
in this place (for it pleases me quite well)
my soul shall dwell both now and evermore.
Hell cannot pursue me into this hollow

Der Taubenfels / ist diese süsse Höle:
die ich allein zur Wohnung mir erwehle.
JESU / mein Fels! ruff mir zu dir hinein:
ich flieg / ich kom / ich wil dein Täublein seyn.
Der Vogel hat bey dir sein Haus gefunden.
In dieser Kluft / in deinen edlen Wunden /
an diesem Ort / (dann er gefällt mir wol)
fort ewiglich mein Seele wohnen soll.
Es darf ja nicht die Höll' in diese Höle
mir folgen nach / darein ich mich verstehle.
Es ist auch diß der Fels / der von sich gibt
ein klares Naß / das eine Taube liebt.
Aus Sion ist das rohte Heil gerunnen.
Ich halte mich zu diesem Felsenbrunnen /
Den GOTT gesandt / die Seel zu waschen rein.
Du Sions / Burg / solst mein Parnassus seyn.
Hier find' ich recht den schönen Hippocrene.
Hier werdet naß / ihr Himmel Musen Söhne!
Hier man sich trinkt voll Liebe / Feur und Geist /
und seeliglich ein Himmels-dichter heist.

104. In both editions of the meditations on the passion, the text reads "spilt." The word intended must be *split,* from *splitten,* which means "to split open." In these lines Greiffenberg plays with a conceit of Jesus' wounds as the topography of Jerusalem, thus conflating them with the image of Jesus as a rock as described in Is 28: 16: "Therefore thus says the Lord GOD, 'Behold, I am laying in Zion for a foundation a stone, a tested stone, a precious cornerstone, of a sure foundation: He who believes will not be in haste.'" Jesus is called a rock in 1 Cor 10: 4. The doves may refer to the baptism of Jesus when the Holy Spirit descends as a dove into the Jordan River (Mt 3, Mk 1, Lk 3). I thank the Rev. Paula V. Mehmel for pointing out the possible significance of this imagery.

wherein I steal away and hide myself.
This is the rock too that originates
the clear, pure moisture that a dove does love.
The scarlet salvation flowed forth from Zion.
I will stick to the wellspring of this rock,
sent by our Lord God to wash the soul clean.
Be Thou, Fortress of Zion, my Parnassus.
Here lovely Hippocrene I'll find quite well.[105]
Here shall you bathe, you sons of heaven's muses!
Here one drinks one's fill of love, fire, and spirit
and is blissfully called a heaven's poet.

ON THE SUPREMELY HOLY AND SUPREMELY SALVIFIC SUFFERING OF JESUS: ELEVENTH MEDITATION

[The eleventh meditation commences with Mt 27: 51–54—the tearing of the curtain, the quaking of the earth, the splitting of the rocks, and the opening of the tombs. When the centurion and those with him behold these events, they declare Jesus the Son of God.]

And the women who had followed him from Galilee.[106]

Not merely a few, but many women were standing with these intimates afar off.[107] The female sex has always been devoted and attached to our dear Lord Jesus. The fear (and love) of God dwells only with women who are chosen.[108] Their simplicity and tenderness made them capable of loving

105. Hippocrene is the fountain of the muses on Mount Helicon, formed by the hoof of Pegasus, who had been sent by Poseidon to make the muses contain their noisy merrymaking. The fountain was regarded as a source of inspiration.

106. Lk 23: 49.

107. Lk 23: 49. Luther refers to these people as *Verwandten* (relatives); the RVS calls them "acquaintances." Greek *gnostoi* means "intimates," those who really knew him. In keeping with Luther's attempt to indicate something more than acquaintances, I have chosen the word "intimates." I thank the Rev. Paula V. Mehmel for her assistance with the translation of this word.

108. Greiffenberg took the rare step here of citing one of her sources in a footnote. In this case it is a verse from Jesus Sirach (Ecclesiasticus), one of the books of the Apocrypha. Sir 1: 15 in Luther's translation corresponds to Sir 1: 13 in the RSV, namely, "She made among men an eternal foundation, and among their descendants she will be trusted." Whereas the English translation speaks of "men," the German translation reads "bei den Frommen" (among the pious or faithful). Greiffenberg takes full advantage of the gender-neutral term and relates it specifically to women, probably taking her inspiration from the verse that precedes it, namely, Sir 1: 12 (RSV; Sir 1: 14 in Luther's translation), "To fear the Lord is the beginning of wisdom; she is created with the faithful in the womb." This verse has been understood to mean that women are espe-

Jesus; for He chose what is paltry and despised in the eyes of the world. What is, however, more despised than woman who is not regarded by some as capable of salvation? To be sure, many women make themselves despicable through their frivolity or stubborn stupidity—I too utterly despise and exclude them from those who love Christ. But in general the fear of God has always found more of a place with women's simplicity than with men's cunning, and they have always followed Christ in greater numbers and more frequently, as did then these women from Galilee.

No land should be too far away and no home too dear to follow our dearest Jesus. One should not consider one's goods when trying to come to this heavenly Joseph.[109] To follow Jesus, many [of these women] must have abandoned their husbands, children, friends and relatives, and also their household and housekeeping for a few days and perhaps did not leave them all that well provided for and instead in danger of unpleasant occurrences. The heavenly bridegroom must be given precedence not merely for a few short days but always over all earthly things, the Son of God over all the children of man, the Eternal One over all temporal friends, even though they would jeer at it. One has to persevere in one's intention with heroic courage and to think of Christ's words: "He who does not love me more than his own family is not worthy of me."[110] As long as we strive not just for the kingdom of God but also for the ruler of this kingdom, the other will come to us according to His Word.

We choose that good portion: Christ. It shall not be taken from us.[111] The primal source of all love will not allow love to cease in the heart of our dearest ones in the meantime, for we only gain renewed strength from Him to love them dearly. Insofar as the fathers follow His begotten son to kiss Him, God, who is a father to all that is called father in heaven and on

---

cially chosen by God. On the subject of the wisdom tradition with its symbol of personified female Wisdom, see, e.g., Johnson, "Wisdom Was Made Flesh," 95–117, and Gössmann, *Hildegard von Bingen*, 92–113. See also above, n. 37.

109. The text refers here to Gn 45: 20, where Pharaoh says to Joseph: "Give no thought to your goods; for the best of all the land of Egypt is yours." Pharaoh tells Joseph to command his father and his brothers to join him in Egypt where they will eat "the fat of the land." The "heavenly Joseph" is Jesus.

110. Mt 10: 37: "He who loves father or mother more than me is not worthy of me; and he who loves son or daughter more than me is not worthy of me."

111. The text refers here to Lk 10: 42: "But one thing is needful. Mary has chosen the good portion, which shall not be taken away from her." This is the story of Mary and Martha, the sisters of Lazarus. Martha is concerned with the things of the world; Mary, by contrast, sits at Jesus' feet and listens to his teaching.

earth, will suffer their children to be commended to Him.[112] Friends, if they are devout and true friends, will enjoy the same friendship with the highest heavenly friend and thus comprehend and not begrudge this divine love for the friend of one's soul. If they do otherwise, then their worldliness is to be disregarded with heavenly magnanimity. The heavenly father will take care of domestic matters quite well and not allow the temporal to go astray while one is seeking the eternal good. If this does happen, then He can soon replace with pearls what has been lost in the way of beans, and it is easy for Him to give a hundredweight of sugar for a handful of salt.

In the end there will certainly not be many earthly things demanded of them whose goal is heaven—if only they ask for enough earthly means from Him to serve Him so they can be relieved of earthly business and not be forced to make bricks when they are to slaughter the Easter lamb for Him.[113] It is sweeter to live simple and poor and in peace with the complete freedom to serve God than to be a serf on a splendid and glorious throne of vanity. Material goods are desirable only insofar as they are necessary to preclude the struggle for them (since we are kept from heavenly exercises by that struggle) and insofar as they further the following of Jesus. As soon as they, however, preclude the latter, they are comparable to what Dido deemed a treasure and that ought to be sunk into the sea.[114] Thus these pious women in Galilee did not let themselves be prevented from following Jesus, these women who without a doubt must also have suffered many impediments. For the path to Jesus is always lined with thorns; one must break through them.

Saw these things.[115]

They saw the complete and full suffering of Christ from the beginning to the end with most ardent sympathy, their hearts breaking as if they themselves suffered all this personally. They always followed Him everywhere. When they saw Him emerge from the praetorium scourged, crowned with

112. With the image of followers of Christ who kiss him, Greiffenberg probably alludes to Ps 2, where the rule of God's son is described. Here one is commanded to serve the Lord and to kiss the son. Ps 2: 12 in the Luther Bible, as in the King James Bible, reads, "Kiss the son," whereas the RSV reads, "kiss his feet."

113. Greiffenberg uses the German word for "Easter" *(Ostern)* here when referring to the paschal lamb that is sacrificed and eaten according to specific rites as part of the Passover seder. In Christian tradition, Christ is seen as the paschal lamb. See above, note 15.

114. Dido was married to a wealthy man of Tyre named Sychaeus. After the murder of Sychaeus by the tyrant Pygmalion, who was also Dido's brother, Sychaeus appeared to Dido in a dream, telling her where a treasure was hidden and instructing her to flee with it. She did so and set sail with all those who opposed the tyrant. The expedition eventually landed in North Africa, where Dido according to legend founded Carthage.

115. Lk 23: 49.

thorns, and dripping with blood, they must have poured out all the fountains of ardor and mercy at once and practically have dissolved in tears from pity. His bearing of the cross and sinking under it must have been unbearable for them, and each one must have been eager to help Him. But prevented by the band of soldiers, they were unable to get to Him to perform a service of love, and they must have envied Simon because he was permitted to do something that they wished to do.[116] But with what anguish must they have beheld His crucifixion? They hardly were able to see through their copious tears the blood flowing from His pierced hands and feet. Yet now and then they temporarily stayed [their tears] solely for the purpose of fully viewing everything that happened there—the parting of the garments, the casting of lots for the coat, and the mockery, His head bowing, and His giving up His spirit, and other wondrous sights. They could hardly look for heartache, and yet for love of Him they did not avert their eyes from Him whom they loved dead as they did living.

Among whom was Mary Magdalene, and Mary the mother of James the less and of Joses, and Salome, the mother of the sons of Zebedee.[117]

The Holy Spirit suffered these women, especially the sinner and penitent Mary Magdalene, to be named by the Evangelist here as well as later in describing the Resurrection so that no sinner, man or woman, would despair of the grace of God and true repentance.[118] If she is deemed worthy of the true love of Jesus and of touching His sacrosanct body living and dead with her mouth, hands, and hair, she who had once given her body over to the most unclean sins, then no one who truly repents should lose heart in the midst of sin. If the Holy Spirit with His sevenfold gift (as He did when He kindled love of Jesus within her) hovered over her, from whom Christ had cast out seven devils, then no one should deny oneself the presence of the Holy Spirit. If He wished to have this woman suffer with His suffering, this woman who once had lived in shameful pleasure, then He will all the less deny those who their whole life long found their only pleasure in Him, even if they otherwise were surrounded by sin and weakness. For her, kind Jesus, who is virtue and gratitude itself, spills His ruby blood from the feet that she once moistened with tears. He therewith washes clean of her sins the woman who washed His feet with her tears.

116. Simon of Cyrene, who carried the cross for Jesus (Mt 27: 32, Mk 20: 21, Lk 23: 26).

117. Mk 15: 40 and Mt 27: 56. Greiffenberg conflates these two verses when she adds from Matthew "the mother of the sons of Zebedee."

118. It is not clear which evangelist she means. Matthew, Mark, and John all name the women and specifically Mary Magdalene.

Mary the mother of James the less, a sister-in-law of Joseph, was there too. It was not, however, the fact that she was a relative but rather a heavenly inclination that she followed when following Christ. But it may also be that the calling of her son to the office of apostle drew her to Jesus. And it is a fine thing when parents do not oppose the spiritual illumination of their children and instead thereby suffer themselves too to be illuminated spiritually. Thus Salome too, the mother of the children of Zebedee, suffered herself to be set right and, backing off from her vain request, followed Christ out of true love, inasmuch as the sight of His bitter suffering crucified all worldly desire and pride within her.[119] This is one of the loveliest fruits of His suffering that the world was crucified for us and we were crucified for the world. For whoever tastes the crucified Christ no longer relishes the world with all its carnal pleasure and charm.

Who, when he was in Galilee, followed him, and ministered to him; and also many other women who came up with him to Jerusalem.[120]

All of these followed Him, not in idleness or out of curiosity but instead from most ardent love, devotion, and desire to serve Him, which they also put into practice (like Martha), and they served Him in all conceivable ways by cooking and lending a hand in all kinds of things that arise on journeys.[121] O blessed hands that cooked for His mouth which itself is the food of life! Yes, the blessed hands that can prepare and serve [food] for Him who prepared and served the heavenly banquet for us. With what joy must they have poured drink for Him who shall water us with delight as with a river, who shall also

119. Mark specifically calls her by the name Salome, whereas Matthew refers to her in the verse as the "mother of the sons of Zebedee." According to the *New Catholic Encyclopedia*, comparison of the two verses makes probable the identification of the Salome of the former with the mother of the sons of Zebedee in the latter, mentioned also in Mt 20: 20–23 as the woman who petitions Christ, "Command that these two sons of mine may sit, one at your right hand and one at your left, in your kingdom." Christ responds that she does not know what she is asking for and that this request is not his to grant. Salome is thought by some to be the sister of Mary mentioned in the parallel passage in John (Jn 19: 25). Greiffenberg's text follows another tradition that identifies Mary the mother of James as the sister of Mary, i.e., Joseph's sister-in-law. According to the *New Catholic Encyclopedia*, "sister" can also mean "sister-in-law," i.e., this Mary is married to Joseph's brother Clopas (*New Catholic Encyclopedia*, s.v. "Cleopas").

120. Mk 15: 41.

121. Two women named Martha appear in the Gospels. In Luke, Martha hurries to take care of Christ's bodily needs but is told that Mary, her sister, who has chosen merely to sit at Christ's feet and listen, has chosen the good portion (Lk 10: 38–42). In John, Martha is the sister of Lazarus who, when she laments her brother's death, is told by Christ that if she believes, she will see the glory of God (Jn 11: 1–40). Even though the Martha of the Gospel according to Luke is reprimanded, Greiffenberg probably refers to her here, inasmuch as she is the one who is performing material services for Christ. See above, note 111.

pour out the rivers of the spirit over us! How overjoyed they were that they could physically serve Him who freed us from the servitude of the devil.

It was, however, not only these women but many others whose names are written in heaven although not in this book. The Holy Spirit would not have omitted them, if it did not suffice for them to be recognized there to greater glory. He takes from those sacred to God no glory that He does not intend to replace a hundredfold in heaven. It is enough here for Him to say "many other women who came up with him to Jerusalem." To come up with Jesus in contemplation of peace is a lofty and laudable undertaking, be it physical or spiritual. They pushed through all impediments and did not let themselves be prevented from following Him who is eternal life. But, oh, wonder! They go to contemplate peace and behold the bloodiest war, to contemplate the presence of salvation and behold the greatest devastation, the wounds and the death of their beloved. It still goes that way: when one seeks in Jesus salvation and peace, one meets with the greatest storm and opposition. But one must not look at what is visible, which is transitory, but instead at what is invisible; seek repose where the greatest storm is and peace in the most obdurate opposition, just as these women found salvation in Jesus' wounds and peace in His strife.

[The meditation concludes with Jn 19:31–37, which describes how the Jews asked that the legs of the convicts be broken in order to keep the bodies from remaining on the cross on the Sabbath. Jesus' legs are, however, not broken because he is already dead, but a soldier pierces his side. Thus, according to John, is Scripture fulfilled: "A bone of him shall not be broken" and "They shall look on him whom they pierced." Greiffenberg is effusive on the subject of the blood that flows from the piercing of the side, which she conflates with the water of baptism and salvation, and she longs for every part of her body and soul to turn into words of thanks and praise in an effort to convert the entire world.]

Explanation of the Emblem

A kernel of wheat we sow in the spring[122]
passes and dies ere it springs up anew.
The winter wheat, as green as it shoots up,
it had all the same died away.
Thou didst give us this parable of Thee

122. See figure 7. This emblem introduces the twelfth meditation. The poem that provides the explanation for the emblem is composed of six stanzas, each of which consists of three lines of ten or eleven syllables, depending on whether the line ends in a masculine or feminine rhyme,

when Thou didst mean to give up Thy life, Jesus:
"Go and sow my body into the earth;
it shall soon be alive again."[123]
So Joseph did this.[124] Thy body was buried—
which my sinfulness so fatally martyred.
When in the earth Thou, Wheat Kernel, wast lost,
rebirth followed again soon.
For us, the earth hast Thou, First Fruit, made holy.
When they strew us there, as was done to Thee,
so shall we surely molder and decay,
yet resurrected living be.
Thy holy death restores us all from death.
By ceasing to be, we return to being.

---

and a fourth line of eight syllables. The first three lines are written in iambic pentameter and the last in iambic tetrameter. The four lines of each stanza rhyme according to the rhyme scheme *aabb*. To suggest poetic language, I have adhered in the translation to the syllabic meter.

Ein Weitzenkorn / das man im Früling säet /
vergeht und stirbt / eh dann es neu aufgehet.
Die Wintersaat / so neben grün aufschiest /
auch so zuvor erstorben ist.

Diß Gleichnis hast du von dir selbst gegeben /
als / JEsu! du aufgeben wolst dein Leben:
Seet meinen Leib nur in die Erd hinein!
er soll bald wieder lebend seyn.

Diß Joseph thät. Dein Leichnam ward begraben /
den meine Sünden todt-gemartert haben.
Als in die Erd du Weitzkorn dich verlohrn:
es ward bald wieder neugeborn.
Du Erstling / hast die Erde uns geweihet.
Wann man uns hat / wie dich / hinein gestreuet:
wir werden zwar verwerden und vergehn /
doch lebend wieder auferstehn.

Dein heilger Tod / uns macht vom Tod genesen.
Zum wesen man kehrt wieder / durch verwesen.
Du Joseph / uns machst wachsen neu herfür /
und öffnest unsrer Gräber Thür.

Ich will dann gern zu dir mich lassen säen /
du Leben du! üm lebend aufzustehen.
Ich werd im Grab auch bleiben nicht / wie du.
So geh ich fröhlich dann zu Ruh.

123. Jn 12: 24: "Unless a grain of wheat falls into the earth and dies, it remains alone; but if it dies, it bears much fruit." The poem calls this verse a parable, though strictly speaking it is not.

124. Joseph of Arimathea, a rich man who retrieves Jesus' body from Pilate and buries it in his own tomb. See Mt 27: 57–60, Mk 15: 43–46, Lk 23: 50–53, Jn 19: 38–40, and Greiffenberg's treatment of the episode in the meditation that follows.

O Thou Joseph, make us spring up anew
and open the door to our graves.
Then will I consent to be strewn in Thee,
O Thou life, to be resurrected living.
Like Thee, I shall not remain in the grave.
Thus I go gladly to my rest.

Figure 7. Unattributed, "Through Ceasing to be to Being" from *Des Allerheiligst- und Allerheilsamsten. . . Christi* (1672). The Beinecke Rare Book and Manuscript Library.

ON THE SUPREMELY HOLY AND SUPREMELY SALVIFIC SUFFERING OF JESUS: TWELFTH MEDITATION

[The twelfth meditation opens with the arrival of Joseph of Arimathea, who asks Pontius Pilate for the body of Jesus. This opening section blends Mt 27: 57–61, Mk 15: 42–45, and Lk 23: 50–52. The following excerpt commences with Greiffenberg's treatment of Mk 15:46 and continues to the end of the twelfth and final meditation.]

And he bought a linen shroud.[125]

O blessed flax bolls, blessed above all pearls and gold bolls, flax bolls that had these flax seeds in them![126] O blessed earth in which it is sown! O blissful hands that collected this flax and rippled it! O blessed earth or water, on or in which it was retted! O happy breaking and hackling that broke it, drew it out, and combed it! O most blissful fingers that spun it, wound it to make a warp, reeled it, and wound it onto the beam.[127] O still more fortunate weavers, washerwomen, and women bleachers who had something to do with it! O all you blissfully happy people who not only did seventy-two tasks but the hundred some tasks that flax requires (I myself have counted them) to become the linen shroud that was needed for Jesus' body or rather His corpse.

Oh! Why did I not live at that time so that my linen cloth, on which I spend most of my effort and work in running my estate, could have come to serve and honor Him? I would not have sold it to Joseph but instead have joyfully given it up to wrap my dearest living decedent in it. Oh! How joyfully would I have borne all thirst, heat, dust, and discomfort if I had known such a noble purpose for my effort! How diligently would I have selected the yarn, weighed it, and helped it to become the softest and purest linen cloth.[128] I would have joyfully forgone sleep and food, company and entertainment, and would have busied myself with this blessed flax work. I would have learned how to weave and work it myself and herein have tried to

125. Mk 15: 46.

126. A boll is a seed-bearing capsule; the term is used especially for flax and cotton.

127. Greiffenberg refers here to the way spun fiber is attached and wound onto the breast beam of a loom (a bar at the front of the loom) and attached to the cloth beam (a bar at the back of the loom) to form the warp (the lengthwise threads of the cloth that is to be woven) in preparation for weaving. The two beams keep the threads of the warp under tension to make possible the weaving in of the web (the cross threads). During the process of weaving, the warp is reeled from the breast beam to the cloth beam, that is, the cloth, which gradually comes to be though the weaving of yarn crossways across the warp, is wound onto the back beam.

128. Yarn is supposed to be weighed first to make certain that the weaver has put all of it into the linen cloth being produced (Zedler, *Grosses Vollständiges Universal-Lexikon*, s.v. "Leinen").

surpass Minerva and Arachne.[129] With what joy would I have bleached and smoothed and polished it, with what pleasure have cut and sewn it, and yet would have sprinkled and washed it with infinitely many tears, if I had been permitted to hope that the purple bloodied body of my Redeemer would be wrapped up in it. Since this happiness cannot be mine, grant then, O Thou Creator of all things, Jesus, that my manifold flax effort and the linen cloth produced by it may serve and honor Thee in other ways. For I cannot be satisfied with mere external use and benefit, and I regret and am vexed over work when it does not actually serve the lauding and loving of Thee.

Nicodemus also, who had at first come to him by night, came.[130]

Nicodemus, who once dared to go by night to the living Jesus, comes now by the light of day to the dead Jesus. He who shrank from coming to the Jesus who back then was only suspect now comes undaunted to the Jesus who is already damned and executed. He means to embalm Him, whom others consider a curse and an abomination, and true-heartedly to help bury Him in the earth. This was a noticeable change that made him brave in danger, loyal in death, and loving when he lacked hope. It was fitting that just as the night had once covered over his weakness, the day now became a witness to his courage. The Heavenly Master proved His divine masterpiece on him by thus making stouthearted and heroic one who was by nature fearful and fainthearted. The Teacher who came from God gave a sign with him, which no one can do unless God be with him—and He did it even when He was dead; He thereby attests that even in death He is inseparable from God.[131]

Nicodemus is one born after the death of his father. The wind blows and the spirit operates where and when it wills.[132] Just as the Lord Jesus did

129. According to Greek mythology, the mortal Arachne, who was an excellent weaver, dared to compete with Minerva, the goddess of wisdom. Both produced beautiful work in the competition, but although Minerva admired Arachne's work, she nevertheless punished her for her impiety, changing her into a spider.

130. Jn 19: 39. The story of how Nicodemus the Pharisee came to Jesus by night is told in Jn 3: 1–21.

131. A paraphrase of Jn 3: 2: "The man came to Jesus by night and said to him, 'Rabbi, we know that you are a teacher come from God; for no one can do these signs that you do, unless God is with him.'"

132. A paraphrase of Jn 3: 8: "The wind blows where it wills, and you hear the sound of it, but you do not know whence it comes, and whither it goes; so it is with every one who is born of the Spirit." Nicodemus's assistance is understood as a sign of his conversion. He has been reborn after the death of his heavenly father. In Jn 3: 3–8, Jesus explains to him that one must be born again of the spirit to enter the kingdom of heaven.

not want to come when Lazarus was dying but instead not until Lazarus had already lain four days in the grave, thus this rebirth did not come to pass until Jesus lay in the grave and not during His lifetime so that it would become clear that, dead or alive, He loves conversion.[133] How should Nicodemus not have been converted, inasmuch as he saw the Son of Man, according to his own words, raised up like Moses' serpent?[134] What else could he do but believe in Him, from whom he had seen such signs that appertain to God alone? If he believed in Him as the true God, then he must of course have desired to honor and serve Him, especially since he saw Him suffering this martyrdom for the sake of him and all humankind and he knew that He gained eternal life for him and everyone who believes in Him.

Bringing a mixture of myrrh and aloes, about a hundred pounds' weight.[135]

Faith that is not attested in love and love that is not attested in works is deader than the dead man whom one claims to lament. If the means are present, the work must be the translator of faith; otherwise, as the ingenious poet says:

> If works are wrested from faith,
> Who then will have faith in faith?[136]

133. According to Jn 11: 5–15, Jesus deliberately delays going to the dying Lazarus whom he intends to raise from the dead. He tells his disciples, "Lazarus is dead; and for your sake I am glad that I was not there, so that you may believe" (Jn11: 14–15). John recounts then how Jesus goes to Bethany where he promises, "he who believes in me, though he die, yet shall he live, and whoever believes in me shall never die" (Jn 11: 25–26) and goes on to call Lazarus forth from the tomb (Jn 11: 38–44).

134. The text refers to Ex 4: 1–5 when God proves to Moses who he is by performing miracles, here by turning Moses' rod into a serpent. In his first meeting with Jesus, Nicodemus acknowledges that Jesus must be from God, for no one can perform the miracles that he has performed except someone from God (Jn 3: 2).

135. Jn 19: 39.

136. Werke von dem Glauben rauben: / wer will da ein Glauben glauben? I have been unable to identify the unnamed poet whom Greiffenberg claims to quote here. It is remarkable that she here emphasizes good works, since Luther's reforms specifically opposed Catholic beliefs about salvation with the tenet "by faith alone" *(sola fide)* based on Rom 3: 28: "For we hold that a man is justified by faith apart from works of law." In her closing pages, indeed, she emphasizes the Lutheran tenet "by faith alone." According to the Lutheran creed good works can be manifestations of justification but do not contribute to justification. In the paragraph preceding the quotation, Greiffenberg paraphrases Jas 2: 24–26: "You see that a man is justified by works and not by faith alone. And in the same way was not also Rahab the harlot justified by works when she received the messengers and sent them out another way? For as the body apart from the spirit is dead, so faith apart from works is dead." I thank the Rev. Paula V. Mehmel for identifying the paraphrase.

How should one not give everything to Him to whom one gives one's heart? True love gives itself. Why not what else it has? Even if true love looks not for gifts, it sees in gifts the nature of the love that is reciprocated. How can the person who opens his heart close his hand, when the two are pulled by a single nerve? True love tolerates no parsimony; thus Nicodemus does not bring some few but a hundred pounds of myrrh and aloes. One hundred is the most perfect number. That thing with which one means to serve Jesus must be perfect—at least in the will and purpose, should one not have the power and the means. Myrrh and aloes are both hot and dry in the second degree and thus efficient and serviceable for preserving and embalming dead bodies that are thereby dried out and desiccated. This is why the first [of the two] is also called paradise wood.[137] Myrrh was presented to Christ in His childhood too as a sign of His true humanity. Thus one sees how the beginning and the end accord in Him who is the alpha and the omega.

They took the body of Jesus, which had been taken down [from the cross], and wrapped it in a clean linen shroud and bound it in linen cloths.[138]

The most alive and immortal being in heaven and on earth, indeed eternal life and immortality itself, suffered His corpse to be handled as they wished. He suffered Himself to be taken down, lifted up, turned over, wrapped up, bound, and laid out, however they wanted, not just, as people are wont to say, *as if* He were dead, but because He was truly dead. Life was dead as far as the body and humanity were concerned, yet it still lived in the soul and in the divinity that is eternal life itself. And what is still more, divinity remained inseparably united to humanity even in death, although the soul had departed from the body. Life was in Him, even when He was in death, and yet He was truly dead within the source of life. His holy limbs were completely stiff and immobile, and so they could bind and wrap them as they pleased.

Oh! If I had been there instead of Joseph and Nicodemus! How would I have caressed and kissed, worshiped and adored the dear body? How would I have counted the weals and have responded to them with a thousand love-

137. The text has it wrong. Aloes, not myrrh, was known as paradise wood. Aloes acquired the name paradise wood because it was thought to come from the only tree preserved from Eden (Zedler, *Grosses Vollständiges Universal-Lexikon,* s.v. "Agallochum").

138. In the doubling, characteristic of Greiffenberg's writing, this quotation of Scripture combines language from Jn 19: 40, "and bound it in linen cloths," and Mt 27: 59, "and wrapped it in a clean linen shroud." The explanatory relative clause "which had been taken away" refers to Jn 19: 38: "So he came and took away his body." The German translation of this verse employs the verb *herabnehmen,* which means "to take down from."

wounds? How would I have sunk my heart, soul, mind, and being into the sacrosanct five wounds and pressed them to my heart? I would not have ceased to suck on the loveliest of all heads until all of the thorns were pulled out, the little holes closed up, and all of the bloody drops in my mouth. Oh! Not until I was in His side, in His most loving heart, would I have drunk myself completely to death and suffered myself to be thereby struck dead, like Cyrus with the Scythian wine.[139] I would have embalmed this wound with my blood or rather embalmed myself with its blood. My regret and penance would have had to be the myrrh, and my faith the aloe that shoots up quickly in a single night and unexpectedly begins to bloom. My heart, the cotton moistened with these liquids and put in the wounds, would have filled them up.

Oh! Once again blissful linen cloth wherein the Supremely Holy One was wrapped, He who in His entrance and departure from this earthly life chose to make use of it! By being deemed worthy, all linen cloth on earth is blessed and sanctified as something that touched, made holy, and consecrated the Supreme Holiness. Who would not gladly have to do with such a creation that surrounded the Creator Himself when He became a creature and when He redeemed all His creatures? The linen cloth will give us an eternal pictorial souvenir of the birth and burial of Christ. Flax, which is commonly called women's martyr, will represent Christ for us, Christ for whose torture the first woman was at fault. Because it is, however, not merely their torturer but also their suffering of torture, godly women ought to recall the passion of Christ when at their flax work, all of which could be interpreted with reference thereto.

I mean, however, to make this comparison only in my thoughts whenever I have to do with flax making. I mean to strive to wrap Him really in my linen cloth through constant contemplation. Whenever I am weighing, I shall weigh His passion; whenever I am winding, I shall think of how He got free and how He prevailed.[140] When measuring, I shall measure His anguish. While bleaching, I shall recall His snow-white innocence. While folding over the cloth, I shall turn over in my mind His infinite atonement, and when I lift up the pieces, I shall ponder in this imperfect piecework the

139. Herodotus reports how the Scythian queen Tomyris took her revenge on the Persian king Cyrus after he killed her son. When Cyrus fell in battle, Tomyris ordered a wineskin filled with blood and put Cyrus's head in it, saying that he would now get his fill of blood (Herodotus, *Herodotus,* 1: 269 [1.214]).

140. Greiffenberg plays with the verbs *winden* (to wind), *sich auswinden* (to extricate oneself), and *überwinden* (to overcome or prevail) when she writes here "bey allem Winden / seiner Aus- und Uberwindung gedenken."

perfection that He gained for us.[141] I shall also consider it a pleasure if I can wrap His poor limbs in my linen cloth and shall regard all my effort as blissful and blessed if I can be of service to Him with my arms and bind Him with my cloth and bind Him to myself.

With the spices, as is the burial custom of the Jews.[142]

Since the Lord Jesus had been circumcised, presented in the Temple, and raised in the Jewish manner, and had lived accordingly, He wished to be buried in the Jewish manner so that He could arise as the Lion of the House of Judah.[143] If I had been with these two men at the burial of Jesus, I would have hoped out of the abundance of love that He might be restored to life through my shrieks and tears as well as through the power of the strong odor. But no! The time of arising was not the moment of burial but was to take place on the third day as the awakening of Lazarus took place on the fourth. His dying was not a ceasing of agitation but a real lifelessness, not a contraction of the life spirits but instead a true loss of them. Thus it was impossible to shriek Him to life and reanimate Him.

Now in the place where he was crucified there was a garden, and in the garden a new tomb [which was Joseph's], which he had hewn in the rock, where no one had ever been laid. They laid Jesus there.[144]

Since the first sin was committed in a garden and our redemption was thus also initiated there, the Lord Jesus Christ also chose to consummate [our redemption] in a garden and thus to be buried and resurrected there. In the garden of paradise the bloom of innocence was lost; in the garden at Calvary its seed was sown again. In the former the forbidden fruit grew out of the earth; in this one the blessed fruit of the body was buried in the earth. In the former the tree of life stood on the earth; in this one it lay beneath

141. The text refers to 1 Cor 13: 9–10: "For our knowledge is imperfect, and our prophecy is imperfect; but when the perfect comes, the imperfect will pass away." Luther translated what in the RSV is translated as "imperfect" as *Stückwerk* (piecework). This is the word used here. Greiffenberg invokes two senses of the word: "piecework" in reference to the making of flax and "patchy work" in Luther's sense of imperfection.

142. Jn 19: 40.

143. Rv 5: 5: "Then one of the elders said to me, 'Weep not; lo, the Lion of the tribe of Judah, the Root of David, has conquered, so that he can open the scroll and its seven seals.'"

144. The verse reproduced here conflates Mt 27: 60 ("and laid it in his own new tomb, which he had hewn in the rock; and he rolled a great stone to the door of the tomb, and departed") and Jn 19: 41–42 ("Now in the place were he was crucified there was a garden, and in the garden a new tomb where no one had ever been laid. So because of the Jewish day of Preparation, as the tomb was close at hand, they laid Jesus there").

the earth. That one had a river that divided into four rivers; this one has the holy wounded heart of Jesus, along with the four blood-fountains of His hands and feet.[145] A cherub guarded that one with a hewing sword; this one, the guards watch, although in vain. Since gardens offer the greatest delights, this one must therefore bring forth the Resurrection of Christ. What is more pleasant than a garden in the spring? Thus the most pleasant and charming one of all chose to have Himself buried in the earth of a garden to give us temporal and eternal delight. He is the seed, bulblet, and root of all delight and begins in thousands of ways to sprout up green.

Oh! That we too were such gardens and living Jesus-graves! He who does not green and bloom in faith and yield fruit through love cannot be a Jesus-grave. Only this earthly realm of the heart is capable of receiving the body of Christ, which is full of flowers of virtue and fruits of faith. To be sure it does not bear these naturally, but through the planting of the heavenly gardener, the Holy Spirit. Just as no garden brings delight in and of itself but must be dug and planted by an industrious hand. Joseph could well say, "Let my friend come into his garden!" And Jesus could answer, "I am coming into my garden; I have plucked my myrrh along with my spices! I am sleeping, but my heart (my divinity) wakes!" Joseph stood there, his hand dripped with myrrh, and myrrh ran over his fingers to embalm the one who is incorruptibility itself.

He laid Him in a new grave. Fittingly He had to have a new grave in which no one had ever lain, He who had a mother's womb in which no one ever lay but Him. The place where Jesus was to lie, rest, dwell, and stay had to be new, pure, and for Him alone. He who renews all things and is the source of new birth had to have a new burial place. It was also a completely new and special person who was buried there. He who was life itself, the immortal deceased, the living dead, and dead living, He who thus had the key to death and hell suffered Himself to be shut up in the grave. He through whose mouth this place, garden, rock, and earth were created suffers Himself to be laid within it and buried there. Oh, what a miracle! Oh, what newness! He who made everything new and shall in future make it new, indeed He who is Himself the most amazing newness suffers Himself to be laid in

145. These are the five wounds of the crucifixion: the pierced side and the pierced hands and feet nailed to the cross. The text refers here to the "wounded heart" rather than the "pierced side," perhaps intending to recall the "sacred heart" of Christian iconography that depicts Christ's heart with the five wounds and a crown of thorns. The devotion to the Sacred Heart is, however, associated with Catholic practice. Greiffenberg's contemporary, the French Catholic nun Saint Margaret Mary Alacoque (1647–90), brought new life to the centuries-old devotion to the Sacred Heart and established its modern form (see *New Catholic Encyclopedia*, s.v. "Sacred Heart, Devotion to," "St. Margaret Mary Alacoque."

a new grave so that as His mother had once been, the earth might now be pregnant with new joy and wonder.

Thus every heart in which Jesus is laid shall also be new so that none of these things—neither sin, devil, world, pride, lust, nor avarice or other such vices shall lie therein—or rather that through this renewal they shall no longer lie therein. [The grave] had to belong to a Joseph, a man whose virtues were ever increasing. It is also necessary to newness that it be hewn in a rock like this one. The repose of Jesus rests in the constancy of the heart. Whoever is not a rock of confession cannot be Jesus' resting place. He must be a rock that defies all the waves of persecution and can laugh at all the stormy winds so that it can be said of him, as the poet writes: "Casareus [*sic*] scorns the waves / that do rise up against him; / Scylla makes the waves to bark / but this too he pays no heed. / He who would vanquish virtue / shall ever be defeated."[146] There must be a rocklike irrevocability in a Jesus-grave and heart so that it dashes to pieces whatever offends it and itself remains indestructible. One needs the imperviousness of a rock that considers all worldly opposition temporal and trifling and is sensitive and tenderhearted only toward what concerns Christ's glory and story.[147]

Thus be a rock, my heart, in steady constancy, in edifying avowal [of faith], in unflinching patience, in impervious firmness of belief, and in all-

146. Greiffenberg loosely quotes Paul Fleming's ode from *Gedichte Auff des Ehrnvesten und Wolgelahrten Herrn Reineri Brockmans / Der Griechischen Sprache Professorn am Gymnasio zu Revall / Und der Erbarn / Viel-Ehren und Tugendreichen Jungfrawen Dorotheen Temme / Hochzeit* (Leipzig, 1635), Faber du Faur, no. 316 (New Haven: Research Publications, 1969). For easy access to the complete text of this rare publication, see http://gutenberg.spiegel.de/fleming/brockman/brockman.htm. Greiffenberg rearranges the lines of this ode and changes a pronoun so that the meaning is somewhat different from the original. In her text, the Caphareus of the original poem has become Casareus. Caphareus is a cliff where Poseidon brought about the destruction of the Greek fleet during the Trojan War. As a result of Greiffenberg's substitution in the fourth line of a masculine pronoun for the feminine one that originally referred to the feminine noun "virtue" her lines appear to speak of Casareus as a stoic person rather than as a place. Whereas Fleming writes of the imperviousness of stoic virtue to strife, Greiffenberg refers to the need of those who follow Christ to be impervious to all persecution.

Paul Fleming	**Catharina von Greiffenberg**
Wer der Tugend an wil siegen /	Casareus verlacht die Wellen /
Pfleget allzeit zu erliegen.	so sich an ihm lehnen auf;
Caphareus verlacht die Wellen /	Scilla läst die Wogen bellen /
Die sich an ihm lehnen auff.	auch nicht so viel gibt er drauf.
Scylla lest die Wogen bellen /	Wer der Tugend an will siegen /
Auch nicht so viel giebt sie drauff.	Pfleget allzeit zu erliegen.

According to Greek mythology, a jealous Circe turned the nymph Scylla into a hideous sea monster. Below her waist she was composed of monsters that barked incessantly like dogs.

147. "Ehre und Lehre" (glory and teaching).

resistant courage. Permit all torments, troubles, adversities, and misfortune to accomplish nothing other with you than hewing you out into a grave and resting place of Jesus. All of their iron tools—crowbar, borer, and drill—can do you no harm but making you capable of the repose of Jesus. They knock off, break loose, and bore out everything that impedes receiving Him. They empty you of all worldliness to enclose this heavenly treasure in you. They vault you so that you can, as it were, draw a heaven over Him.

One benefits from earthly robberies inasmuch as one is thereby made more ready and able to be a spiritual vessel. Nothing is taken from us through the cross except what impedes honor and glory in heaven. As little as the hewn-out rock can complain of losing its gravel and dust when it has thereby become a splendid tomb, so little can we complain about the loss of temporal goods or fortune because we thereby become heavenly mausoleums and pyramids of the fortress of pain of our dearest Jesus.[148] The devil and the wicked world cannot harm us except to our advantage. Their tools of torture beautify us. Their robberies have no power over us except over what impedes our perfection. We can indeed suffer these expropriations because they make us fit for God's glory. Although we feel it when they are carried out and it is not without pain, it is still desirable and delightful, because we thereby receive Jesus in us.

Through this burial of the Sacrosanct One, indeed Holiness itself, all our graves are sanctified and consecrated. Indeed, the Resurrection interred Himself with this dead man and will bring forth all the dead on Judgment Day. He who filled heaven with joy and clarity is lowered into the dark grave; into the hard rock [is lowered] the most delicate tenderheartedness, into the earth the ruler of all the heavens, into the vault the tip of the beams and pinnacle of all majesty and heavenly sublimity. Oh, wonder! Mortal men bury the immortal God. The grave in the rock encompasses Him who spanned all the heavens with a span. Oh! If it could only be said of me as well: they laid Jesus there! Where then? In my heart, in my soul and thoughts, in my mind and mood, in my conscience, spirit, and memory, in my body, mouth, and tongue, in my works, words, and pen, in all my movements and powers, life and conduct. Oh! Let them lay Jesus in there often and everywhere, they, the servants of Christ, the teachers and preachers, confessors and those who tender Communion, indeed the Heavenly Father

148. Greiffenberg makes clear here by indicating with a footnote that with the word "Leidburg" (fortress of pain) she means the *castrum doloris,* the decorations accompanying the catafalque in seventeenth-century funeral practice. The elaborateness of the decorations indicated the importance of the deceased.

and the Holy Spirit through governance and illumination, through their impetus, operation, and inspiration so that all people would feel and confess it from their very being, words, and works. Let Jesus too rise from the dead there and let His praise be spread throughout the entire world from there. For this is certain: once a person serves Jesus as His resting place, Jesus will thereafter also use that person to spread His glory.

They did this because of the Jewish day of Preparation, and the sabbath was beginning, as the tomb was close at hand.[149]

On the evening of the Jewish day of Preparation, when the Sabbath was beginning, these pious men had to hurry, because they were not allowed to be busy or restless in order not to give offense or to set a bad example. Should we not rather neglect and break off our corporeal business to celebrate the day of the Lord in a Christian manner, when these men hurried even with the holy body of the Lord Himself in order to lay Him to rest before the Sabbath? No corporeal thing ought to impede the sanctification of the Spirit, since the most blessed body of Lord Christ itself was not to do so. He suffered Himself to be buried hastily to show that we should hurry with all corporeal things in order to reach repose in God as the true Sabbath.

For a good design, everything has to fit in the end: just as here Joseph's grave and garden had to lie near the place of the skull. Fathoming the hearts of all humankind, unfathomable, omniscient Providence had previously spied the pious desire of those who loved God and had cleared away all incidental impediments that could be contrary to their holy zeal. If some remain, they must serve to refine and sharpen this zeal, and it will in the end be revealed that the impediments were nothing but spurs and the delays winds to guide into the desired harbor. The grave of all erring must be close at hand as was Christ's grave here. Divine Dispensation always arranges a place to bury the adversities that impede our heavenly repose and work. When billows of fog darken the sun of the spirit and become much too thick, a heavenly, beaming, golden spirit comes to burn them up. It makes the earth open up its mouth so that they are engulfed and buried. In short, the grave must be close at hand when the Sabbath of the soul is to dawn: the grave of the sins in the wounds of Jesus, the grave of sadness in the spirit of joy, the grave of misfortune in the omnipotence of God, and finally the grave of the world in the dawning of the glory of Lord Jesus. Then

149. This verse conflates Lk 23: 54 and Jn 19: 42 and adds "They did this."

the true, eternal, and heavenly Sabbath will dawn, whose repose is eternal and whose celebration is endless, whose sun has no setting and whose comfort has no end.[150]

They rolled a great stone to the door of the tomb, and departed.[151]

They did this to prevent wild animals or wicked people from doing any harm or mischief to the holy corpse or mocking it. Dearest Lord Jesus, the cornerstone and foundation stone of our salvation, suffers Himself to be covered with a stone. He allows Himself thus to be put safely away so that in future His omnipotence will break out all the more gloriously. Whoever means to serve Jesus must, like these men, not let himself be discouraged by any effort, work, danger, or trouble in rolling the heavy stone. Many a stone of misery, opposition, burden, and affliction must be rolled forth. How heavy will many a person find the stone of his office and profession so that his strength gives out carrying it! There is always someone who nearly rolls himself to death on the stone of his desire and intention and yet cannot get it anywhere. Another pushes the stone of his disinclination with all his might toward the grave and yet in vain. There is no one for whom it is not a burden to bring that burden to the grave.

To be sure, our faithful Lord Jesus appears meanwhile to be sleeping or dead. But He observes our work invisibly and imperceptibly infuses His power into our weakness and mobility into our immobility so that the stone becomes fluff; the load a puff of air; and the work a delight. He makes the yoke so light that a fly could pull it.[152] His ability to penetrate everything goes into the stone, so that while it was previously like Hiero's ship not to be moved by innumerable people and horses, it can now be set into motion like that ship with two fingers by means of Archimedes' art.[153] It may be said of this: He came to me and made easy for me what otherwise appeared to

150. Greiffenberg imagines the Sabbath as beginning with the dawn; in Jewish custom it begins at sundown.

151. The plural subject comes from Jn 19: 42. Mt 27: 60 has therefore been edited to read "they" rather than "he."

152. The last two sentences may be an allusion to Mt 11: 30: "For my yoke is easy, and my burden is light."

153. Hiero II (d. 215 BCE) was the king of Syracuse during the second Punic War. Archimedes (d. 212 BCE) designed the defense of Syracuse when it was attacked by the Romans. Greiffenberg refers here to the well-known account of how Archimedes demonstrated to Hiero that a heavily laden ship could be launched single-handedly with the power of a small engine composed of levers and pulleys.

me to be nearly impossible. Only Jesus has a place to stand on outside of the earth (like what Archimedes wished for) and can lift it up out of its place or give a gnat the power to accomplish incredibly mighty works.[154] He was to be sure dead when He was buried, but His omnipotence lived and moved the stone through inner strength so that the rolling of it became all the lighter for them. Omnipotence wants to have something large and strong as an impediment so that it can show its colossal greatness and strongest point.

The way out must be blocked for Him whose way out is eternal so that He can invent a miraculous way out through His divine power. The door to the grave is put in the place of the door to life[155] so that [the latter] will not burst forth living. But in vain! This door, which to be sure needs no door for a way out, could make a door right through the stone where it is the hardest and thickest. With this rolling shut of the door they create no difficulties for Christ our Lord or for the angel who afterward rolled the stone away. But they certainly do thereby grieve the good women, and they do supply a proof of our Lord Jesus Christ's omnipotence and glory [by showing] what powerful grave tenders and personal servants He has keeping His grave. After they had honorably buried and interred Jesus, these good men departed in sadness and thought they had left Him lying in rest, Him who had no rest until He had gained eternal rest for them and for us all through His unrest.

Mary Magdalene and the other Mary were there, sitting over opposite the sepulcher. The women who had come with him from Galilee followed, and saw where and how his body was laid.[156]

The trusty recorder, the Holy Spirit, who keeps good deeds like a signet ring, cannot extol and praise these enough, even those of the greatest sinners, men and women alike. He certainly mentioned the discipleship and constancy of Mary Magdalene and of the other women who loved Jesus. How He lauds their presence and persistence, not only in living and suf-

154. Archimedes is said to have written to Hiero that if given a place to stand outside the earth and a lever long enough and a fulcrum strong enough, he could move the world.

155. The "door to life" is Jesus. In Jn 10: 9 Jesus says, "I am the door; if anyone enters by me, he will be saved."

156. Up to "the sepulcher," the text quotes Mt 27: 61. It switches mid-sentence with the insertion of "the women" to Lk 23: 55, where the two Marys are not specifically mentioned. "The sepulcher" is here replaced with "where" as a transition into Lk 23: 55, and thus the two verses are seamlessly blended.

fering, but also in death and at the sepulcher of Christ! He does not fail to touch upon or describe a single testimony of loyalty but instead makes them known to the entire world. This must please the Most High most highly because He cannot get enough of writing and extolling it. This happens perhaps because poor womenfolk, on account of being completely despised and defamed by most men, seek and find their honor in the apologia of the Holy Spirit. And why ask in the end about the disgrace of people who have God Himself eulogizing them? If it is God who takes care of our honor, we are thus free from care.

See what a detailed account He gives of all their actions and undertakings and how He leaves not the slightest thing unnoticed! They sit over against the sepulcher out of heartfelt love and painful sadness. They would rather have laid themselves in it and been buried with their beloved, but the fear and dread of committing an unnatural novel act (which to this day prevents many a holy and doughty undertaking) must have held them back from it. To be sure it would not have been completely unheard of, but in another way. At other times, many brave and true women have had themselves cremated with their loved ones and have jumped joyfully into the fire with the corpses of their loved ones. Indeed, praiseworthy Indian women have even struggled and quarreled over which among them should have the honor of following their consort to the funeral pyre. If this happened among the heathens, why should not the lovers of Christ who were burning through and through with the spirit have just as much and even more zeal for dying? They cherished Him without a doubt, but Christ chose them not as companions in death but as messengers of Resurrection. Thus they had only to sit over against the sepulcher and merely have their hearts buried with their beloved. They observed everything precisely, that is, where, in which cave, in which corner, in which pier-arch of this catacomb, and also under what circumstances, in what kind of clothes He was laid so that they would know for certain how to find Him according to their holy intention. Love and reason want to be sure of their ground.

Then they returned, and prepared spices and ointments.[157]

With Jesus in their hearts and their hearts in the sepulcher, they returned to the city. Often one must seem to turn away from Jesus to serve Jesus, quit the places where His body and repose are, and go into the godless city where He is slandered. The undertakings of the saints and the godly often cannot be fathomed, and many of them have a purpose different from

157. Lk 23: 56.

their appearance. Often what is most horribly slandered has the best intentions. It suffices that God knows their hearts and will make their righteousness shine forth like the sun on that day. Meanwhile they are often with these holy women busy preparing the spices for anointing the holy body of Christ, when people regard them as the most removed [from God] and most godless. These good women must doubtless have been regarded as heedless lovers, of whom it is said, "Out of sight, out of mind!" And such judgments come from that very same mindset. These women testify, however (although secretly), with their deeds that nothing is more on their minds than Jesus who has fallen out of sight.

They go about preparing the spices for the embalming of the corpse in the most industrious manner. All that Joseph and Nicodemus had done was too little for them. Love is never content in the honoring and tending to the well-being of the beloved; it always wants to do still better. By taking their time, they intend to make good what making haste did not permit these men to do, namely, to see to it that the corpse of the Eternally Living One would be treated properly. Love lived powerfully in them, but faith was as if dead. They certainly had an undying love for Him, but no hope of His immortality. They could not neglect His holy body, but they had lost sight of His Holy Word. From this it appears that loving is easer than believing and that faith is at times weak even in the holy ones. Thus they are sorely in need of the power of God.

On the sabbath they rested according to the commandment.[158]

Quiet generally comes with godliness. A soul that loves God also loves the quiet in which God is wont to reveal Himself, particularly over the Sabbath. What is sweeter and more delightful than being quiet and being spared all vanity and emptiness on the Sabbath so that eternity and spirit do their work in us; celebrating so that God works in our hearts; being quiet so that we can listen to the music of the Holy Spirit and the angels and can hear what Jesus says in and to our souls. Oh, blessed quiet of the sea that makes us hatch this heavenly halcyon in us![159] But oh! how Satan and the wicked world oppose this quiet! Unfortunately the Sabbath of all days never allows for quiet. All of the meetings, visits, trips, and festivities take place then. One is supposed to leave God behind and attend to the world, to set knock-

158. Lk 23: 56.

159. The halcyon (Greek for kingfisher), a mythological bird, is said to breed in the winter when the sea is calm and the weather fine, laying and sitting on its eggs on the surface of the water.

ing on the door of heaven at naught and dance to the tune of vanity, to push away the Bible and take up cards. If one does not do it, one is considered a foolish woman or what is worse a pious hypocrite.[160] One does not have a choice; rather one is disturbed against one's will in one's peace and quiet in God, for one is flushed out everywhere like a solitary little bird. If it does not happen on account of company, then some task and domestic matter comes along, a matter that at other times might hold the promise of sundry benefit. Even if this does not happen, there will still be such a lot of needling, mocking, and complaining that one can no longer collect oneself in the quiet.

Oh! The stillness of the Sabbath really does have just too many enemies. It must be a precious thing since the devil simply cannot abide it, and his bride, the world, can so little tolerate it. What turbulent storms, confusions, and disorder must arise in a soul before it can enjoy even a short hour of quiet in God! Unfortunately the commandments and laws of the Lord are despised and neglected, but none more wickedly than the commandment to keep the Sabbath holy. People say openly: "Who can pray the whole day long? You need to seek amusement!" As if the greatest delight did not consist in intercourse with God! Furthermore, they say, "I am not a monk or a nun who has to pray all the time; I am no Jew either who has to live so strictly according to the law," and they make all sorts of similar excuses, when it is really the highest obligation of every Christian to observe the laws of his God, to speak, sing, and tell of them day and night. We are all priests before God; we are all betrothed virgins and brides of Christ; we are all Jews (confessors of our faith) and the people and family of God, and the Ten Commandments apply to us as they do to the Jews.[161]

But a damned abuse has spoiled everything. Even the most honorable and holy people approve of this abuse through their graciousness and amicability when they should be frowning at it and openly casting blame. They say, "People do need their delight!" As if it were not the greatest delight to delight in their Creator! One cannot (they say) spend all one's time doing spiritual exercises. But no one is asking for that, but merely for the seventh part of the week. Of this seventh, one third is lost to sleep, and of the 16

160. Greiffenberg uses the word "Pharisäisch," which I have translated as "pious," with reference to a pious sect of Jews, the Pharisees, who because of their condemnation of Christ and his teaching in the Gospels have a negative connotation in Christian circles.

161. "Betrothed virgins" refers to Mt 25: 1–13, the parable of the wise and foolish virgins who are to go out to meet the bridegroom. Only five of them bring oil for their lamps and are thus ready to meet the bridegroom (Jesus Christ) when he comes and go in with him to the marriage (heaven).

hours, at least 4 to eating, dressing, and undressing. Thus of 168 hours a week barely 10 or 12 remain for devotion, during which short time the spirit really ought to be able to hold still. We are (they say furthermore) not yet angels or spirits that we could live in contemplation.[162] We certainly are not, but we hope to be, and in our temporal existence we should accustom ourselves to practicing what we are to do in eternity.

Thus it is ever strange that we must be forced to accept our good fortune. Everyone would joyfully hold out his hat if it rained pearls; why not his heart and ears to the pearls of the Divine Word? If gold fell in pieces from heaven, nobody would absent himself on account of being too weak and incapable of picking it up. Why then does one invent for oneself an inability to receive the greatest treasure of heaven? It is ignorance, the indifference to divine goodness, that causes one to hold in such low esteem what is so enormous; to esteem so little what is so great, and to slight what is the dearest thing in heaven and on earth. Oh! Be not ashamed, you wicked despisers of the Sabbath, to learn from these women how to be still over the Sabbath. I recommend repose and quiet above all. I feel like David: if my heart were not calmed and quieted, then my soul would be weaned.[163] Oh! How often will the world try to wean me? I cry, however, for Thy breast, O Jesus! The law of Thy mouth is dearer to me than gold, even fine gold.[164] I say with that pious man: "Lead me, Thy little child, into the wilderness; press me to Thy loving breasts."[165] I consider being quiet on the Sabbath one of the truest indications of love from a person who is loved by God and who

162. Greiffenberg uses the German word "Beschaulichkeit" here and then adds a footnote defining it with Latin *contemplative.*

163. Ps 131: 2: "But I have calmed and quieted my soul, like a child quieted at its mother's breast; like a child that is quieted is my soul." David, the second king of Israel, is the presumed author of many of the psalms.

164. Ps 19: 9–10: "The fear of the LORD is clean, enduring for ever; the ordinances of the LORD are true and righteous altogether. More to be desired are they than gold, even much fine gold."

165. Although this quotation reads as though it reproduces Scripture, I have been unable to identify it as such. Greiffenberg may refer obliquely to Sg 8: 1–5, which both mentions bringing the beloved to the mother's breast and refers to a woman coming "up from the wilderness, leaning upon her beloved" (I thank Paula V. Mehmel for this reference). If Greiffenberg indeed has these verses in mind, then the "pious man" would be Solomon. Greiffenberg has also just quoted a psalm attributed to David, and therefore the "pious man" whom she mentions may be David instead. The notion of being led into the wilderness might suggest the deliverance praised in Ps 136: 16 "to him who led his people through the wilderness." According to Ex 15: 22, the Israelites, led by Moses, wandered into the desert after escaping Pharaoh. When they were starving, God fed them with manna and quail (Ex 16: 13–16).

loves God. For whoever has tasted the sweetness of God will not deliberate for long about being quiet so as to cling to [God's sweetness] still more. Whoever loves God will not need a host of admonitions to have intercourse with Him. One can thus soon see by way of this sword of Solomon who is the true mother.[166]

Next day, that is, after the day of Preparation, the chief priests and Pharisees gathered before Pilate and said, "Sir, we remember that the imposter said, while he was still alive, 'After three days I will rise again.' Therefore order the sepulcher to be made secure until the third day."[167]

Hatred and evil are as immortal as love because they come from the devil. The high priests, who are supposed to keep people from being ugly, make themselves ugly with this vice. The Pharisees, a special holy sect, are not ashamed of the most intransigent wickedness.[168] They think night and day of nothing else but how they can vent their hatred of Jesus after His death, annihilate all of His words, and prevent the fulfillment of His prophecy of His Resurrection. They do not cease displaying malice toward Him even when He is sleeping in His grave. They would have preferred to have cremated Him and to have seen His ashes scattered in the air or over water rather than that He should lie in a grave. Thus they do not celebrate. Instead they gather before Pilate to make a plea in one voice. Nothing is denied to an entire group of people (they think). They had already learned that this judge could be confused with screaming and unanimity. Thus they meant to make further use of this power. They also employed all deference and eloquence to make him favorable to them. "Lord!" they say, "we consider and recognize you as our lord who has the power to command us and who grants us the freedom to make a request."

"We thought," they continue. Here one sees that their cogitating and thinking has a wicked purpose. They think evil thoughts in their hearts. They conspire against the Lord and His anointed. All of their thoughts are directed toward doing evil, toward twisting the words of Christ, toward

166. 1 Kgs 3: 16–27. These verses recount the famous judgment of King Solomon in which he determines the true mother of a disputed child by judging the reactions of the two women when he orders that the baby be cut in half with his sword.

167. Mt 27: 62–64.

168. The Pharisees were a social political sect of pious Jews who aimed to keep out what they considered heathen influences and who stressed the separateness of the Jews. They are frequently named in the Gospels as especially opposed to Jesus' teachings. In Mt 23, for example, Jesus takes them to task at length. See above, note 160.

malicious interpretation of them, and toward refuting them with their deeds whenever possible. But [His words] are still true, even if the world should be split asunder over them. Out of hatred, they do not even want to give or grant Jesus His name; rather they call the very Way of Truth a seducer. Is He then a misleader who leads into heaven? Can one lead better than into heaven? Shall He perhaps be called that because He leads strangely? Oh, no! Lord! Lead strangely, but blissfully! Or because He leads to the cross and trouble? By no means! Where Jesus is, is where heaven is, even if it were in hell. With Him, paradise is in the icy tundras; the hall of cheer in the vale of tears. To lead in a singular fashion is not to mislead but to lead to glory. If one could ask the malefactor, he would tell us whether Jesus was a misleader or whether He was not rather the leader to the heavenly Jerusalem. But Jesus was thus forced to suffer scorn even in the grave so that our reputation would bloom on our graves and that we should retain an honest name after death; for often our reputation does not blossom until then and our innocence is not brought to light until then.

The enemies of Christ kept His word much more firmly in their memory in order to do their evil with it than did His friends to strengthen their faith with it. Of the latter there is nothing written about their ever recalling His words at the cross or the grave, but the former can cite them subtly in order to prevent [what they] falsely alleged [as] fraud. They are not satisfied that He is dead and buried. They even desire, as it were, to put the grave in prison and not to free His dead body. They request that the grave be made secure. Envy, hatred, cunning, and wickedness against Christ must always have worldly power as its arm. Order this and that to be done, they say. They give commands and have put into effect what they have evilly devised. But let them devise and command! He who is in heaven as well as in the grave laughs at them, and the Lord mocks them. Let them make guards of the entire world and turn all the rocks into gravestones! He will still get through them. Let their guards stand watch for the three days during which the truth of His words shall be asserted or prevented: the tiniest dot will not be lacking in time or truth.

They are all about untruth and deception, and inasmuch as they are always pregnant therewith, they also suspect others on this account and measure innocence according to the yardstick of their own wickedness. Suspicion is commonly an indicator of native malice and rarely lodges in a heroic heart. How should he who is conscious of nothing good in himself suppose that there is good in others? He whose hands are sticky with malice presumes that everything is sticky that he touches. Because they deal in nothing but lies, they suspect the same of Christ's disciples. Therefore they said,

"Lest his disciples go and steal him away, and tell the people, 'He is risen from the dead,' and the last fraud will be worse than the first."[169]

Lying, deceiving, and stealing perennially move the godless heart. If it cannot do these things itself, it must accuse others of doing them. After they have robbed Christ of His honor—indeed, His blood, life and limb—with lying and deceiving, they impute this damnable vice to what little remains of Him, namely, to His disciples. It is unfortunately the all too well known way of the world that one attributes wrongdoing to a person that one has done to him oneself, that one stabs him and then afterward puts the iron in his hand as if he had wounded himself. Oh! The horribly painful double-edged sword! If they would at least let a person be unhappy in his innocence and not rob him of the comfort of virtue [as well]! But we cannot have it better than did Christ. He was martyred, crucified, and slain and needlessly mocked, maligned, misrepresented, and misused to death, indeed, to the grave. What true Christian heart can hope or dare to wish that he should have it better? Whoever would be my disciple, it is said, must follow my example.[170]

Like scattered little sheep, the poor apostles ran back and forth in confusion and sadness and probably thought of nothing less than of lying, deceiving, and stealing. But these people come along then and impute to them these gross vices. This is what often happens. When one is in the deepest ecstasies of love of Jesus and in the midst of innocent exercises, thinking nothing bad and merely looking pensive and melancholy and languishing, the world quickly interprets it as hostility, displeasure, and animosity and creates an uproar and commotion. The evil spirit cannot stand for a Christian to be either blessed or blissful, much less for him to be that way for any length of time. Oh! Let the world have the latter things for itself, and leave me for the sake of God only the former things! Because they themselves always put off the common people with lies, they judged the disciples accordingly.

They could not, however, with all their might prevent what the Al-

169. Mt 27: 64.

170. Greiffenberg expresses here as elsewhere the idea that Christians should expect to suffer as did Christ. This idea is articulated in Jn 15: 18–21: "If the world hates you, know that it has hated me before it hated you. If you were of the world, the world would love its own; but because you are not of the world, but I chose you out of the world, therefore the world hates you. Remember the word that I said to you, 'A servant is not greater than his master.' If they persecuted me, they will persecute you; if they kept my word, they will keep yours also. But all this they will do to you on my account, because they do not know him who sent me."

mighty intended. The last fraud will not be worse than the first one, for there was no fraud here. But the last truth will indeed be clearer than the first one, when Jesus is resurrected unimpeded by anyone. Their last fraud is certainly worse or rather more foolish than the first one, for previously they took only His temporal life from Him; now they mean to rob Him of His divinity by presuming to suppress His omnipotence and truth. A valiant soul can sooner bear that someone murders his body than murders his honor. But Jesus, the alpha and omega, the beginning and end, the first and the last, will have nothing to do with deceit, indeed, will have no need of it to reveal His glory. He is accustomed to driving His works ever higher and to making the last one greater than the first one was. His birth was initially mean and wretched in a stable but in the end made splendid by the proclamation and songs of praise of the angels. Thus baptism too was at first a commonplace thing but in the end made splendid by the voice of God and the appearance of the Holy Spirit. This is how it went with His entire life and conduct as well, where the last thing was always more splendid than the first had been.

Thus with the faithful the last thing will always be better than the first. The unbearable making of bricks (as with the people of Israel) will be followed by a splendid sea journey; the woeful wildernesses followed by the Canaan they desire.[171] It is the opposite with the godless; there the last fraud will be worse than the first. The first one made them take lumps of coal for pearls; the last one will give them flames for roses. Here they take the chaff for the wheat and the wind as substance; there, however, the devil, after he has removed his mask, will give them worms for beauty, serpents for delight, sulfur and pitch for money and goods.

Pilate said to them, "You have a guard of soldiers; go, make it as secure as you can."[172]

The wicked get a hearing and a concession in their evildoings sooner than do the pious in their supremely holy desires. The happiness of the godless would be lamentable if their good beginning were not to be followed by a miserable ending. People commonly say, as they do hereabouts: "So you have your heart's desire!" But the miserable chosen people say, "Heaven is made of iron and brass; no prayer can get through; God has forgotten how

171. Exodus recounts how Pharaoh sets taskmasters over the Israelites and forces them to make bricks. When the Israelites are later pursued by the Egyptians, God enables Moses to part the Red Sea so that the Israelites can pass through it (Ex 5). Their pursuers, however, are drowned (Ex 14). After crossing through the Red Sea the Israelites wander for forty years in the wilderness until they come to Canaan (Ex 16: 35).

172. Mt 27: 65.

to be merciful; He has changed into a cruel one; the gates to a favorable hearing are closed; the bridges of succor drawn up." But be of good cheer and undaunted! Everything will yet get better. The right hand of the Most High can and will change everything. The metalline heaven will melt, indeed, even become an incense burner for saying prayers like the incense of the saints. God will be mindful of them and have in mind nothing but grace and mercy, which can change Him back into the most tenderhearted and cordial friend. [The right hand of God] is the gatekeeper who opens up the gate to a favorable hearing and closes it to no one. It can make the almighty finger of God into a bridge and find happiness even if [happiness] were beyond the earth so that people will joyfully say: "So you have your heart's desire!"

So they went and made the sepulcher secure by sealing the stone and setting a guard.[173]

They besieged the sepulcher with guards like a fortress that one intends to starve out, and they secured the stone as the door to it. But, oh, foolish precaution that strains against God's Providence! Vain securing that means to crush omnipotence! Miserable guards who are supposed to enclose the one who fills up everything in a grave that is as wide as a span! Risible sealing that means to seal fire with wax so that it will not break out! They think that everything is over since the enemy is dead and His friends are by means of trickery prevented from seeing to it that His Word is fulfilled. Yet they are way off the mark! God granted this power to them to make His omnipotence known and to revile their impotence. He makes them guard and watch, seal and stamp, and is minded not only to go through the stone but through all of their minds. Let the flies stand watch; the lion will find the way out. The stone will become a plum when the Omnipotent begins to stir. Since mountains melt before the Lord, how shall the wax stand before the flame of His divinity? Their impotent guarding is but an indication of the nullity of human assaults on the Lord.

But the children of light ought to learn this clever thing from the children of the world and keep the sepulcher of Christ or rather Jesus in their hearts so that He is not stolen from them and so that the last vexation does not become worse than the first one. They ought to ask God for guards to secure their hearts well like the sepulcher of Jesus. They ought to ask for the Holy Spirit, for mercy, power, strength, courage, and patience so that the sepulcher of the heart is manned and surrounded over and over so that no one can break in and steal this treasure. They ought to ask for the holy

173. Mt 27: 66.

angels who stand guard day and night and make the rounds so that nothing can be plotted secretly. They ought to ask for the stone of constancy to be sealed with the Holy Spirit and the blood of Christ so that neither the devil nor the world may push it aside. Oh! My chosen Lord Jesus, who put Thyself in me, be Thou at once the guard who preserves and protects me, the stone that covers Thee up in me, and the seal of inviolability so that even eternity cannot part us. Indeed, press me like a seal onto Thy heart and Thee onto mine that we may be buried together, melted together, and lowered together [into the grave], inseparable in all infinite eternity.

What praise I owe Thee once again, dearest Lord Jesus! Praise for Thy burial: that, dead, Thou hast awakened Joseph to bury Thee. Oh! Awaken in me all thoughts of thanks that can occur to a thankful heart, all words of praise that Thy glory can put into a mouth, and all proofs of praise that a human mind could ever think up to crown Thy sepulcher with glory and jewels. I praise Thee for granting Joseph courage after his long faintheartedness so that he dared to go in to Pilate to ask for Thy corpse. Oh! Make me too—so that I can be thankful to Thee—bold and stouthearted to dare to do everything that serves Thy glory and repose. May stouthearted daring, the goddess of all miracles, draw me forth with all her might and make me go in among lions and dragons so that I, undaunted, may desire to honor His body and to bury it in its proper sepulcher and resting place, which would be the most pleasant service and thanks for its burial. Since I have accomplished with words and thoughts everything that was possible for me [to accomplish]—oh!—so grant me at last a gratitude expressed in deeds.

For the surrendering of Thy holy corpse, which came to pass with Joseph, let me surrender to Thee in gratitude my own body (unworthy as it is), not only in every way to serve Thy holy name but also to die for the sake of Thy glory. For Thy humble consent to be wrapped in linen, let me thank Thee with real wrapping of Thy poor limbs in the linen that Thou grantest me. For the mercy of generosity that was granted Nicodemus who was previously so fainthearted, I mean to show myself thankful by means of Thy power through manly steadfastness, although I am a weak woman. For tolerating that Thou, Immortal, Heavenly, and Imperishable One,[174] wast embalmed and anointed with perishable plants of the earth, I mean to praise Thee with immutable imperishable praise in my writings, which with Thee

174. The text of the second edition incorrectly reads "vergänglichen," meaning "perishable one." The edition of 1672, by contrast, correctly reads "=vergänglichen," the "="standing in for "un," meaning "*im*perishable one" (Greiffenberg, *Des Allerheiligst- und Allerheilsamsten Leidens und Sterbens Jesu Christi* [1672], 999).

as the content will outlast all the columns and statues of marble, steel, and bronze of earthly heroes.

I owe Thee special praise, O flower of all beauty and fragrance, for the charming wish to be buried in a garden. I want to thank Thee in a real way by touching all the flowers and to recall Thee most lovingly whenever I behold such a garden treasure. Each scent shall make me sigh over Thy burial. My entire garden delight shall commemorate Thy grave. For the memory granted me when Thou didst permit Thyself to be laid in a new grave, let me thank Thee with a new heart-grave. Oh! Renew Thy grace in my heart; otherwise nothing new will come to be. Renew me with a blessed grave so that in the grave I may become a new grave for the blessed Resurrection. I so desire to thank Thee with a new mouth and lips that I will gladly die to renew Thee. I have a great desire herein to thank Thee really so that no one but Thee shall enter my heart and soul. I allow no one to open my heart: "Lamb who for me art wounded / Thou art my only bridegroom," I sing with a dear spiritual teacher.[175] Thou art the one and only true ruler of my heart, the innermost peace, and the most ardent pacifier of it. "Everything, all / is like to a ball, / doth rise and fall," I say in the words of the poet.[176] Jesus, Jesus alone shall be the heart of my heart. I will put Him in it. Indeed, may He put Himself therein and let it not disturb His peace.

I thank Thee too for the haste on account of the Sabbath. Oh! Make me hasten and be prepared to prepare in me Thy repose. Oh, hasten to drive the balance wheel in my soul that prevents me from keeping the Sabbath properly. Oh, how lamentable! Shall Satan and the world be so powerful as to keep a Christian from the celebration of the Sabbath when the holy corpse of Jesus itself does not prevent them from it, but instead must be buried hastily so as not to do so? Grant that to show my gratitude I may cast aside, drop, and leave everything behind me, rather than disrupt the Sabbath of my soul; grant too that I may abandon not merely my worldly affairs but also the concerns of my soul, that I may deal with the pain of scorn and antipathy, throw shame and honor to the wind, endure hatred and anger, despise despising, and crush everything bad that as a result happens to me

175. Angelus Silesius (pseud. Johann Scheffler, 1624–77). Greiffenberg quotes two lines from the seventh verse of his hymn "Die Psyche sehnet sich nach Jesu alleine": "Du für mich verwundtes Lamm / Bist allein mein Bräutigam!" *Heilige Seelen-Lust oder Geistliche Hirtenlieder der in ihren Jesum verliebten Psyche. 1657. (1668.)*, ed. Georg Ellinger (Halle a.S.: Max Niemeyer, 1901), 13. Scheffler converted to Catholicism in 1653 and became a priest in 1661.

176. "Alles ander alles / Hat die Art des Palles / Der steigt und fällt." Greiffenberg here once again quotes the poem "Tugend ist mein Leben" (Virtue Is My Life) by Paul Fleming (see *Gedichte von Paul Fleming*, 86).

just to be able to kiss and caress Thee in undisturbed peace. Oh! That I were but drawn into Thee so that I remained insensible to the world! If I am indeed already that way when it concerns the delights of this world, oh, let me be that way too when it concerns its troubles.

Grant that to praise and laud Thee for the rolling of the stone over the door of the sepulcher I may roll the stone of constancy over my heart so that it shall nevermore be opened to the world or vanity. For their going away and leaving Thee alone, let me nevermore go away, but instead sit with eternal solicitude by Thy sepulcher and guard my heart so that Thou wilt nevermore depart from it. I desire to replace in gratitude the grace of persistence lent to the weak women with my own persistence in Thy blood and suffering until I die. But what sort of substantial thanks shall I be able to give for the slander that Thou didst suffer after Thy death and for the name of misleader, given Thee by the envious Jews? Even if I give Thee the most glorious name in the world [as compensation] for this, it is merely what I naturally owe Thee and it by no means amounts to a delectation and compensation. But I want to do what I can, and mindful of their deceit, thank Thee, in divine and worldly things, with the purest truth and with the simplest sincerity. For their malice in trying to hinder Thy Resurrection, I shall wish that this malice be revealed to the entire world, and I shall ever endeavor to make the last honor and transfiguration of Thy glory greater than the first. For Thy willingness to allow Pilate to set guards upon Thee, grant me the willingness to thank Thee, out of the grateful love so greatly owed Thee, to do whatever Thou mightst desire or that might be desired of me in Thy name and on account of Thy love. For the mockery that Thou didst suffer from the securing, let me with extreme care and ardent desire secure in my heart Thy presence and dwelling and seal the stone of steadfastness with Thy blood. In the meantime I desire to burn, smoke, sigh, sing, say, and write: Unto Thee, most praiseworthy Jesus, may there be praise, honor, thanks, glory, fame, splendor, might, magnificence, and immortal exaltation for Thy bitter suffering and dying until my death, which I wish to wish were soon, in fact today, except that I would like to extol Thy immortal fame properly.

Nothing else detains me in this mortal cottage but the desire to lead with my sighing an entire army of devout souls to the honeyed meadow of Thy holy suffering and dying. I would like to open up the eyes of understanding with this heart-honey so that the slain lion of the house of Judah may be given all glory, power, might, strength, and vigor. He is likewise the slaughtered lamb before which I would like to make not only the twenty-four elders there fall on their knees, but here too make all the emperors, kings, and princes fall on their knees and lay their crowns, might, honor, and power at His feet.[177] My heart alone is just too little for me. I would wish to laud and praise my Jesus with hearts and tongues as innumerable as grains of sand.

So come then, you rulers and heads of the realms of the world, with the army of your subjects, which covers everything with dust and dries up rivers, and help me to thank my dearest darling a thousand million times for the many lashes and all the torment, for the death that He suffered for our sakes. It happened for you as well as for me, and He gained for you as much as He gained for me. Therefore do not refuse to aid me in praising. If there be a Christian vein in you, then do not fail to accept this invitation to laud the suffering of Christ. I implore you by your crowns and thrones, indeed, by the blood and wounds of Christ (insofar as you wish to have a part in them), to assent to this pact of praise with me and to urge all your underlings to it. You cannot do otherwise than to accept such a reasonable demand! God inclines His head, Christ's blood and weals move, the Holy Spirit drives, the angels entice, and your own conscience admonishes you to do it. You will certainly not be able to resist all these heavenly inducements. Your own and the salvation of the souls of those who belong to you depend on it and could be lost if you did not want to be a part of it.

But I am completely certain that you will not exclude yourself from such a concluding cadence of praise but instead, as Christian knights, will joyfully accept this challenge to praise and will compete with one another to glorify the loveliest Deoglori.[178] My spurring you on now will start you on this glory track. It is easy to allow oneself to be urged to do pleasant things and to tend to sweet obligations. Noble souls are soon moved and flaming spirits easily drawn up into the air. Thus do I see, my sweet Jesus, that I shall succeed, indeed, that I have already succeeded, in praising and worshiping Thee with a millionfold army of jubilation for Thy wounds and many weals. Oh! Holiest Savior! Accept it as if I accomplished all of it with

177. Rv 4: 4: "Round about the throne were twenty-four seats: and seated on the thrones were twenty-four elders, clad in white garments, with golden crowns upon their heads." Rv 5: 6: "And between the throne and the four living creatures and among the elders, I saw a Lamb standing, as though it had been slain, with seven horns and with seven eyes, which are the seven spirits of God sent out into all the earth." Rv 5: 14: "And the four living creatures said, "Amen!" and the elders fell down and worshiped."

178. The "Deoglori" (glory of God) is the word that Greiffenberg uses in connection with her quasi-mystical experience of spiritual illumination at age eighteen, when in her words she saw the "Deoglori-Licht" (the light of the glory of God). Here she imagines the Deoglori (a feminine noun) as the lady whom knights seek to honor by jousting in a tournament.

my mouth. Let it be pleasing to Thee and let the sun of Thy praise reflect to their salvation.

The highly important, necessary, useful, and blissful duty to thank and praise—the duty by which you, you most august lights of the world, acknowledge yourself to be bound to the Most High on account of His suffering and dying—demands of you the greatest thanksgiving in every way conceivable. Now the greatest gratitude must be the purest gratitude, for what is not pure cannot soar into the air. The purest gratitude is when one ascribes to our Redeemer, Jesus Christ, alone all honor, merit, strength, might, deed, and gaining of our salvation; it is when one gives Him alone the glory of our salvation, excluding the merit and deeds of all the angels and all humankind, when one robs His wounds of not a single droplet of their liquor of redemption but instead ascribes to them the infinite love of universal reconciliation, and when one believes that all the sinners in the world are called to salvation. The purest gratitude is when one believes that there is nothing in nature and creation that can cleanse sin except the blood of Jesus Christ alone, when one places one's trust in it absolutely, believing that it alone—without any help, deed, merit, and addition of humankind—has the divine omnipotent power not only to cleanse us of sin but also to give heaven and salvation to all those who believe in it. It is the purest and consequently the greatest gratitude for the blood and the death of Jesus Christ when one lets His wounds alone be the gates of heaven, indeed, heaven itself. He who would make earthly things into agents that strive alongside Christ to gain these things has not thanked Him purely and greatly for His suffering. Purity is pleasing to the celestially pure Lamb of God.

Pure prayer of the mouth is necessary for the purity of the heart's trust. How can there be pure faith where there is no pure prayer? Out of the abundance of the heart the mouth speaks.[179] What kind of purity is it if I call upon the angels who were created or upon miserable human beings and set them alongside the Creator and Redeemer? It is not pure praise when it is coupled with such a prayer. No person is to be worshiped or called upon for intercession except Him alone who is one person with the Eternal Divinity. His blood, which cries to the heavens, is done a great injustice when we want someone else as our intercessor. It has as many tongues as drops and speaks most eloquently on our behalf with His heavenly father. The mouth of one single such drop is more powerful than all the words of angels and men, even if there were a hundred thousand million of these. One ought to

179. Mt 12: 34.

ask Him alone for intercession, and He suffers Himself to be prevailed upon immediately as He then speaks and promises: "Him who comes to me I will not cast out."[180]

With His drops of blood, the Eternal Word divided Himself up into pure pomegranate seeds, and from each seed a word came to be to speak the word to us. In each ruby of blood resides heavenly eloquence, and [it] wins over the heart of the Omnipotent Father so that He grants the wish. Why then do we want, for God's sake, to run after a handful of water when the divine primal spring gushes forth in superabundance? How should a little wax candle light [the way] for us in the bright midday sunshine? If God (Jesus) is for us, who can be against us?[181] How should the words of this Word that in eternity emerged from God not enter into God's heart to be granted a favorable hearing, especially after He has done penance for our sins and so superabundantly atoned them. But whom can one have eternally more capable as an intercessor with God than Him with whom God Himself conversed about our creation and redemption? With what sort of cordiality can one thank Him anyway, if one does not consider Him the sole sufficient Word and calls on others in addition to Him? Just as He wants to keep the trouble for Himself, so He wants to keep the glory for Himself as well. Thus once again it is the purest thanks that desires no human intercession but hangs onto Him alone who alone hung on the cross for us.

Furthermore, the highest thanks must be the greatest as well. What rises up must necessarily be great; otherwise it would not have force and could not be seen either. So gratitude derives its greatness from the thing that was bestowed and earned for us, namely, here from redemption and salvation. The greater the latter is, the greater the former. Thus we accordingly give that worthy person who gained it for us the greatest thanks when we consider our salvation perfect, certain, sure, pure, and eternal, excluding all further penance, doubt, uncertainty, need for purification, torture, and agony of the soul here and there, all of which runs contrary to and diminishes that perfect thing that He gained for us. His body was itself tortured and tormented for us by the angry fire of the Heavenly Father and hellfire, when at the same time the sins that He took upon Himself from us were swept away and purified so that we would become in Him the righteousness that carries weight with God. Now no righteousness that still requires purification carries weight with God. Thus we became in Christ, before we ever were, the righteousness that surpasses the purity of the angels and that car-

180. Jn 6: 37.

181. Rom 8: 31.

ries weight with God; we therefore had no need of any other purification, but we did need a faith as pure as gold to acquire such and to give God the greatest thanks of all with it.

The highest thanks is also the most humble and reverential thanks. Now a person is neither properly humble nor reverential if he does not consider everything divine that comes from and out of Christ, such as His redemption, Word, wonder, and wounds. If one considers His redemption divine, then one must believe it perfect, superabundant, solely valid, firm, certain, sure, and immutable, all of which are divine characteristics with which no human contingencies can be mingled. If one considers His words divine (as they indeed are), then one must not deny them the judge's office in religious matters and disputes of faith, which is appropriate to divinity alone. If one believes them to be divine, one must respect them clearly and without obscurity, for God is a light in which there is no darkness. If one considers them divine, one must consider them perfect, for God is the highest perfection. If they are perfect, then they suffer no addition, no alteration, and no reversal, all of which is incompatible with perfection. If one considers them divine, then one must necessarily consider them the highest wisdom, which in everything is to be believed and followed without contradiction. For the highest wisdom can in divine things pronounce the best judgment and be the most just judge of all—like Solomon in earthly things.[182] If one considers them divine, then one must consider them the highest goodness as well, whose desire it is that every person derive life and comfort from them and that would not want us to make them the cause of quarreling and a discordant bone of contention, but rather would want them to serve us as a clear well in which we see the will of the Heavenly Father, Christ's merit, and the beams of the Holy Spirit, which ignite us to do nothing but laud and love God and humankind on account of the glorious redemption. Furthermore, if we consider them divine, we must actively believe in them. For divinity is subject to no death; instead everything in it is full of spirit and life. If they are alive, then they can speak; for speech indicates life. If they can speak, then they can mediate disputes and pronounce the most just verdict.

Thus it demonstrates the utmost reverence toward God to consider His Word holy, wise, good, and living; to leave all decisions, verdicts, and judgment to Him; and to submit obediently to His teaching and tenets and also not to allow the slightest thing to be altered, diminished, increased, or

182. Solomon (848–796 BCE), king of Israel, was known for his wisdom. The Luther Bible attributes authorship of three books of the Bible to Solomon by naming them "The Proverbs of Solomon," "The Preacher Solomon" (Ecclesiastes), and "The Song of Solomon."

decreased in them but instead to regard these, like a single divinity, as the only guiding principle of life and faith. Without this submissiveness, one cannot give God the highest thanks, and without the highest thanks, no one is pleasing to him. The Most High wants the highest, and the highest issues from the most profound obedience. Thus the highest gratitude is also the most obedient thanks, which cannot consist in one's own choice of the manner of serving [God]. Only wisdom that is just as profound as God's highness knows the way in which divine majesty is to be served. All service outside of the command of the divine majesty is disobedience or disservice, and good intention is at the very least a childish transgression. In order to guard against such failings, the Infinite Goodness revealed His will in the Divine Word and thereby opened up a wide field of action in which to fulfill our duty to obey Him and to realize our eagerness to serve Him. Thus refusing to be mindful of grace and wanting to serve according to our own lights amount to the utmost disobedience and ingratitude, especially since pleasing is always connected to obedience.

How can there be greater delight and pleasure than drinking in Holy Communion the blood of the Redeemer out of the well of sweetness itself according to the command of His holy words? One is easily urged to pleasant things, but to despise the commanded and offered greeting of sweetness itself is as unnatural as it is sinful. Shall His Divine Word give way to the insanity of a brooding human brain? Oh! Not that! Let us stay with Christ's words! He will, like the rod of Moses, swallow the serpents of doubt and smash the rocks of wrath so that the ship of our obedience may enter the port of His wounds without danger of crashing against them.[183] Following Christ is pure certainty. How can the Way itself lead us astray, mock truth, and dispatch life to death? Obedience is better than sacrifice, and all the more so, the more unerring is God's Word compared with the thoughts of humankind.

I say with my Jesus: Shall I not drink the cup that my heavenly father has given me?[184] How would Scripture, the words of my Jesus, be fulfilled: "Drink of it, all of you"?[185] Obeying God blindly is being the most prudent,

183. Ex 7: 9–12. At the command of God, Moses and Aaron go to Pharaoh. Aaron casts down his rod, and it becomes a serpent. When all of Pharaoh's wise men and sorcerers cast down their rods, these likewise become serpents, but Aaron's rod swallows up theirs. This event is to serve as one of the many wonders and signs preceding the Exodus.

184. Jn 18: 11: "Jesus said to Peter, 'Put up your sword into its sheath; shall I not drink the cup which the Father has given me?'" These are Jesus' words to Peter after Peter attempts to defend Jesus when he is first arrested.

185. Mt 26: 27.

and one thereby shows that one places infinite trust in His eternal omnipotence. Obedience is and remains an obligation that cannot be neglected, without which God and Christ can be neither properly served nor thanked. If one does not wish to obey Christ in sweet things like drinking His holy blood, what must He expect from us in bitter things? If one deigns not to drink the ruby nectar of His blessed cup, how then should one ever take from Him the embittered cup of myrrh of the bitter cross? If one wants not the roses, what will happen with the thorns? Oh! Shall the earth make bold to chop down the well pipes of heaven? Shall it appropriate the power to forbid what the former commands? [The earth] certainly cannot nullify the last will of Him who created it from nothing! No creature has the right to alter the laws of the Creator. Thus the spirit of Christ cannot teach contrary to Christ. Anything other than what Christ says is not from the Holy Spirit, for He and the Father and the Son are one being and of one mind. How can one give God obedient thanks for His wounds when one refuses to stretch out one's hand for their dear blood?

If one were to believe Christ complete in one form and to seek the holy blood in the body, how would Christ's commands and will be done, and what would become of obedience to the letter? He speaks not only of eating but also of drinking. He commanded us to drink the blood, not the blood in His body but that which was spilled for us from it. And when, as we know, one of them is just as holy as the other, how can either of them be denied to laymen?[186] Did the All-Provident One neglect to do something that could be improved upon? Shall the immortal God be guided by mortal men? Must Heavenly Wisdom suffer herself to be justified and complained about by her children?[187] Oh, no! It is a divine matter that has been wisely thought out from eternity and that the world can as little alter as improve. God certainly handed over the keys to His heavenly goods, treasures, and sacraments to His church and its servants on earth—just as a potentate hands over the keys to his chancellor—so that they may apportion and administer them

186. Greiffenberg goes to battle here against Catholic Communion rites whereby the celebrants need receive only the wafer, the body of Christ. According to Catholic theology the bread that has become Christ's body through transubstantiation also contains his blood. Luther argued that both should be distributed to the congregation. See Lee Palmer Wandel, *The Eucharist in the Reformation: Incarnation and Liturgy* (Cambridge: Cambridge University Press, 2006), 94–138, esp. 99, and 217.

187. Greiffenberg most certainly means God here, but when she employs the feminine noun *Weisheit* (wisdom) and speaks of wisdom's children, she again fleetingly appears to speak of God in a feminine aspect, that is, God as wisdom personified as woman. I have for this reason again chosen here by way of exception to make obvious the feminine personification. See above, note 37.

according to His command. He did not, however, surrender them to them so that they could do with them as they pleased or keep a part of them for themselves.

Thus it remains incontrovertibly true that the highest gratitude due the Highest One for His suffering and dying has to be the most obedient one. Just as no obedience can exist without humility, it therefore follows too that the highest must be the most humble gratitude, because before God humility and lowliness are the highest. It is, however, proper humility when one submits to all the laws and commands of God and suffers oneself to be reminded of them and thus instructed, even by a most unimportant person; when one is ashamed of no regret and no change; when one endangers one's own high standing in order to make the humble words of Christ prevail; when one places one's honor in the dust in order to further the honor of God; when one denies one's own power and reputation in order to allow for the authority of the Divine Word; when one surrenders one's reason and wisdom to divine obedience; when one lets go of one's old opinion and habits when a beam of divine truth shines in one's eyes; when one falls down before divine majesty, regrets and casts off one's contrariness, recognize it and freely and openly confesses it, and submits oneself along with all one's underlings to the Word and will of God. Nothing is low enough for humility to demonstrate its unending submissiveness. Dust and ashes, shame and dishonor, are the elements in which it is wont to live and remain safe and sound.

This humility must, however, be heartfelt; otherwise it is supreme hypocrisy. The highest thanks must be the most heartfelt thanks. What does not come from the heart is not taken to heart either. He who created the heart wishes to enjoy its sweetest fruits, which are love and gratitude. Just as nothing in the nut is good but the kernel, nothing in gratitude is good but the heart. Heartfelt gratitude is the pouring out of all ardent powers and desires into laudation and love of Jesus, indeed, the spurting out of all emotions of love. It is a turning round of the heart into the sea of God's goodness, there where it, as it were, swims and floats with delight and becomes so intoxicated with the contemplation of the divine infinity of love that it reels with rapturous knowledge. This knowledge bursts out in the most ardent desire to employ the whole possibility of the power of love to serve and praise God in the extreme. The entire bettering of one's life depends on this desire to praise. The smallest blood vessel will not go unchanged. Everything is willing to submit to purity and ability to praise. The resolve to give thanks is so ardent that it must weep bloody tears over all hindering weaknesses that occur daily with human frailty. One wishes to be outside of one's body in order to escape the hindrances that it is wont to create. What then prevails in the soul are thoughts of thanks, at whose feet all other thoughts must fall. Not only is the entire heart there, but it wishes for everything to become heart just so one could thank God quite heartily.

Cordial gratitude toward God also commits us to cordial love of our neighbor. "What therefore God has joined together, let not man put asunder."[188] Since God gave us only one heart for both loves, one cannot thank Him in a heartfelt manner when they are not both to be found therein. Gratitude wants the heart with all of its dispositions, as it is most pleasing to God. Now there is nothing more pleasing to God than love, which He Himself is and which He commanded in the highest and practiced to the utmost.[189] Thus all of Christian life and the complete fulfillment of the law flow from heartfelt gratitude, which is nothing other than heartfelt love of God and one's neighbor. From this it becomes clear how every single thing depends on the heart, just as the fulfillment of the law must come from the Gospel and good works from faith and gratitude for the suffering of Christ. For gratitude from the heart must also be gratitude in deed. Just as little as a heart lacks a beat, so little does its love lack effect. A spring cannot do otherwise than pour out a brooklet. As little as fire can leave off burning, all the less can a heart leave off giving indications of its love. As surely as a stone will fall to the earth, so unfailingly does the plumb line of love plummet into the foundation of completion. When the heart applies the spurs, the horse can—as their effect—do nothing but gallop. When the weight of desire raises the little hammer of the will, it has to strike. The cup of the heart filled to overflowing must flow over into works.

The highest gratitude cannot be accorded the Eternal Weaver either, if it be not true gratitude. It must consist of deed and substance that are pleasing to the Infinite Primal Being. He whose words are pure genesis is not to be contented with words of gratitude that are void of deeds. Because His speech is pure doing, our gratitude should also be pure deed. Since He is wont to effect with His words, He thus requires our works too as words of gratitude. When God gave the law of the sacrifice of thanksgiving, He said explicitly: he shall bring it with his hand![190] From that we see that the hand,

188. Mk 10: 9.

189. 1 Jn 4: 8: "He who does not love does not know God; for God is love." 1 Jn 4: 16: "So we know and believe the love God has for us. God is love, and he who abides in love abides in God, and God abides in him."

190. Lv 7: 30, which Greiffenberg herself cites, belongs to a description of the ritual of sacrifice in which the person wishing to make a burnt offering to the Lord is to bring it to the alter himself: "he shall bring with his own hands the offerings by fire to the LORD; he shall bring the fat with the breast, that the breast may be waved as a wave offering before the LORD."

that is, the deed and effect, must be present. Good works and deeds can just as little be excluded from heartfelt gratitude as can the midpoint or center of the circle from the compass. For God created humankind so that He could communicate to them His goodness and do good for the one through the other.

What is to be the highest must also be perfect, for without perfection nothing can attain the highest, because the highest has nothing to do with increase. What suffers no addition is perfection. That which is to please the Highest Eternal Perfection must be perfect. However, because it alone is perfect, it cannot be otherwise thanked to perfection and in the highest except through perfection, namely, through Jesus Christ. Now giving thanks through Jesus Christ is when one ascribes all the glory of one's righteousness and salvation to His merit alone; when one seeks heaven only in the hollows of His wounds; when one demands intercession and a plea for mercy from His holy mouth alone; when one allows His Divine Word to be the scepter, oracle, and guiding principle in all matters of faith and the soul; when one receives with the ardor of a rutting stag His holy blood, according to His command, neglecting all human fancy; when one clothes oneself with His gentleness and humility, applies oneself fully to [imitating] His obedience and virtuous life, and takes from Jesus' heart the sincerity of one's own; when one completely and deliberately submits to His will with the infinite confidence that His perfection, to its glory and our salvation, will in the most glorious manner work and set right everything in our nothingness.

This is the most perfect kind of gratitude, which is pleasing to God and can be accomplished in our imperfection. Our lowliness and weakness cannot manage anything higher, and God does not demand anything higher either. Rather He accepts it as perfect because it happens in perfection, in His son, who makes everything perfect that happens in His name, however weak and frail those things may be. This gratitude is then so lofty, you lofty ones who assist in praising, that you cannot be ashamed; so reasonable and obliging that you cannot work yourselves loose; so deserving that you cannot refuse it; and so pressing that you cannot put it off. What can be more glorious and proper to your highness than when you see to it that the highness of the Most High is praised most highly? What is more fitting than your giving utmost thanks to Him who made you uppermost on earth?

You are captured for the most glorious freedom. You are entangled by the most binding bonds of the sweetness of the laudation of Jesus. No one can absolve himself of this obligation, not even heaven itself that desires it above all to be fulfilled. Your crowns do not hinder you in this; rather they incite you to do it, for the Highest One demands of those high up the highest praise. You are the wheels of His triumphal chariot of praise that all underlings must follow as serfs of laudation. The scepters of great potentates should be victory and glory columns of the heavenly Deoglori. It is a pressing obligation to praise God to the highest degree with one's land and people, for God will seek in the head what the limbs neglect to do. The sun must account for illumination for the stars, and the staff must be responsible for the shadow's being identical with it.

Oh! You illustrious ones! With however many millions you fall at your Savior's feet here in highest gratitude, you shall see yourselves surrounded by as many stars streaming from heaven on that great day. Not only your duty but your heavenly bliss incites you to do this. As many souls as you lead with your lofty example and command to the highest gratitude, as many paradises filled with joy shall await you there. Oh! Increase your blessed heavenly state then by increasing the glory of God on earth. Do not be ashamed to follow a little footpath that leads to great splendor. You can make eternal your estate that you have here on earth; you can become princes of heaven and suns among the elect, just as you are now earthly princes and suns under the sun. Honor God, you earthly gods, who so highly honors you here and will in turn honor you there eternally.

I think that you overlooked the importance [of praising God] when I made my first simple appeal to you to praise [Him] and that you are somewhat taken aback by this manifesto. But how can you complain of me when after merely admonishing you to go with me to the little shepherd's cottage, I now take you to a splendid palace? When I promised you simple milk and now proffer you a holy soup of pearls like Cleopatra?[191] I promised you miserable plums and now serve you pomegranates. You expected crystals and now get rubies and diamonds instead. Can you even say that I deceived you? What king or prince would not, if a second Columbus came before him to discover a new golden world for him, be eager to seize it with the greatest haste?[192] But what is this one compared to the world that I present you to be seized through the highest expression of gratitude? Who would not gladly follow a Virgin of Orleans if she meant to make him seize a kingdom?[193] But

191. The text refers to a story reported by Pliny of Cleopatra. In the presence of Anthony, Cleopatra took a precious pearl earring from her ear and dropped it in a concoction that dissolved it. She then drank it. Pliny the Elder, *Natural History*, trans. H. Rackham, 10 vols., Loeb Classical Library (Cambridge: Harvard University Press, 1950) 3: 243–46 (9.58.119–21).

192. The text refers to Christopher Columbus (1451–1506), whose four voyages led him to the Americas, which at the time were for Europeans uncharted territory.

193. The text refers here to Joan of Arc (1412–31) who, compelled by voices that she thought came from God, rallied Charles VII of France during the Hundred Years War to fight back

why not all the more gladly follow these admonitions to give thanks when one can conquer an eternal kingdom in the Kingdom of Heaven?

Is it then wrong to learn the art of the angels, which consists purely of divine praise, and thus to become a great angel? What have the seven wonders of the world gained in the way of great fame and name? But what are they compared with the love and the Passion of Christ and compared with the praise and gratitude that we owe Him for this? Him—the most splendid mausoleum conceivable is due Him. I will take the place of His beloved, His bride, His queen; I will herewith erect to His memory and my love the most beautiful marvel of a grave.[194] You august princes ought to be the jewels and towers on it, your realms and lands ought to be its walls of constancy and its gates of praise. Oh! Come to it, you artists of the Holy Spirit, and help me carry out this construction of wounds and wonders. I will meanwhile scatter the holy relics of my darling (His body and blood) in my food and drink to eat them with the bread and wine (in Holy Communion). I intend to mix the ashes of repentance among my tears and sighs and to make them my food and drink until the glorious glory temple of His death and the mausoleum of His immortal memory is finished so that I can have myself buried there with Him.

An Egyptian pyramid or a column of fire, built purely of the flames of the Holy Spirit, is due Him, my sweetest Jesus.[195] His glory, which towers above all the heavens, deserves from us a colossus of praise that reaches to the clouds like the sun of justice and the fountain of illumination.[196] We ought to set up to His glory an eternally burning Pharos torch to light up the corners of the earth so that those who float on the sea of vanity will have a light to spot and find the landing place for heaven.[197] We ought to thank

against the English and Burgundians, which led eventually to Charles's coronation in Reims. Ultimately Joan was taken captive by the English, tried and convicted as a heretic, and burned at the stake in Rouen. In Greiffenberg's day she had not yet been canonized.

194. The text refers to the mausoleum at Halicarnassus, one of the so-called seven wonders of the ancient world, built by Artemisia for her husband Mausolos. Before the monument was completed, Artemisia ingested the ashes of her husband so that she could serve as his funeral urn.

195. The text refers to the great pyramid of Giza, one of the so-called seven wonders of the ancient world.

196. The text refers to the Colossus of Rhodes, one of the seven wonders of the ancient world.

197. The text refers to the lighthouse of Alexandria on Pharos Island, which is part of Alexandria. The lighthouse, one of the so-called seven wonders of the ancient world, was said to be the tallest building in the world. It lit up the sky by night with fire; by day, it used a great mirror that reflected the sun's rays.

Him infinitely, the heavenly Jove or Jehovah, by setting up His marvelous image, the new human being, in the temple of the heart and by holding the Olympic (heavenly) games.[198]

One ought to build to His incomparable Deoglori, the chaste Diana, the eager huntress of our souls, the silvery white moon of Christ's church, a temple of glory to the teaching of Saint Paul of Ephesus, a temple of white marble of the purest fear of God. The Amazons, the bellicose women, destroyed the first temple constructed there.[199] Oh! Would that on the contrary many pious women would assist me in fighting for God's glory and help me lay the first cornerstone of the temple of the Deoglori. You, however, you august pillars of the world, be pillars of God's glory and support this edifice as did the 120 Asiatic kings in that one.[200] You European grand seigneurs! Do not fail to match their feat—just as you match them in number, indeed, probably even surpass them, if one were to count all the exalted houses and heads. Oh! Begin soon and hurry, you august venerators of God and holy heroes! No one can promise you that you will have as much time as they did. So further your edifice of heaven and bring about in time what can delight you in eternity, namely, the glory of God.

I was promised to this while still in my mother's womb and have since then myself devoted and offered up all my life and doings to it. I knew of no better way of attending to this offering and vow than with this public eulogy and expression of gratitude for my Savior's holy suffering and dying. I herewith place this [work] once again most humbly at Thy feet, O Jesus, who art most worthy of being praised by all the angels and ask Thee graciously to accept it. You, however, you august persons of high rank, I charge you in conclusion by the Supremely Holy Trinity and by the supremely

198. The text refers to the statue of Zeus at Olympia, one of the so-called seven wonders of the ancient world. The statue of Zeus enthroned was so large that it barely fit in the temple. The Olympic Games were held in Zeus's honor. The text also picks up on Gn 1: 27: "So God created man in his own image, in the image of God he created him." Jesus himself is referred to as the second Adam as he redeemed humankind from the sin brought into the world by God's first creation, Adam. Rom 5: 15–20 describes the new being with Christ. I thank Rev. Paula V. Mehmel for this last reference.

199. The text refers here to the temple of Artemis at Ephesus (in Asia Minor), one of the so-called seven wonders of the ancient world. The temple held statues of Amazons, who were said to have been the founders of Ephesus. Paul preached in Ephesus at a time when the temple was still standing.

200. According to Pliny, the temple of Artemis at Ephesus had 127 pillars, each of which had been constructed by a king. It took 120 years to construct it. Pliny the Elder, *Natural History*, 3: 243–46 (36.21.95). In Greiffenberg's text the number of years is confused with the number of pillars.

holy blood of Jesus Christ to realize and to write in the hearts of your subjects what I have written in this book. Persevere now at the end of the world to make the glory of God infinite so that His grace places you in the infinity of joy. And when you have fulfilled my wish that this be spread throughout the world, God will in turn fill heaven with you and your subjects. Oh, yes, Lord Jesus, fill

> the heavens and the earth with souls and glory;[201]
> what I yearn for
> grant me fully.
> Amen! In the name that can do all things!
> Lord Jesus, Thou truth! Say Thou amen too.
> Yes, Jesus! On earth make come to pass in splendor
> whate'er increases Thy glory without ending.

201. Greiffenberg employs here the rhyme scheme *aaabbcc*. The first, fourth, and fifth lines are written in dactylic tetrameter and are ten or eleven syllables in length, depending on whether they end in a masculine or feminine rhyme. Lines 2 and 3 have two beats each to the line, end in feminine rhymes, and consist of five and six syllables, respectively. The final two lines are written largely in dactyls with five and four beats to the line, respectively; they consist of twelve syllables each and end in a feminine rhyme.

> Himmel und Erde / mit Seelen und Ehren;
> meine begehren /
> mit vollem gewähren.
> Amen! im Namen / der alles vermag!
> JEsu / du Warheit! das Amen auch sag.
> Ja / JEsu! auf Erden höchst-herrlich vollende /
> was mehret dein Ehre / ohn einiges ENDE.

TWELVE DEVOUT MEDITATIONS ON THE SUPREMELY HOLY INCARNATION, BIRTH, AND YOUTH OF JESUS CHRIST

by his most ardent lover and most zealously devoted admirer,

Catharina Regina Frau von Greiffenberg, née Baroness of Seisenegg.

WRITTEN AND EXECUTED TO MAGNIFY GOD'S GLORY AND TO AWAKEN TRUE DEVOTION

Nuremberg

PUBLISHED BY JOHANN HOFMANN, DEALER IN BOOKS

AND ART. PRINTED BY ANDREAS KNORZEN

IN 1678 A.D.

Figure 8. H[ans]. J[acob]. Schollenberger, "Grasp of the Ungraspable" from *Der allerheiligsten Menschwerdung, Geburt, und Jugend JEsu Christi* (1678). Herzog August Bibliothek, Wolfenbüttel: Portrait Collection (Th 1058).

II
MEDITATIONS ON THE INCARNATION OF JESUS CHRIST

To the one, true, living and infinite eternal God, Father of Our Lord Jesus Christ Almighty, Creator of Heaven and Earth, My Dearest Heavenly Father.[1]

MOST HUMBLE DEDICATION

Thou infinite source of all things, Thou substance of all substance, Thou wellspring of divinity and all good, Thou eternal beginning without beginning and infinite end without end! Thou didst create us in the beginning for the purpose of eternal enjoyment of Thine uncreated joy-infinity, and when we, as a result of our disobedience, allowed Thy Word to slip from our hearts and thus made ourselves incapable of this sweet end of creation, Thou didst turn Thy Word and heart to us anew, indeed didst share it with us, or rather didst give it to us wholly and in it didst give Thyself when Thy begotten son became flesh in order for us to become the children of God. A thousand times a thousand tongues of seraphim cannot express this miraculous grace and gracious miracle. Not satisfied with this, Thou givest me too Thy Holy Spirit, which with His flaming tongue writes this into my heart and suffers me to write of it: that I, among many thousands (Jews and Turks) who neither know it nor wish to know it, perceive it, and that I, among countless many who do know it but pay it no heed, honor and worship it to the greatest degree possible and that I delight in it too. How can

1. This translation of the meditations on the incarnation of Jesus is based on the reprint of the one and only edition of Catharina Regina von Greiffenberg, *Der Allerheiligsten Menschwerdung / Geburt und Jugend JEsu Christi,* vol. 3 of *Sämtliche Werke,* ed. Martin Bircher and Friedhelm Kemp (Millwood, NY: Kraus Reprint, 1983).

I, since Thou hast given me Thy heart in and with Thy self-sufficient Word, do otherwise than give Thee in turn my heart in and with these words that tell of and extol that Word? To whom else can I dedicate the description of His birth than to Him who suffered it to be made known to us several thousand years ago and who gave Him eternal birth? To whom ought I more properly to dedicate this, my writing, than to Him who gave Himself to me myself for myself in the image or script of His heart? To the Father of the primordially self-sufficient Word are properly due all words that speak of and honor the Primal Word. To the father who means to be honored only in the son, one properly ascribes all honor that shall be written of the son. I can therefore present this honoring of the birth of Thy Son to no one better than Thee, the Omnipotent Father, from whose grace without beginning He and all salvation and honor infinitely spring forth. Receive it graciously, Thou unfathomable Archgrace, and let it be pleasing to Thee in and through that person whom Thou wast pleased to favor with Thy good will. If there be something good therein, then it is of Thy Spirit, which inspired it in me. If anything be unfit, then these are my mistakes, which I hope Thou wilt graciously forgive. Thou heavenly all-encompassing eye! Thou seest the project I tender in Thine honor. Dispose of it through Thy supremely wise wondrous disposition and let it achieve its desirable end. Let these swaddling clothes of Jesus be the thread that winds Thy glory out of the labyrinth and suffers it to be worshiped by the entire world. If I have achieved this, then I have achieved enough and well invested my time and industry, which have my whole life long spun and woven this thread and these swaddling clothes. If it does not come to pass here, then it will nevertheless come to pass there, and all the angels will praise the Deoglori along with me, just as here I have sung the Gloria in excelsis along with them.[2] In the meantime, let this [project] be agreeable to Thee in Thy most agreeable one—[let it be] favored in the beloved—and do not disdain as a nanny a poor shepherdess, for whose sake Thou once didst find the shepherds worthy to witness this miracle.[3] Graciously let my childish babbling about Thy child, who is wisdom itself, be pleasing to Thee until, with the tongue of an

2. "Deoglori" (God's glory) is the word that Greiffenberg applies generally to her mission to spread the glory of God in word and deed during the last days of the world. "Gloria in excelsis" is the Latin for "glory to God in the highest" (Lk 2: 14), that is, part of the greeting that the angels sang to the shepherds when Jesus Christ was born.

3. Greiffenberg asks God to favor her writing because she writes about his beloved son. When she invokes the shepherds who witnessed the miracle on her account she recalls again that the birth of Jesus Christ saved all of humankind. She refers here to the shepherds who were keeping watch by night and to whom angels appeared announcing the birth of Jesus (Lk 2: 8–20).

angel, I laud and praise Thee in heaven, O Heavenly Father, together with Thy Divine and Incarnate Son and the Holy Spirit. In the meantime permit me, Almighty Creator of Heaven and Earth, to call and confess myself before the entire world to be

The most humble obedient handmaiden of Thy divine majesty,
Catharina Regina, Frau von Greiffenberg
Seisenegg, 27/17 *Jan.* 1678[4]

PREFATORY REMARKS TO THE NOBLE READER

Be not amazed, high-minded reader, if you hear me speaking childishly of the childhood of our Eternal Father and babbling immaturely about the immaturity of the substantial Word. Consider that the angels themselves cannot speak worthily enough of it.[5] What, then, shall I, unworthy woman, do? Since Wisdom itself was not afraid to become a child, you should have no reservations about hearing something childish from me. Do not expect lofty words: I speak of a child who humbled Himself among all creatures and not of lofty Wisdom. I make it my calling to be abased, small, and childish with Him. You will not find what you seek if you seek something here other than love and simplicity. Love, which drew my Redeemer from heaven, draws me to His crib and opens my lips to proclaim His glory. I seek His glory and not mine. I seek nothing with this but the joy of having the world praise and laud Him with my words and thoughts. I seek not my own glory but God's, thereby to spread the Deoglori in the world. Thus I did not choose to follow the wise and clever advice of several learned good friends to append to the work, as is fitting, a Latin digest of the Church Fathers, which thing I certainly could do, but which I have refrained from doing to show that I flee from all vain honor and glory.[6] A learned and well-read person will certainly see that I have not cited them falsely and improperly but in-

4. Greiffenberg marks the date by both the old Julian calendar (17 January 1678) and the new Gregorian calendar (27 January 1678), which was introduced in 1582.

5. Greiffenberg here again uses the words "unmündig" and "Unmündigkeit," which I have translated here as "immaturely" and "immaturity" to retain her wordplay. These words have several meanings and can refer to the inability to speak or do certain things as well as the legal status of children and women who cannot represent themselves. Here Greiffenberg refers to Jesus' submitting of himself to the normal human process of being carried in the womb, being born, and of growing up.

6. The text refers here to "allegata" (sayings, allegations), presumably a digest of patristic writing on the subject of incarnation.

stead have made well-founded and truthful reference to them. Others would not have taken the trouble anyway to follow up and look them up. It thus would have been a vain vanity such as I have long since renounced. Be not surprised either, dear reader, that only in the first meditation on the eternal divinity of Christ do I make use of the testimonies and pronouncements of the Church Fathers and First Church and that afterward in the others I have mostly omitted these; [it may look] as if I intended merely to display a lot [of knowledge] and then accomplish little or only to start off high and afterward let everything drop. No! It is not meant that way, but instead occurs with forethought and deliberation. Since this very point about the divinity of Christ was the main foundation and cornerstone of the entire work, it had therefore to be well established and proven. For if this thing is believed, all the rest is true and credible in itself so that it does not require much more proof. If I have from time to time been too long-winded or if I have repeated the ineffable miracle of incarnation too often, one ought to consider that no person can say too much about Him of whom all the angels cannot get enough. If I have perhaps made too much use of prosopopoeiae or used them in a fashion other than what is customary, namely, not [just] for inert things but also for animated and activated people, then be it known that the holy fathers did it before me.[7] Inasmuch as it was permitted to them, it is not forbidden to me. Furthermore, I mean not to excuse my mistakes, hoping that the courteous reader will do it for me and also be forbearing with the printer's mistakes. Whoever desires the honey of the love and worship of Jesus will not precisely trace out the little wax houses with a compass to determine whether they are aligned diametrically and are hexagonal but instead will be contented with the sweet liquid even if it does not come from a cell that is a [master]work of architecture. Whoever desires highly intellectual, ingenious, learned, and profound things must seek them not here but instead with highly intelligent Aristotle, with wise Plato, with eloquent Cicero and Demosthenes, and with those who in our own time fill their

7. Richard A. Lanham describes prosopopaeia as follows: "an imaginary or absent person is represented as speaking or acting." *A Handlist of Rhetorical Terms: A Guide for Students of English Literature* (Berkeley: University of California Press, 1969), 83. Prosopopaeia refers in other words to staging absent, dead, supernatural or inanimate beings through writing. Pierre Fontanier, *Les figures du discours* (Paris: Flammarion, 1977), 404. Greiffenberg's language in this sentence is opaque, but it appears that she makes an apology here for recreating religious figures in her text, e.g., the Virgin Mary, Joseph, and Elizabeth, and putting words into their mouths. In the doubling that is characteristic of her style she speaks of "lebend- und einkommenden Personen" (people who are becoming alive and coming in [to the work]), presumably meaning persons whom her writing is reanimating.

shoes.[8] With a poor shepherdess, one must expect nothing but a simple lullaby, with which she sets love and devotion to singing. If it is received kindly and I am redeemed from my enemy, I shall further employ my life to meditate on my Redeemer's life and shall soon give the well-disposed reader something more to read. If not, this will be my last work and perhaps it will be more charming when its author lies in the grave, where she is to be laid as the constant friend of all those who love God and virtue.

Catharina Regina, Frau von Greiffenberg.

Explanation of the Copper Frontispiece

The infinite God, whose summit cannot be reached,[9]
whom angels' fiery understanding cannot grasp,
whom heaven's circles leave off attempting to grasp,
I have Him now, oh, miracle, in mine own hand.
Substantial Wisdom that lights up everything,

8. Aristotle (384–322 BCE), Greek philosopher and student of Plato; Plato (ca. 427–ca. 347 BCE), Greek philosopher; Marcus Tullius Cicero (106–43 BCE), Roman orator, statesman, and political theorist; Demosthenes (384–322 BCE), Greek orator and statesman.

9. See figure 8. The sixteen-line explanation of the emblem in verse that follows is written according to the rhyme scheme *ababcdcdefefghgh* and consists of alexandrines, that is, twelve- or thirteen-syllable lines, depending on whether the line concludes with a stressed or unstressed syllable. While the translation that follows does not attempt to reproduce the accentual meter or the rhyme, it does observe the syllabic meter. See above, chap. 1, note 1. I have followed this same practice with all of the poetry in this chapter.

Dem unendlichen Gott / des Höh' nicht zu erreichen /
und unbegreifflich ist der Engel Feuer-Verstand /
dem alle Himmel-Kreis / ihn zu begreiffen / weichen /
den hab' / O Wunder! ich anjetzt in meiner Hand.
Die wesend Weisheit so das ganze All' umstralet /
aus Liebes-Witze wird ein Einfalt-volles Kind.
Dem unbegreifflichen auf diese Weis gefallet
von uns begriffen seyn / sich in die Windeln windt.
Der in Drey-Einigen vollkommen wahres Wesen
Selbständig höchster GOtt / nimt nun die Menschheit an!
zum Heiles Werkzeug / daß in solcher wir genesen /
in der Unendlichkeit / begreifflich uns seyn kan.
O Wunder! meine Hand demselben kan begreiffen /
der unbegreifflich doch der Himmel Himmel ist.
Wie? ist sie weiter dann als Aller Himmel Reiffen?
Nein: Allheit wird ein Mensch / ein Kind mein Jesus Christ!

Kathleen Foley-Beining points out that the title of the emblem, "Grasp of the Ungraspable," is meant both literally and figuratively. She furthermore speculates that the German title, "Begriff des Unbegreifflichen," may be intended to play with the author's name, Greiffenberg (*Body and Eucharistic Devotion*, 43). *Greifen* means "to grasp" in German. The punning continues in the poem.

from the wit of love a simple child comes to be.
It pleases the ungraspable to be grasped by us
in this way by wrapping Himself in swaddling clothes.
The being, completely real in the Trinity,
supreme, self-acting God, takes on humanity
as salvation's tool that we be thereby restored,
that all of us could grasp it in infinity.
O Miracle! My hand can grasp the very one
who is ungraspable yet is the heavens' heaven.
How? Is my hand broader than all the heavens' rings?
Oh no: Allness becomes a man; a child, my Christ!

[Greiffenberg opens these twelve meditations by contemplating the divinity of Christ. To speak of Christ's divinity, she must also ponder the nature of the trinity, that is, of the hypostatic union of Father, Son, and Holy Spirit. She reflects on what it means for the Son to be uncreated and everlasting, and distinct from, co-equal, and co-terminal with the Father and the Holy Spirit in the trinity, and what it means to be eternally begotten by the father and yet to become incarnate in history. She thus begins the first meditation, not included here, with the first verse of the Gospel according to John: "In the beginning was the word," which she here as elsewhere also applies to her own writing as she asks for divine help in understanding the Gospel, finding the right words, and making a beginning. She bases the rest of the meditation on Jn 1: 1–5 and Jn 1: 9–14, omitting the self-referential verses Jn 1: 6–8.]

Explanation of the Emblem

The vast and wide sea flows, completely without stopping,[10]
round this great orb, encloses it within itself
and holds it in its arms. Thus nothing can be found
that in the globe could contain it within itself

10. See figure 9. This emblem introduces the following meditation. The explanation of the emblem that follows consists of twenty lines, written in rhymed couplets, some of which are imperfect. The lines themselves are all alexandrines.

Das weit / und breite Meer ganz unaufhaltlich fließet /
um dieses große Rund / dasselb in sich beschließet /
und in den Armen hält. Daher sich nichtes findt /
daß in dem Erden-Ball in sich es fassen künt /
dieweil es viel zu groß. Doch ist die Kunst noch größer /
wann solcher sperret auf die Weisheit ihre Schlößer
des innersten Verstands. Dieweil die Seh-Kunst macht /
daß es in eine Schal durch Perspectiv gebracht /

Figure 9. H[ans]. J[acob]. Schollenberger, "The Most in the Least" from *Der allerheiligsten Menschwerdung, Geburt, und Jugend JEsu Christi* (1678). Herzog August Bibliothek, Wolfenbüttel: Portrait Collection (Th 1058).

---

von Felsen zugericht / die in die Schmäl es bringen.
Kan dieses nun die Kunst / solls nicht viel mehr gelingen
der Künste Ursprung GOtt? daß Uberschwänglichkeit
werd in ein schwachs Gefäß der Sterblichkeit geleit /
das weite Gottheit-Meer / in eine änge Schale
des Jungfräulichichen Leibs? daß gleich die Gottheit walle
in und auch auser ihr / daß sie den wahren Gott

since it is much too great. Greater still is the art,
however, when for this, Wisdom opens her locks
of inmost understanding. Meanwhile optics' art
uses perspective to cast it into a basin,
prepared by cliffs that force it into the narrows.
If this art can do, shall not God, source of the arts,
even better succeed in guiding boundlessness
into a fragile vessel of mortality,
the wide-flung godhead-sea into the narrow basin
of the virgin's womb? So the divine can float both
in and out of her, she can conceive the true God
real-substantially, and yet the remaining sea,
without miscarriage, free, unhindered, plunges forth;
the wave-infinity is painterly foreshortened,
perfect within the basin, complete outside it,
a God in the womb and in the Trinity's sea.

MEDITATION ON THE INCARNATION OF CHRIST

Divine truth, which had many thousands of years ago prophesied itself, chose now to fulfill itself. The self-sufficient Word that promised itself in paradise now suffers itself to be announced by an angel. The seed of woman promised by the Word to the first woman intends through the seed of the divine message to be sown in a woman in order to take on from her the seed of Abraham, human nature. The ascension from on high will enter lowliness to conduct us lowly ones to heaven. The highest work possible in heaven and on earth begins to make a humble, childish, and small beginning so that it can achieve a sublimely glorious and triumphant end.

The angel Gabriel was sent from God to a city of Galilee named Nazareth, to a virgin betrothed to a man whose name was Joseph, of the house of David; and the virgin's name was Mary.[11]

Inasmuch as the Most High chose to send His substantial power to earth, it was fitting that He had it proclaimed by the angel empowered by Him.

---

würk-wesentlich empfang / und doch ohn Abgang-Noht
das übrig hohe Meer / frey unbeschränkt fortstürzet /
die Well-Unendlichkeit ist mahlerhaft verkürzet /
vollkommen in der Schal / vollkommen auser der /
ein GOtt in Mutter-Leib / und in der Dreyheit / Meer.

11. Lk 1: 26–27. Greiffenberg's text omits from the verse quoted the prepositional phrase "in the sixth month," which refers to Elizabeth's pregnancy.

An angelic ambassador was to announce the God who was being sent. The power of God in the angel was to indicate the power of the unification [of the divine] with humanity—just as this angel had once revealed to Daniel the seventy year-weeks, after which the Holiest of Holies was to be anointed, [this angelic revelation] being an indication of the holiest work possible.[12] He had six moons prior announced the miraculous conception of the precursor of this Wonderful.[13] Thus it appears that all lofty things must be learned and understood from divine power. God is [true to] Himself and loves order. For this reason, He suffers His plan to come to pass and be realized in an orderly fashion. This is, however, the kind of order that, by means of divine mediation, unites things that are separated in the extreme and makes one follow from the other.

The highest God above all the heavens sent an ambassador, one of the most glorious angels, down to earth, to Galilee, a poor, obscure spot on the way to Nazareth, an unimportant little hamlet, to a virgin who was the most insignificant and lowliest of maidens, the betrothed of a simple, common carpenter. In this simplicity, however, the Divine Trinity showed its greatest wisdom in that it knew both how to find in the greatest lowliness capacity for virtue and how to impart the capacity for divine things to the most wretched incapacity. It shows its omnipotence in its ability to exalt a little speck of earth to heavenly spectacles and splendid miracles. It displays its goodness by electing the most miserable things for the purpose of its elevation, and it displays its freedom by turning with its grace there where, at the beginning, one—and all of the rest of the world—would not have expected it.

Who would believe that the King of Kings, the Lord of all the potentates, would dispatch an angel as an ambassador to a poor maiden or the wife of an artisan? What is more absurd before the world and yet better disposed for the dispensation of heaven? Poverty and lowliness are no hindrance to

12. Dn 9: 20–27. During the time of Israel's captivity in Babylon, the angel Gabriel appeared to Daniel with the prophecy that a time period of seventy weeks of years, that is 490 years, was to pass "to finish the transgression, to put an end to sin, and to atone for iniquity, to bring in everlasting righteousness, to seal both vision and prophet, and to anoint a most holy place" (Dn 9: 24). Biblical exegetes have understood this prophecy to find its fulfillment in the life and ministry of Jesus Christ.

13. Lk 1: 11–13 and Lk 1: 26–27. An unnamed angel appears to Zechariah to inform him that his wife Elizabeth will bear a son who will be called John. Gabriel appears to Mary when Elizabeth is in the sixth month of her pregnancy. John as the messenger is to prepare the way according to the prophet Isaiah: "the voice of one crying in the wilderness, 'Make straight the way of the Lord,' as the prophet Isaiah said" (Jn 1: 23, Mt 3: 3, Is 40: 3). "Wonderful" is the name given to the Messiah in Is 9: 6: "For to us a child is born, to us a son is given; and the government will be upon his shoulder, and his name will be called Wonderful, Counselor, Mighty God, Everlasting Father, Prince of Peace."

divine calling: as little as they could take from her the right of inheritance of her royal birth from the house of David and still less the gracious election by God, whose piercing eyes see through all the mountains of misery the small flash of the metal of virtue that His hand has placed within them. He selected her from the very beginning of eternity for this high honor and from that same beginning made her fit for it. And so He therefore suffered her to be called to it too. For all divine calling has its roots and foundation in eternal Providence.

The raising of her in particular, however, to this honor is divine freedom of choice. Yet one must believe in holy humility that the Very Best must have chosen best, and the Greatest Wisdom, the most wisely. There is, however, no denying that Providence is omnipotent and infinite and therefore could have endowed someone else with these same virtues and capacities. Yet we must consider divine will the highest and utmost end of all righteousness and wisdom in the assurance that God does everything in the most inscrutable and unsurpassably best manner so that all eternity will have in its revealing plenty to praise in the cleverness of His choice.

But He elected a virgin to show that virginity and chastity are an undeniably pleasant and beloved workshop of divine miracles and effects. God created man in the greatest perfection—which is incontrovertible. So He created him, and subsequently woman, in the state of chastity and virginity—as is undeniable. Thus it follows that this [state] constitutes the greatest perfection. Since Jesus too was conceived and born of it and dwelled and lived in it, thus it certainly is and remains the most holy and praiseworthy thing on earth and the highest gift of grace that a mortal being can be given. I cannot refrain from composing an encomium for this most beauteous commander of my soul.

In Praise of Chastity

  Divinity's image, angelic undertaking![14]
You Jesus-Element wherein He swam and floated,

14. The following sonnet is written in alexandrines with the rhyme scheme *abba abba cdcd ee.*

  Du Bild der Göttlichkeit / du Englisches Beginnen!
Du JEsus-Element / in dem er schwamm und schwebt /
Sein See in Mutterleib / die Luft in der er lebt!
  Die Sonne / die so schön schien in der Jungfrau Sinnen!
  Die Königs-Tochter war ganz herrlich / ja von innen /
mit güldnem Stück bekleidt: Daher sie auch erhebt
zum Thron der Allmacht war / die doch vor Demut bebt.
  Durch Keusch- und Demut sich die Wunder stets anspinnen.
Sie ist der Weisheit Haus / der GOtt-Geheimnis Schul /

His sea in the matrix, the air wherein He lived!
The sun that shone so brightly in the virgin's thoughts!
The king's daughter was most splendid—yes—inwardly,
dressed in gold garments. Thus to the Almighty's throne
raised up was she, yet trembling with humility.
From chast- and humil-ity are wonders e'er spun.
'Tis wisdom's house, the school of mystery divine.
As prove Joseph, Daniel, and thousands of examples;
Throne and crown of beauty, the seat and stool of bliss.
Health, might, and strength sweetly incline to chastity.
In short: It is the flower that loves God and angels,
that gives every virtue strength and praise eternal.

You wondrous virtue, who are never praised enough! How beautiful are you in those eyes, illuminated by God, because you so thoroughly pleased your Maker that He deigned to become the Redeemer of the World through you.

Nevertheless He did not despise the state of holy matrimony, which He Himself had instituted. Rather, He wished to bring about this lofty work within conjugal chastity, for He called upon a virgin who was promised to a man. The outward marriage had to be the cloud of shadow over the sun of chastity. It appears that nothing serves divine works better than a misty clarity so that the sublime delightfulness of God is lightly covered with another [sort of delightfulness] that it may shine forth all the more gloriously. God needs a curtain for His works so that the world cannot peer into the brightest obscurity. The splendor of divine works must be contained like an eyeball between the eyelids and the eye socket of humility and propriety so that it is bearable and pleasant.

Variation and darkness are necessary for all beautiful things to acquire perfection. If an entire face were nothing but eyes, it would be a horror. The various parts and colors constitute its delightfulness—even the darkness that falls from its plumpness into the dimples and depths and from which the cheeks, lips, and eyes are rounded and where the light is delightfully lost. Thus in diamonds, pearls, and other precious gems, the clouds, water, and darkness provide the most delightful play.

Therefore in taking on human nature, God chose also to practice that

---

Wie Joseph / Daniel / und tausend Beispiel zeigen;
Der Schönheit Thron und Kron / des Glückes Sitz und Stul.
Gesundheit / Kraft und Stärk sich lieblich zu ihr neigen.
Kurz: Keuschheit ist die Blum / die Gott und Engeln liebt /
die aller Tugend Kraft und ewigs Lobe gibt.

which is instilled in the most beautiful things, namely, the darkness that enhances all beauty. He shaded off the beauty of chastity with marriage, which is entangled in the world. Thus all its beauty was preserved, but hidden by humility. It is not always useful and necessary to have an awareness of all virtue. God knows the proper time to reveal it. In the meantime it must remain hidden, like the seed in the earth over the winter. God has His reasons for not always making virtue visible. The more hidden His works, the more important they are; the more unfathomable, the more glorious.

To be sure, this virgin was promised to a man by her family and her own consent, yet it was through the most precise Providence of God who had such in His power and wanted this most chaste woman to have a spouse to overshadow the most chaste work on earth, a spouse who would not only not prove a hindrance but also hinder all evil gossip.[15] God loves the honor of His pious ones and does not suffer them to be reviled. Chastity is well taken care of with chastity and often better than in a stone tower since indeed one knows to seek it where no one can have suspicions about it. This kind of virtue must be pleasing to God, for He alone is its weaver and confidant, inasmuch as it is hidden from the world and thus lies beneath the shadow of humble darkness, which God will lift in His own time.

She was, however, promised to a man from the house of David to show that she came from the same ancestral home and line. For Joseph's pedigree and the genealogical table are written solely for this reason and listed two different times by the Evangelists to prove the family, birth, and origin of the holy Virgin Mary, for in the Old Testament no one was permitted to marry into another tribe.[16] They by no means did this on account of Joseph, whose blood stock was not to play any role, but instead merely to establish the lineage of Mary as the true daughter of David and thus also of Jacob, Isaac, and Abraham, from whom was to be descended the promised Messiah, the Son of David, who up above was the Lord our God and the Blessed Seed. God is just as precise in the fulfillment of His promise as He is merciful in the bestowal of it, and no more beautiful order can be seen than what emerges at the conclusion of God's works. For God is pure active memory, the very epitome of understanding, and the omnipotent dispensation of all things.[17]

15. "Freunde," the word I have translated here as "family," can refer to friends, relatives, or family.

16. Mt 1: 1–17, Lk 3: 23–38.

17. I have translated "wesentliche Gedächtnis" somewhat freely here as "pure active memory" to get across Greiffenberg's point, namely, that God's memory unlike human memory is eternal and ever active. A more literal translation would be "substantial memory." I thank Carl Starckloff, SJ, for his advice on the translation of this locution.

Thus must everything proceed according to the most exacting selection and in the sweetest harmony.

Moreover, no little dot, as in the writing of the Hebrews, can be without significance. Thus the names also indicate something. Joseph means an increase or growing. Under his care, the tender youth or human nature of our Savior certainly increased and grew. Mary means bitterness or bitter sea. This little drop from the sea of humanity that Christ, the Eternal Word, took from her most certainly became for Him a bitter sea of pain and agony. There would be here a thousand mysteries to contemplate, but there are so many great ones that there is no time left for the small ones.

For us to listen to the angelic words, the human ones must be silent, and to contemplate the heavenly sweetness of grace, one must cease contemplating the bitterness of the sea and lend one's ears fully to the power of God in the angel.

And the angel came in to her and said, "Hail, O favored one among women, the Lord is with you!"[18]

Since the angel came in to her, she had to have been in a room or a chamber, and doubtless she was praying or reading. For prayer and solitude prepare us for angelic visitation. Quite different things happen to a roaming Dinah and a Tamar sitting at the roadside.[19] Gabriel flies only to the praying Daniel, the sacrificing Zechariah, and the devout Virgin Mary.[20] Where God effects something, there too are the angels of His power. God is, however, everywhere where one seeks Him and calls upon Him, which fittingly comes to pass in prayerful solitude.

The more emptied of the world, the more filled with heaven! Never-

18. Lk 1: 28. The German translation of this verse uses the verb "hineinkommen," which indicates entry into an enclosed space. I have added "in" to the RSV to indicate an enclosed space; otherwise Greiffenberg's argumentation makes no sense. Furthermore, the Luther Bible reads "gebenedeit unter den Weibern" in anticipation of Elizabeth's words in Lk 1: 42, whereas the RSV reads simply "favored one." I have added "among women" to the quotation of the RSV to make the verse conform with the Luther Bible more closely and also to make it clear that Greiffenberg here ponders Mary's being singled out from among those of her sex.

19. Dinah, the daughter of Jacob and Leah, is raped when she is on her way to pay a visit. Her story is told in Gn 34. The story of Tamar, who is said to be an ancestor of Jesus (Mt 1: 3), is told in Gn 38: 6–30. Both women are mistaken for harlots.

20. Daniel recounts a vision in which Gabriel appears to him (Dn 8: 16–17 and 9: 21); Greiffenberg refers specifically to the second mention of Gabriel, who visits Daniel when he is praying. Gabriel also visits the priest Zechariah, the husband of Elizabeth, in the Temple and announces to him that his wife is pregnant with John, who will prepare the way for the Lord's coming (Lk 1: 8–21). These three passages are the only ones in the Bible in which the angel is called by the name Gabriel. The unnamed angel of the annunciation is, however, traditionally assumed to be Gabriel as well.

theless Christian communion is not thereby despised; rather we speak here only of the remaining hours for special devotion. One can never have too much intercourse with God. Each and every hour that is spent with God wears the crown of bliss. All things do well at their point of origin. Thus it is with the soul in God, who is the soul's element, primal substance, goal, and center. Fish languish on the earth—thus too the soul when it must have intercourse with earthly things. Birds are burdened and weighed down by water and sigh for the air—thus too the spirit when watery vanity hinders its flight to heaven. Seed seeks the earth—thus too divine love its progenitor, God's love. The flame rises up above through all resistance—thus was the soul created by God for heaven. For all these natural things it is never too much to be in the primal element[21]—thus it is never too much for godliness either to be in God.

Of course this will always come to pass everywhere, but never more easily than in solitude. When the windows are covered, good painters get the best lighting. A good marksman must keep one eye closed, and during exquisite lute playing there must be complete quiet. Thus must one cover up the baseness, need, and misery too, close the one eye that is turned to the world, and be completely quiet in the spirit when the Most High wishes to paint, aim at, and play within us. If the angelic larks of comfort are to be caught in the little springe of our thoughts, it must be completely quiet and dark and one must wield the rope of divine word and prayer most gently.[22] All mysteries demand quiet and solitude, especially this greatest one of all in heaven and on earth when the angel of God came in to Mary. The mercies become ever greater. First an angel came in to her, thereafter Almighty God Himself. First he appears. Then he even speaks. It was not merely speech but a salutation, that is, a congratulating and a blessing. His clever nature and divine intuition permit us to hope that an angelic wish is simultaneously a prophecy and an assurance of the greatest happiness. He first of all congratulated and rejoiced in the very message that he meant to bring her before he delivered it in order to demonstrate that holy angels are spirits of joy and that they so rejoice in our well-being that they can hardly proclaim it for pure joy. He does not know how he should find mellifluous and uplifting words enough to present this happiness to her exquisitely, delightfully, and sweetly.

21. The text reads "Ruhwesen" (literally, "peace-essence" or "stillness-essence"). This word is probably a neologism. Below Greiffenberg reverses the order of the two elements of the compound to produce another neologism, namely, "Wesensruh" (literally, "essence-peace," "essence-stillness"). See below, note 25.

22. Greiffenberg here uses the metaphor of a snare for game by which a noose (the rope) is attached to a branch under tension.

He says, "Hail!" Not merely that the greatest imaginable happiness is wished you, but also that which no person, indeed no angel, could have imagined, but one that could have been imagined by Him alone who is above all faculties and understanding; such a thing the like of which neither the beginning of all beginnings nor infinite eternity has [seen], a happiness that has never come and never will come to any human being, indeed, to no creature in heaven or on earth, a happiness that in a way has only Almighty God Himself as a companion. I rejoice in such bliss that has not its equal not merely in its nature, but in its honor, majesty, worthiness, and greatness. All earthly bliss is filth by comparison: Alexander's, Cyrus's, Caesar's, and Croesus's world conquests and wealth mere child's play; the capturing of the hearts of all the empresses, queens, and princesses and the heroic ardor in love of them, merely chill dew.[23] Indeed even ours—the delights of the angels—are a paltry thing; they too are less delightful and ardent. In short, heaven itself has nothing of the kind; it will not be possible for this to befall anyone else, even in salvation, which is otherwise completely and totally delightful. So contemplate now what I announce to you that will befall you from God.

O you lovely woman who are endowed above all princesses on earth with God's favor! Right well full of grace because the Most High has chosen you as the treasury of His grace, as the temple of His glory, the seat of His grace, the Ark of the Covenant, the vessel of the sea of divinity and heavenly dawn, from whom divine dew will be born. You gracious rose of paradise from whom the Holy Spirit will draw the honey of salvation! You gracious grape who will bring heavenly nectar! You excellently redeemed miracle of grace and miraculously favored one![24]

The Lord is with you! In a miraculous and special way as He never was with anyone on earth, with an omnipotence and wisdom unfathomable to

23. Alexander the Great (356–323 BCE), aka Alexander III, king of Macedon (336–323 BCE), was one of the most successful military commanders of antiquity. He conquered vast territories from Macedon eastward as far as modern-day India and southward as far as Egypt. Cyrus the Great (ca. 576 or 590–529 BCE), aka Cyrus II of Persia, was the founder of the Persian Empire. Gaius Julius Caesar (100–44 BCE) was a Roman military and political leader who helped to transform the Roman republic into the Roman Empire. He is known, among other things, for his conquest of Gaul and for leading the first Roman invasion of Britannia in 55 BCE. Croesus (595–546 BCE), who was legendary for his vast wealth, ruled as the last king of Lydia in western Asia Minor.

24. The epithets listed here recall the language of Catholic prayers such as the litany of the Blessed Virgin Mary or litany of Loreto (approved 1587 by Pope Sixtus V). The repetition of the word "blessed" (*gebenedeit*) in the text also recalls the repetition of the Hail Marys in the Catholic rosary.

all of the angels and with a uniting of which no example is to be found in all eternity. The Lord is with you much more closely and particularly than He is with even us archangels. For He is not merely with your spirit, with your soul, your mind and heart, but also with your flesh and blood, with your body, and He works from it the greatest miracle in heaven and on earth. Indeed, the Lord is with you in such a way as for all of humanity to be with and in Him. From His being with you, the being and state of the everlasting salvation of all humankind will come to be. Therefore contemplate what kind of being with you that must be, from which such a blissful state ensues.

You blessed among women! Not merely for your own sake but also because this very blessing will come into you and from you. The power, spirit, star, and most intense peace of being of this blessing will take on a tangible body in you so that we can see, hear, smell, taste, and feel it: corporeal and yet heavenly, spiritual and yet at the same time with the body.[25] The very blessing that was desired several thousand years ago and that will be of benefit over several thousand years will descend into your flesh and blood.[26] The seed of woman, the hope of which was sown long ago in the minds of the patriarchs, will arise from your body. The blessed seed of Abraham, in which all peoples are to be blessed, will sprout from the bed of your chastity. The self-sufficient Word that promised itself to the ancients makes its presence known with you. The Word that made all humankind come to be will become incarnate in you.

You, blessed woman among women, will alone provide the tool for blessing all of humankind according to the advice of Wisdom that is pleasing to God and not because necessity requires it. You blessed woman, I say, blessed among all women—who alone among all of them has the honor to bring into the world the Blessed One and Dispenser of all Blessing. Blessed above all the empresses and queens on earth! So what if a woman can pride herself on being the granddaughter, daughter, sister, consort, mother, and grandmother of an emperor? Or another that she was the matriarch of all Christian kings and princes and gave her daughters to all the great houses as consorts? What is all that compared with your being the bride of God the Father, a mother of God the Son, and the workshop of God the Holy Spirit?

25. "Wesensruh." Greiffenberg reverses "Ruhwesen," which she used above to express the idea of the primal element, to express here an idea of divinity. See above, note 21.

26. The benefit of several thousand years into the future refers to the remaining time of the earth from Christ's birth until Judgment Day and the end of time. Like many in her day, Greiffenberg believed that the final days were close at hand. See Birken, *Der Briefwechsel zwischen Sigmund von Birken und Catharina Regina von Greiffenberg*, pt. 1, p. xvii.

In short, the one in whom the Divine Trinity means to work this unique and greatest miracle in this unique way.

Although there are many blessed and famous people among women and although there will be more, you are nevertheless the most blessed of all. What is their pregnancy in comparison with yours? Even if they have given birth to saints (that is, to more than kings), what are these saints in comparison with the Most Holy of Holies?[27] Little stars in comparison with the sun, specks of dust in comparison with a rock? What is the fame of those famous among the heathen in comparison with yours? Whereas Semiramis and Artemisia built two wonders of the world, you will bring Wonderful Himself into the world. Whereas the Amazons and Zenobia fought kings and emperors, you will have beneath your heart Him who will triumph over all.[28] The women martyrs too cannot assume superiority over you, for you will have in your womb the chief martyr and the crown of all those martyred.

The blessed women who arise after you will be those who little by little convert most of the kingdoms and countries to Christ and the true faith—as for example Empress Helena, who extolled the cross and the glory of the crucified one in the Roman Empire; Shirin, who will bring the Christian religion to Persia; Theodolinda, to Italy (Lombardy); Clotilde, to France; Ingunda, to Spain; Margaret, to England; Gisela, to Hungary; Dubrawka, to Poland; Walpurga, to Germany; and many others whose names still remain secreted in the mysterious chasms of God's hidden decree.[29] But your

27. As a Lutheran, Greiffenberg presumably feels the need to define "saints" here so as not to be seen to stray into Catholic doctrine.

28. Semiramis, goddess and legendary queen of the Assyrians, was associated with the hanging gardens of Babylon, one of the seven wonders of the ancient world. In the fourth century BCE Artemisia built the mausoleum at Halicarnassus, another of the seven wonders of the ancient world, for her husband Mausollos. In Greek mythology, the Amazons were a legendary nation of women warriors. The militaristic Zenobia reigned as queen of Palmyra (Syria) and the Palmyrene Empire 267–272 CE as regent for her infant son Vaballathus.

29. Empress Helena, that is, Flavia Iulia Helena, aka Saint Helena (ca. 248–ca. 329 CE), was the consort of Constantius Chlorus and the mother of Constantine I, Roman emperor, who famously converted to Christianity. She is traditionally credited with finding the relics of the true cross. The text reads here "Cäsarea," presumably from Latin *caesarea*, meaning "of or belonging to caesar (emperor)." While I have been able to verify the name only as one of several place names in the Middle East, my best guess is that Greiffenberg refers here to Shirin (d. 628), the Armenian Christian wife of the Persian shah Chosroes II. On Shirin, see Wilhelm Baum, *Shirin. Christian—Queen—Myth of Love. A Woman of Late Antiquity: Historical Reality and Literary Effect* (Piscataway, NJ: Gorgias Press, 2004). Theodolinda of Bavaria, queen of Lombardy (591–628), helped to convert the Lombards to Christianity. Clotilde (474–544) was a Burgundian princess and wife of the Frankish ruler Clovis (475–545), whom she converted to Christianity. Ingunda (ca. 567–585), the Frankish wife of Hermenegild, the son of the Visigoth king in Spain

blessed bliss surpasses all of them, for you will have in your body Him at whom all of their arrows of love will aim, and you will also yourself be the female originator of their teaching and manner of conversion in that you will say, "Do whatever he tells you."[30] Thus you are and will remain the most blessed among women.

But when she saw him, she was greatly troubled at the saying, and considered in her mind what sort of greeting this might be.[31]

When God is present, He does not permit us to marvel at anything that is different from Him and less than He. The angelic figure that is otherwise marvelous elicited no marvel here. She was frightened, however, by his speech, not by his person, which no doubt was very beautiful and lovely. Since the greeting was especially auspicious and filled with comfort and joy, it thus must not have been a troubling fright, but instead a God-fearing fright and a humble paralysis at God's goodness. For pious souls, even if they are the most beloved among all humankind, are always fearful and frightened when it is a matter of God's glory and story and when God bestows His undeserved grace upon them.[32] The grace of God always has as its holy companion a humble fright. A virtuous terror is the morning star of a glorious wondrous sun.

She considered in her mind what sort of salutation this might be! Not

---

Leovigild, helped to persuade her husband to renounce Arianism. Hermenegild then revolted against his father and was executed in prison in 586 and later declared a saint. Hermenegild's conversion is said to have influenced his brother Reccared's conversion, which led to the establishment of Catholicism in Spain as the religion of the state. Saint Margaret (ca. 1045–92), was the wife of Malcolm III of Scotland and a daughter of Edward "Outremere," or "the Exile," by Agatha, kinswoman of Gisela, the wife of Saint Stephen of Hungary. Margaret was known for her piety, her zeal in instituting religious reforms, and her founding of numerous churches. Saint Gisela (d. 1095), sister of Saint Henry, emperor of Germany, and wife of Saint Stephen of Hungary and first queen of Hungary, was known for her charity. In the tenth century the two wives of Prince Mieszko furthered the spread of Christianity; the first of these was Dubrawka (Dobrawa/ Domberta, ca. 933–971), a sister of the king of Bohemia. Saint Walpurga (710–779) followed her brothers Willibald and Wunibald from England to Germany to assist Saint Boniface in the Christianization of the populace. Greiffenberg refers to these figures as Helena, Cäsarea, Theodelinda, Clothildis, Undegunda, Margarita, Gisela, Damburea, and Estelberga, respectively. I have identified them to the best of my ability and have substituted the commonly used English versions of their names.

30. Jn 2: 5. At the wedding at Cana when the wine runs out, Mary commands the servants to do as Jesus tells them. Jesus then turns water into wine as what John the evangelist calls "the first of his signs" (Jn 2: 11).

31. Lk 1: 29. Greiffenberg adds "But when she saw him" to this verse.

32. "Ehre und Lehre" (glory and teaching).

expecting particular grace is a proof of humility, namely, that one does not consider oneself uncommonly worthy or capable. Grace of the highest sort comes as a rule to those who least expect it, unless God, through hope, gives them a foretaste of it, which then makes their anticipation as holy as this terror. What sort of greeting might this be (she considered in her mind) from an angel whose words are serious and true? What lofty wishes and superior words of praise, which are hardly believable and can hardly be listened to? Is this perhaps happening to test my humility or credulity or to exercise my trust in God which He appears to charge with something of importance? If only I knew with what sorts of gestures I should praise God herein and what it is that God desires! If it were to deflect high expectations, then no serpent would ever have stoppered its ears before its oppressor as I wish to stopper mine before these archangelic words. As majestic as they sound, as sweet as they ring, so shall they seem to me only as terrifying cliffs and lethal siren song, before which humility should creep away and hide.

If it is, however, the power of faith that heaven seeks to test in me, oh, then there is no thing so difficult that I do not trust that He can do it, no impossibility that I do not regard as possible, and no unlikelihood that I do not regard as likely, as long as they have divine will to support them. God's will alone is capable of extracting the poison of impossibility from wonder-snakes, of giving mountains the wings of removal, and of expanding the bounds of nature.[33] He can restrain the unstoppable and set the immovable in motion, make the sea into walls, the cliffs into fountains; remove the ardor from fire and the ability to extinguish from water. It is easy for Him to accomplish difficult things through insignificant ones and to carry out the lofty works of His wisdom through lowly ones. God's will and omnipotence do not leave room for doubting anything that is even more impossible than impossibility itself. The world can imagine nothing that heaven cannot give. But because it is so much greater than the earth, heaven can certainly give much more extravagantly than the earth can imagine. Thus it is on account of God's will alone that I have complete trust in God's omnipotence. Not that I doubt His goodness and inclination, but instead that I merely lack the knowledge of whether it pleases His unfathomable, well-intentioned wisdom to have something special in mind for me or whether I should fear to sin against humility through credulity and thus to bring down God's wrath upon me.

33. With the words "giving mountains the wings of removal," Greiffenberg borrows language from 1 Cor 13: 2: "And if I have prophetic powers, and understand all mysteries and all knowledge, and if I have all faith, so as to remove mountains, but have not love, I am nothing."

And the angel said to her, "Do not be afraid, Mary, for you have found favor with God."[34] God permitted the angel to see her thoughts; such thoughts are otherwise concealed from all angels, not to mention from devils. But these thoughts become known now to the former, now to the latter when divine will deems it appropriate. Now Gabriel sees into the holy fear that will, as it were, create an obstacle to trusting in the Supremely Holy God. As often happens with pious Christians, their pious worry that they will do harm to their humility and presume too much for themselves keeps them from trusting gloriously. Probably they too, as here, require an angel who curbs the fear and renews the trust. Gabriel does this here with Mary, fully answering her thoughts. "Do not be afraid," he says. For where God suffers the sweep of His goodness to pass, there is nothing to fear. Where His glory enters in, all fear must retreat. Fear not that you might believe too much of that which you could not believe exhaustively [even] with the faith of the entire world, even if there were a thousand such worlds. Fear not that you will do injury to humility by believing in lofty things, for God's majesty is wont to become manifest in lowliness. The loftier the grace, the deeper the humility needs to be in order to be fit for it. Humility is the case in which the diamond of glory will be held. Do not be afraid to be all too credulous, for faith is obedience to the Holy Spirit. Now one cannot, however, be too quick to obey the spirit of God. Indeed, do not be afraid that such majestic things, spoken of generally, perhaps might not pertain to you. Oh, no, Mary, you are called by name; this lofty message truly pertains to you.

You, you, you have found favor with God. Whoever has found grace need fear no wrath. You have found favor. Therefore fear not. You have found favor that no person has found or will ever find in all eternity, indeed, such a favor as you never sought, one that surpasses both imagination and desire, that flies on the wings of eagles above all hope even if it were the highest hope on earth or even divine. Therefore give your faith the reins, your trust wings, and let Divine Providence run free. It is impossible to do so much that this lofty matter would not require still more.

"And behold, you will conceive in your womb, and bear a son."[35]

Behold, just consider what an unimaginable miracle I must announce to you. You will conceive in the womb! Conceive—you who are the epitome of chastity, for your thoughts and actions are well known to me through divine

34. Lk 1: 30.
35. Lk 1: 31.

concession. You will not alter your heart and life, and yet what I say will come to pass. You will not give up your chaste being and yet you will be pregnant.[36] You will not perchance become pregnant in the sense of lofty thoughts or the fruit of the intellect. No! Instead [you will become pregnant] in your womb with a son who will be in the form of other human children and will be discovered to conduct himself like a human. [To understand] that this is, however, a great thing, devised by God long ago, then learn and think back and remember what the prophet Esaias prophesied many hundreds of years ago concerning it.[37] Behold, a virgin shall conceive and bear a son. You who love God and His word doubtless must have often read and contemplated these words. Now you yourself are this virgin who was in God's word and mind long, long ago. In you will be fulfilled what has been hoped for so ardently for several thousand years. In you the one promised in paradise will begin to be what He is not, even if He is everything!

"And you shall call his name Jesus."[38]

Because there is a certain kind of certainty in knowing the name, thus know herewith what you shall call Him, namely, Jesus, that is, a Savior. A name that is above all names! For all knees in heaven, on earth, and beneath the earth must bend to it. A name due no human, because divinity alone is capable of bringing us eternal salvation! Even though a few people did bear [this name]—although by special decree—then they did so only to presage this one. Joshua led the people of Israel into the Promised Land as an adumbration of this true Joshua or Jesus who will lead all peoples into the much-praised promised land of heaven.[39] No one will be called this name after Him, for when the real thing comes, the adumbration [of it] must end.

This name is a sea, unfathomable to all thoughts, inexhaustible to all understanding, unpronounceable to all tongues, ungraspable to every spirit except the one from which it emerged. It is a sun in which the heat and radiance of all salvation and bliss inhere. It is a nomenclature of all names of salvation, whatever names they may have; a point from which issue all the lines, circles,

36. The text actually reads "Beginnen" (undertaking) and "beginnen schwanger zu werden" (literally, begin to become pregnant) where I have substituted "being" and "be pregnant" in order to retain Greiffenberg's rather forced wordplay.

37. Greiffenberg uses the Greek form of Isaiah here when referring to the prophecy of Is 7: 14: "Therefore the Lord himself will give you a sign. Behold, a young woman [virgin] shall conceive and bear a son, and shall call his name Immanuel."

38. Lk 1: 31.

39. According to the Book of Joshua, Joshua, the son of Nun, Moses' minister, led the Israelites into the promised land after Moses died (Jo 1–8).

angles, pictures, and figures of all our salvation's surveying. The name Jesus is the glow of love, the desire of salvation, the sea of sweetness, and the land of the living, a foretaste of heaven, and the quintessence of all good deeds of Christ. [It is] a brief compendium of all of Holy Scripture, where everything flows into the name Jesus, as though into Holy Scripture's center.

It is a root word from which infinitely many names of the Son of God sprout, such as seed of woman that will crush the head of the serpent, which thus amounts to saving humankind; angelic Redeemer; hero; star; scepter; ruler; prophet; priest; Redeemer; anointed one; king; my son; the most beautiful among the children of man; God; the only one who can bring salvation; the Chosen One; a servant; David's first son; the son of a virgin; a child; Immanuel; Salvation of God; Wonderful; Counselor; might; hero; Everlasting Father; Prince of Peace;[40] the Gracious Word; the Righteous Root of David; a benevolently reigning king; the lord who is our justice; the Angel of the Covenant; a shepherd; a son of man; the Supremely Holy One; the comfort of all heathens; a plant; the Holy One; the arm of God; the right hand of God; the Wisdom of God; friend; the servant of God; the Horn of Salvation;[41] a grapevine; the beloved; a duke; the hope of the people; a light of the heathens; the Just One; a cornerstone; fortified rock; a treasure; Son of the Most High; the Word: the only-begotten son of the Father; Christ Son of God; the root of the house of David, a bright morning star;[42] the son of the living God; the lamb of God; the Almighty Son of God; the likeness of God;[43] the firstborn among all creation;[44] Savior of the world; the reflection of His glory; the stamp of His being;[45] the firstborn in the world; a light of the world; the life; the way; the truth;[46] the power of God; the water of wisdom; the door to the sheepfold;[47] love; hope; the Son of Man; the Word that became flesh; our peace; our intercessor; representative; crown of God;

40. Greiffenberg loosely quotes from Is 9: 6: "his name will be called 'Wonderful Counselor, Mighty God, Everlasting Father, Prince of Peace.'"

41. Lk 1: 69.

42. Rv 22: 16: "the root and the offspring of David, the bright morning star."

43. 2 Cor 4: 4.

44. Col 1: 15

45. A loose quotation of Heb 1: 3: "He reflects the glory of God and bears the very stamp of his nature."

46. Jn 14: 6: "I am the way, and the truth, and the life."

47. Greiffenberg conflates Jn 10: 1 and Jn 10: 7. The word "Schafstall" (sheepfold) that Greiffenberg uses here occurs in Jn 10: 1 ("He who does not enter the sheepfold by the door but climbs in by another way, that man is a thief and a robber"), but in 10: 7 Jesus states, "I am the door of the sheep."

bread of heaven; the head and bridegroom of the church;[48] a living tree; the kingdom of God; a wellspring of life; the holiness that was born; the Almighty Son of God; God above all; a faithful shepherd; a lion of the race of Judah; Melchizedek;[49] our justice, wisdom, sanctification, reconciliation, redemption; the Gospel. These and countless more names all sprang like a little branch from the root name Jesus.

"He will be great, and will be called the Son of the Most High."[50]

Your son will at the same time be the Son of the Most High—thus great because He has His father in heaven and His mother on earth; great because He fills heaven and earth with His majesty. Indeed great because He is totality itself and thus everything in everything. Great because His greatness is ungraspable, incomprehensible, unimaginable, and what is most wonderful, it most greatly proves itself by reducing itself to a little tiny child. For the most ungraspable work of all of God's omnipotence is to make what is ungraspable graspable in the tiny body of a little child; and the Godhead can thus display its supreme majesty in no better way than through the supreme capacity to become a child.

Therefore you will be a blissful mother to have a son who is at once called the Son of the Most High, not as a matter of hearsay, but [called that] by the Most High Himself, who will say, "This is my beloved Son with whom I am well pleased!"[51] From the Holy Spirit who long ago said through David: "Kiss the Son, lest he be angry!"[52] Through the inspiration of the Holy Spirit, He will also be called the Son of God by the apostles and the Evangelists.

"And the Lord God will give to him the throne of his father David, and he will reign over the house of Jacob for ever, and of his kingdom there will be no end."[53]

God will make Him the spiritual king of Judah and Israel. He will be an eternal king and will govern and rule in the hearts and souls of humankind. His kingdom will be completely astonishing. As long as He dwells on the earth with His body, He will of course not have a corporeal or earthly kingdom.

48. Eph 5: 23, Col 1: 18. Church is used here in the sense of "community of believers." Jesus is referred to as "bridegroom" in Mk 2: 19–20, Mt 9: 15, Lk 5: 34–35, and Jn 3: 29.

49. This name occurs in Gn 14:18 and Ps 110:4.

50. Lk 1:32.

51. Mt 3:17. When Jesus is baptized, the heavens open and he sees the spirit of God descending from heaven and hears a voice speaking these words.

52. Ps 2: 12: "Kiss his feet, lest he be angry."

53. Lk 1: 32–33.

However, after He goes to heaven He will exercise all power on earth. God will not only give Him the throne of His father David but lay all of the kingdoms on earth at His feet. David, who is your natural ancestor and thus also the father of your son, would be able to say more reasonably than King Philip: "Son, seek a greater kingdom; mine is too small for you."[54] What would an earthly throne be for a heavenly king anyway?

Thus everything is directed toward heavenly and spiritual rule. Nevertheless the physical choice is also possible for the incarnate God, and all the kingdoms can, indeed will, be conquered and captured by His kingdom. He will be the eternal king of the house of Jacob. But then nothing that is temporal is eternal. Thus He must not be a temporal king. For what is visible is ephemeral. Thus on this account He remains an everlasting eternal king, although at times invisible in His majesty and without splendor, which at a time when it pleases God can also become visibly and temporally manifest and gloried. Invisibility takes nothing from its reality. His kingdom is just as real and true in invisibility as if it stood before our very eyes—just as the sun is neither darkened nor diminished by the night.

He will remain a king throughout eternity even though His glory is hidden from our eyes—and specifically a king of the house of Jacob, which He will exalt now in spirit and afterward in reality. God's promises are incontrovertible, unfailing, and unstoppable. Even if a thousand counterblows are struck, [God's promises] will still all have to hit the target. If the house of Jacob is now wretched, scattered, darkened, and in ruins, as it were, it will nevertheless return to prosperity, because it has such a glorious and—what is more—eternal king, even if this should be delayed longer than one thousand five hundred years, if Jerusalem be in the meantime destroyed and if the Jews become the most despised people on earth. Your son will be king in the house of Jacob forever, both uninterruptedly and perpetually, although in the most hidden and secret manner, which neither angel nor human can fathom, in a manner that nevertheless will appear most truly and ultimately in the greatest clarity and majesty.

There will be no end to His kingdom. What is endless belongs to God. Earthly lords do not reign endlessly. Thus there is also nothing on earth that is not without end. Since [the earth] itself is not without end, it follows that His kingdom will be superterrestrial, heavenly, spiritual, and divine, since it

54. Philip II of Macedon (382–336 BCE), father of Alexander the Great. According to Plutarch, when King Philip witnessed his son's taming of the horse Bucephalus, which was thought to be unridable, he exclaimed, "O my son, seek out a kingdom worthy of thyself, for Macedon is too little for thee."

is to be without end. But it will extend over the world too, inasmuch as the rule of the same is necessary to the heavenly reign. It will be the great stone that will crush all realms and fill up the entire world.

And Mary said to the angel, "How shall this be, seeing I know not a man?"[55]

What one loves most is what one worries about most. What is closest to one's heart is the first thing on one's tongue. The most chaste virgin worries most about her chastity, which is her most ardent love and only life. It is the artery on which her heart is suspended. Thus her mouth is moved to speak of it. She does not gainsay the divine annunciation but instead asks only how it shall be, given her chastity, which, she knows for certain, is pleasing to God. It is not, however, some absurd Nicodemus-question but instead a God-fearing request for elucidation as to how two divine dispositions that appear to contradict one another can exist simultaneously.[56] She asks for an angelic account as to how it shall be that fertility and chastity, motherhood and virginity, corporal integrity and giving birth will exist side by side. She had so firmly concluded that she would remain eternally chaste that she did not commit the error of thinking that God had changed His mind but instead stuck by the principle that it would come to pass in chastity. She merely asked how it should come to be.

It is worth thinking about the fact that she said, seeing I know not a man, when she was engaged to Joseph who was soon to bring her home as his wedded wife. She must, however, have certainly been assured of her own chastity and perhaps of his too (as some of the ancient teachers maintain and as finally may well be the case), or, however, more likely, she quite accurately understood the angelic message that it had to occur in the purest chastity. Thus she did not ask from lack of faith as if she doubted the fulfillment, but instead (as Ambrose says) she wants to know how it will work.[57] It was not in her case an expression of lack of faith or of impertinence but instead one of necessity and ready obedience so that she would know how she was to conduct herself herein.

55. Lk 1: 34. Here it becomes necessary to quote Mary's words from the King James Bible since it is closer to the German. Greiffenberg's commentary does not make sense if one uses the wording of the RSV, namely, "How can this be, since I have no husband?"

56. Jn 3: 1–9. Here the Pharisee Nicodemus questions Jesus about the incarnation in essentially the same words: "How can this be?" (Jn 3: 9). After chiding him, Jesus again explains the incarnation and the importance of believing in the son of God (Jn 3: 10–21).

57. Saint Ambrose (ca. 337–397), one of the four major Church Fathers, who among other things was known for his love of and writing on virginity, author of many works including *On Virgins* and *The Mystery of the Lord's Incarnation*.

And the angel said to her, "The Holy Spirit will come upon you, and the power of the Most High will overshadow you."[58]

Here we see that the holy angels speak and answer when it is necessary and beneficial and that they do not fail to discuss any holy and necessary question and that this question was not an impertinent one, because it was dignified with an angelic answer. But in order for me to meditate on such angelic words and to write of the Holy Spirit coming upon her, suffer, O heavenly Father, the Holy Spirit to come upon me too in the way necessary for me to think and write properly about these things. Overshadow me too with power from above that I may understand properly and praise most highly the power of this overshadowing.

It will take place (the angel means to say) in a completely holy and special way in which it has never before taken place. In this work, the Holy Spirit will not just come upon you in your spirit, but upon your body. He will cleanse your blood and form the supremely holy body of the Son of God from it and in it in the holiest, purest, and most inconceivable manner, a manner that is impossible not only for you human beings to fathom and praise sufficiently but for us angels as well. The Holy Spirit who at the creation of the world moved over the face of the waters will now, in the incarnation of the Redeemer of the World, move over you and your blood.[59] Not that the Holy Spirit will effect this procreation as a father, but He will instead put it in your body as a creator. For the corporeal conception will ensue not from the substance and being of the Holy Spirit but instead from His power and effect, indeed from the power and effect of the entire Most Holy Trinity.[60]

The power of the Most High, namely, the Son of God, the Eternal Word, the Power from on High, which is in God and God in it, and thus God the Father, Son, and Holy Spirit will effect this miraculous conception in you. Yet only God the Son will be born of you. For God the Father can-

58. Lk 1: 35.

59. Gn 1: 2: "The earth was without form and void, and darkness was upon the face of the deep; and the Spirit of God was moving over the face of the waters."

60. Greiffenberg writes here of incarnation using an understanding of human reproduction derived from Aristotle, one that had been taken up by Christian theologians, most notably Thomas Aquinas. The sperma is understood to work "by intellection" on the matter provided by Mary's body (see Laqueur, *Making Sex*, 54). Thomas Aquinas writes of incarnation, "But it was according to the natural mode of conception that the matter from which Christ's body was formed was similar to that which other women furnish for the conception of a child. According to Aristotle, this matter is the woman's blood, not of any sort, but blood which has been brought to a more perfect secretion by man's generative faculty, so that the matter is rightly disposed for conception." Saint Thomas Aquinas, *Summa Theologiae*, Latin text and English translation (New York: McGraw Hill, 1969), 52: 270 (3a.31.5).

not change His name and become a Son; rather, God the Son, who was forever and from the beginning of time a Son of the Father, means to be born in time of you as a son of man and thus retain the name of a son, which no other person in the Godhead bears.

Thus the infinitely injured God must be reconciled and appeased by His most dear one in heaven and on earth. Now this is His only begotten son, His heart, which is at once the Self-Sufficient Word and the Eternal Wisdom. He must be the child of a human being so that all children are aided. Through Him, through whom everything was created, must everything also be restored: all this came to pass in and through Christ and must continue to come to pass [in and through Him]. The Holy Spirit must, however, beget Him as a separate person and not be the one who takes on human nature, even though [Christ] is with respect to the Godhead precisely one and the same.[61] Precisely that very God, but not the same person from the Trinity. The perfect God will become incarnate in you, but not all of the persons of the Holy Trinity. He who is in the Father but is not the Father. He from whom the Holy Spirit emerges and yet is not the Holy Spirit! He is certainly most holy and, as God, also a spirit but not the person who is called the Holy Spirit.

The begotten Son of God will be your begotten son, and thus you will be the bearer of a God—not that you will bear divinity, but God, who will take on a human body in you. These two differing natures will wed in your body and come forth in one person. Divinity will not be changed into humanity or humanity into divinity, as little as man and woman can change into one another. Rather through their unification they will generate the blessedness of humankind. The Holy Spirit will come upon you with His omnipotent effects.

The power of the Most High will overshadow you, as does an eagle its eggs, which thereby receive life and movement, like a morning cloud that bears the dew, as once did the glory of God when it covered the tent of meeting with mist, as did the incense the mercy seat in that most sacred place.[62] This shadow will be a tent of the hidden miraculous effects of God, a curtain of secrecy for the unfathomable incarnation of Christ, a dark cloud that shades His arrival. It will be dark beneath His feet: that is the way and the manner in which He will come into you. His tent is dark all around,

61. Greiffenberg wrestles here with the doctrine of the trinity, according to which three coequal and co-terminal persons are united in hypostatic union.

62. Ex. 40: 34. "Then the cloud covered the tent of meeting, and the glory of the LORD filled the tabernacle." The "mercy seat" (*Gnadenstuhl*) is specified in Ex 25: 17 as a feature of the ark of the covenant. Christ is also referred to as the "mercy seat."

black opaque clouds in which He is hidden. Oh, wonder! The heavenly clarity comes in darkness, the most substantial substance in shadow, and this shadow must be a tool of the sun of justice. God makes use of shadow, in which He means to bring light into the world—as when a good painter covers up the windows when he means to paint a pretty picture.

To make preparations for His heavenly undertaking, God placed the greatest power of many arts in the shadow. Shadow must give painting rounding and augment the light. Without it, it would be a flat and stupid thing. Shadow must also serve optics, that is, the study of light and sight in its variations, and must make its illusions visible. It lends many resources and powers of observation to surveying as well as to architecture. It serves telescopes, sundials, and compasses as a guiding principle. [Although it operates] without sorcery, [shadow] is almost a supernatural artist that can be observed [at work] in all beautiful works. Thus God wanted to use it too in that most beautiful painting of the incarnation of Jesus Christ in order to exalt through its secrecy the inconceivability and miracle of [that occurrence].

The most beautiful piece of optics of the holy love of Jesus must fall in this shadow onto the slate of chastity. The Immeasurable must receive by the power of this overshadowing a proportioned human body. He who made the world makes for Himself a palace of purity in accordance with the perspectival art of the camera obscura.[63] The shadow of divine power generates and indicates the hour of our blessedness. Through this divine shading, the embroidery and tapestry of this holy humanity was worked. Oh, heavenly shading where, as it were, the darkness of humanity exalts the light of divinity through the rounding of perfection! A Methuselah's lifetime would be necessary for contemplating this overshadowing of power, and yet one would fathom only a shadow of this shadow.[64]

Now I mean to listen further to the angel who says:

"Therefore the child to be born of you will be called holy, the Son of God."[65]

Since everything will proceed in such a holy fashion through the operation of the Holy Spirit and the overshadowing of the power of the Most

63. In the seventeenth century the camera obscura was used as an aid to drawing and painting, in particular to aid composition and the rendering of perspective. The camera obscura is a darkened chamber or box that receives a real image through a small opening and focuses that image (inverted) on an opposing surface.

64. According to Gn 5: 21–27, Methuselah, one of the patriarchs before the flood, lived 969 years.

65. Lk 1: 35. In order to enable Greiffenberg's commentary to make sense, I have added "of you" in accordance with the King James Version and the Luther Bible. The RSV itself notes that other authorities add "of you" here.

High, that holy thing to be born of you will be called the Son of God: God from God, holy from the Holy Spirit, the Son from the Father, born from eternity; a true human because He is also born of you. I am not saying here the holy *person* (he means to say), even though He is undeniably this, but instead the holy *thing*; namely, [I am saying that] human flesh and blood will be united in His person with divinity and thus be holy as well. I speak not only of His divine nature but at the same time and principally of that nature that He will take on within you and that you will bear from your substance and blood: that holy child will also be called the Son of God. The child will not be merely called that; rather all the angels and all those who believe will honor Him as such, teach it, know it, and profess it—not just with words but with their blood and life.

Indeed, not just the angels and humankind, but God Himself will call precisely Him, whom you will bring forth from your body, the Son of God (namely, His Son). For this reason He is indubitably God and human in one person; for He is at once God's son and your son. For no pure human being can be the Son of God from nature and being; and you can bring forth from yourself no pure God without humanity. Thus it must follow that this God is human, because He is at once God's son and your son, is a true God from God and a true human being from your flesh and blood.

It is no diminution of His divinity and glory that He becomes incarnate in you, but rather the highest proof of the same: for no one but the selfsame divinity could bring immeasurability into a strait and inconceivability into a human belly. The Omnipotent proves Himself most gloriously by wrapping Himself in weakness; Wisdom, in that it knows how to become a child without displacing its omniscience; Inconceivability, in that it causes Him to be contained in a speck of dust that is nevertheless greater than heaven and earth. Inimitability shows its art, amazement its splendor, unattainability its sublimity; in short, all the divine powers their extremity in the incarnation of Christ.

It is thus no wonder that such majestic things seem strange to you and confound you. But if you consider that everything is possible for God and that the limits of nature and possibility are in His hands and that He can disarrange these as He wishes, it will not seem hard to you. For

"Behold, your kinswoman Elisabeth in her old age has also conceived a son: and this is the sixth month with her who was called barren."[66]

You can behold a living and visible proof of divine omnipotence and mastering of nature in your kinswoman Elisabeth, whom age and natural infertility

66. Lk 1: 36.

have made as incapable of being pregnant as has your chastity (by its nature). Yet she is pregnant, and this is not just something that is thought, but it is certain in the feeling and stirring of the child, for it is the sixth month with her. Thus you see that God has power over all kinds of impossibilities. He can give age new powers so that it renews itself like the eagles. He can make infertility pregnant and make possible impossibility itself. He who made the dry rod of Aaron green, bloom, and bear fruit overnight could also awaken this fruit of the body out of desiccated age.[67] Indeed, He who was able to raise up children for Abraham from these stones can of course also do it for infertile people when it benefits His glory or our salvation.[68]

"For with God nothing will be impossible."[69]

Every impossible thing that can be imagined is possible with God. What is more impossible than walking through the sea? Still He made it come to pass. Than a rock giving forth water? Still He made it flow forth. Than to stop the sun? Still He made it stand still, indeed, made it go back to where He wanted it to be. Nature can have nothing and the sharpest mind think of nothing that would be impossible for God.[70] He who set limits to nature holds sway in complete freedom outside of the bounds of nature. Nothing is impossible for Him except finding something impossible for Him.

One could of course say that in Him there is the impossibility of doing evil. But evil is not a power but instead a weakness and does not belong to the things of nature but is the corruption of Satan, of which thing the Divinity is of course incapable. But nothing is impossible for God in any effective thing that can be imagined or invented. He could make the mountains into pearls, the stars into tinsel; in contrast, sand into stars and the sea into flames. He could make jewels grow on trees and in mussels, cherries. He could make it so the rocks gave forth oil and the grain bore ore. He could make nature turn around or create a new such thing in which what is now unnatural would be natural.

Everything is not only possible for God but also easy for Him. It is as easy for Him to place in your womb Him who fills heaven and earth as it was easy for Him to create your womb through Him. It is as easy for Him

67. Nm 17: 5–8.

68. Mt 3: 9, Lk 3: 8.

69. Lk 1: 37.

70. The Old Testament miracles to which Greiffenberg refers here are the parting of the Red Sea (Ex 14: 22–31), Moses striking the rock in Horeb to bring forth water (Ex 17: 6), and God making the sun stand still until Joshua's army defeated the Amorites (Jo 10: 12–14).

to light up the world with a glowing bit of dust as with the incomparably large globe of the sun. He can catch elephants with spider webs, use teetering stems of flowers as masts, use delicate hairs for camel columns, and make weakness itself into the Atlas who held up the world.[71] With a little rabbit, He can collapse the tallest towers; with a swallow, build a royal palace. An ant can at His command feed an entire empire with its eggs, and a little bee can produce so much wax and honey that many lands and peoples are illuminated and fed with them. A despicable pond mussel can yield the purest pearls (rivals to the oriental ones) with which empresses and queens adorn themselves.

The omnipotence of God can see to it that a little lamb conquers the lions; a dove, the eagles; a doe, the dragons; and an insignificant nightingale, the great ostriches; that the columns and walls of the world tumble down not from the blowing of trumpets but from the weak sound of this [nightingale]; that the sea becomes walls, not only through Moses' magic staff but through the point of the needle of a poor shepherdess. He can make the sun stand still not only at the behest of a powerful field commander but also at the wish of a miserable person abandoned by the world; make it go back at the request of a zealously praying woman as well as that of a king who has found favor with God. With Him, one sigh of the lowliest person lying in the dust can accomplish as much as all of Nineveh doing penance.[72] A little strand of hair's worth of faith pulls on Him just as hard as do thick ship's ropes of many thousands [of strands]. He is just as ready to reveal Himself to a simple Samaritan as to grant the splendid King Solomon His wisdom.[73]

He, the Almighty, can do whatever He wants and chooses to do, which is the most useful and most proper thing but generally also the most singu-

71. The camel is a beast of burden in Christian art that symbolizes obedience and humility. *Lexikon der Symbole*, ed. Udo Becker, Spectrum 4698 (Freiburg: Herder, 1998), s.v. "Kamel." By camel column Greiffenberg probably means either a camel serving as a pillar, perhaps in a frieze, or a camel supporting a pillar. According to Greek mythology, Atlas, a Titan, who joined the revolt against the gods, was placed by Zeus as punishment at the western end of the world where he was forced to hold up the heavens.

72. Nineveh is the wicked city to which God commands Jonah to preach. When he finally does God's bidding, the city repents and God spares it (Jo 1: 1–2, 3: 2–8). The book of Nahum is also filled with prophetic denunciations against this city. The repentance of the city after the preaching of Jonah is cited again in the New Testament in Mt 12: 41 and Lk 11: 32.

73. Greiffenberg refers here to the parable of the good Samaritan (Lk 10: 25–37) and to King Solomon of Israel, who is traditionally said to be the author of three Old Testament books, Proverbs; the book of Kohelet, i.e., Ecclesiastes; and the Song of Solomon, as well as of one deuterocanonical book, the book of Wisdom. God granted him great wisdom at age twelve (1 Kgs 3: 7–13).

lar thing. So do not be surprised if He proceeds in a singular fashion with you. What He plans to do with you will be singular. Wonderful has to have a singular birth and bearer, and He cannot receive a human body without a miracle, He who will work such great miracles on the bodies of humankind. Therefore have complete faith in the omnipotence of God who is able to do even more than I say and than you can hope for.

And Mary said, "Behold, I am the handmaid of the Lord; let it be to me according to your word."[74]

Humility is always a companion of gifts of grace and a precursor of sublimity and bliss. It is the white rocky matrix that indicates the ore of heavenly exaltation and the dawn of the divine sun of grace. It is the capability for becoming great by means of smallness, the primary feathers for flying high by means of lowliness, the most adept loathsomeness for bringing about its opposite, the dead scorpion that serves as antidote to the bite of the living one. Humility is the giver of what was given over; it brings home what was left to God. It makes one worthy of that of which one considers oneself unworthy, and it makes worthy of being lifted up those who see themselves unworthy to lift up their eyes. Humility is finally the glorious workshop and at the same time the matter of God, where and from which He works all His miracles, particularly this miracle that humility does not recognize itself, wanting to be not what it is but instead nothing at all.

This excellent virtue reigned then also in that woman who was to bear the Lord of all Lords. Thus she said, "Behold, I am the handmaid of the Lord." She did not say I want to be His bride or the bearer of God, but instead, "Behold, I am His handmaid, His humble servant and serf, over whose body and blood, mind and movements He can hold complete sway. Not merely from natural dominion and the power of creation, or merely from the inborn submissiveness of the Jewish race, but instead also from voluntary subjection and servitude so that I would choose God by my own volition for my lord and master even if there were otherwise no obligation or duty, and I would bind myself to Him as His most humble handmaid and slave."

Let it be to me according to your word. Generally the greatest faith takes to following the deepest humility, and it is the gold scale of godliness when humility and conviction are evenly balanced, when trust is as lofty as obedience is lowly, when one expects just as much good from God as one means to deprive oneself of in order to honor Him. Without faith nothing

74. Lk 1: 38.

can be pleasing to God. Since, however, this most chaste wonder of virtue was pleasing to God, she had to have above all an incomparable faith too. She believes not merely external things that happen to the sun, moon, and stars, but such unheard of and never before experienced miracles that are to take place in her own body and blood. She believes contrary to her knowledge and her [clear] conscience so to speak; for she knows herself to be chaste and believes herself to be pregnant. She has known no man and believes that there is a son in her belly.

She believes God more than herself—as of course is fitting. She is certain of her chastity and yet believes to be certain what He has suffered to be announced to her. She believes that the Creator of Nature can change its course and can rule and hold sway without it and over it. She believes the impossibility where there is no impossibility, because she well knows that the God who created her can do with her as He likes. No miracle is too great for her faith as long as it is marked with divine will, which is the foundation of every edifice of all trust. On this rock, faith can build incredibility itself. What is more unbelievable than conceiving in a tiny womb the totality that fills heaven and earth? Yet she believes it, the mirror of all those persons of deep faith, and it comes to pass too. She believed God and conceived God. When she lends credence to the words of the angel, her body is given the Self-Sufficient Word of God. She assents to divine promise and receives thereupon the heavenly effect.

In all things, God so loves action based on free will and faith that in this totally divine work too He means to have the approval, confirmation, and consent of the poor maiden. Is it not a startlingly supreme miracle that He who in the making of creation said "Let there be!" suffers a weak woman to speak thus in the incarnation of His substantial image, of His Son, and thereupon suffers it to come to be?[75] Indeed, the Word itself, through which everything that is created was created, put this word instead in the mouth of the woman who with this word was to bear a mouth for Him, the substantial Word.

This single "Fiat" or "Let it be to me," this word of the tender virgin in a certain way (one could say) accomplished more than the oft-repeated "Let there be" in the creation; for in the latter only finite and transient things

75. With "wesentliches Ebenbild," which I have translated as "substantial image," Greiffenberg uses the language of Luther's translation of Heb 1: 3, "Ebenbild seines Wesens," which has been translated variously into English as "the very stamp of his nature" (RSV), "the image of his person" (AV), and "the very imprint of his being" (NAB). The word "substantial" refers here to what makes God a person. I thank Carl Starckloff, SJ, for identifying the reference to Hebrews and for assistance with the translation.

were created; in the former, however, the eternally glorious incarnation of Christ. This "Fiat" is not, however, the prime mover, but instead merely a contingency pleasing to God, and Christ's incarnation did not come from the power of this word as did heaven and earth in the creation. It is one thing when something comes to pass upon a thing; it is another when it comes to pass from it. It is certainly true that a great miracle followed upon this Fiat, but not from it, but instead from the overshadowing of the power of the Most High and from the operation of the Holy Spirit. For that reason she said as well: "Let it be to me according to your word!"—not just, "Let it come to pass." The "Let it come to pass" of the devout must come to pass according to God's word and promise. Without this foundation they can speak no Fiat.

"Let it be to me according to your word!" she says. Let the Holy Spirit come over me, the spirit of God, purity, the spirit of wisdom, the worker of all miracles, the conqueror of all hardship, the executor of all impossibility, the fire of powerful effect, the fountain of all holiness, the air of salvation, and the comforter of all hearts. Let Him come, let Him come, oh, yes, let Him come over me, the blessed dew from on high! Let Him drop His droplet into my womb, like the dew on Gideon's fleece.[76] Let Him come over me like the sun with its beams upon the pure crystal! Let Him come over me in a heavenly inconceivable manner. Let the divine spirit work in a spiritual manner so that an incarnate God and a human being united with God emerge from it. Let the power of the Most High overshadow me so that the sun of the power of the Most High may operate in a profound weakness: unification without mixing of strength and weakness, of omnipotence and helplessness, of totality and meagerness, infinite and finite, immortality and mortality. In short, let this overshadowing make a person appear who has something like [both] what is in heaven and on earth, but has no equal.

If it shall be to me as you have said, then the thing that has never before come to pass must come to pass in heaven and on earth. So let it come to pass because He who suffers it to be announced knows no impossibility in His works. Since I have known no man at all and cannot give birth on my own either and nevertheless shall become pregnant through the spirit and power of God and shall give birth to a son, He simply must be holy and the Son of God; for supernatural things require supernatural power, and no one can rule over nature save Him who created it. God alone has done this

76. Jgs 6: 36–38. In order to assure himself that God means to save Israel through him, Gideon tells God that he will put a fleece of wool on the ground. If the dew falls only on the fleece and not on the ground around it, he will take it as a sign from God that he is to become the savior of Israel.

then. He alone can work in me what surpasses the bounds of nature when He suffers to be born of me Him whom He from the beginning of eternity bore from His divine being. It is just as easy for Him to rule over adamantine chastity as over withered fertility: the latter naturally, the former through the miraculous force of the spirit.

Of Him for whom nothing is impossible I shall believe all things that He chooses to promise and command; for the entire cause of possibility in an impossible deed is the omnipotence of Him Himself who does it. When God is the one who promises, then the promise is divine and thus omnipotent. When God promises it, then truth, which is infallible, promises it. Thus it is fitting for me to lend incontrovertible credence to this message.

She believes and conceives what she believes and as she believes. She speaks the Fiat with her mouth; God speaks it with the deed and truth. Let it be to you as you have believed! He says as in the creation: "Let there be!" and it was there. The Word became flesh, at once a body and a living rational soul personally united with the divine nature. Mary believed God in the angel Gabriel just as Eve believed the devil in the serpent. Since the latter assented to the devilish deception, the former had to assent to the angelic utterance. The latter took thereupon the cursed forbidden fruit from the tree; the former received the promised and blessed fruit in her body. Irenaeus says that through her obedience the obedient Virgin Mary untangled the knot that the disobedient Eve pulled tight.[77] What Eve bound through her unbelief, Mary unbound through faith. Epiphanius says that Eve became for humankind the cause of death because death came into the world through her;[78] Mary is, however, the cause of life, because from her, Life, that is, the Son of God, came forth. Just as through the serpent and the woman the devil achieved his purpose of corruption on the path of unbelief and disobedience, so God used precisely the same path of belief and obedience by means of the angel and the virgin to reach His goal of salvation, and thus everything is restored as it was lost.

77. Irenaeus (ca. 130–202 CE), bishop of Lyon and one of the Church Fathers. Irenaeus is one of the first to draw comparisons between Eve and Mary, contrasting the faithlessness of the former with the faithfulness of the latter. The text paraphrases his *Adversus haereses* 3.22. For a brief summary of writings of the Church Fathers on Mary as new Eve, see Thomas Halton, *The Church*, Message of the Fathers of the Church 4 (Wilmington, DE: Michael Glazier, 1985), 206–11. On Irenaeus's writings on Mary, see Luigi Gambero, SM, *Mary and the Fathers of the Church*, trans. Thomas Buffer (San Francisco: Ignatius Press, 1999), 51–58.

78. Epiphanius (ca. 310/20–403 CE) was a Church Father, a heresiologist, known for pursuing deviant teachings. In his *Adversus haereses*, he compares Mary with Eve: while Eve is the cause of death because through her death entered the world, Mary is the cause of life, because through her life came into the world. On Epiphanius's writing on Mary, see Gambero, *Mary and the Fathers of the Church*, 120–30.

And the angel departed from her.[79]

Since he had delivered his message duly and inevitably and had received her assent and consent, he departed. Holy angels do not remain visible longer than is necessary and useful. Their appearance ends right with the attainment of the ultimate purpose for their coming. They do nothing superfluous or unnecessary. They are the precise clockwork that runs according to the weight of divine will. They are therefore orderly and incessant in their working. This one was the heavenly Hymenaeus who wed in Mary the divine and the human through his message.[80] Now he must as an exalted power soar up to heaven, as a gossamer spirit raise himself up to God, and as a star above the heavens assume his place in the celestial sphere in the band of the archangels. He must shine once again as a bright lamp in the temple of eternity, play the part of a torch on the stage of salvation, and be a pillar in the palace of immortality. For this reason he hurries away in order to assume his place of lilies in heavenly paradise. He does not tarry long on earth so that he is not too late to play the part of a mirror of the uncreated sun in heaven. He departs because she no longer needs him but instead already has in her belly Him who is better and more glorious than all the angels.

She could also certainly comfort herself over the departure of this angel, for she now had God Himself not merely in her heart but under her heart, Him who is the Lord of all the angels. This archangel departed from her as a special divine messenger, but from then on she remained surrounded by angels who protected her and treated her with great tenderness. For where God is, there too are the holy angels. Thus because God was in her, she never lacked for angels just as those too who have Christ in their hearts never lack for angels. There is always an invisible soul- and bodyguard surrounding her that is just that much more unimpeded since it is invisible and all the more glorious because it is inconceivable. We enjoy its protection, even though we do not see its struggle, and we can take all the more comfort in it the less we can see it with earthly eyes; for heaven prefers to offer miraculous aid that is imperceptible and exercises its power in secret.

Thou commander of all the angels! How can I thank Thee sufficiently for this angelic envoy on which the resolution of heaven and the gaining of my salvation depended; and not merely mine but that of the entire world, of all the potentates of the world, and of all the rulers of the earth? Oh! Grant that for this heavenly dispatch they direct all of their envoys and engagements at other courts and places to Thee alone, that their entire purpose be

79. Lk 1: 38.

80. In Greek mythology, Hymenaeus is the god of weddings.

directed to Thy glory. Let this glory be contained in all alliances, included in every resolution, and intended in all agreements. Bless also through this angelic legation all envoys and dispatches that occur to honor the heavenly Deoglori. Suffer the spirit of success to imbue all of their plans. See to it that they always hit the mark of the most blissful Fiat or Let it be! Let there be Gabrielian nets of eloquence that no one can escape, archangelic sweetness of amicability that captures hearts so that they cannot slip away, an incontrovertible proof of omnipotence so that neither fear nor impossibility has a base or place. Indeed, let all such legations and envoys everywhere in the world find an obedient, believing, and humble Mary who responds with "Let it be" to every petition so that the holy plans are accomplished and Thine honor is spread throughout the world.

But what do I do? I should give and thus I desire to take. I intend to give thanks for the good deeds shown me and make bold to ask for new ones. While I intend to take care of debts, I do not realize that I am incurring new ones. But that is how it goes. One can make no sacrifice to God without taking wood from His forest and cattle from His herd. His blessing must make the wheat and olive trees grow from which one makes the sacrifice in praise of Him. Thus He must also ensure the success of the plans to praise Him, since proper thanks has to occur in works.

But until that comes to be, I shall praise Thee, O incomprehensible God, with my insatiable heart and ardent words for dignifying her with Thy divine envoy and for sending the angel of Thy power to her, weakness itself. Oh! Dignify me, wretched woman, with your spiritual envoy in the spirit and assure me through Thy spirit alone that the stirrings in my soul that honor God are these sorts of invisible angelic emissaries from you so that the fear of God does not prevent me from lending full credence to them.

How can I thank Thee sufficiently for the angelic greeting by which salvation was wished not just the virgin but all of us, indeed, by which salvation actually came to us? O wish replete with deeds, words replete with substance! Angelic wish! Divine fulfillment! Who can imagine Thee or thank Thee fully? An angelic answer of thanks would be appropriate in return, but I must save it until I by the grace of God am like the angels. In the meantime I shall remain completely enraptured in humble servitude. Nevertheless, because it is permissible even for weak humankind to praise Thee, indeed, it is commanded, I shall, O holy God, praise (although with a weak mouth) Thy wisdom that lent the angel such divine eloquence and such a heavenly art of speaking in order to herald on earth this otherwise ineffable activity of heaven.

Oh! Grant that all those who desire to speak of Thy glory make manna fall like dew, rain nectar, and pour out ambrosia, make honey and milk flow so that those who are listening are satiated with delight and yet remain hungry with desire. Make the sermons that strive to honor Thee into mistresses of the will, queens of the soul, and conquerors of hearts. Let nothing slip through their nets, let nothing escape from their snares; rather, let succeeding be the eternal end of their point and compass.[81] Lend them, as here the angel, clever swiftness to swallow up all opposition, as does the sea a spark, and to break out with a thousandfold power of proof.

I thank Thee from all the powers of my spirit that Thou hast suffered Thy Holy Spirit to come over Mary in order to form the supremely holy and purest body of Christ in her. Oh! All-provident God! Let Thy Holy Spirit come over me too so that I may praise Thee sufficiently for this boon. Oh, come, God Holy Spirit, Thou heavenly fire, Thou divine flame, Thou holy wind! Ignite, inflame, and transfix me that I, glowing and fiery, go up in smoke in praise of Thee. Oh! Come over me with the most forceful drive to praise so that I bring it forth full of rapture and undaunted by the world. Yes, come over me with that power of praise that transfixes all hearts, all thoughts, and all the heavens; that leaves nothing empty like the air, but instead fills everything with love and laudation. Oh! Come to make us thank Thee for this coming over in which Our Savior received a body that makes our bodies come into heaven. Thou weaver of the holy body of Jesus! Form in our bodies too the love and the laudation of the same. Take the most delicate of our stirrings and form His glory and praise from them. I praise Thee with infinite swelling of praise for the overshadowing with Thy power (the power of the Most High). Oh! Shadow that begot for us the sun, O power that begot for us the weakness that healed our weakness and gave us heavenly powers! How shall we praise and exalt Thee? Thou art to be praised far more for the forming of this weakness than for the creation of the firmament or the powers of heaven. The latter would not have helped us if the former had not redeemed us. When God created light, He beheld it and said, "It is very good!"[82] I, however, and all of Christianity, and indeed God Himself see and say, "This shadow is better still because the best of the best in heaven and on earth is produced from it." May anyone who is so inclined rejoice over the light; I rejoice over this shadow and would gladly be so simple as to take this shadow for the sun, indeed, for the being of the

81. The point and compass refer to geometric calculations that might be undertaken in navigation or surveying. The word for compass is identical with the word for circle in German. "Circle" might also be an appropriate translation. Either way, the idea remains more or less the same.

82. Gn 1: 4: "And God saw that the light was good."

entire world, because it is filled with divine being. Oh! If only I could give thanks substantial enough for this beneficent act of overshadowing! I would gladly let my substance perish in order substantially to praise this shadow in the heavenly substance.

But how shall I begin to give thanks for the holy thing that Thou hast suffered to be born of Mary, that holy thing which is called the Son of God? For this, all thanks shall be given as a sacrifice to Thee, all thanks that the Godhead itself can imagine and conceive. For God's becoming incarnate for humankind is more than if He (if it were possible) became a god for them: for the latter accrues to His honor and glory; the former, to His disgrace and agony. For this incarnation shall all people become pure thank-essence; [let them] draw spirit, power, oil, and salt out of all their capacities, faculties, and powers in order to praise God. No drop of blood shall remain uninflamed, no marrow unmoved. Everything that is human shall extol and honor this taking on of human nature. No tiny vein, little hair, or little spot the size of the point of a needle shall exist on this God-man that is not covered and imbued with a million thanks and laudations. He shall live not so much in the flesh as in the raising of His praise.[83] All the air around Him shall be nothing but praise and honor, the air in which he commences to walk.

My thoughts never have a surfeit of honoring Him and thanking Him for still more events and circumstances. I praise Thee, Almighty God, for making the angel of your omnipotence praise and prove how nothing is impossible for you. Oh! Let my wishes not be [impossible] either, my wishes that all go to Thy glory. If they appear impossible before the world, reveal then that thou who art in me art greater than the world. Even if they are [great] in my own heart, oh, Thou art a thousand times greater than is [my heart] and canst wield extravagant abundance over everything that we can ask for and think of. Oh! Assure me too in the spirit through Thy comforting angel of Thine unstoppable omnipotence and of how nothing in heaven or on the earth is impossible provided it is designated for Thy glory and our salvation.

Make not me alone but all Christian hearts capable of recognizing Thine omnipotence. Oh! If we considered this rightly we would not strive so much for temporal things and money, which people think they can do anything with; we would be neither so fainthearted in danger nor so negligent in carrying out Christian acts of heroism. We would set out with the boldest courage against the enemy of the Christian name, believing that not

83. The original reads "Er soll nicht so viel im Fleisch / als im Fleiße seines Preißes leben." I have taken some liberties with the translation to reproduce the assonance.

he but rather the one who is on our side is almighty. We would not find it impossible to conquer [the enemy], if we did not believe it impossible. It would bring infinite benefits if we could make the treasure of omnipotence of good use to Him. One could thereby become the master of the entire world, indeed of heaven, and what is far more, of God Himself. But all this only to serve and honor Him.

Thus one ought to take heed of this angelic asseveration and ask God on one's knees for the knowledge of His omnipotence. God is to be thanked not only for angelic eloquence but also for virginal assent, that He made her believe the most sublime and difficult thing in the world, a grace that came from heaven, that is, the Son of God Himself. And this thing is close to being not much less [marvelous] than His conception; for He came through faith in the spirit into her body just as He did through conception into it. God is the dispenser of all the virtues, and He not only put the Savior in her body but also put in her heart the beams of the virtues that shine forth from the very sun of perfection, virtues like faith, obedience, humility, conquering of reason, willingness, and trust so that it would be to her as God had promised: in short, [He imbued her with] complete devotion to God, which is the mother of all the virtues, just as Mary is the mother of Jesus. And she could not have become the latter without the former, because in the work of redemption God meant to have everything free and uncoerced.

Thus we should praise Him in the extreme for this infusion of virtue, and praise her as blessed for being a temple of virtue, a treasury of grace, a wonder of faith, and a gem of endowment, from whom the beams of the beauty of all the angels shone, for having her spirit as well as her body filled with God. Oh! Should not one for this reason laud and thank God who showed such great mercy to humankind? Should not one say, Our Holy Lord did great things for her?[84] We shall doubtless fulfill her wish on earth and the first one in heaven if we help to praise her God for the grace granted her; for the holy ones have no more ardent desire than the desire for the glory of God, and the greatest honor is shown them when one is wont to honor God for their sake. In the state of holiness in heaven there is no wish for anything other than the glory of God. The holy ones are capable of nothing but lauding God, and we can in no better way act in accordance with their wishes than by praising God.

So let us fill her will then with the praise of God because He filled her womb with His Son for our salvation. Thus may there be unto God glory, laudation, glory, praise, thanks, force, power, strength, victory, triumph,

84. This line refers to Lk 1: 49: "For he who is mighty has done great things for me."

fame, and splendor from eternity to eternity for each little vein, limb, bone, and droplet of blood of the most holy body of Jesus, which He, through His Holy Spirit and power, formed in and from Mary. Let each little spot on this holy body be transfixed with millions of beams of glory! For each little crumb of marrow, let a sea of praise be poured out! And may God soon grant that we, having given up the ghost, may in all eternity express our fullest gratitude to Him.[85]

Explanation of the Emblem

Oh, Wonder! Do I see spots even in clarity?[86]
My limpid pure spring is not free of blemishes.
What is this shade that aims to obscure eyes and heart?
Surely what mine own eyes perceive deceives me not?
The bright surface of my spring is besmirched with darkness.

85. The concluding subordinate clause, which has a singular verb "möge" (may), lacks a subject. In the context of the paragraph, it would appear that the subject should be "we" and the verb therefore plural. It is also possible that the author meant to write "I," or she may have meant to use a passive construction here, in which case the German should read "gegeben werden möge." In any case, she expresses a wish that in death humankind and she in particular will be better able to express perfect gratitude to God.

86. See figure 10. This emblem introduces the following meditation. The twenty-line explanation of the emblem is written in alexandrines with the rhyme scheme *ababcdcdefefghghejej*. The translation does not attempt to reproduce the accentual meter and rhyme but does conform to the syllabic meter of the alexandrine, that is, twelve or thirteen syllables, depending on whether the line ends with an accented or unaccented syllable.

O Wunder! sehe ich dann / selbst in der Klarheit / Flecken?
Mein klarer reiner Brunn ist ohne Mackel nit.
Was für ein Schatten will mir Aug und Herz bedecken?
Mich trieget ja nicht das / was selbst mein Auge siht?
Mein Spiegel-helle Qwell mit dunkel ist beschmieret.
Nichts rein auf Erden ist / weil diese es nicht war.
Ach weh! ich will demnach sie lassen unberühret /
und machen in geheim mit Schmerzen mich von dar.
So dacht der fromme Sinn / und sah nicht / daß das Trübe
vom Himmel selber kam / daß dieses war sein Bild /
was sich in ihr ereigt / daß ihre Klarheit bliebe
von solchem unverlezt / in Schatten eingehüllt.
Ach! Joseph that also: der Schatten macht' ihm Schatten
das Liecht die Dunkelheit / weil er nur abwarts schaut[.]
Er sorgte / übel sich mit dieser zu begatten:
Die doch / sowol als er / der Höchste selbst getraut.
Der Gottgeliebten Werk ist anderst / als sie sehen.
Gar oft das Gute selbst dem Bösen gibt den Schein.
Es ist des Himmels Trieb / das trüb' herüber-gehen.
GOtt / wie der Engel hier/ wird dort Entdecker seyn.

Figure 10. H[ans]. J[acob]. Schollenberger, "Overshadowed but Unblemished" from *Der allerheiligsten Menschwerdung, Geburt, und Jugent Jesu Christi* (1678). Herzog August Bibliothek, Wolfenbüttel: Portrait Collection (Th 1058)

There is nothing pure on earth since this spring was not.
Alas for me! I shall therefore leave it untouched
and secretly depart from there with aching heart.
Thus thought the pious mind seeing not that the trouble
came from heaven itself, that what came to pass there

was its image, that its purity would endure,
enveloped in shadow, uninjured by this trouble.
Oh! If Joseph did this, the shadow would make shadow;
the light the darkness, because he looked downward only.
He feared it was wrong to take this woman to wife:
but she and he were wed by the Most High Himself.
The work of God's loved ones is other than they see.
Goodness itself so often appears to be evil.
'Tis the impetus of heaven, this obscure passing.
God, like the angel here, will be there the revealer.

MEDITATION ON THE PREGNANCY OF MARY

In those days Mary arose and went with haste into the hill country, to a city of Judah, and she entered the house of Zechariah, and greeted Elizabeth.[87]

What the Holy Spirit suffers to be recorded merits the most intense meditation and ought not to be merely read but most devoutly fathomed and pondered. It is pure pearls that the sharp vinegar of meditation must dissolve and render salvific. Nothing has been written that does not in some sense call for an imitation of virtue as well as demand to be read. The most holy pregnant woman Mary, who was indeed pregnant with that very holiness, arose—without a doubt from prayer, meditation, and praise and laudation of God; after the angel's annunciation, she must have persisted on her knees in this for several days. Oh! With what lofty humility must she have assented to this high honor! For one can attain no heavenly majesty without earthly abasement. With what holy terror must she have pondered this singular miracle and how must she have been beside herself with rapture over such unheard of tidings, which, in the presence of the angel, she could not fully absorb!

In the first beaming of joy, the faculties are dazzled from pure splendor such that they cannot see.[88] But when one gathers the beams into a single point in the darkness, the entire sun can be observed quite clearly. Thus when Mary, in dark solitude, gathered all the beams of these angelic words

87. Lk 1: 39–40.

88. The original text reads "Seinen," which makes no sense and therefore must be an error. The context calls for the word "Sinnen," the plural of "Sinne" (faculties, senses). See Johann Heinrich Zedler, *Grosses vollständiges Universal-Lexicon aller Wissenschaften und Künste* (1732), s.v. "Sinne." http://www.zedler-lexikon.de/index.html.

into the point of her faith, she could see into the sun of glory. Oh! How must the beams of the Holy Spirit have shone into the eyes of her heart in that dark chamber! What leaps of the heart must she have felt! What stirrings of joy from the child of joy that was coming to be under her heart! Since the heart is the first thing formed in the womb, she must have thus been stirred in her heart when He who stirs hearts began to receive His heart from her. Her thoughts must have swirled toward God with praise, honor, laudation, gratitude, glory, and splendor, like an infinite number of little specks of dust. Her entire spirit must have been replete with stirring emotion that her tongue was incapable of articulating, as still comes to pass in the sacramental receiving of the body of Christ [in Communion]. Sighs must have expressed most of this and then gestures, which cannot be contained within the individual.[89] With what blazing eyes of faith must she have looked heavenward; with what humility and fear of God, back down to the earth! What rejoicing must have convulsed her; what astonishment in turn paralyzed her! Love and fidelity must have caressed one another within her; joy and jubilation kissed and embraced.

As God entered her body, her spirit must have flown away into God. As the spirit of God wrought the body of Christ in and from her body, her spirit must have brooded God's praise and glory—Augustine nearly speaks in this manner.[90] The power of the Most High over her, the Son of God in her body, and the Holy Spirit in her spirit must have moved her so that she was nearly immobile and breathless from worship, love, and laudation. Yet because human nature cannot endure the power of divine stirrings for any

89. The German reads "in der Einsame." Grimms' *Wörterbuch* refers to usage of "meine einsame" in Ps 22: 21 and 35: 17, meaning something like "individual self," which is translated in the RSV simply as "afflicted soul" and "life," respectively. I have translated the expression as "the individual" to indicate Greiffenberg's idea that Mary experienced emotions too powerful to be contained within an individual person. *Deutsches Wörterbuch*, ed. Jacob und Wilhelm Grimm (1854–1954), s.v. "einsam."

90. Saint Augustine of Hippo (354–430 CE), Latin Church Father. In the *Sermo de Nativitate Domini*, he puts the following words in the mouth of the archangel: "He is more with you than he is with me: he is in your heart, he takes shape within you, he fills your soul, he is in your womb." *The Navarre Bible: Gospels and Acts. Text and Commentaries*, trans. Michael Adams (Dublin: Four Courts Press, 2000), 321 n. 28. Greiffenberg may refer here to the idea that Augustine expresses in sermon 215.4: "Mary herself conceived by believing the one whom she bore by believing." Augustine explains that when the angel explained to Mary that God would overshadow her, "she [Mary] was so full of faith that she conceived Christ in her mind before doing so in her womb." "Mary believed, and what she believed came about in her." Augustine of Hippo, Sermon 215, in *Sermons*, trans. and notes Edmund Hill, OP, ed. John E. Rotelle, OSA, vol. 3/6 of *The Works of Saint Augustine: A Translation for the Twenty-first Century* (New Rochelle, NY: New City Press, 1993), 162.

length of time in this life, God permits them to last only as long as they do not impair earthly life, and He does not permit us to pasture in heavenly delights so long as we can be of service to Him in this mortal life. He does not permit us to take any more of the poppy juice of holy rapture than the short sleep of awakening for a few sweet moments. Only when our hour comes does He permit us the full, long sleeping draft. So long as we have something to do in this world, He does not come to us as a fully blazing Jupiter but sees to it that He makes himself tolerable to our nature by checking the flames.

Thus He saw to it that Mary arose from this most holy rapture, precisely because, after a while, her weak human nature could not have borne the divine power and she also had to do the most important thing in the world, namely, bear the Savior, and therefore she was not to perish in these flames of the spirit. Because she had already spent several days doing this, because the angel's words were for her not simply out of sight out of mind, and because instead many days had passed in contemplation and thanksgiving, she thus finally arose so as to observe the visible sign of the omnipotence of God. After her spirit has seen plenty of miracles in the spirit of God and her body has perceived and felt His power within, she wishes to feast her eyes on His truth as well and to see in a barren belly the fruit of his omnipotence; for the godly can never get a surfeit of the glory of divine omnipotence.

Therefore she goes into the hill country. She, who was certainly of royal lineage but had grown up in poverty and lowliness, went on foot and did not shrink from walking such a long way as it was from Nazareth to Hebron to witness a divine miracle. She went not to stroll and take in the air, for it was not yet the most pleasant time of year. Nor was it a beautiful region; rather, it involved arduous climbing. Instead she pursued her devotion to delight in God's manifest omnipotence and divinely inspired operation. She finally went her way, that is, nimbly, swiftly, and without stopping, constantly thinking of the end and goal of her undertaking. She had no other purpose; rather, the goal of her journey was a most high and true one: the glory of God. The holy and innocent pretext was to visit and serve her dearest friend. This act is an irreproachable undertaking and provides both comfort and the lesson that one should arrange all journeys like this.

She entered the house of Zechariah, an honorable old priest, and her kinswoman, the honest, aged Elizabeth, whom God had blessed through divine intervention and whose pregnancy the angel had cited as proof of Divine Providence. All praiseworthy and important visits are herewith justified that are undertaken for the purpose of the greater exaltation of God's glory; for the meeting of godly people is a lute whereupon the Holy Spirit plays God's praise. A single string yields no harmony; there must be more than one of them.

She greets Elizabeth—doubtless not in an ordinary way, but rather with special congratulations and rejoicing over her divinely inspired bliss that at her age her womb was blessed with fruit and that she had angelic assurance that the Most High would accomplish something especially lofty with the fruit of her womb, since He had created it within her in such an uncommon way. She probably also told her something of the divine and miraculous thing that had happened to her, or she at least mentioned that she had something unheard-of and miraculous to reveal to her when she would lend her ears to it. For according to the dictum of the angel who accompanied young Tobias, one should gloriously praise and reveal God's works; and as Epictetus, a wise heathen, said, beautiful and praiseworthy things always desire the light.[91] Divine works are not to be hidden among the godly. He who knows [something] demands a confidant, who, as it were, helps him to taste, ruminate, and digest it. When God's glory does not have a doubled and multiplied echo, it believes that it has not resounded sufficiently. The Magnificat or the amplified praising of God requires a company that will be made to listen to it through the telling. But before the praise rings out, hearts must first be tuned and their tuning pins tightened through the motion of the Holy Spirit.

And when Elizabeth heard the greeting of Mary, the babe leaped in her womb.[92]

The Holy Spirit is not bound to human reason, age, tongue, or mouth but so free in His movements that He can communicate them to children before they have acquired reason and the use of their mouths and tongues. The Holy Spirit can make God's praise peal forth from those who are not yet capable of speaking and make not only those in the cradle but those lying in the womb liven and quicken, as He does here with the unborn John.[93]

91. The story of Tobias is told in the Book of Tobit, one of the books of the Apocrypha, which are accepted in Roman Catholic versions of the Bible but not in Protestant ones. Tobias was accompanied by the angel Raphael when he went to fetch ten talents from Gabael the son of Gabrias at Ragae in Media (Tb 4: 21–11: 17). When the angel later identified himself to Tobias and his family as Raphael, he told them: "Praise God and give thanks to him; exalt him and give thanks to him in the presence of all the living for what he has done for you" (Tb 12: 6–7). Epictetus was a Greek-born Roman slave and Stoic philosopher (55–135 CE).

92. Lk 1: 41.

93. Greiffenberg speaks of "den Unmündigen" here. This term can refer to various kinds of incapacity, including physical weakness and legal limitation. In this context, Greiffenberg is

For when Elizabeth heard Mary's greeting, namely, her rejoicing over the testament of God's omnipotence, the babe leaped in her belly. The Holy Spirit, the spirit of joy, likes nothing better than bestirring and setting Himself into motion at the recognition of divine miracles. When one speaks of God's Word and miracles, one tugs at the little artery where the Spirit has to bestir Himself. The Spirit lives beneath the palms of God's praise like Deborah.[94] He is the fourth one in the fiery furnace of devotion, like the angel with the three men in Babylon.[95] Wherever one speaks of heavenly things, He sits upon the tongue, as upon His throne or in His triumphal chariot, and holds the splendid victory wreath. Why should it surprise us that when one touches and strikes the keyboard of an instrument, the jack or quill pluck leaps up? Since Elizabeth's heart was moved, John's little body had to leap and be moved. It is said not merely that the Spirit blows where He wills[96] but also that He hops and leaps where He wills; in the hall of the maternal belly as well as in the Temple in Jerusalem. The Holy Spirit sets a half-grown, still premature babe ablaze with joy just as He once did a glorious king so that he danced before the Ark of the Covenant.[97] The Spirit suffers the little legs and limbs, which are still quite soft and incomplete, to move and leap for joy toward the Savior. Before the little feet have their little footsteps, toes, and little nails, they desire, through the driving force of the Spirit, to walk toward their Savior, who is still younger and even less grown. Out of ardent desire to do good for humankind, the Holy Spirit, as the true God, can hardly wait to be animated and fully formed. Thus the Spirit begins already to work within the child.

As soon as a child is alive and even before it has a little mouth, the Holy Spirit emits sighs for eternal life from it. Indeed, the entire Holy Trinity is

---

specifically interested in the inability of children to speak. Here as elsewhere she plays on the false etymology of the word as coming from *Mund* (mouth).

94. Jgs 4: 5. The prophetess Deborah "used to sit under the palm of Deborah between Ramah and Bethel in the hill country of Ephraim; and the people of Israel came up to her for judgment."

95. Dn 3: 13–30. Nebuchadnezar has Shadrach, Meshach, and Abednego cast into a furnace for refusing to worship a golden image that he has erected. When the three men do not burn, the king decrees that those who speak against the god of these men will be punished, and he thereafter promotes all three of them. According to Dn 3: 25, there is a fourth man in the furnace who "is like a son of the gods."

96. Paraphrase of Jn 3: 8, where it says the "wind blows where it wills." With these words, Jesus answers Nicodemus's question "How can a man be born when he is old? Can he enter a second time into his mother's womb and be born?"

97. Greiffenberg refers here to 2 Sm 6 where King David, filled with the Holy Spirit, dances before the ark of God. I thank Paula V. Mehmel for this reference.

active within the child before it is fully a real human being. God the Father, the Almighty Creator, forms its body within its mother's belly. Jesus Christ strengthens it with His holy body and blood while it is still in the womb and rules mothers so that precisely when they can bring along such a dependent little guest they most prefer to go to Holy Communion. Probably many a child leaps in the womb then, and I heard from one of my friends herself that her child quickened and stirred for the first time at the moment she received the holy sacrament.

In some children the Holy Spirit precedes language and speech, so that before they can speak they point to heaven and give to understand with pious gestures that the Spirit of God drives them. In the case of other Christian children, the Spirit does not wait for them to be taught but is Himself their teacher and puts words in their mouths and suffers them to pray spontaneously what they have never heard from their parents or nursemaids. I know one girl to whom this happened when she could scarcely talk; she knelt down and stammered in broken speech: "My God, preserve me from the evil spirit, amen!" Many other pious children of five or six prayed like that at the end of their lives, uttering dictums, psalms, and thoughts on dying that no one would have expected from them; they also had such visions and such a foretaste of the joy of heaven and made such speeches that we must recognize that the Holy Spirit was undeniably active and powerful within them.

Oh! For this reason Christian parents should not be too saddened by the loss of their unborn, and thus unbaptized, children. God is not limited by His own conditions and means; to be sure He can hold dispensing with baptism against a person if baptism is disparaged, but not when it is impossible to carry it out. His lying in the womb saved those in the womb as well; if He had not intended thereby to benefit them, then perhaps He would not have had Himself conceived and carried in the womb, but rather would have come into the world in another way. But for the sake of babes lying in the womb He too lay in the womb, thereby intending to make them holy and to take them into heaven.

And Elizabeth was filled with the Holy Spirit and she exclaimed with a loud cry, "Blessed are you among women, and blessed is the fruit of your womb!"[98]

Oh, most sublime bliss in heaven and on earth, the bliss of being filled with the Holy Spirit! To have the sea filled with pearls, the mountains filled with gold, the fields filled with armies, indeed, heaven filled with angels would be

98. Lk 1: 41–42.

nothing in comparison. Oh! The Holy Spirit! The divine spirit! The heavenly spirit! The eternal spirit! The spirit of joy, of comfort, of peace, of love and harmony! The heavenly anointing, the oil of joy, the balsam of paradise, the flame of God, the dove of faith! The rain of nectar and river of blessing! The preserve of the soul! Favonius of the heart and wind of life![99] The most fervently desired revivifying breeze! Musky breeze and refreshment of the mind! In short, inconceivable total delight! Oh! For what more can one ask when one is filled with this [delight]? Nothing but that it be unceasing.

O Holy Fulfillment! Fill me too with Thyself; there is no droplet within me that sighs not for this fulfillment. Nature, learned men write, tolerates no vacuum. Oh! Then tolerate no vacuum in me, Thou most kind Godhead-nature who fills up all things!

Elizabeth was, however, filled with the Holy Spirit, from which can be clearly seen that the Holy Spirit also dignifies women with His fulfillment and excludes from His grace neither sex, nor estate, nor age. Mary was a virgin, Elizabeth a wife, Anna a widow; all of them were filled with the Holy Spirit.[100] He excludes no one except him who opposes Him and resists Him with the resolve to sin. He does not show partiality toward one sex or the other, and even if weak women are otherwise despised, He does not despise them. He works, sings, plays, shouts for joy, and jubilates in their hearts as in men's. He makes them courageous, strong, joyful, and brave too, when it is a matter of professing God's name and the Christian faith, as when, by the power of the Holy Spirit, the pious Apollonia feared not the fire and instead leaped into it rather than deny the Christian faith.[101]

He armed the incomparably enthused Agnes with strength so that she suffered all the torture that Symphronius undertook to inflict on her so as not to abandon her heart's bridegroom, Jesus.[102] And He made her so bold

99. Favonius is the Roman god of the gentle west wind, the herald of spring.

100. That is, the prophet Anna, the woman mentioned in Lk 2: 36–38, who had been a widow for eighty-four years and served in the temple. When Jesus was brought to the Temple for the first time, Anna praised him. Greiffenberg calls her Hanna in keeping with Luther's translation.

101. Saint Apollonia suffered martyrdom in Alexandria (end of 248 or beginning of 249 CE). She was seized by a mob that broke all her teeth and then threatened to burn her if she would not repeat the impious words they dictated to her. When given a little freedom at her request, she jumped into the fire that had been prepared for her.

102. Saint Agnes is honored as one of the four great virgin martyrs of the Christian church. She was martyred in the early fourth century during the reign of Diocletian (284-305 CE), the Roman emperor who ordered the last great persecution of Christians, beginning early in 303 CE. Procopius, the son of the Roman governor, tried to persuade Agnes to marry him, but she refused since she had dedicated her life to Christ. When Procopius failed to win her hand and

that before she would make a sacrifice to the idol Vesta, she, relying on Jesus' omnipotence, was prepared in all her chasteness to be undressed and led to the common brothel, but the Holy Spirit created brightness around her so that no one could look at her—as with the sun. Subsequently, He preserved her in the midst of the fire and, instead of burning her up, made it burn up those who would burn her up. Nevertheless He granted her the honor of spilling her blood in death for the sake of Him who with the spilling of His own blood delivered her from eternal death.

Saint Crispina anointed this spirit of joy right well with the heavenly oil of joy. Her motto was "Always merry!"[103] For she rejoiced when she was taken prisoner and brought before the judge, when she was thrown into prison, when she was taken out again and tied up, when she was put up on the block, when she was questioned, and indeed above all when she was sentenced to death. She rejoiced in all of this and sang God's praises with the holy angels and happily suffered her head, blood, and life to be put to the sword for the glory of Him who created her, redeemed her, and sanctified her with joy.

The spirit of strength guided the heroic Blandina so that her executioners—not she—became tired of torturing her, when she was, after all, by nature a timid, weak, and despised woman and the other Christians were worried about her endurance on account of her weakness.[104] The Holy Spirit wanted to show in her that He is powerful in the weak. He lent her such strength that everyone, even her worst enemies, had to confess that no woman had ever surmounted so much and so great an agony with such valor and steadfastness.

The Spirit of Wisdom enlightened the learned Alexandrian Catharine so that she prevailed over fifty of the wisest philosophers, drove them into a corner, and converted them to the Christian faith, and thereafter so that she acquired the boon of strength to proclaim her Savior with her blood and to lay down her head and life for His glory and teaching, which for a righteous Christian is a cardinal honor and grace.[105]

---

fell ill, his father, Symphronius, the governor, attempted to persuade her by means of force. Greiffenberg recounts here only two of the torments to which Agnes was subjected. In the end Symphronius's subordinate, Aspasius, saw to it that she was executed by the sword.

103. Saint Crispina, like Saint Agnes, was martyred during the Diocletian persecution. She was beheaded in Numidia on 5 December 304 CE.

104. Blandina was a virgin martyr of Lyons, France, who in 177 CE suffered at the hands of a fanatical pagan populace. After surviving exposure to wild animals in the amphitheater, she was flogged, placed on a red-hot grate, thrown before a wild steer that tossed her into the air with his horns, and finally stabbed to death.

105. Saint Catherine of Alexandria was martyred under the reign of Emperor Maximinus, who was violently persecuting the Christians. According to legend, at age eighteen Catherine con-

The Spirit granted Anastasia comfort and at the same time the learnedness to write highly comforting and learned letters to the holy martyrs as to how they should be comforted and steadfast in their faith.[106]

He sharpened the memory of the pious Paula so that she was able to learn the Holy Scripture by heart.[107]

He clothed the manifoldly gifted Dionysia at once with strength as well as with wisdom, chastity, and bravery so that she declared herself ready to suffer all torment but asked only that she not be stripped.[108] When this, however, had come to pass and her entire body was stained with blood, she said that all earthly humiliation would serve to prosper her glory in heaven. She admonished those standing around her with very moving words to be steadfast and bade her son, whom she had carried in her body, joyfully to sacrifice his body to Lord Jesus. When that thing had been done, she cordially thanked God for it, buried her son in her house, and feeling all the more comforted, said her prayer upon his grave to be permitted to follow Christ.

When she was given the choice of losing her rights or denying Christianity, the true joyful spirit made the virile, indeed, right valiant Julitta say, "What do I care for my riches? What do I care for my life?[109] I would prefer to die a thousand deaths to offending my Creator." Indeed, He made her give thanks that the world cast her out so that she could gain paradise all the sooner. He possessed her as it were and said through her to those women that they had been created by God in the image of God for the highest

---

fronted scholars sent by the emperor to persuade her to abandon her faith. She, however, emerged victorious, having converted several of her adversaries, who declared themselves Christians and were at once put to death. Maximinus had Catherine scourged and imprisoned. She was eventually condemned to die on the wheel. After this wheel was miraculously destroyed, the emperor had her beheaded ca. 310 CE.

106. According to legend, Saint Anastasia was martyred under Diocletian in Sirmium where she had gone to visit the faithful. She was allegedly beheaded on the island of Palmaria on 25 December and buried in the house of Apollonia, which had been converted into a basilica. There is no historical record of her.

107. Saint Paula (347–404 CE) became the model of Christian widows. Inspired by Saint Jerome, she studied ardently, mastered Hebrew, and eventually followed the monastic life in the east. She died in Bethlehem in the midst of trials and good works.

108. According to legend, the widow Dionysia encouraged her son Majoricus to suffer martyrdom and buried him in her own house. She made it a practice to pray unceasingly at his tomb. Her own martyrdom took place in North Africa under the Arian Hunneric the Vandal. She was arrested in 484 CE and scourged in the public forum for her faith.

109. Saint Julitta was martyred under Diocletian in Tarsus in Cilicia ca. 304 CE. The pious widow was burned at the stake along with Saint Cyricus after her child was killed before her very eyes. According to one version of the legend, her adversary exposed her as a Christian when she tried to get back her stolen property.

good, for the most sublime virtue, with a heart just like the men—yes!—that they were made of the man's rib and bones so that they would remain strong, firm, and immovable in all agony for the sake of God's glory. As she said once and for all after many parries, she wanted to be a perpetual servant of Christ. Thereupon, with the fiery spirit of joy within her, she leaped into the fire with an unbelievable belief and desire until her spirit was in heaven with Him, who would once again quicken her body too.

The heavenly anointing, the divine oil of joy, the Holy Spirit, poured Himself out over the beautiful and chaste Potamiana and eased her pain and made it bearable when the tyrants had poured hot pitch on her beautiful body, which thing the Holy Spirit made her bear with glorious steadfastness.[110]

Publia, who was filled with the Holy Spirit, praised God with sacred songs and psalms, unimpeded by Julian's prohibitions.[111] Indeed, she was undaunted by the blows that he had dealt her on this account, which she considered nothing but an honor, and continued her joyful praising and singing.

The chaste Spirit of God fortified the Christian virgin Trabula so that when she was falsely accused of witchcraft, she was prepared to suffer herself to be sawn in half rather than to submit to the will of one of the Persian wise men.[112]

Saint Victoria did not have to overcome death, but something much more difficult, namely, conjugal and maternal love and loyalty. The Holy Spirit not only helped her withstand all agony but also helped her to overcome the exhortations and impulses [that arise from this love and loyalty] and to go about her work.[113] One must obey God more than humankind and

110. Saint Potamiana was an Alexandrian martyr whose execution during the persecution of Septimius Severus led to the conversion to Christianity of the officer of the court Basilides. The officer himself was martyred immediately thereafter.

111. Saint Publia (ca. 370 CE) was an abbess in Antioch who sang with her religious order Ps115, "The idols of the heathen are silver and gold" and "May their makers become like them," as Julian the Apostate (Roman emperor 361–63 CE) was passing by. When he ordered them to be silent, they responded with Ps 68, "Let God arise, let his enemies be scattered." The emperor ordered her to be slapped and severely rebuked. The women were, however, spared execution as Julian died soon thereafter.

112. Trabula was the pious sister of Symeonis, the archbishop of Seleucia, who was sawn in half in the year 368 CE by the command of Saporis, the king of Persia. See Johann Heinrich Zedler, *Grosses vollständiges Universal-Lexicon aller Wissenschaften und Künste* (1732), s.v. "Trabula." http://www.zedler-lexikon.de/index.html.

113. Saint Victoria and her sister Anatolia both refused importunate suitors who denounced them as Christians. Thereafter they were imprisoned and starved. When Victoria refused to make sacrifices to pagan gods, she was executed.

all human emotions and impulses. This the devoted women Felicitas and Perpetua did as well through the power of the oft-mentioned Holy Spirit, when the child that Felicitas was carrying under her heart and the child that nursed at the breast of Perpetua were not spared and [Felicitas], along with the child, was thrown to wild animals, and the other woman instead of feeding her child herself became the food of ferocious animals.[114] They must have achieved thereupon what their two names indicated, and in the end all martyrdom aims at the names of these last-cited three women, namely, at *Victoria & Perpetua Felicitas*! At victory and eternal bliss!

Thus one sees that not only Elizabeth but innumerable other women have been filled and will yet be filled with the Holy Spirit, if they but make room for His force and do not resist. For God despises not what is despised by the world but rather wields His highest power in the powerless and shows Himself powerful in the weak, for which reason He filled Elizabeth.

The Spirit will not be hidden where active, not quieted where playing, just as a gushing river does not allow itself to be tamed but takes the shore and bank along with it. As the wind suffers no limits and fire no bounds, thus the Spirit is completely free to radiate as He wills, like the sun that penetrates all glass and water. He is also not quiet, but instead loud like a blaring horn that one hears from several miles away and that quickly makes the next one resound until the entire land is filled with it. Thus did Elizabeth when she was filled with the Holy Spirit; she called out loudly. The Holy Spirit does not activate silent and mumbling impulses but loud, heroic, and fearless confessions that dare to enter the world free and undaunted, cost or matter what it may. He is not tepid but ardent, for the former sort will be spat out; He does not strike dumb, like the evil spirit, but makes one speak that which serves God's glory.

The first word that He spoke through Elizabeth was blessed. Thus He makes our mouths and lips into pure wellsprings of blessing, sanctify-sources, and salvific rivers, and it is the first proof of the spirit when thriving and blessing hover on our tongues. Here to be sure it is something very spe-

114. Saint Felicitas and Saint Perpetua were martyred in 203 CE in Carthage during the persecutions ordered by Emperor Septimius Severus. Felicitas, a slave, who was far along in her pregnancy, and Perpetua, the wife of a man in a good position and the mother of a small child, were imprisoned with three other prisoners. After many trials, Perpetua's child, who was still nursing, was removed from her. Miraculously neither Perpetua nor the infant suffered discomfort from this forced weaning. Meanwhile Felicitas, who feared that she might not be permitted to be martyred with the others because she was pregnant, gave birth to a daughter who was adopted by a fellow Christian. The two women were exposed to a mad heifer, and when they survived the attack, they were turned over to the gladiators who killed them. In Greiffenberg's version, the children both perish as well.

cial, but in general redemption and blessing ought to be the watchword of all Christians, and there is no more beautiful mouth than that which is both a sea of God's glory and the fount of the redemption of one's neighbor.

But to come back to this special blessing, thus she said, "Blessed are you among women, consecrated, dignified, made happy, favored, and supremely blissful among all women on earth, because you will have the blessed seed in your body, the blessing under your heart, the inestimable in your womb, the joy of the world in your hands, and the fount of all grace at your breast." Oh! You miraculously blessed woman, whose body and blood He will receive and personally unite with His divinity, He who is the archspirit of all blessing. Heavenly blessed woman, from whose body the body that will gain heaven for us will take itself! Divinely blessed woman, for God will become incarnate in you and thus capable of suffering for us. Angelically blessed woman, for you will bear what all the angels worship, the Son of God. Blessed woman among all women, she alone who will have the heavenly bridegroom both in and under her heart, she alone who will have a son who is also God's son, she alone who will nurse and nourish the Savior of the World as a child at her breast! Indeed, she alone will wrap with mean swaddling clothes Him who spreads out heaven like a carpet. Oh! You alone, blessed in this manner by God, above all empresses, queens, and princesses in the entire world that He may take on humanity from you, He who redeems all people who believe in Him. O woman who is blessed through and through, from whom God takes the matter that He uses as the tool of our redemption.

Primarily and above all, the fruit of your womb is blessed. This is the root, foundation, kernel, marrow, and essence of all blessing and benediction. All blessing is assembled in this fruit (like Theophrastus's gold powder in the pommel of a sword); it is the essence of blessing, the source of redemption, and the soul of all benediction and benefit.[115] Heaven and earth, our body and soul, which will feel the infinitely blessed fruit of this in heaven all the more, are witnesses thereof. I say the "fruit of your womb," thereby indicating His true humanity and your great bliss. The former: since He is the fruit of a human womb, He must therefore be a true human, for God created nature (in Christ Himself) so that each thing begets its like; each seed, tree, animal, and little bird begets its like. Thus the fruit of a human being must certainly also be human and the fruit of the body must

115. Gold powder was said to quicken the life forces and to protect against infectious diseases. See Johann Heinrich Zedler, *Grosses vollständiges Universal-Lexicon aller Wissenschaften und Künste* (1732), s.v. "Gold-Pulver." http://www.zedler-lexikon.de/index.html. Theophrastus (370–ca. 285 BCE) was a Greek philosopher.

also be a body, but not only and merely a human or a human body but an incarnate God and divine human being; for your womb did not bear this fruit on its own but conceived it of the Holy Spirit which wrought the unification of both natures in your womb.[116] Just as metal and gems (as the natural philosophers write) are to be sure born in the earth but have their substance and effect from water, thus He is born a true human being from you but is born a God from God from out of you, and He will be the fruit of your womb, which was itself the fruit of His creation. The high and mighty trunk becomes the fruit of its little branch; the sea flows out of its droplet; in short, a mote will bear the sun.

Your bliss arises from and inheres in precisely this, namely, that it is called the fruit of your body, that precisely your body was found worthy and chosen to carry such a divine and human fruit—which happiness will be granted to no body on earth before or after it is granted to yours. You alone are the divinely inspired bearer of God, who will transmit to Him human nature, and the mother of Him who will be a father of His mother and a son of His daughter, of Him who with His Word created the flesh and blood from which His mouth and entire body are formed. Oh, blessed fruit! All blessing be unto its fruit! Blessed fruit that has concealed within it the lord of all victory and benediction!

"And why is this granted to me, that the mother of my Lord should come to me?"[117]

How is it that I have received this great honor and happiness that the mother of my Lord comes to me, that I alone among many thousands have the bliss of knowing my Creator to be in her womb and to embrace, caress, and kiss the body that has hidden in it such a divine miraculous treasure? Why? From what heavenly turn of fortune comes this grace that the alabaster tower wherein the commander of heaven and earth dwells itself comes to me?[118] Why, oh, why is it granted to me that the heaven in which the son of God now resides comes into my dwelling place? That the cloud where the glory of the Most High resides comes down to me?[119] That the tent of the

116. Mt 1: 18, 1: 20. Greiffenberg will turn to these verses in Matthew over the course of this meditation to stress that what is in Mary is conceived of the Holy Spirit.

117. Lk 1: 43.

118. Greiffenberg probably means to refer to the "tower of ivory" here and has simply replaced or conflated one precious white substance with another. Taken from the Song of Songs (Sg 7: 4), the tower of ivory is one of the common epithets for Mary as recorded in the Catholic litany of the Blessed Virgin Mary or litany of Loreto, originally approved in 1587 by Pope Sixtus V, a prayer that lists a series of epithets for Mary.

119. According to Ex 13: 21, during the day God, in the pillar of a cloud, led the Israelites out of the wilderness of the Red Sea on the flight from Egypt.

great God Zebaoth comes into my chamber?[120] Oh, ineffable bliss, that I in my pregnancy am permitted to see the one who is pregnant with that same holiness? Good friends who come together when they are pregnant often promise their children to one another. Since, however, we shall both have sons, I thus promise mine to be the obedient servant and yeoman of your son so that from this moment on he shall serve and wait upon him in most willing obedience and most ardent loyalty until his death.

"For behold, when the voice of your greeting came to my ears, the babe in my womb leaped for joy."[121]

My helpless little boy appears to confirm my offer of service by receiving his lord and master with a leap of joy.[122] As soon as I heard your voice greet me, he stirred and leaped for joy, because he does not yet have a voice to speak and cannot offer his service in any other way than through movement. The presence of Jesus always kindles joy, even when it is hidden and is with hidden things. Jesus, hidden in His mother's womb, gladdens John, who is likewise lying beneath his mother's heart. This shows that no darkness or seclusion, no invisibility or concealment, neither flesh nor blood, nor corporeal or natural thing—nothing—can impede joy in Jesus.

This joy in Jesus penetrates all obstacles, illuminates all darkness, enters through all locks, grants in the midst of prison the most pleasant freedom, makes visible within invisibility the gleam of its beams, and in the deepest obscurity does not conceal itself before those who love Him; it employs flesh and blood, which to be sure are by nature incapable of this, as a tool of its operation; it makes even of unborn children an instrument for its music. And since the child as yet has no little mouth with which to speak, thus must its entire body be the tongue that reveals the presence of joy in Jesus through its movement.

Thus shall it be with all those filled with the Spirit; they will indicate the impetus of the spirit not merely with their mouths but rather with their entire bodies and all their movements. Everything in them will leap and jump for joy and desire to go out to meet their Redeemer with praise. As soon as one hears the voice of one's mother, the Christian church, the motion of joy will follow, for joy in the Holy Spirit is the Christians' splendid

120. The text refers here to the tent over the tabernacle of the ark of the covenant (Ex 26: 7–14). In other words, Mary provides the shelter or dwelling place for God.

121. Lk 1: 44.

122. "Helpless little boy" approximates the immaturity and helplessness indicated by the word used in the text, namely, "Unmündiger." See above, note 5.

jewel, the spiritual kings' beautiful crown, a precious pearl of the Kingdom of Heaven on earth, and the true golden ornament with which the daughter of the heavenly king is splendidly adorned within.

"And blessed art thou who believed."[123]

Oh, how joyful and overjoyful that you, believing, accepted the divine calling, for without faith one cannot be pleasing to God, and if you had not been pleasing to God, you would not have received this high honor. It is faith that brings and bestows all bliss, as said this holy matron replete with the Spirit. Thus Our Lord Jesus, the judge of the quick and the dead, from whom the Holy Spirit issues, will say on Judgment Day: "Blessed art thou who believed!" To faith, oh, to faith, shall all bliss be attributed. He, on that day, He shall receive crown and wreath, ring and jewel.[124] There, there, shall this "Blessed art thou!" resound within and among all the faithful, each of them rejoicing and exulting in the other's salvation through faith, such that this joyous sound shall fill heaven and earth. All the angels and archangels shall sing this bliss; one's own heart and mind shall rejoice and delight in it. But all the unbelievers shall lament, gnash their teeth, and regret (fruitlessly to be sure) that they did not believe that faith redeems.

Oh! For the sake of God and one's own salvation, let no one rob himself of salvation. Let everyone believe! Let everyone believe that faith redeems. Let each person believe what this matron, replete with spirit, says. Let everyone believe the supremely angelic divine word, like the holy Virgin Mary, so that, like her, they too shall be saved. Let us follow her in this and thus believe (as she did the angel) the Son of God himself, whom she received through her faith into and under her heart. Let us believe that the belief in Jesus Christ redeems us. Let us believe that God gives the Holy Spirit to everyone who calls upon the one who will make the fruit of faith and good works active in all those who believe so that they will have not a dead faith but a living one: if we believe and trust in the power of God, then [that power] will make faith active through love.

When Our Lord Jesus celebrates the beautiful fruits of faith on that great day, we shall glorify the trunk of faith that bore them. He will celebrate what pleased Him: without faith nothing can please God. Thus He will celebrate faith. All good that is done is done through God, for He says

123. Paraphrase of the first half of Lk 1: 45.

124. According to Scripture, "the Son of man comes in his glory, and all the angels with him, then he will sit on his glorious throne" (Mt 25: 21). In the scenario of Judgment Day, the enthroned Christ sits in judgment over all nations.

Himself, "Without me you can do nothing"; but then He does everything in and through faith; it is the conceptual power of all divine gifts and effects. Then shall it be said, "Blessed are you who believed what was ostensibly impossible to believe and what was unbelievable to practically everyone." The greater the impossibility, the more blessed is the glory of faith that overcame it.

Oh, blessed is he who, at the instigation of God, believed things most derided by the world, things that appeared to be nonsensical foolishness, and blessed is he who suffered all manner of scorn and reproach for it, he who finally triumphs with success and sees all derision prostrated. The greatest bliss on earth that could be thought up by all wise men, indeed, by those very angels, is to gain through faith a victory thought impossible by all the world; the unnatural rock basin supplies the sweetest nectar of victory; the Israelite walls of the Red Sea please me more than all seven wonders of the world because they are the triumphant proof of possible impossibility.[125] The course of the sun, which renews and rejoices the world, is never so pleasant to me as its standing still, halted by Joshua's faith, and its resuming its course upon Hezekiah's demand.[126]

The most pleasant things are those impossibilities achieved through faith. I like no animal in the world better than those lions tamed by the power of Daniel's faith, and I can think of no more choice display of fireworks than the fiery oven of the three men whose burning coals became roses through faith.[127] After the beholding of God, this will be the great-

125. The text refers here to the parting of the Red Sea, Ex 14: 21–23.

126. "Then spoke Joshua to the LORD in the day when the LORD gave the Amorites over to the men of Israel; and he said in the sight of Israel, 'Sun, stand thou still at Gibeon, and thou Moon in the valley of Aijalon.' And the sun stood still, and the moon stayed, until the nation took vengeance on their enemies. Is this not written in the Book of Jashar? The sun stayed in the midst of heaven, and did not hasten to go down for about a whole day. There has been no day like it before or since, when the Lord hearkened to the voice of a man; for the Lord fought for Israel" (Jo 10: 12–14). Hezekiah was the king of Judah (715–690 BCE). "'This is the sign to you from the Lord, that the Lord will do this thing that he has promised: Behold, I will make the shadow cast by the declining sun on the dial of Ahaz turn back ten steps.' So the sun turned back on the dial the ten steps by which it had declined" (Is 38: 7–8); "And Hezekiah said to Isaiah, 'What shall be the sign that the LORD will heal me, and that I shall go up to the house of the LORD on the third day?' And Isaiah said, 'This is the sign to you from the LORD, that the LORD will do the thing that he has promised; shall the shadow go forward ten steps, or go back ten steps?' And Hezekiah answered, 'It is an easy thing for the shadow to lengthen ten steps; rather let the shadow go back ten steps.' And Isaiah the prophet cried to the lord; and he brought the shadow back ten steps, by which the sun had declined on the dial of Ahaz" (2 Kgs 20: 8–11).

127. When King Darius puts Daniel into a den of lions, the angel of the Lord closes the mouths of the lions, and Daniel emerges unscathed (Dn 6:16–23). Likewise, when Nebuchad-

est joy on Judgment Day, that is, when one is saved because of one's trust in God. Thus because this was so at the beginning of eternity, thus it must rightly be the supreme pleasure in this temporal life to be saved on account of a faith confuted by the world.

Oh, that I too could gain such glory! I would prefer this crown of honor to all of the crowns of empire, because no one but the one who is in heaven can place it on my head. Oh! I shall gain it without a doubt, for that very God who exhorts and makes me believe will also suffer me to be redeemed, because He is the very one who sent the angel Gabriel to Mary and who filled Elizabeth with the Holy Spirit so that she spoke this praise! He will not suffer to be promised what He does not intend to fulfill. What, however, He does suffer to be proclaimed and accepted, He does fulfill, and He suffers those to be redeemed who did not resist Him and who instead believed in Him and did not let themselves be deterred by nature and reason's denial of what appears impossible to attain.

"For there will be a fulfillment of what was spoken to you from the Lord."[128]

Oh, blessed is he who has faith, for faith is followed by the coming to pass of what one has been told. Faith has as its first object invisibility, but not in perpetuity; it has this invisibility in no other wise than the painter his empty panel, which he fills with color and forms, or as in needlepoint the woman has her names, which she embosses with gold and pearls. Fulfillment is the end of faith: a full end—not an empty one—follows upon its effects; an end replete with miracles, replete with blessings, replete with fruit, and replete with joy crowns its ending. From its initial shadow there will ultimately be a bright sun; from its ostensibly empty air a substantial and solid fortress; and from its dark silhouettes a perfect miraculous image.

The virgin's confirmation of impossible things, the glorious fulfillment, ensues herewith. Thus will it also ensue with everyone who imitates her herein. Elizabeth, who is filled with the Holy Spirit, promises her fulfillment in precisely that spirit that came over her and also wrought faith within her. It is a spirit, but of manifold nature and effect. Oh, blissful time in which will be fulfilled what was ordained from the beginning of eternity and prophesied four thousand years ago: blissful fulfillments that joyous eternity has as

---

nezzar casts Shadrach, Meshach, and Abednego into a fiery furnace, an angel of God rescues them (Dn 3:19–27).

128. Lk 1: 45. The translation provided corresponds to Luther's translation. The RSV reads, "And blessed is she who believed that there would be a fulfillment of what was spoken to her from the Lord."

its infinite end.[129] Now that four thousand years of expectation have finally been fulfilled, who shall still doubt a thing that is promised by the Lord and that is not equal to this most impossible of impossible things either in the length of the delay or the ease of accomplishment?

She speaks in the spirit, thus saying with certitude, unerring and assured, "There will be," and not "There shall be a fulfillment." The Holy Spirit is a certain and joyful spirit; He removes all doubt and gives the greatest joy in the confirmation of pleasant, (even if) impossible things. The certitude in the Good is the proper foundation of bliss. What will all consolation profit me when I am neither certain nor assured of happiness? The certainties of grace, love, and the receiving of God, indeed, of eternal salvation are precisely the greatest grace, love, and salvation themselves, and they come from nowhere else but from God, who grants them to us out of grace. Without His grace, there is no assurance of salvation for us—neither in heaven nor on earth. Grace is the only certitude of salvation, and it is the Holy Spirit who assures us of grace. Therefore everyone who is thus wont to confirm it speaks from the Holy Spirit with certitude and assurance. Thus it follows that we should lend credence to them and accept their assurance, as did Mary that of the enthused Elizabeth.

Oh! There are still many more spirits who assure us of the Spirit and crown the beauty of salvation with the crown of certitude. Oh! May heaven send such reassuring spirits to all those who thirst for certitude in their God-fearing doubts. To be sure, the fact that what the Lord said will come to pass requires no further assurance, since holy reason assures us that God is truth and that this truth is unfailing.

And Mary said, "My soul magnifies the Lord."[130]

Since nothing is sweeter than the assurance of a happy fulfillment of the grace promised by God, Mary could therefore no longer contain herself, and like a full sea, burst out praising and glorifying God. This chord of delight touched the strings of her heart, making them spring, sing, and ring. This flame made the heated-up sugar of the praise of God rise, effervesce, and boil over. Indeed, this oil of the Holy Spirit, poured into the fire of her love, rose with glory and thanks toward heaven; as little as gunpowder, when it is lighted, can keep from blowing up, so little can a spirit moved by the Spirit keep from shooting upward when the fuse of assurance draws nigh. When one tells a person who trusts in God of the fulfillment, it is like

129. Jesus was thought to have been born four thousand years after the creation of Adam.

130. Lk 1: 46.

to when one pulls the plug in a barrel so that the wine of spirit and joy must run out of it unimpeded.

"My soul magnifies the Lord!" said this true daughter of David, doubtless learning this from her grandfather:[131] my soul, spirit, feeling, heart, mind, and everything in and on me; my reason, understanding, will, memory, motions and emotions, my blood, in which the soul lives, and my entire body, which it animates; no blood vessel is in me but it praises the Lord; they are not as full of blood as they are full of His praise. My legs have less marrow than divine praise in them; I have not so much hair on my head as I have heavenly desire for glory, and my interior is completely filled with it. Thus I magnify the Lord above all the heavens, making great His honor and glory: not, of course, that I can enhance His being (for it cannot be augmented even by all the creatures and their utterances), but rather that I magnify his praise, honor, glory, renown, splendor, and illustriousness and let it be praised by the entire world, that through grateful magnification I once again bring forth His renown, which has been suppressed by oblivion, and His honor, which has been buried in the earth by neglect, indeed, that I make great the glory, praise, and name of Him who made me the greatest among all women on earth.

How then should I not make this omnipotent vastness vast, since it made Him who is vastest small in me? Shall my soul not magnify Him who magnified my body to give His divinity a body? Oh! There is no manner of magnifying God that can be devised on earth—or indeed in heaven—that can sufficiently magnify this abasement and make this diminution sufficiently vast. If all the seraphim poured out their fiery intellects and all the cherubim their flaming abysses, it could not be praised sufficiently. I perceive much more than I can give thanks for, and yet even the thousandth part remains hidden from my perception; thus all my magnifying hardly reaches as high as a nail in comparison with the boundless heights of heaven.

"And my spirit rejoices in God my Savior."[132]

My spirit, spurred by the Holy Spirit, leaps for joy in God my Savior; it trembles, jumps, raves, praises, and exults with joy and ardent longing to love and praise in no other way than when the flame makes water, or whatever kind of liquid it be, boil so that the bright bubbles leap up and rise out of and above the vessel and do not suffer themselves to be stilled or damped.

131. Greiffenberg presumably means her "ancestor" here and thus refers to David, as the author of psalms.

132. Lk 1: 47.

Thus joy effervesces and rises up in my spirit, which makes the sweetness of God's grace overflow from the heat; I feel a joy that my heart is too small to contain, since this joy is the sort that makes the pomegranate burst and split thus that the kernels of love can be seen therein.

The joy that is in me forces me out of myself, for what remains within itself and master of itself is no true joy of the spirit. The proper joy of the spirit effervesces, flames, flies, rises, and sends smoke up to heaven; it renders one drunk in heavenly ecstasy so that in the spirit one reels, dances, leaps, and shouts for joy, and knows not how to contain oneself. One is not in control of oneself; instead one suffers the Omnipotent One to hold sway in one's weakness. One is not frightened of the world, because one has the ruler of it in one's heart whence all the little spirits, blood vessels, and drops of blood come forth, like artificial fireworks when they have been lighted and are to catch fire and burst into a million sparks of praise.[133]

This single spirit inspires thousands and thousands of flames of joy: now a rocket of the eternal joy of heaven goes off, now a fire of joy flies up over God's glory; there a ground rocket over the love of Jesus; here a sunburst over the force of the Holy Spirit; on the one hand, a ball of jubilation over the creation of the world; on the other hand, a burning time-fuse over the wondrous rule; there a spark of thanks leaps into the air, here a mine that scatters in a thousand stars of praise.[134] The mercies promised for the future drive the brightest little stars of praise to such heights that they seem to compete with the fixed or static stars in the eighth heaven.[135]

133. Greiffenberg uses the word "Geisterlein" (little spirits) here, a word that she has likely borrowed from alchemy. The "little spirits" are released when fire is applied to matter; spirit is thus the pure essence of a metal or person. See Abraham, *Dictionary of Alchemical Imagery*, 188.

134. What Greiffenberg calls a "Springflamm" here probably corresponds to what Brock describes as a type of "ground rocket," "a rocket less fiercely burning, charged solid, fixed to a support so that it remains stationary whilst burning, the fire being thrown out in a jet." Alan St. H. Brock, *Pyrotechnics: The History and Art of Firework Making* (London: Daniel O'Connor, 1922), 97. Greiffenberg's "Strahlen-Ball," literally "ball of beams," here translated as "sunburst," may correspond to what John Babington describes as a type of firework "which as soone as it breakes, the springs will cast forth your fisgigs, and make them seeme like the sparkling beames of the sunne, and the mixture in the center will seeme as the body of the same; this will continue a while, and then you shall see it breake with divers reports." *Pyrotechnia; or, Artificiall fire works [1635]* (Amsterdam: Theatrum Orbis Terrarum; New York: Da Capo Press, 1971), 50. Finally, with the word "Zunder-Fahnen," Greiffenberg probably refers to the time fuse that burns as the shell rises into the air, leaving a tail of sorts. The time fuse ignites the shell when it has reached its zenith. It is also possible that she refers to the tail of a rocket, which, however, technically speaking is in fact produced not by a fuse but rather by its burning composition. Alan St. H. Brock. *A History of Fireworks* (London: George G. Harrap, 1949), 206.

135. Aristotelian-Ptolemaic cosmology had it that the earth was surrounded by nine heavens, the first seven being the location of the moon, Mercury, Venus, the sun, Mars, Jupiter, and Sat-

The Holy Spirit is always ready to catch fire as long as the powder of our spirit does not become heavy and damp from the air of vanity. Yet even if it comes to pass, the spirit soon can drive away the damp air and purify it, dry the powder, and summon a dry wind that makes it ignitable. The Holy Spirit is certainly the one and only and best fire worker, in both the preparation of the charges and the machine: He is also the dove that is released from the hand of God artfully, charmingly, to ignite the entire firework display; whatever He ignites goes off, even if the entire sea were to pour out over it and all the clouds burst above it.

The glorious and holy joy of the spirit is an inextinguishable light in all the abysses of the sea and the waters of heaven. Oh! The glorious heavenly fire of joy of the Holy Spirit—how it ignites and transfixes me so that for joy I cannot describe the joy. I rejoice not merely from the prompting of nature or the spirit but rather from the greatest cause in the world, namely, in and over God, my Savior. I rejoice in God who is in me and over God who is under my heart. I rejoice in Him who is a vessel of all joys and who is now contained by my body (when He is otherwise unconstrained); in Him who, to gain eternal joy for the entire world, takes on within me the capacity to experience sorrow so as to deliver us from all sorrow.

My spirit rejoices in God, my Savior, who takes from me the tool of my own salvation, for I as well as others will be saved through His powerful suffering and death. Oh! I rejoice infinitely on this account over the ineffable grace of God that from me (who, myself born of Adam, would have been damned) took the means, matter, and tool by which I and all of the children of Adam will be saved. Oh! Should I not rejoice that He who is one with God the Father is also of one flesh and blood with me, that I am to be the mother of the one of whom God is the father, that within me the Creator of my body is provided with a body, that I can embrace the one who embraces everything, conceive the inconceivable, and with my weak body encompass the one who encompasses heaven and earth, that I carry in my body the one who carries heaven and earth, me, and all things?

Oh, joy above all joy! The source of the first living beings takes on a new being within me to gain for us living joy and salvation. What bliss, which no angel can sufficiently conceive, to clothe with my flesh and blood the animator of all the angelic spirits! What bliss to give from my body a body to the one who is a lord of all spirits! What unimaginable joy to have the Spirit in heaven and God in my body; to see, nay, feel my insignificance;

---

urn respectively, the eighth one being the location of the fixed stars, and the ninth the location of the prime mover.

to become a casket of the sum of everything; and to place upon Him a nature that even in death and in all eternity is indivisible, a nature by which our sinful nature would be purified and made holy.

I would have to be dumb and lacking in all human reason, faculties, and sensitivity if I did not experience the most fundamental joy conceivable that the fount of all reason took on a humanly rational soul and all senses and sensations within me. Is it not reason for rejoicing that the most beautiful king of angels and divine prince betook himself to me, miserable shepherdess that I am, and not only loved me divinely but even took on a heart from me so that he, wounded with a million arrows of love, could deliver it back to me; that he acquires arms within me so that he can embrace me; hands with which he can caress me; a mouth so that he can kiss me; and a breast against which he will caress and press me? Is there a cause for joy on earth that is as great and important as mine, the one that comes from rejoicing in my Savior, who is at once in my body and in my heart? I challenge all causes of joy, but none will be able to measure up to this one, for having Almighty God as a companion, having love itself in one's body and the Holy Spirit in one's spirit, surpasses everything that can be felt and imagined of joy. In short: nothing can compare with this joy.

Thus, my spirit, let your desire run its course and rejoice in God your Savior with all your heart, with all your soul, with all your might, and with all your power. Let entire rivers of joy flow forth from my mouth and let the wellspring in my heart overflow with heartfelt ecstasy. Joy in God and in the spirit commands divine praise as well. Therefore praise the Lord, my soul, in the most ardent and extreme way that a creature can praise Him; let all your stirrings be urges to pray; your every breath, the breath of praise; every drop of your blood, rubies of praise; and all your deeds, praise of God's miracles. If you consider the heavens, then praise God's loftiness, which is higher than heaven; [if you consider] the earth, [then praise] His kindness, with which it is filled; [if you consider] the sun, [then praise] His brightness, which is a wellspring of [the sun's brightness]; you yourself, [then praise] His grace, by whose power you are what you are. May everything that comes into your sight be a divine detonator of praise; may all my powers of perception and reason prime and chime God's praise. Do it so vigorously that you might perish doing it, so incessantly that neither time nor eternity can disturb you while you do it, for praising God is your greatest obligation and the reason why you were created and why God created for Himself a new nature within you, one that will once more restore sinful nature so that it can again fulfill the original purpose of creation.

Thanks be to you on this account and to you eternal praise that rises above all the heavens for your still higher grace! Just as sight gets lost high above in the air and sees infinite blue, so all pronouncements vanish within the majesty of the heavenly joy of the spirit; especially in my case, I who received the greatest and most special mercies and who thus for sheer joy and desire to praise hardly know what to say.

"For he has regarded his wretched handmaiden."[136]

The majesty of a thing is always recognized in its opposite, lowliness: the deeper the foundation, the higher the edifice; the deeper the spring, the higher the waterfall; the deeper the wretchedness, the greater the grace of exaltation, which now appears with me; for God has regarded his wretched handmaiden. God, the Most High, me, the lowliest; the Most Glorious, me, the wretched one; the Almighty, me, who am nothing; the King of Heaven, me, the little earthworm; the Ruler of all the Angels, me, the wretched handmaiden on earth; the Omnipotent One, me, the worthless one; the Immutable One, me, the fleeting little speck of dust; He who is everything and makes everything come to pass has regarded me, poor nothing; the King of all Kings, me, His wretched handmaiden, the servant of His soul, His serf who was not worthy to kiss the footprints of His omnipotence. He has regarded her, that is, He has blessed, given grace, made happy, and exalted [her]: for God's regard is blessing, granting mercy, making happy, exalting, and redeeming in time and eternity.

This regard amounts to the same thing as directing the entire river of grace at a person, emptying out the entire cornucopia of salvation over a person, suffering the cloudburst of ecstasy to rain down upon a person, indeed suffering the entire sun-fountain of all the beams of the spirit to flow and flash at once; for the eyes of God are sources of bliss, which when they are trained upon us can do nothing but overflow with pure blessing and life, as I have experienced it myself with the most ardent joy.

The glorious beams of grace of the Most High seek a broad space so that they can spread out unimpeded, a space found nowhere more truly than in humility where no earthly being gets in their way. So for this reason He regarded the humility of His handmaiden so that He could operate unimpeded in her most profound lowliness. If a single inkling of desire for majesty or of presumption had been in me, it would have repulsed His effect, for God's glory does not tolerate the slightest presumption to the paltriest worthiness. All capability of the divine operation of grace is lost if one har-

136. Paraphrase of Lk 1: 48: "For he has regarded the low estate of his handmaiden."

bors the smallest presumption, and it is nothing but nothingness in which the Omnipotent One means to operate.

Oh! If the world understood this and learned from me that one is deemed worthy of becoming the tool of God's grace as a result of the most fundamental sense of one's own nothingness, the world would not fall into the deepest rung of hell through arrogance and sink into the unfathomable slough of affliction on account of pride.

Oh! Consider! If the Most High has regarded humility, it must indeed be the most beautiful and virtuous thing in the entire world. For He regarded nothing but this in me, not my form, not my royal lineage, my youth, my chastity, my respectability, decency, piety, or devotion; not my eloquence, art, or skill either, but only my humility and my humility alone, and not so much as a virtue but merely as an unimpeding convenience into which He could release Himself, since no manner of earthly presumption was in the way. Also it was not that I as a human being possessed such perfection but that I through His grace recognized my imperfection and through true illumination of the spirit felt myself to be completely insignificant and wretched. I did not force myself to be humble by imposing humility on myself; rather I was from the bottom of my heart conscious of myself as wretched and worthless. He who probes our hearts regarded my personal confession and my unvarnished testimony to my good conscience, and from this miserable insignificance He took the substance that He united personally to His divine being.

Thus humility learns from the Most High, who took on substance from substantial insignificance and put it in the company of His divinity. Since He put the sum of the universe itself in the dust, why should He not demand all the more that obligatory, nay, natural humility be in the creatures of the earth? Should not the worms of the earth bury themselves in [the dust] all the more, given that it is their element, primordial being, and origin? Oh, folly! How should insignificance wish to be something when the sum of the universe itself becomes nothing?

There is no greater folly on earth than pride, no worse error, since it takes and regards everything wrongly. It means to climb and falls into the abyss. It means to fly and sinks thereby into a pit. What it considers laudable reaps it the greatest scorn, and it does not know that its vaulting is a plummeting; its elevating a foreshortening; its heaven hell; and its stars hell's sparks. To be sure, other vices lead people imperceptibly astray from the path of virtue; pride, however, leads in exactly the opposite direction. All the same, people cannot let go of it. Thus they not only sully themselves with pride but also want to pin it on the dead, indeed, even on those who already dwell in heaven, namely, by imputing and attributing undue honor to them, honor of which one is incapable in that blessed place where one desires only to honor God in persons three. If this (as I imagine it) should happen to me too, I would want to ask and to stipulate that I demand no honor due the divinity; rather, if the least dust speck of honor and worship due God were given to me and done to me, even were it with the best of intentions, I would want to be horrified and indignant about it in heaven too, were that possible.[137] I am content, and that is enough abundance and glory for me, and thus I can say,

"For behold, henceforth all generations will call me blessed."[138]

Just consider what an ineffable honor this is! From now on and on account of this, all those who come after me, those who are born over the centuries, will call me blessed. From now on, from that moment on, when I conceived the Redeemer in my womb, all people who are redeemed by Him would consider and call me blessed, should they know of this, my good fortune and theirs. All the angels in heaven will call me blessed—to be sure it will not help them because they are already redeemed, but they rejoice in our salvation and exult in the miracle! There is no praising of salvation in heaven and on earth that will not be given me by and by.

It will, however, not be the dignity and excellence of my person that are herewith praised, but rather the ineffable grace and kindness of God, the unfathomable love and humility of the Most High; the highly amazing and admirable abasement of the sublime divinity in the person of Jesus Christ, the sublime and only begotten son of God; and the inconceivable miraculous operation of the Holy Spirit, who within my weakness wrought a tool of omnipotence in order to conquer hell and the world. This [miracle] will be extolled by all creatures, and I myself [will be extolled] only on account of having been chosen as the matter, tool, shelter, and vessel beloved of God, in which He aimed to form, provide, work, and prepare this miracle.

I shall be called blessed or blissful by the entire world because such great things have come to pass within me and upon me: not that I through my own capability and powers, art or virtue, should have wrought these, but rather that God deemed me worthy and performed this most sublime work within me.

God's grace will be extolled in me, not my merits, of which I have none; rather, I am a wretched handmaiden and unworthy tool of His gracious hand. And even if over the centuries people should arise who praised me for my person and not just merely and purely for the divine grace [that I

137. Greiffenberg alludes here to the Catholic cult of Mary, which she as a Lutheran rejects.

138. Lk 1: 48.

received], but instead wanted to ascribe the slightest part of it to my merit, I hereby aver—with divine true knowledge, in complete illumination of spirit—that I would not favor it. Nor would it please me; rather it would offend and pain me if the tiniest speck of dust of God's honor were to be taken from Him and attributed to me: for blessed souls (which mine will without a doubt be at this time) consider as no honor that which is taken from God's honor and attributed to them. Their honor is honoring God; their wish is for it to come to pass that the whole world honor Him and Him alone; their action is to remove their crowns and lay them at His feet; their aim is to inspire everyone through their example in this life to make it their ultimate goal to give Him alone, the Infinite One, infinite honor now and forever.

And thus when people ascribe excessive honor to me or to any creature, they act against my honor, wish, work, goal, and end and against those of all the blessed ones, thus doing us no honor or service but rather the greatest disservice and offense; for our aim and desire to adore the one and only, the supreme God, are thus countermanded. A blessed spirit has completely divested itself of self and has its honor, its joy, its glory and praise—everything—in God; God means everything to it. [It regards] whatever of such things that are given to God as given to itself. [A blessed spirit] rejoices in them; it delights in them. Whatever [honor] is ascribed to [a blessed spirit] insults it, and it regrets that these people sin by not giving all honor to the one to whom it is due, namely the God in Persons Three.

I say this in the present illumination of spirit as a future warning that people must not afflict me in that joyous eternity by honoring me inappropriately; for in my heart I will consider it the greatest honor when people give that honor to Him alone, who lay beneath my heart. I shall, however, delight in being called blessed for having the good fortune to be His mother. My worry is and will be and will forever remain how to praise God enough. I shall apply all my thoughts and powers, muster all my doings and undertakings, direct all my thoughts and plans toward letting the whole world sound his glory and letting his glory resound throughout the world. Through the ineffable grace and charity of the almighty God, I am most firmly and inexorably bound to this.

"For he who is mighty has done great things for me, and holy is his name."[139]

He has done great things for me, indeed, the greatest of everything that He could ever do for a mortal but had never done before or will ever again! Great things in that from me and in me He has made the greatest of all become small—wedded strength to weakness, omnipotence to impotence,

139. Lk 1: 49.

and the divine to the human; in that He made me the mother of the one who from His Word created and bore me and my mother and her mother's mother. Great things in that in me He made the very Creator of all seed into the seed of woman to redeem us, the sinful seed of Adam. Great things in that precisely through me, a wretched handmaiden, He intended to fulfill the promise of grace made in paradise and thus must have thought of me, unworthy one, when I had (otherwise) not yet been thought of.

What can really be greater on earth than carrying in one's body the one who is greater than heaven and earth to that end that He be made capable of the greatest deed on earth, namely, redeeming the human race through his blood and suffering? This greatest of all things, then, has He done for me to form from and in my body and blood a holy body and blood that in the deepest unity with the divine can serve heaven by spilling blood that redeems the entire world (even if there were thousands of worlds): indeed, that will also spill its blood for that from which it came, for I, just as well as others, will be saved through Him.

Oh, great things! A worm as the jewel case of the divine, a speck of dust as the case of the sun, and a little tiny ditch as the vessel of the sea of totality! Who can speak of these great deeds of God and glorify His laudable works sufficiently? I stiffen, go silent, and am enraptured over it!

Angels perceive that one gloriously ponders
Divine power's most exceptional wonders.[140]

When the time comes that brings the Eternal One into the world, these angels will also sing and shout, extol it, and tell about it.

I, but I, oh!
I cannot rest either meanwhile;
the great doings of the great God
stir up my soul in me.[141]

140. My translation adheres to the syllabic meter but unlike the original ends in an unaccented syllable, adding an extra syllable to each line.

Engel gehören / daß Göttlicher Macht /
Sondere Wunder man herrlich betracht.

141. My translation adheres to the syllabic meter of each line but leaves off the last unaccented syllable of the final line.

Ich aber / Ach!
Ich kan indessen auch nicht ruhn /
Des großen GOttes großes Thun
Erregt mir mein Gemüte.

Oh! Shall such great deeds not elicit great feelings and emotions? Shall they not drive love forth from the mouth and eyes in a hundred thousand flames? Shall they not transform all the blood that is left into heat and cinders? Oh, yes! It comes to pass and is more than I can express. Even if I use divine language, it remains nevertheless an unreachable ineffability. Yet I will sing praise as much as I can:

1
My soul! Put yourself upon[142]
the spirit's eagle; fly up,
even if it upward flew,
heavenward, displeasing you,
because it is still too low.
Above the highest of heavens,
take the cymbal of God's worship,
since you are deeply indebted.
From these lofty heights praise God
as needs His divinity.

2
Heave as high as could the spirit
possibly raise anything;
even should it melt perforce

142. The following poem consists of seven numbered verses, written in trochaic tetrameter according to the rhyme scheme *ababcddcee*, etc. (The first verse, however, deviates from this rhyme scheme.) The concluding couplet of each verse alternately consists of the impure rhyme of "Gott" (God) with "Not" (need [require], necessity, misery) or "Gott" with "Tod" (death). I have reproduced only the syllabic meter, which consists here of either seven or eight syllables, depending on whether the line ends in an accented or unaccented syllable. Stanza 6, line 8 likely contains a misprint and should read "bekränzt" (wreathed, garlanded) rather than "beklänzt." Grimm records no such word as *beklänzt*.

1. Meine Seele! setze dich
auf des Geistes Adler / fliege /
wann auch solcher schwünge sich
Himmel-an / dich nicht vergnügt /
weil es noch zu nieder ist /
über aller Himmel Himmel /
bring die GOtt-Verehrungs Cimbel /
weil du hoch verpflichtet bist.
Preiß in solcher Höhe GOtt /
die zu seiner Gottheit Noth.

2. Heb so hoch / als je dem Geist
müglich ist / was zu erheben /
ob er von Gewalt zerfleust

from the superhuman striving,
heed it not; to praise the highest,
to praise His goodness as well
be your diligent intention
(in your heart no strength shall linger!).
Be prepared even through death
to magnify your Lord God.

3
Magnifying, your strength, spirit,
heart, and life shall pass away.
If God's glory but remain
floating in divine clouds,
passing away means arising
into rapture everlasting.
God's laudation is my crown,
His glory, my ornament.
I, to magnify my God,
disregard passing's misery.

4
Be it my art, way, and practice
to make golden and make shine
the whole wide world with His praise,

---

durch das über-menschlich streben /
acht es nicht; deß Höchsten Preiß
seiner Güte gleich zu treiben /
(solt kein Kraft im Herzen bleiben!)
sey dein Seel geflißner Fleiß.
zu erheben deinen GOtt /
sey bereit auch durch den Tod.

3. Im Erheben / soll vergehn
deine Kraft / Geist / Herz und Leben;
bleibt nur GOttes Ehre stehn /
und in Gottheit-Wolken schweben /
ist Vergehn ein Aufgang mir
in die unvergänglich Wonne /
GOttes Lob ist meine Krone /
seine Ehre meine Zier.
Zu erheben meinen GOtt /
acht ich nicht Vergehens-Noth.

4. Alle Welt mit seinem Preiß
zu vergülden und beglänzen /
sey mein Ubung / Knust [*sic*] und Weis /

to garland everything
and give laurels with God's glory.
To fill all the world with it
is my will's principal aim.
My heart desires naught so much
as magnifying my God,
as in life, so too in death.

5
Were my will but a column,
I would raise it to God's glory
and would not merely raise up
in the air the highest part,
inscribed with stories of praise.
Yes, even the highest heaven
with the bright sparkling of stars
would lie far, far beneath it.
I must magnify my God
more than heaven's heights require.

6
Soul, use your divinity,
in eternity grown strong,

---

zu verlorbeern und bekränzen
alle Ding mit GOttes Ehr /
alle Welt damit zu füllen
ist der Haupt-Punct meines Willen.
Nichts verlang mein Herz so sehr /
als erheben meinen GOtt /
wie im Leben / so im Tod.

5. Wär mein Willen eine Seul /
wolt ichs GOtt zur Ehr aufrichten
und nicht nur das oberst Theil
in der Lufft / voll Lob-Geschichten
angeschildet / überhöhn.
Ja selbst aller Himmel Himmel
mit dem hellen Stern-Gewimmel
müste weit darunter stehn.
Zu erheben meinen Gott
mehr als Himmels-Höh ist Noht.

6. Brauche deiner Göttlichkeit /
Seele! deinen GOtt zu loben /
die sich stärkt in Ewigkeit /

to sing the praise of your God.
Offer proofs of the spirit's might
to Him, infinity-crowned.
Show the freedom to serve Him;
the life forces green in praise
so a wreath adorns earth too.
Look for the freedom in death
to magnify your Lord God.

7
Oh! Soul! High as He may be,
magnify Him, your Lord God.
Since you too are infinite,
let His praise ever endure,
let your devotion to God
soar like His divinity
that it rise up higher still
above the choirs of the angels.
You must magnify the Lord
more than all the angels need.

Of course more than all the angels! For nothing so very great as this has come from God to all the angels together, nothing so great as what has come to me, wretched one, expressly from Him who is so powerful. When He with His omnipotence could have created an angelic child bearer for

---

Leiste Geist-Vermögens Proben /
den Unendlichkeit bekränzt;
zeig die Freyheit / ihm zu dienen /
Saft und Kraft im Lobe grünen /
das die Erden mit beklänzt [*sic*].
zu erheben deinen Gott
such die Freyheit durch den Tod.

7. Ach! erheb so hoch er ist /
Seele! deinen GOtt und HErren /
weil du selbst unendlich bist /
laß sein Lob auch ewig währen /
seiner Gottheit gleich hoch schweb
dein erhebtes GOtt-Verehren /
daß es ob der Engel Chören
noch was höher sich erheb.
Du hast zu erheben Gott
mehr als alle Engel Noht.

Himself, I, miserable one, have the grace of clothing Him in my flesh. He who with His power could have made me into nothing, as I was before His creation and my birth, He with His goodness made His coequal omnipotent person take on within me the nullity of human nature. He who has dominion over all crowns and thrones was pleased to become a little worm within me; He whose name, nature, kind, being, will, and works are holy, He purified for Himself within me, poor sinner, a little drop of blood that is capable of uniting with His divinity and cannot be consumed by its purifying fire. Indeed, that very holiness and purity itself sanctified for itself a dwelling place in my weakness and took away the sin of a little speck of dust of it and made it into the purest twin nature in one person.

O holiness! How do I come to Thee, I, sinful wretch? Or rather, how dost Thou come to me, Thou who art inconceivable to all people, so that Thou art thereby conceived as a human being? He who is holy works wonders of holiness in me, wretched handmaiden. He will cause that very Holiness to be born of me, sinner, so that everyone who believes in Him will thereby be made holy. The embodied Holiness will come forth out of my body so that all of our bodies will become holy. He will put Holiness in me to make it into a human being and thus, in a way, to communicate it to all humankind.

For just as His purest human nature was conceived and prepared in a most holy fashion without sin within me, sinner, thus shall His righteousness be fully received through faith in those poor sinners. For He who is holy works great wonders of holiness; He places these [wonders] in them who were not holy and makes them holy, contrary to their own worth and capacity.

Holiness is not diminished when it takes up sin and takes on the sinners and takes away their frailties. It becomes only that much holier in the hearts of those made holy when it swallows up their unholiness, heals their frailties, and brings about sanctification in them, namely, through precisely that spirit that undertakes to form the Savior's body in mine.

Oh, holy miracle! God makes a cloak for God within me so that He can make the cloak of righteousness for me and all poor sinners. The Most High builds for His equally majestic person in me, the lowly one, a palace that all humankind will worship and in which all people will be given a favorable hearing. Omnipotence makes use of my weakness to produce a work of the most powerful pith of omnipotence. [Omnipotence] grants Highness the material of its effect by descending into the deepest abjection; it engages in the most important business of eternity by playing with a child, and Omnipotence's inconceivable miracle makes conceivable inconceivable heaven, which is spanned in a place as wide as a span, that is, makes conceivable even when it is invisible. This is much more amazing and a much greater grace than the creation of all conceivability. For

"His mercy is on those who fear him from generation to generation."[143]

Since His mercy endures from generation to generation, He has thus invented an eternal redemption. Because the mediator between God and humankind, between time and eternity, is to accomplish this, thus must He also be temporal and eternal, be born and partake of both natures, so that time and eternity are united in and through Him. The Eternal One had to become temporal so that we who are lost in temporality could take in eternal joy. To make His mercy endure forever and ever, the merciful God Himself had to become that which He forever and ever was not. To make His mercy great in blessed eternity, the Eternal One Himself had to become small; so that it could endure forever and ever, He had to enter the state of transitoriness and at the same time remain the forever and ever imperishable one; for God's mercy could not endure forever and ever if His righteousness were not satisfied. To satisfy this righteousness, God's mercy had to cease toward itself for a while so that it could endure toward us forever and ever, and specifically toward those who fear Him.

Fearing God is as indispensable to our enjoyment of mercy as opening our eyes to see the sun; for the most unimaginable magnanimity is an undeniable characteristic of God. This characteristic can neither show itself nor show mercy except when one lies down humbly at its feet, which happens solely through the fear of God. The fear of God kisses the punishing hand of the Almighty and makes all arrows of wrath fall from it; by humbly prostrating itself, it prevents us from being crushed by [God's] fury. It falls on the sword of revenge and winds the mollifying olive branch around it. Indeed, the Epitome of Magnanimity Himself will not suffer Himself to be overcome by abasement without His goodness becoming greater still. His extravagance aims for victory in the dispensing of charity, and God does not abandon His heavenly leonine manner to show kindness to the timid.

He who fears God opens the window of His ardent mercy so that it blazes forth from [the window] unchecked, like a fire fanned by air. With a childlike fear, he touches God's aorta so that it overflows and flows with grace toward him. Fear of God is the weight that transforms mercy into

143. Lk 1: 50.

eternal motion. It is the North Star of its sort of magnet, the oil of its ever-burning lamp, and in short the dwelling place of its gracious effect; for only those who fear God can hope for mercy. Poor sinners are not excluded here; no one is more afraid than they who have offended God. Their fear is thus no hindrance but instead an enticement to God's grace, which endures forever (even toward the greatest sinners).

Oh, Wonder! Fear is an assurance against fear; the fear that one will anger God refutes the fear of being cast out, and he who fears God alone need not be afraid of anything that is outside of God. Thus it is said: Fear God; otherwise fear nothing. Oh, blissful fear of God that drives away all fear on earth, indeed, fear of hell, and makes us live without fear in secure bliss.

Thus let all the world fear the Lord, for the fear of the Lord is the beginning of wisdom.[144] It is, as the wisest of tutors says, the highest honor, the fairest glory, the sweetest joy, and the noblest crown. It gladdens the heart and brings joy and delight; for it will go well in the final extremity for those who fear the Lord, and they will ultimately receive God's blessing. They must of course fare well in the end, because God's mercy holds sway forever and ever over those who fear God. Thus things cannot of course go badly for them in the end; because eternity has no end, things have to go well for them longer than the end, indeed, beyond the end, and they will have His blessing not merely in the end but endlessly.

Fear of the Lord is the proper way to worship God. It protects and makes the heart pious and gives joy and delight; for whosoever fears the Lord will thrive and be blessed. Fearing God is the wisdom that enriches and brings along all goodness with it; it fills the entire house with its gifts and all the chambers with its treasure, all of which I have indeed experienced, for who can be more enriched than the person who has the root of all riches in her body and her heart? To whom can it bring more goodness than to the one to whom it brought the highest good? It fills not only the house but my entire body with its gifts, indeed, with the gift and the giver of all gifts, and all the chambers of my body and soul, mind, and spirit with the greatest treasure in heaven and on earth. Of course with regard to the body, that is, the corporeal conception for the purpose of the incarnation, it will happen to me alone, but with regard to the spirit, to all those who fear Him.

So fear the Lord, you, His saints, for those who fear Him lack no good of any kind; [they lack] no divinely inspired heavenly blessings; [they lack]

144. Sir 1: 12 in the RSV.

no angels, for [angels] surround those who fear Him and assist them; [they lack not] for God's care, for the eyes of the Lord look down upon them who fear Him; [they lack] not for wisdom, for the fear of the Lord is the beginning of wisdom and refined intelligence; [they lack] not for praise and crowns of glory, for whosoever acts in accordance with this shall be eternally praised, and the fear of God is a crown of wisdom. It makes people true and wise and lends [them] honor; [they lack] not for blessing, for He blessed those who fear the Lord, always and forever; [they lack] not for salvation and peace, for [fear of the Lord] brings not only ordinary but rich, superabundant peace and salvation; [they lack] also not for ephemeral gifts. [Fear of the Lord] brings grace before the kings and greats of the world and attains freedom—as happened in the case of the God-fearing Tobias.[145]

He who fears God does not lack for joy either (which is one of the greatest of all earthly gifts), for whoever fears God (says Sirach) will achieve joy and he will receive a true friend.[146] In short, fear of God, in which true bliss consists, profits this and that life, for whosoever fears God has no one over him. For this reason everyone should strive for this excellence and humble himself beneath the mighty hand of God. For

"He shows strength with his arm, he scatters the proud in the imagination of their hearts."[147]

His hand is like the mighty thunder that opposes only what is hard and oppositional, that shatters the blade and does not harm the sheath, smashes the bone but does not injure the skin, and works many wonders of that sort by exerting pressure. He exercises strength with His strong arm against the strong who mean to use the strength that comes from Him against the Strongest of All—as Pharaoh, Sennacherib, Nebuchadnezzar, Holofernes, Sisera, and thereafter a whole series of tyrants and bloodthirsty villains

145. See the Book of Tobias (Tobit), a deuterocanonical book of the Old Testament, where the lesson is taught that God is faithful to those who are faithful to him. Tobit is excluded from the Protestant canon.

146. The Book of Sirach or the Wisdom of Jesus the son of Sirach belongs to the Apocrypha. It is also known as Ecclesiastics (church book) because of its wide use among Greek and Latin Christians in moral instruction. Classified among the wisdom writings, the book was written in Hebrew ca. 180 BCE by Jesus ben Sirach. Fear of God is a central theme in this book. The text may specifically reference the verses "The fear of the Lord is glory and exultation, and gladness and a crown of rejoicing. The fear of the Lord delights the heart, and gives gladness and joy and long life" (1: 9–10 in the RSV) and "A faithful friend is an elixir of life; and those who fear the Lord will find him" (6: 16 in the RSV).

147. Lk 1: 51. The RSV deviates from the Luther Bible in Lk 1: 51–53 in its use of the present perfect. Greiffenberg's quotations of these verses are all in the present tense in keeping with her source.

learned and as will learn in the future still many more, who wish to wield their gossamer against the lead of His thunder.[148]

He shows strength with his arm, He who created the world and strength. The origin of all strength—shall He not exercise what He is Himself and make it bubble up and flow like a spring forever and ever? He shows it as does a master his art, as a king his authority, and an effect the success that cannot fail to set in. He has shown it from the beginning of the world and will show it to its end, indeed, in infinity. His strength has the same confines as does His wisdom, namely, endlessness. What miracles will yet emerge? Oh! Who could regard and contemplate them sufficiently?

O adorable strength of God! What manner of miracle wilt Thou not yet work? Almighty arm of God! What more wilt Thou yet effect, especially against the proud? For Thou scatterest them in the imagination of their hearts. When they have gathered their spirits and forces like stone and lime mortar and erect a great Babel in their imagination, Thou scatterest them by not assenting to its completion; when they have set mountain upon mountain, like the giants, to storm heavenward, so must they perish in the sea of Thy might and wisdom.[149] When, like ants, they have assembled their mountains of pillage and smoke, He customarily spreads them out and scatters them with the staff of His mouth so, like those ants, they must run off and hide in a thousand places.

When pride aims, as if on wings, to raise itself heavenward through the dust of its manifold thoughts, He scatters it with His beams and makes an Icarus-army fall into the sea of shame and confusion.[150] He scatters not only their works but their attempts in the imagination of their hearts. Their

148. In Exodus Moses and Aaron ask Pharaoh to let the Israelites go. Pharaoh refuses and proceeds to torment the enslaved Israelites even more than before. Pharaoh finally lets them go after God wreaks ten plagues on Egypt. Pharaoh, however, changes his mind and pursues them with his armies into the Red Sea (Ex 5–14). Sennacherib was the king of Assyria who sacked cities in Judah and besieged the capital city, Jerusalem. According to 2 Kgs 19: 35, the siege of Jerusalem was unsuccessful and Sennacherib returned to Nineveh. The conflicts of the idolatrous Nebuchadnezzar II, king of Babylon (ca. 605–562 BCE), with the Israelites are portrayed in the Book of Daniel and in Jeremiah. Nebuchadnezzar dispatched the general Holofernes to take revenge on the nations to the west that had failed to submit to his rule. The deuterocanonical Book of Judith recounts how when he laid siege to Bethulia, the beautiful Judith, in the guise of seducing him or being seduced, decapitated him. Sisera was the captain of the army of the king of Canaan, Jabin (Jgs 4: 2). God is said to have sold the people of Israel into the hand of Jabin because they had sinned.

149. In Greek mythology, the Aloadai giants attempt to storm the home of the gods in the sky by piling Mount Ossa on top of Mount Olympus and Mount Pelion on top of Mount Ossa.

150. According to Greek mythology, Daedalus fashioned for himself and his son, Icarus, wings held together with wax. Exuberant in his godlike ability to soar upward toward the heavens, Icarus ventured too near the sun, the wings melted, and he plunged to his death.

hearts are to Him nothing but a bowl full of flour or down into which He blows, making everything fly away and disappear.

Shame on you, you proud ones, for having your hearts full of dust that will in the end be scattered by the Most High! They should be filled with pearls instead, pearls that cannot be blown away! Pearls of the fear of God, penitence, worship, prayer, and Christian virtue that are strung on the crimson threads of the blood of the lamb, which is soon to be spilled, and that lace up and adorn the heart so that neither the devil nor hell can open it up! O blind pride, you who are the reverse of your own goal, you who abase when you mean to exalt and who are odious to yourself.

He does not, however, just scatter, but instead when they do not want to pay heed and want rather to continue [as before],

"He puts down the mighty from their thrones, and exalts those of low degree."[151]

In the case of cruel Cambyses, the lancer of hearts, [God] pushed the man's own sword into his heart, thus pushing him from the imperial throne. He toppled Hippias, the bloodthirsty tyrant, from the Athenian throne into wretchedness on the isle of Lemnos and forced blood from his eyes. He had Thrasybulus stab and topple the worst of the thirty Athenian tyrants, Critias, who wanted to make the poor daughters dance in their fathers' blood. Ochus, who cruelly raged against the Jewish church and against everything else, was finally driven away and destroyed with poison.[152]

History books offer many examples of such topplings—of both women and men. Proud Cleopatra, cruel Tullia, arrogant Vashti, and impious Jezebel felt this blow, as well as did wanton Athaliah, and as did both before and after them innumerable arrogant people who believed themselves firmly rooted to their thrones but who were pushed off them like a dog from a precious cushion that it has begun to soil.[153] In contrast He raised up those of

151. Lk 1: 52. The verse is here changed to the present tense.

152. Herodotus recounts the cruel deeds of Cambyses the king of the Persians at length in book 3 of his *History*. In Herodotus's account, Cambyses met his death when he accidentally stabbed himself in the thigh with his own sword, wounding himself in the very place where he had once wounded the Egyptian god Apis (*Herodotus*, 83 [3.64]). Hippias was tyrant of Athens in the sixth century BCE; Critias (460–403 BCE) was one of the most violent of the Thirty Tyrants, a pro-Spartan oligarchy installed in Athens after the Peloponnesian War in 404 BCE; Thrasybulus (d. 388 BCE) was an Athenian general who led the successful resistance to the oligarchic government of the Thirty Tyrants; Artaxerxes III Ochus ruled Persia 358–338 BCE and among other things led a bloody campaign against Egypt and Sidon. The Jews were thought to have joined the fight against the Persians and to have been punished for doing so. One of Ochus's ministers, the eunuch Bagoas, is said to have poisoned the king.

153. Tullia was married to Lucius Tarquinius Superbus (Tarquin II), whom she encouraged to murder her father, Servius Tullius, in 534 BCE so that Tarquin could ascend to the throne. Eventually Rome revolted and the Tarquin family was expelled from Rome in 510 BCE. Jezebel

low degree who never ever thought of any kind of majesty, as for example Joseph, who was put down a well and imprisoned in a tower and who asked to see the light of day but by no means demanded the radiance of glory; similarly it happened to the shepherd David and before him Saul, who was looking for donkeys and thinking of his dumb animals and not about the art of governance.[154] Elisha, who was tending his oxen, probably did not think of the high office of the prophet either, nor did the cowherd Amos [think about] what he was to be called to.[155]

God means to favor with lofty things those who have no thought of them: He transports those who are content with their lowliness into majesty to show the superabundance of His mercy, which can more than delight. Good Abdylonymus was quite delighted with his garden work and wished to wield successfully both the unexpected scepter and the garden tool.[156]

God also exalted by means of wisdom those heathens who hovered in the depths to the highest pinnacles of glory. Socrates, who was named by the oracle the wisest among men and who was, as it were, the heathens' Solomon, was the son of a stonemason, and his mother practiced as a midwife. The father of that researcher of secrets Pythagoras was a ring maker. God brought him so far along that he had knowledge, as it were, of everything on the entire earth and of everything that was encompassed by the ring of heaven. Demosthenes, the most famous of all orators, was the son of a knife maker. Rome had among its seven kings three of quite common and base origins, three whom the Most High raised from the dust to this illustrious rank and placed on the throne.[157]

---

was the wife of Ahab and queen of Judah and a worshiper of Baal (1 Kgs 16–21). Vashti, queen of Persia, refused to obey the king's command that she appear before him. He therefore repudiated her and replaced her with Esther (Est 1). Athaliah, daughter of Jezebel and King Ahab and a worshiper of Baal, usurped the throne of Judah. She herself was also eventually slain (2 Kgs 11).

154. Gn 37: 23. Joseph's brothers cast him into a pit that was empty of water. He was later sold to a band of Ishmaelites who took him to Egypt. In Egypt he was imprisoned after Potiphar's wife falsely accused him of attacking her (Gn 39: 6–23). David was a mere shepherd boy when he entered the service of Saul and then went out to combat Goliath (1 Sm 16–17). When Saul, who was looking for his father's lost donkeys, sought out the prophet Samuel for help, Samuel anointed him king of Israel (1 Sm 9–10).

155. Elisha is an Old Testament prophet who was called by Elijah when he was plowing with twelve yoke of oxen (1 Kgs 19: 19). Amos, one of the minor prophets of the Old Testament, identifies himself as "a herdsman, and a dresser of sycamore trees" (Am 7: 14).

156. Abdylonymus was a gardener for the Persian satrap of Sidon in the third century BCE who protected the gardens under his care from the rebellion against the Persians. When Alexander the Great took the city, Abdylonymus was chosen to be the new king of Sidon.

157. Socrates; from the point of view of the Christian world, Socrates' wisdom makes him the Solomon of the Greek world. Pythagoras (ca. 582–ca. 507 BCE) was a Greek mathematician,

If I meant to recount all the examples of divine exaltation, three moons would not suffice me; for the highest God takes such great pleasure in exalting the lowly that He cannot demonstrate it often enough. I am, however, the principal proof of that since he chose me, the most wretched little clump of earth, to be the jewel case of his divinity, which he lowered into me. And after me, there will come to pass countless spectacular miracles of his wondrous exaltation of the lowly (to be sure nothing like this one, but like the previous ones).

"He fills the hungry with good things, and the rich he sends empty away."[158]

God, who is certainly indescribable and inconceivable, might most accurately be called, among all the names, the Sum of Everything, because all goodness and all wisdom are in Him; He also practices every imaginable manner of blessing and favoring us. He exalts (as stated) those of low degree who never harbored any thoughts of majesty and feeds the hungry who cry out for food day and night. A similar mercy holds sway in dissimilar undertakings: He delights the former by unexpectedly showering them with pleasantness; the latter He delights with the granting of a ravenous desire; He tosses in the lap of the former what they never expected; to the latter He gives the food of Tantalus, which they never before could reach, thus giving rise to a pleasant dispute as to which have the greatest cause to be delighted, those who, as it were, found an unexpected treasure or these whose inflamed ardor was cooled by a spring.[159]

Unexpected mercies are to be sure delightful cloudbursts, floods that practically drown desire, but in so doing, they are the long-yearned-for fulfillment of desire. They are the bread that hunger provides, on which one nearly stuffs oneself to death out of delight.

There is no more raging bodily passion than hunger; all others allow themselves to be satiated and governed; this one, however, demands to be satisfied shortly. Thus its gratification and satiation are a real and perceptible joy and delight that are not merely a figment of the imagination but

---

astronomer, and scientist. Demosthenes (384–322 BCE) was a Greek statesman and orator. The seven kings of Rome are those who ruled for a time span of just under 250 years from Rome's legendary founding by Romulus (reigned 753–716 BCE) through Lucius Tarquinius Superbus (reigned 535–510/509 BCE).

158. Lk 1: 53.

159. According to Greek mythology, the gods punished Tantalus by having him stand in a pool of water with a branch bearing fruit that retreated from him when he reached for it. When, by contrast, he bent to take a drink, the waters receded. He thus stands for desire that is always whetted but never satisfied.

are substantially felt. God, however, fills not with air and shadow but with goodness and blessings, not with chaff and husks but with marrow and pith, strength and sap, spirit and life; with good blessings whose root is His love and the pinnacle of His glory; with blessings that flow forth from the breast of His mercy, bubble up from the wellspring of His being, sail on the sea of His wisdom, and are brought forth from the unknown land of His hidden treasures. In short, God fulfills with those good things that have the highest good within them and thus have a sweetness of which one never grows weary and a pleasant taste that remains savory in all eternity. [These blessings] retain the sting of desire in the midst of satiation so that the flames of appetite swim amidst the sea of plenty.

The Sum of the Universe fulfills as water fills a glass, and yet there is still room for desire for more. Delight and desire balance the scales like two boys on a pole, one of them holding a torch toward the other one; the second one holding a jug toward the first one, with which they are accustomed at once to inflame and fill up. Oh! The good Lord cannot do anything other than fill with blessings the hungry and those most humbly desirous of His grace. The most tender being of love cannot do anything other than break when torn by the points of loyal and zealous desire and flow into the little pipe of ardor and humility wherever it finds an opening.

Tear open a cherry, peach, or whatever kind of fruit it may be and suck on it with your lips; you will soon feel the juice and the sweetness in your mouth: the most tender heart of God is thus replete with pure essences of goodness, so that when it is pressed by the lips of ardent prayer and faith it yields the juice of its very self. That same goodness fills the soul with itself, so that swimming in the sea of totality the soul not only is filled but has in that fullness its infinite intercourse; the spirit is filled with the spirit of everything that is good and with good spirit so that it desires the sea of eternity for its release. Understanding takes so much from the abundance of God that it wonders how it could possibly replace this abundance with equal gratitude, thence to draw anew on the well of grace so as to receive grace for grace so that it can replace grace with grace.

God feeds the mind that hungers for heavenly thoughts with the sweetest recollections and conceits of the Holy Spirit, who leads the mind to recall what it has heard here and there. With the sweet power of faith, He will feed the fancies, which, like a little bee for honey, will henceforth be ravenous for the wounds and blood of Christ, while they, as it were, eat and kiss Him [during Communion]. He will feed, fill, and satiate both faith and the palate, both of which feel the greatest hunger in Holy Communion for the little lamb of the body and blood of Christ, the lamb that is to be slaughtered in future—and certainly not just symbolically, but really, orally and substantially, thus with the greatest good from the greatest good.

Oh, blissful hunger that will be fed with the very same sum of contentment! I experience in actuality everything that the spirit compels me to say: I myself have hungered for God and have had nothing but God in my desire, appetites, and heart; I have hungered and thirsted for God, longed for Him, and sighed for Him, and, lo, He has fulfilled me, not only with His blessings but with Himself, with the highest and eternal good itself, with His son, and with His spirit as an example to all those who hunger for Him that they too shall be fulfilled, one and all, with these things, although not in that manner. Those, however, who hunger for the riches, splendor, and honor of the world and are rich, blessed, and satiated in it, those He will leave empty. To be sure they too have their filling, but a filling without fulfillment; a fullness that leaves [one] completely empty, that fills one with nothing but empty vanity. Its substance is a shadow, its good a dream, its being an illusion, its gratification starvation, and its feeding a devouring of the time and means by which one could attain true contentment.

O you foolish worldly ones who content yourselves with a handful of sand when you could have a Danube full of pearls! You fill your stomachs with bran and grape skins when you would have cakes and pastries to eat. You weigh yourselves down with gravel and leave the precious diamonds and sapphires lying there!

Deceptive cleverness that thinks to get rich in nothing and that abandons everything, that collects the chaff and husks and throws out the grains and fruits, that saves the shells of hazelnuts and almonds and throws out their kernels, that saves the turnips and gives the lemons to the pigs!

Senseless housekeeping that picks up spider webs and throws the flax on the dung heap, that lets the precious wine run out and fills the barrels with puddles of muck, that scatters the tender wheat flour on the path and packs the dust from the street in the crates, that smears the butter on the cart and uses grease to cook food! This is what they do when they seek vain and temporal delights and abandon the eternal and heavenly ones.

Those rich people who are rich in poverty, gratified by nothingness, satiated by froth, and replete with emptiness—God leaves those people empty, devoid of His all-encompassing fulfillment, miserable and languishing with regard to any and all spiritual good living: since they seek their delight in vanity, so may they find their misery in their enjoyment and learn that without the greatest good no goods have even the tiniest drop of good in them and instead [learn] that this very same [good] is the core and root of all of [these goods], just as the origin of all grace and good deeds is the mercy of God, by which I can truthfully say,

"He has helped his servant Israel, in remembrance of his mercy."[160]

He recalls the primeval impetus to goodness, mercies that even before the primeval beginning incited Him to have mercy upon this miserable race; for mercy is the impetus of our bliss. He recalls how pity stirred Him right at the start at the fall of Adam, how ardor melted Him, how softheartedness bowed Him, and how the need of all of us in the misery of these two people moved Him to pity so that He could not allow the day to pass without showing them mercy and instead on the same evening promised the restoration [of paradise].

He remembers His own heartrending mercy, the solicitude flowing with love, the incomparable loyalty and compassion that inflamed the soul that, to everyone's delight, He resolved [to show] once again to aid His poor servant Israel, that is, all the faithful (who are the spiritual Israel). Now this could not come to pass other than through the abasement of the Lord of Glory, through which this sinful servitude was mitigated. Now this very same Lord could not debase Himself more than by having Himself conceived as a little child in my miserable body. For which thing He is to be most emphatically praised, honored, lauded, and extolled, and the memory of this mercifulness too must be remembered in all eternity.

Oh! If all memory were but eternally shifted to this purpose! Oh, if our entire life were but a pure recollection of God's remembrance of mercy! If only this remembrance were the dreams in sleep, the spice in food, the moisture in drink, the object in works, and in everything the support and the shelter! Oh! If only I were allowed to do nothing but praise God, then I could have no other thoughts but of and about Him!

Alas! I am bound to vanity by temporal necessity, when, however, my spirit would so gladly cling to God and be completely free of such things! Thou Knower of Hearts art Thyself my witness with what repugnance I serve the world and vanity and my own body, and there will be many souls ready for heaven after me who will be thus burdened. But comforted! I direct all of you, you dear ones who share my sentiments, to the eternal life where we shall, unimpeded, have complete joy and freedom to contemplate God and His mercies. There, neither the scorched world, nor annihilated vanity, nor damned hell, nor the shackled devils can hinder us. The most ardent impediment, the body, will no longer impede but rather will be of the utmost

160. Lk 1: 54.

benefit; indeed, it will be of service for transforming the purest desire for God into the work of praising the Most High without pause. Then the holy wishes will swim in their element of eternal fulfillment.

In the meantime I shall praise God as much as I can and not fail to speak of the good that He has done for me and in particular for His servant Israel: in order to assist His servant, God on High Himself took on the form of a servant and will become not merely a boy but even a [tiny] child so that He can assist the worthless servant as the loyal servant of God.

Oh, unheard-of fidelity! The highest monarch in heaven and on earth becomes a servant so that the serfs of hell become potentates in heaven. The Prince of Life becomes a serf of death so that we, released from the dominion of darkness, may serve Him without fear our whole life long. The unconquerable universal conqueror makes Himself capable of defeat so that He can aid His servants who are laid low by sin. The Omnipotent alienates His power so that it can raise the powerless. He effects what hope has to be sure long hoped for but what it did not exactly believe: fulfillment pervades all the corners of the earth and all the heavens and begins to effect what one would never have believed possible: namely, the most unimaginable miracle of mercy and inconceivable work of salvation of aiding fallen humanity.

"As he spoke to our fathers, to Abraham, and to his posterity for ever."[161]

He does what He said, He for whom saying and doing are one and the same, He whose Word and deed run along the same line, He who has as much power to fulfill as He has truth in His promise, in short, He for whom nothing is impossible except finding something impossible in the execution of His promises. The Eternal Word, in which all deeds are resolved, executes the resolution of eternity; the Word, in and through which everything was promised, carries out the promises by entering my body; indeed, the very Word that called Himself the Seed of Woman sows His same self in my body in order to become capable of feeling the sting of the serpent in His heel while crushing its head. The blessing granted to Abraham now comes into the world after it has long been absent from it in order to bring eternal salvation in that world to him and his seed and devout descendants.[162]

161. Lk 1: 55.

162. Gal 3: 14: "Christ Jesus the blessing of Abraham." The genealogy enumerated in Mt 1: 1–17 begins with Abraham, who is separated from Christ by forty-two generations. In Gn 28: 4 Isaac blesses his son Jacob with the words "May he give the blessing of Abraham to you and to your descendants with you that you may take possession of the land of your sojournings which God gave to Abraham!" This blessing refers to God's promise in Gn 12: 1–3 to make of Abraham "a great nation."

All promises of happiness and blessedness, from paradise on, through all the patriarchs, the kings, the prophets, and the godly down to this day are confirmed in Him: in Him, I understand, who lies under my heart. He is the heart of all promises, who gives them blood vessels, spirit, fluids, and powers to be realized, not only temporally but eternally. Inasmuch as all of God's mercies generally extend into eternity, time is much too narrow a space for them; they are intended to delight no less than eternally. Those who understand everything only in temporal terms curtail their bliss. They do themselves the greatest harm and the Greatest One the greatest injustice by interrupting His perpetuity, and they expect something incommensurate from the Eternal One, namely, something temporal. It is not that He is not the ruler and dispenser of temporal good and that all temporal happiness and bliss come not from Him, but instead that He measures his greatest mercies not with time but with eternity and it is for Him far too little to make us happy only temporally. Because He made our souls immortal, He wished our delights to be that way too, for what would a finite delight profit an infinite spirit? What would it profit Israel if her dominion extended over the entire world and yet this world passed away? What would it serve? Is it not better to give us the sea of divinely delightful eternity through the Eternal One, who on this account becomes temporal, than to have us enjoy here a finger's worth of droplets?

O blissful Israel! Happy seed of Abraham! Blessed faithful and chosen ones, you who extend all promises into eternity, which are indeed thus intended and understood by the Eternal One! God does as He said. He spoke of eternity and thus he provides eternal help and salvation.

Alas, you erring Israel! By understanding all this in temporal terms you shall eternally regret that you do not direct your thoughts and hopes toward eternity; by desiring only temporal things you shall forfeit eternity; if you would concern yourself, however, with eternity only, then would the fleeting things of this life fall to your lot on their own.

Alas! Open your eyes, you blind people! And consider whether you are not miserable. If your Savior and Messiah were only temporal, if He conquered all foes and yet the ultimate one, death, remained unconquered, what would all His brave deeds and victories serve? Human misery requires one who conquers everything, an eternal helper, an immortal slayer of death and an eternal animator! Almighty God has lowered such a one into my body after promising Him four thousand years ago. This one will exalt Israel and all believers to the highest throne of heaven, unto and into God Himself.

And Mary remained with her about three months, and returned to her home.[163]

After this music of the Holy Spirit and the magnification of the glory of God through this magnificent song of praise that the Spirit of God played upon the harp of her heart and mouth, she abided with this inspired friend. Holy ones gladly abide together; they are bosom friends, because in each of them a God and a spirit dwell whose reflection ignites them ever more and makes them ever more ardent. Who would not gladly abide with those with whom God Himself abides and who can recognize and heed God's presence in others as well?

It is difficult to part from those blessed ones, from whom, like the sun from windows, the power of God beams out toward all words, deeds, and events, ever providing us with a spiritually reviving view and splendid edification: now a holy example, now a beautiful image of the fear of God; now a majestic picture of hope, now a profound goal of humility; now an incredible strength of faith, now a powerful tinder of prayer; now an invincible sign of patience, sometimes a gentle likeness of a sheep; then a chaste chaplet of lilies whose sweet smell excites imitation.

Sometimes there is a praiseworthy guide for generosity, a heroic defiance of death, an example of heavenly heroism that, regarding the world as void and insignificant, does the most courageous deeds and performs miracles—from which we could learn a fair bit. And then again there is an invincible model of patience, the deepest submerging of the will, a clever lesson in discretion and disregard for all vanity. Soon thereafter there is a lively inducement to laud God, a spur to praise the Creator, an ardor to pump the bellows of spiritual fire.

Nothing is more contagious than godliness among souls so inclined. It provides a mirror for a thousand incentives and inducements to emulation. Thus happy is he who can be with such heavenly magnets, and it is no wonder if we are happy to abide with them. It is also good for those being visited. They have a good opportunity to display the wares of their godliness in the cottages of true hearts and to pour out their hearts, which are filled with pious thoughts, into the bosom of the other.

The love of God, which (like all kinds of love) does not gladly suffer itself to be hidden, can give its fiery flight free rein and has the prospect of realizing its hallowed benefit of rendering others all the more ardent. There is no more noble pyrotechnics than increasing the flames of God

163. Lk 1: 56.

through the reflection of God-loving heart-fire-mirrors. A divine infinity of love comes to be from such ardent striving, from which one phoenix after the other rises up.[164]

Blessed gathering where Christ is the center! Oh! That there were no other gatherings or at least that I should find myself in none but those where Jesus was the purpose of the conversation, the goal of the assembly, the spice of the talk, the sugar of the words, and the content of the thoughts; where the table was filled not so much with food as with praise; where His holy body was remembered during the eating of bread, baked goods, and roasted things as well as with meat dishes; where through devotional remembrance His holy blood shimmered in all chalices and wineglasses and holy baptism came to mind in all drinks of water.

Oh! That we were mindful of the Holy Spirit by those lights! Oh! That the confection were partaken of with the sweet memory of the precious words of comfort and the fruit with the desire for the fruits of the spirit and faith! That the most splendid banquet music of the praise of God were struck up, music that would delight both spirit and body! That we seasoned with sugar, that we exacted—one from the other—the sweetest pithy sayings and comforting promises, and that we rejoiced not merely in spirit but also in body in the gifts of God and partook of them with jubilation and exultation!

There ought to be such meals that preview for us the benevolence of heaven in the gifts of the earth and that make us laud the Creator; it would be a jolly affair where earthly and heavenly desire were wont to wed one another, jolly to be with people when the angels were among them. And in a word, one would get on jolly well where one found God at home and in all things and found all in all things.

Mary, who was devoted to God, found this holy all-encompassing delight with her cousin, and for this reason she stayed with her for about three months. They were probably like mere days for her; for no time passes better than the time one spends remembering the Eternal One, and there are no sweeter pastimes than meditating on eternity.

She certainly must have also helped her out physically, along with the spiritual sustenance. For virtue does not miss the opportunity to make itself known in all manner of ways, and a good soul does not let go of its tool, the body, where it can serve a purpose. She must have faithfully lent a hand to her cousin who was fatigued by her years and her corporeal burden, strained

164. According to legend, the phoenix was reborn from the ashes left from a conflagration of itself and its nest. This firebird served as a symbol of rebirth.

by many cumbersome household tasks, and she must have prepared everything for her that she needed for her confinement. Inasmuch as the Most High, in these and other difficulties, often sends such good angels who, when the burden of the household threatens to become too heavy, provide support and make it easier, He can and will certainly in the end not refrain from relieving this misery, which is one of the most difficult ones, even if it is the most ordinary one, especially since He is rightly called the Redeemer from all evil.

There is no misery that does not touch His ardor. No matter how paltry and insignificant it seems and no matter how long no help is forthcoming, this most benevolent heart will still be moved—and the lack of help is the guarantor of a still more beneficial kindness; for He never fails to do us good unless He has something still better in mind. Jesus, who was locked up inside the womb beneath Mary's heart, undertook to serve John, who likewise lay in Elizabeth's belly, to show that He was come not merely into the world but also into the womb to serve humankind, and indeed not merely to assist humankind as born but also to lend humankind assistance [when He was] unborn in the womb so that the unborn too could hope for His help and so that both those in the microcosm and those in the macrocosm would have a helper in Him and so that pregnant women would also be assured that they would be served by Him [who is] now in heaven as were they [while He was] in the womb; for He is always the same person and unceasing in His works.[165]

The Holy Mother of God returned home again. She did not tarry here and there with useless talk as is the wont of the frivolous world, which rolls the precious gem of time in dust and muck, in wanton chatter and idleness. Instead she returned home to honor God in accordance with respectable custom and to serve Him in greater peace and freedom.

These are the things (order and solitude, peace and freedom) that make one seek and desire one's home in order to worship God with greater ease. Even the most pious company can sometimes impede worship; for speaking with God requires shutting out the world, and solitude is the workshop of delighting in God, and speaking to heaven the element of meditation, the clear spring of contemplation, and the mother of all spiritual exercises, as I once declared by means of this little song:

165. "Microcosm" refers here to the body. Greiffenberg stresses here that even in the womb Jesus came to the assistance of both the unborn—those in the world of the body—and those who were born and living outside in the universe (macrocosm). Moreover, the fact that he himself was active in the womb means that his aid extends to the unborn.

Praise of Solitude

1
Solitude, image of the soul[166]
that God's spirit is wont to choose,
you chaste delight of virtue, you!
Mind's stillness, you, rich in effect!
In you can one be refreshed sweetly,
have intercourse with all the angels,
speak even with heaven itself
of many an exalted wonder.

2
Dear stillness, you, desired by God!
where He sinks His most profound will
into the chosen soul, watering
it with fluids of mystery.
You, sister of all art and virtue,
you are like to the year's fresh crop,
the blossoming, beloved springtime,
a thousand heart's delights possessing.

166. The sixteen-stanza poem in praise of solitude is constructed of eight lines in each stanza. Each line is written in iambic tetrameter and is either eight or nine syllables in length, depending on whether it ends with a stressed or unstressed syllable. Each stanza consists of four rhymed couplets.

1. Ach Einsamkeit / du Bild der Seelen!
die GOttes Geist pflegt zu erwehlen /
du keusche Tugend-Wollust du!
du Wirkung-reiche Sinnen-Ruh!
in dir kan man sich süßest laben /
die Engel-Unterhaltung haben /
selbst mit dem Himmel halten Sprach
von mancher hohen Wunder-Sach.

2. Du GOtt-begehrte liebe Stille!
in der er seinen tieffen Wille
in die erwehlte Seele senkt /
sie mit Geheimnis-Säfften tränkt.
Du Schwester aller Kunst und Tugend
vergleichest dich des Jahres Jugend /
der Blüh-beliebten-Frühlings-Zeit /
mit tausend Herz-Ergötzlichkeit.

3. Die safftig-frische Gnaden-Kühle
setzt allen Brünsten Zweck und Ziele
in dieser Seel / die Welt-entwehnt
mit Geist-Bethauung ist verschönt /

3
Grace's moist and refreshing coolness
sets the goal and aims of all passions
in this soul that, weaned of the world,
is adorned with the spirit's dew
and tapestried with good hope's shadow,
since one senses ever-green strength.
It surpasses the nightingale,
with praise resounding up to God.

4
It appears that it makes resound
praise of the Most High: a pure singing
it seems to be, and a plain voice.
Echo never makes words resound
as clearly and purely as that
when she delightedly responds
at the pleasure of him who thrills her
according to the will's resounding.

5
It has too a wellspring of grace
that flows forth from the cliffs of heaven,
that, its source in goodness's sea,
gushes from there into the soul,
keeps and refreshes virtue's fruits,

---

und Hoffnung-Schatten tapeziret /
weil ewig grüne Krafft man spühret.
Sie kommet vor der Nachtegall
mit GOtt-erhebten Lobes-Schall.

4. Sie scheinet / daß sie mach erklingen
des höchsten Lob / ein lauters Singen
und eine bloße Stimme seyn.
Die Echo nie so klar und rein
die Wörter machet wiederschallen /
Als ihres Helfers Wolgefallen
auf alle Frage sie vergnügt /
nach Willens-wiederhallen fügt /

5. Sie hat auch einen Gnaden-Brunnen
vom Himmels-Felsen hergerunnen /
der von dem Ocean der Güt
ursprünglich springt in das Gemüt /
die Tugend-Frücht' erhält und frischet /

quenches all improper desires;
nor does it ever desiccate,
since it springs from eternity.

6
Though the waters above the stars
ever retreat from those below,
the winding crystal, spring of life,
still flows into the vale of tears;
thoughts, burning desires, goal, and will
sparkle like purest silver threads.
Thereafter grace's rivulet
delights and moistens the heart's tree.

7
Heaven sees with astonishment
all it has helped to edify;
origin of love and joy's meadow
expand this lovely brook of grace;
increasingly they give each droplet
such strengths with miraculous fluids
that one lacks strength to celebrate
their consummation and effect.

---

unordentliche Lüst auslischet /
vertrocknet auch zu keiner Zeit /
weil seine Qwell die Ewigkeit.

6. Obschon die Wasser ob den Sternen
sich von dem untern stäts entfernen /
noch fliest das schlänglende Krystall /
die Lebens-Qwell / ins Jammerthal;
Gedanken / Gierden / Ziel / und Willen /
als reine Silber-Fäden spielen /
es netzet / und ergetzt hernach
den Herzen-Baum der Gnaden-Bach.

7. Der Himmel mit Verwundetn [*sic*] schauet /
was er erbanlichs [*sic*] mit-gebauet;
die Freuden-Weyd und Lieb-Ursach
mehrt diesen schönen Gnaden-Bach /
von Blick zu Blick / mit Wunder-Säften /
giebt jedem Tröpflein solche Kräften /
daß ihre Wirkung und Vollzug
zu rühmen man nicht Kraft genug.

8
The birds are able to see also
how things tend to be in the soul
that serves the Lord in solitude,
that does not make bold to alight
on limbs of delight, greened with bliss.
Since its darling, the best and fairest,
on the arid tree died and suffered,
it coos just like the turtledove.

9
Like a true phoenix it will build
a nest of confidence and hope,
sweet smelling from the fire of love,
from the mind and force of the will,
like to wings, wondrously unfurled;
but not 'til the full flame ignites
from God's grace and the sun of faith
in which it expires, filled with joy.

10
How could there possibly be eagles
that praised solitude even more
than does this soul's sharp spirit-sight,

---

8. Es machen auch die Vögel sehen /
wie in der Seel es pfleg zu gehen /
die in der Einöd GOtt bedient /
die sich zu setzen nicht erkühnt
auf Glück-begrünte Wollust-Aeste:
Dieweil ihr Schatz / der schönst' und beste /
litt und verschied auf dürren Baum /
girrt wie der Turtel-Tauben-Gaum.

9. Als wahrer Fönix will sie bauen
ein Nest / von Hoffnung und Vertrauen /
wol-riechend aus dem Feur der Lieb /
aus dem Verstand und Willen-Trieb /
als Fliegeln / Wunder-aufgewehet;
doch erst die volle Flamm angehet /
aus GOttes Gnad und Glaubens-Sonn /
in der sie stirbet voller Wonn.

10. Wie könnt ihr immer Adler haben /
die mehr berühmt die Einöd gaben /
als dieser scharfes Geist-Gesicht /

whose steady glance aims the heart's beams
at the clearest divinity,
beams their mother ne'er casts aside,
the church that impels them to flight,
since she ever looks to the sun.

11
The more the soul ventures through trust
to observe the king of the stars,
the more He gives it understanding,
the more it loves His streams of light,
the more He shows His noble being,
the more it would read mystery,
it grieves to curtail this delight
when bodiliness makes its claims.

12
With one eye, like the dove, the soul
regards the kernel; in true faith,
it contemplates God with the other
as the Creator of the earth;
though birdsong can approximate

---

das in die klarste Gottheit richt /
mit stetem Blick / die Herzen-Strahlen /
die ihre Mutter nie läst fallen /
die Kirche / die sie reitzt zum Flug /
weil sie die Sonn schaut stet genug?

11. Je mehr sie trauet / durch Vertrauen /
den Sternen-König zu beschauen /
je mehr er ihr Erkäntnis giebt /
je mehr sie seine Strahlen liebt /
je mehr er weist sein edles Wesen /
je mehr sie will Geheimnis lesen /
mit Schmerzen sie der Lust abbricht /
wann Leibes-Nohtdurft sie verpflicht.

12. Sie schaut das Körnlein wie die Tauben
mit einem Aug / durch waren Glauben
sie mit dem andern GOtt betracht
als Schöpfer / was die Erd ihr bracht /
die Vögel-Musick sich kan gleichen /
die doch im wol-laut-Streit muß weichen

the sweet sounds of the soul's rejoicing
on the bushes' throne, fresh with hope,
it must retreat in the song match.

13
The ciphers, notes, point, and strings too
are all heart-sensibilities
that yet another spirit touches
so one feels the work's harmony;
the purpose is to repay Him
with lively praise for the life given,
even if one sung one's heart out—
like many noble little birds.

14
Who would not cherish such repose
wherein such sweet singers rehearse,
where living-cool wellsprings reside,
where one finds sylvan glades of virtue
with serenities filled with blessing,
where one contends not with the world,
and where the tongue is wont to be
quite free to extol God alone!

---

der Seelen süssen Jubel-Thon /
am Hoffnung-frischen Büsche-Thron;

13. Die Zifern / Noten / Punct / und Saiten
sind alle Herz-Empfindlichkeiten /
die noch ein andrer Geist berührt /
daß man die Werk-Einstimung spührt;
der Zweck ist / vor gegebenes Leben /
belebtes Lob ihm wieder geben /
wann (wie manch edles Vöglein thut)
man schon versänge Leib und Blut.

14. Wer wolte solche Still' nicht lieben /
Wo sich so süße Sänger üben /
wo lebend-kühle Brunnen sind /
und wo man Tugend-Haine findt /
mit Seegen-vollen Ruhigkeiten;
wo man nicht mit der Welt zu streiten /
wo pflegt die Zunge nur allein /
zu preißen GOtt / recht frey zu seyn?

15
Steal away, all you Christian senses,
in times of worldly undertaking
and seek out sweetest solitude
quite far removed from vice's burden;
eat of its noble fruits of virtue,
a dish for the soul, sweet as angels;
solitude is not solitary
when Jesus Christ thus comes to us.

16
Withdraw from the sludge of the earth,
on earth start to be heavenly,
by your estate however burdened;
consider that a mere short time
can you elect to worry over
and put in order your house in heaven.
Withdraw from the earth's company
to be with that in heaven's kingdom.

All of this comes to pass in solitude. Who then would not love it, seek it out, and delight in it, when he can have it? Oh! How well must the blessed bride of God, the mother of Jesus, and the lantern of the Holy Spirit, the pure temple of the divinity, the holy wondrous virgin, and the woman who made God incarnate have fared in her solitude? How must she have thought about all the words of the inspired Elizabeth and those of her own song of praise?

---

15. Entziehet euch / ihr Christen-Sinnen!
zu Zeiten allen Welt-beginnen /
und sucht die süsse Einsamkeit /
von der der Laster Last sehr weit /
eßt ihrer edlen Tugend Früchte /
ein Engel-süsses Seel-Gerichte;
die Einsamkeit nicht einsam ist /
wann zu uns kommet JEsus Christ.

16. Entziehet euch dem Schlamm der Erden /
hebt himmlisch an auf Erd zu werden /
wie Stand-beschwehrt ihr immer seyd /
seht / daß ihr nur ein kleine Zeit
euch könt zu sorgen auserwehlen /
eur Haus im Himmel zu bestellen.
Entzieht der Welt-Gesellschaft euch /
zu seyn bei der im Himmel-Reich.

For the Holy Spirit leaves room through [these] intervals for people's spirits to contemplate what they have said and written at His prompting. Thus she must have been engaged in the most holy pastime, thinking clearly through all this.

However, even as she deals with purely spiritual and divine things and has her heart in heaven and its ruler in and under her heart, even as her body is a throne of the Most High and her flesh and blood become clothing for the Son of God, even as (I say) her chastity becomes a divine miracle and a wondrous spectacle, even as heaven itself thinks to make a show of this very thing, at precisely that time, in fact at that moment, she is placed by the world (and indeed by the pious) under suspicion of being unchaste.

When she had been betrothed to Joseph, before they came together, she was found with child of the Holy Spirit.[167]

We ought to wonder at the fact that it was possible for the omniscient and most righteous God to permit the most innocent woman and His most holy and only child Himself to be endangered by the suspicion of a dishonorable conception, [that it was possible] for Him, who has all time and hours in His hands, to ordain that her pregnancy be revealed before she came together with Joseph so that piety was angered by holiness and God Himself came under suspicion among the godly.

The Son of God, our dear Lord Jesus, intended to take all human scorn and misery upon Himself, and for this reason, also the suspicion of a dishonorable conception, because this is practically the first misery that can befall an innocent person. Thus there would be no evil that He had not tasted for our sake. Since many large-spirited people regard having their honor impugned as the only real misfortune, He therefore wished not to remain untouched herein either (in the way of suspicion), so that, inasmuch as nothing remained untried by Him, so should it also not remain unblessed. He wanted to suffer this as a child so that all children—likewise innocent—would have consolation and company in Him and also so that their guiltless disgrace would hurt them as little as it hurt Him.

In His entire life and suffering, the Lord Jesus never suffered any [difficulties] having to do with chastity and honor, but He did have to suffer evil suspicions regarding these virtues. This is the most unbearable suffering. Thus He did not want to leave people who have been injured in this way without comfort, but instead [He meant] to taste the honor-agony [that

167. Mt 1: 18. "She" has been substituted for "his mother Mary." Greiffenberg now returns to Matthew for more information about Mary's pregnancy.

they experience] from being blamed when they are innocent and to gain for chaste people strength to bear unearned calumny with patience.

And how should one not be patient in one's innocence when one considers that the same thing happened to the very wellspring and source of chastity and that the purest virgin sanctified by the Spirit had to fall under false suspicion, regardless of the fact that she was purity itself and that she carried the father of purity as her son in her body. Did she then have to suffer this like others, who, even if they were honorable, nevertheless conceived in sin and were, unlike her, not pregnant with holiness?

How must it have pained this most innocent woman that her shame came to light before her honor did, that it was rumored that she was pregnant rather than that she was the bearer of God, that the effect was visible before the cause was known, that she could not hide her big belly and could not uncover the holy secret of salvation! How she must have shrunk from Joseph and been ashamed and hardly dared to look at him! For she knew full well that he knew nothing of her secret, which she had also not dared to confide to him. But heaven, which laid this burden upon her, also helped her to bear it. He who imposed external shame upon her gave her inner comfort. He placed a cool restorative wellspring in her heart that could cool the heat of the external shame, namely, a good conscience, which cools all fear, extinguishes all heat, sweetens all bitterness, and is a restorative and refreshment for all anguish.

It was the consolation that she was pregnant with the Holy Spirit. This sweetened all the bitterness of evil gossip, for being conscious in oneself of the work and operation of the Holy Spirit is a delight that outweighs all of the world's judgments and suspicions and is as if one sat in heaven and from far off heard a little dog barking but nevertheless did not allow oneself to be prevented from listening to the music of the angels.

It is a special gift and virtue to take pleasure in and be satisfied with our own virtue and innocence when we are the only ones who are certain of it, even when the world does not know that the Holy Spirit is working within us. For he who is too keen on having his innocence made visible to the world reveals his vanity, showing that he desires to please the world more than God.

To be sure, one should love the honor of a good name and reputation above all, but wherever the honor of God can be increased with the darkening of one's own, it is better to let one's own remain invisible than to reveal divine mysteries before their time. We must deny our love of self even in the matter of honor itself and submit ourselves to the honor of God as did here this most chaste of all virgins, who would rather allow all shame and suspicion to come over her than reveal her glorious secret.

It is, in my opinion, the greatest test of self-possession and humility that a person can undergo when, to increase God's honor, that person renounces his own wish for honor before the world and when, although he has the means in his hands not only to prove his innocence but to become celebrated, he does not attest it and instead allows his name to remain under evil suspicion. This is true selflessness and the life in Christ, who is also so faithful that He will acknowledge these faithful deniers of self before His heavenly father, before all the angels, and before all humankind and will make their honor shine forth a millionfold like the sun.

Ought we not therefore to think that God causes only rash and careless people (probably even without actual guilt) to come under evil suspicion and that whosoever refrains from the deed is also spared the gossip (as the common saying goes) and thus that honest people will never ever come under suspicion? Oh, no! The contrary is evident here and often elsewhere too: those who are most eager for honor and those who are most chaste are often subjected to the worst suspicions where they have circumstantial evidence as their worst enemies.

Who was more chaste and innocent than the mother of God? What was, however, more self-evident than that she was pregnant before she had come together with Joseph? If God allowed this to happen to His very own flesh and the fount of His blood, then He may still allow many chaste hearts to be burdened by charges of which they are innocent: either so that in that world they shall wear an even more beautiful and shining crown of lilies and innocence or so that they shall serve in this world as a miracle and remarkable example of the divine miraculous Providence [of Him] who, to be sure, is wont to cast down His own [people] but in the end to honor and transfigure them in the most glorious manner—as He did with this woman, this purest woman who made Him a human being, who lay under the suspicion of a few neighbors, but who now is honored and blessed by all of Christendom. For this reason one ought to be careful about harboring suspicions about those who are otherwise virtuous and proceed cautiously and gently; one can soon find oneself sinning against Divine Providence if one puts a wrong construction on His miraculous ways and lets oneself be deceived by appearances.

Her husband Joseph, being a pious man and unwilling to put her to shame.[168]

Divine Primal Prudence arranged everything in such a fundamentally benevolent way and order that virtue was never subjected to any more misery

168. Mt 1: 19: The RSV of this verse reads "and her husband Joseph, being a just man and unwilling to put her to shame." The German translation of this verse that Greiffenberg uses here

than what was necessary to polish it to bring out its fine grain and never so much [misery] that its trusty vassals were injured or abandoned. It ordained that the pregnancy of chastity be revealed without the revelation of the true cause, and it gave her, moreover, a man as a companion, in whom it had incorporated chastity and piety beforehand so that hers was preserved and was not defamed before the world.

Precisely the God who made her a wonder-mother and bearer of Wonderful also gave her a betrothed who was a wonder of piety and who did not want to punish [her for] this thing that appeared to be wrong (although it was innocent). I say a wonder of piety, for ordinary piety is not bound to let such things that are contrary to honor go unpunished—and it is not, as it were, praiseworthy either; punishing wrong constitutes neither a lack of piety nor a sign of evil, but a kind of justice that is pleasing to God and that is to be loved as well as practiced.

But with special occurrences, special miracles must come to pass. When the epitome of chastity comes under suspicion, piety must expand to include what itself is right. God's gracious ordinance arranged things so wisely that in this point chastity and piety had to coincide, because only the innocence of the former was capable and worthy of the abundance of the latter so that the former was not afflicted and the latter not ridiculed. Joseph was pious and with this piety benefited not only his betrothed but himself so that he did not need to feel remorse or shame that he had done something bad to purity and had accused innocence innocently.

Virtue, which is its very own reward, rewards his piety with personal delight in its own benevolence and in the end gives it the sweet fruits of patience to enjoy, that is, the joy of a good ending. Herein one sees that it is not just all gifts and virtues that come from God, but also their time and governance. If Joseph's piety had been in the days of Phinehas, it could not have been praised, just as the zeal of Phinehas, on the other hand, would have been in no way appropriate to this event.[169]

The continuous sovereign rule of God has each virtue come in its own

---

reads more like "Joseph, however, her husband, was a pious man and did not want to blame her" (Joseph aber / ihr Mann / war fromm / und wolte sie nicht rügen). As a compromise I have used the RSV, substituting the word "pious" (German *fromm*) for "just" since the meditation that follows focuses specifically on Joseph's piety.

169. According to Nm 25: 1–12, in a time when the Israelites were generally beginning to follow the ways of idolaters, the zealous Phinehas became angry when a man of Israel married a Midianite woman, that is, an idolater. Armed with a spear, he entered their private rooms and impaled both of them. God approved of Phinehas's action, as it was intended to prevent and atone for idolatry, and he promised Phinehas his covenant of peace.

time (season); it makes piety overflow with generosity when innocence is associated with it and pricks zeal with spurs when vice oversteps the boundaries. It has every virtue on its leash like a hunter the whippets and ordains the course for each one to track down its quarry in the most appropriate manner. Here patient making of allowances was unleashed—not that Joseph's soul was forced to do it, but because God found that virtue in Joseph's soul, He ordained that it be unleashed. He, however, found it in there as His own work that He had wrought there, not as Joseph's own fruit, but rather as that which He had caused to bloom and grow within him.

For God is the fount and source of every virtue. Humankind is nothing but the air in which the virtues hang and hover. As one makes a wreath of fruit, weaving together the most appropriate fruits, thus God conjoined here modest piety to innocent purity so that the latter would be preserved through the former, for he did not want to blame her. As her betrothed husband, he would certainly have had the power to shame and accuse her, but he put into practice the words of Paul some years before they were written: "'All things are lawful for me,' but not all things are helpful."[170] The spirit that dictated it to [Paul] put it in the mind and practice of [Joseph]. He did not want to reprimand her so that she would not be scorned and punished before the world, yet as an honorable man he was not completely capable of getting over and tolerating the presumed wrong.

Resolved to divorce her quietly.[171]

Here we see how virtues seldom come alone but generally in company, namely, piety with honor. He was so kind that he did not even want to dishonor and injure the wife he presumed to be unfaithful, but he also had such zeal for honor that he did not want to cohabit with a woman who was not righteous. He felt the wrong as he should, even if he did not want to punish it as he could. Benevolence is all the more noble that arises not from stupid indifference but from clear knowledge and active feeling.

If wisdom and bravery are not with piety, it is only worth half the praise; they lend it spirit and life, splendor and charm. Joseph's sense of honor made his piety much more worthy of praise, and it is this deepening that lends it the contours of perfection; for it is natural for simple people to let something go out of stupid indifference, but it is as heroic as it is kind [for people] to spare something that is intolerable to [their] honor from shame and punishment and yet themselves feel [the injury to their honor] in the

170. 1 Cor 6: 12.

171. Mt 1: 19.

extreme. This reveals his kingly mind and line, regardless of his station as a carpenter; [this royal disposition] forgives out of kindness, yet will tolerate no disgrace. We also see his modesty and discretion when he merely thinks it over privately and neither confers nor consults with anyone about it; thus he must have revealed it to no one.

Piety bears the most beautiful fruit when it draws the shadow of discretion over the error of its neighbor, when it keeps to itself what it cannot let out without the loss of a good portion of itself. Holding one's tongue on the subject of the failings of others is a piece of one's own perfection, and one deserves praise in the same portion as the disgrace that one helps to avert from one's neighbor.

The more virtues work in secret here, the more glorious shall their revelation be there. It is virtue's most beautiful virtue to remain secret, and it would be desirable for all [virtues] to be so secret that even they themselves knew not [their own virtue], as Moses knew not the radiance of his face.[172] The left hand of memory should not know what the right one of action has done, and the oblivion of Emperor Claudius would be desirable here so that one could forget one's good deeds as he forgot his murders.[173]

Pious Joseph intended to divorce her quietly so that people could blame it on misfortune or even on him rather than on her so that she would neither be endangered nor come under suspicion, and he showed this loyalty to a woman whom he thought unfaithful—and even though some are of the opinion that one is not obliged to show any loyalty to such people. His punishment consisted only of thoughts, and these are so secret that they are hardly cognizant of themselves. But however secret they may be, He sees them nevertheless, He who sees everything, He for whom all secrets are a clear mirror and a bright spring, indeed, a microscope, for He sees them larger and clearer than they actually are, as one sees through it the eyes and ribs of the smallest little animal, indeed the points on a speck of dust that are otherwise invisible.[174]

172. Ex 34: 29. Moses' face shines brightly after encountering God at Sinai, an episode to which the story of the transfiguration of Christ also alludes when Jesus' face shines brightly.

173. Claudius was known for his "absentmindedness and blindness." Suetonius writes in *Lives of the Caesars* that Claudius would summon people to consult with him after he had condemned them to death the day before. *Lives of the Caesars*, trans. J. C. Rolfe, Loeb Classical Library (Cambridge: Harvard University Press, 1914), 73 (5.39). I thank my colleague George Pepe for this reference.

174. The text reads "Kunst-Vergrößerungs-Glaß," literally art-magnifying glass. I have translated it as microscope given the description of what one sees through the device. Experiments in optics that allowed a view of minute things had taken place at least a hundred years before Greiffenberg wrote her meditations. Galileo, among others, had written of the view through

God sees more mystery in those mysteries than the very heart that hatched them is aware of. Before a single little spark has ignited, He has the poker in his hand by means of which he intends to curb and turn them. Before thoughts are transformed into deeds, an angel must come from heaven to prevent it.

But as he considered this, behold, an angel of the Lord appeared to him in a dream.[175]

Because he harbored pure thoughts and because in all innocence he innocently found fault with the innocent woman, God sent him a pure angel, who remained in a state of innocence, to declare the innocence of the purest among women; even as he considered this, the angel appeared to him.

Angels are nimble spirits and masters of our thoughts, which they know and into which they are initiated through a concession of God. These very same thoughts are the stage upon which they appear and hold their debates. Thoughts are the air in which the angels dwell: in the pure and innocent ones, the good angels; in the evil ones, however, the wicked angels. Although Joseph's thoughts were unjust, they were nevertheless not evil, and those who err most of all need the council and proper guidance of the holy angel.

An angel of the Lord appeared to him in a dream. Here we see that our dreams too are surrounded by angels and that dreams at times are their workshop. If one lies down with holy thoughts, one tends to get up with angels; they prefer most of all to be around the soul when it is most like them, that is, during sleep, when it is free from all corporeal activities. Then the angels join it and give it their sweet imprint. The nature of the apparition, however, must have been spiritual, for because it was a dream, it must have happened during sleep when the body was as good as dead and robbed of its senses; this apparition thus must have been visible to the soul alone and have occurred in its realm.

Its being called an angel of the Lord is not to be understood as if not all angels were of the Lord, but rather it means that it was one of the special, high-ranking angels that served the Lord Jesus Christ in his incarnation and attended in the sublime work of the birth of Christ. Some think that it was probably the angel Gabriel, which is plausible but cannot be determined for certain, since that is beyond what is explicitly stated in Holy Scripture. It is

---

the microscope. In 1665, Robert Hooke had published his widely circulating *Micrographia,* a set of drawings of views through the microscope including a well-known enlarged image of a flea.

175. Mt 1: 20.

enough [to know] that the angel appeared to him while he was considering this. How can he, however, have been considering such things when he was sleeping and dreaming? He doubtless had fallen asleep over these thoughts so that the soul, which is not idle and never sleeps or rests, was still preoccupied with them in his dreams, so that the angel found [the soul preoccupied] therein and thereupon responded to it. For it is written,

Saying, "Joseph, son of David, do not fear to take Mary your wife."[176]

It cannot be determined whether this was a language that rang in his ears or whether it was perceptible only to his mind. It is certain and enough to say that the angel answered his thoughts, as those of faithful, God-fearing souls are still answered—not only by the angels but even by God Himself, who, as it were, (as that blessed teaching of Hr. M. says) puts His ear to the heart, thus catching up, collecting, intercepting, and answering all sighs and thoughts.[177] We find these conversations of the heart described frequently and in many places in the writings of the ancient holy fathers, especially of Augustine, Tauler, and Bernard, where they are considered the greatest bliss on earth.[178] For this reason they renounced the world and sought and loved solitude so that they were all the more capable of [receiving] this divine address and could enjoy it unimpeded.

And this is in truth praiseworthy and beneficial also because it happened in the right way without superstition, for the tumult of the world impedes repose in God, and this godly address of the soul has to take place in deepest repose. Repose is the proper chapel of devotion, the halcyon stillness in which the kingfisher or rather the bird of paradise, the Holy Spirit, broods and heats up our icy hearts with His flames so that we feel His holy stirrings, which are His language.[179]

176. Mt 1: 20.

177. Greiffenberg likely refers here to Rom 8: 26–27: "likewise the Spirit helps us in our weakness; for we do not know how to pray as we ought, but the Spirit himself intercedes for us with sighs too deep for words. And he who searches the hearts of men knows what is the mind of the Spirit, because the Spirit intercedes for the saints according to the will of God." "Hr. M." is probably an abbreviation of "Herr [Mr.] Martin Luther."

178. Saint Augustine of Hippo (see above, note 90); Saint Bernard de Clairvaux (1091–1153) was a doctor and monk, known for piety and worship of Christ (see above, chap. 1, note 76). Johannes Tauler (1300–1361) was a German Dominican monk and mystic whose sermons were devoted to practical life and the ascension of the soul to unite with God.

179. Two myths are conflated here. The kingfisher (halcyon) was believed to lay and hatch its eggs on the surface of the sea during the fourteen calm days in the winter. The bird of paradise is an alternate designation for the phoenix. The phoenix is said to be reborn in fire out of its own ashes and has been used in Christian art to represent Christ, resurrection, and immortality.

The stillness of the soul is the desert where the angels show us the wellspring of the living and seeing. In repose and solitude one sees, like Moses, the burning bush of God's love. There one receives the magic wand of the divine mystery of the spirit, and one must be on a Patmos-island if one is to experience divine revelation.[180]

This is to say, however, not that one should abandon one's trade and estate and run from the world and that for this reason one should above all else seek such places, but only that those whose hearts God has so disposed ought to remain in repose and be left in it, and furthermore, that in general everyone ought at times to retreat from the world for a brief hour and praise and serve God in the stillness. Again, repose is as necessary to devotion as air is to life.

I do not, however, exclude a church filled with many thousands from such repose, but only the earthly tumult of purely mundane and temporal things. The more streams of devotion flow into the river of the spirit, the stronger it will become; the more it roars, the sweeter will be the repose into which He causes the reverent soul to sink and pass away; for because this solitude has the capacity for the totality, it also has the capacity for the multitude, and nothing is excluded other than nothingness, namely, vanity that impedes the conversations of God and the angels.

Who would not—in order to hear beautiful music—gladly lock up or chase away the dogs and cats, when their yowling and hissing would disrupt it. What is, however, all music compared with the divine and angelic expression of the soul? Why then should one not chase the vain and flattering substance of the world from one's heart in order to lend an ear to the Holy Spirit and His angelic spirits? Why would I not prefer to speak with those whose words are pure sugar, cinnamon, amber, and musk rather than with the world, whose speech is full of poison, gall, and deadly stings?

Every one of God's words is a balm poured into the soul that permeates body and spirit and makes everything joyful, lively, and pleasant. By contrast the words of the world leave wrathful snakebites in their wake, or when they are the most pleasant, they leave behind certain suspicions of flattery or ambiguity so that one does not know how they were intended. The heavenly and angelic ones, however, are so full of assurance of the good that one cannot entirely conceive of it. Who then would not prefer to eat

180. See Ex 3: 2 where God appears to Moses in a burning bush. Patmos is a Greek island where John the evangelist is supposed to have received his revelation. See Rv 1: 9: "I John, who also am your brother, and companion in tribulation, and in the kingdom and patience of Jesus Christ, was in the isle that is called Patmos, for the word of God, and for the testimony of Jesus Christ."

sugar rather than gall? Not prefer to deal with musk rather than poison and not gladly flee from the yowling owls in order to listen to the most charming nightingales? Why then is it surprising if once in a while one retreats from the world for a brief hour to attend to its Creator?

The lovely angel said, however, "Joseph!" To give him full assurance that it pertained to him, the angel called him by his name, for the holy angels know our names, because they are written in heaven. Here we see that it is an angelic virtue and wisdom to announce a thing to a person clearly, candidly, and intelligibly and that ambiguous and contorted deceitful speech resembling the riddle of the Sphinx and the Apollonian Oracles has one and the same origin with them.[181] In contrast, it is angelic when one makes one's pleasure known to a person clearly and at length.

Since, however, there are many Josephs, the angel also said, "son of David!" thus making him all the more certain and assured that it concerned no one but him; [the angel] even named his clan and family so that the miracle should seem to him even more credible, because it was to come from precisely this clan and house.

Angels are not given to idle talk; each word has the import of a hundredweight. There is hidden in each one a sea of wisdom. How much more so in those godly ones, that is to say, their depths? They express in brief figures great sums of intelligence and use few words for many proclamations. People who want to be angelic should also take pains to achieve brevity replete with spirit and power, for superfluous chatter is bestial rather than angelic; for sheep, calves, and rams bleat incessantly. The ducks and geese and crows and magpies too carry on a constant quacking and gabbling, screeching and fussing, and superfluous words indicate a lack of intelligence, just as speech is otherwise a marker of the human being.

When speech does not have as its purpose praising God and benefiting one's neighbor, it is a clock that strikes the hour out of time and order. It ought to be an infinite resource for these two things; otherwise, however, it ought to be a precious liquid that falls only drop by drop and mostly then when it can delight and refresh, as here when the pleasant angel says, "Fear not!" There is no sweeter command than when one is forbidden to be afraid, for nothing is more burdensome than fear, which is almost worse than the

181. According to Greek mythology, the Sphinx was a daughter of Typhaon and the snake Echidna. She appeared near Thebes and killed anyone who could not solve the riddle "What goes on four legs in the morning, on two legs at noon, and on three in the evening?" Oedipus guessed that she meant a human being. The Apollonian Oracles are prophecies of the most famous oracle of the ancient world, the shrine of the Greek god Apollo at Delphi. These prophecies were enigmatic and required interpretation and were thus subject to misunderstanding.

evil itself. Here, however, the command means that he should not be afraid to take the epitome of chastity, although she is already pregnant.

"For that which is conceived in her is of the Holy Spirit."[182]

For precisely this announcing of her transgression is the effect of that very holiness. What makes her honor suspect should lead you to be mindful of her honor before God and all the angels. What makes you mistakenly believe that she is unworthy of you makes all of your merits too paltry for you to be worthy of her. What makes you think of divorcing her is exactly why you should go to her from the ends of the earth. Therefore, be not afraid to take Mary, your wife, for her pregnancy (which is what all this is about) is not natural and therefore not dishonorable, but of the Holy Spirit. The Holy Spirit is the mover of this sea of chastity from which shall come the Savior and salvation for all of you. What is born in her has as its maker Him who is a fount of all purity. The Word, through which everything came to be and which is everything, will become in her something that the Sum of the Universe previously was not.

This is how it works with such holiness, namely, the Holy Spirit Himself is the maker and purity the substance in which it is wrought. The source of all purity makes itself capable of pouring out a river that will make the impure pure. In this cloud of chastity the snow of innocence will be born that makes your scarlet sins like snow. In this virgin-retort the quint-essence of the body is prepared, from which afterward will come the five holy wounds that heal the entire world.[183] In this enclosed garden the Creator of Paradise is made into a flower of paradise. The glory of God fills the temple of this virgin body so that glorious heaven will be filled with your bodies.

God entrusts your betrothed with His co-terminally eternal son, and you would not dare to take her to you, when God Himself (in a certain manner) took her as His wife? The heavenly Adam will be constructed of her body and blood, and you do not want to take to you this reversal of Eve?[184] She is pregnant with holiness, and you are afraid that it will bear you disgrace to have her with you? Oh, no, fear not! It will bring you everlasting

182. Mt 1: 20.

183. The five holy wounds include the four marks of the nails of the crucifixion on the hands and feet of Jesus and his pierced side, as described in Jn 19: 34. By hyphenating *quintessence,* Greiffenberg stresses *quint* as the number five. In alchemy, the quintessence, the fifth element after earth, fire, water, and air, is thought to be the highest element and the substance of the heavenly bodies.

184. Jesus is understood to be the second Adam because he saved humanity from the sin brought into the world by Adam's disobedience.

honor to have a wife who is married to God Himself and is pregnant with holiness.

"And she will bear a son."[185]

She will, however (the angel means to say), not be pregnant in eternity, but finitely, and will give birth at the proper, natural time. It will not be a hope that is always delayed and never attained, one that eternally feeds and never satiates, one that always manifests and never gives, always blossoms and never bears fruit. Oh, no! She will be as fruitful in the realization as she is charming in the blossoming; she will delight with the fulfillment as she consoled with the food of hope; she will certainly give in the degree to which she long manifested, and in short, she will emerge as glorious as she was hallowed in hiding; for this virgin replete with holiness will bring forth a son who is the Son of God and the Father of all of nature. The world will consider Him your son and you will be His foster father. Therefore do not refuse to assume such a holy office.

It is no small thing to be the foster father of the Prince of Heaven. Caring for that tender little mouth, from which the entire being of the world emerged, is not an honor that one ought to refuse. Therefore, accept this holy honor. It is so great that it has never fallen to any of the most exalted potentates or powerful of the world. They rule over worms and at most are the fathers of fatherlands of dust and ashes. You, however, will become the foster father of the Eternal One and the provider for Him who provides for everything. Their subjects are wretched human beings; yours will be He who otherwise rules over all.

The childhood of Him who is older than the world will be under your control, and you will be able to do and deal with Him who has to do and deal with all the angels and all the heavens. Therefore fear not to take to you your spouse, who is blessed with a heavenly child. For you do not so much take her to you as you take to you, with her, the center of the heaven of all the heavens, for she will bring forth such a son.

"And you shall call his name Jesus, for he will save his people from their sins."[186]

You can recognize in this name and the effect of this newborn who He must be. Since you are to name him Jesus, He must be a Savior, for the Most High would not have commanded it from heaven to no purpose and would not have sent me to you. To be sure there were in former times a number of

185. Mt 1: 21.
186. Mt 1: 21.

people who were called this name—like Joshua, Jesus Nave, Jesus Sirach, and still others—but only by their kin and not by an express command from heaven.[187] These same men were to be sure valiant heroes and wise men, but all this only as a prototype of Him who is the true commander of the army of God and the fount of all discipline and wisdom. You shall give Him the name of salvation, under which the greatest act [of salvation] in heaven and on earth will come to pass.

Oh, wonder! You shall give a name to Him, who existed before the name, and to the being of the world from whose mouth all wisdom, and thus all names, issued; indeed, you shall give a name to the Eternal Word, in which all words and names exist and which is the hypostasis of all meanings and utterances. In short, you shall create a name for the Creator of heaven and earth. Because it would, however, be too difficult for you, the Creator Himself created it and has it announced to you. He will have the name with the deed, indeed, the deed before the name, or rather both at the same time from eternal eternity. He will make come to pass in time what He decided at the very beginning, and by means of His temporal wretchedness He will save His people for all eternity.

His people, I say, that is, those who believe in Him; all those who recognize Him as their Lord and Savior; everyone who trusts in His grace and mercy; everyone who seeks protection and rescue, help and comfort, in Him; all those who place themselves beneath His banner and wing; everyone who finds solace in His goodness and love. In a word, all those who call upon Him in truth and the spirit are His people, whom He will save from their sins.

He will, to be sure, redeem the sins of the entire world. However, the blame for the fact that not all the world will be saved, even though everyone is redeemed, lies with them and not with the Savior, because they do not accept Him and choose not to believe in Him. He obtained the jewel and offered it to the world. What can He do about their thoughtlessness, which prevents them from seizing or accepting it? He stretches out His hand to a disobedient people the whole day long, entices, calls, charms, entreats, and requests them please to accept His grace. What more can He do? He hands them the jewel of salvation; they do not want to seize it believing. He invites them to the table of heavenly communion that is fully prepared for them; they do not want to come. He offers Him-

187. Jesus Sirach, author of one of the deuterocanonical books of the Bible known as Ecclesiasticus; and Jesus Nave or Joshua, author of the sixth book of the Old Testament, the Book of Joshua. The name Joshua is cognate with Jesus.

self and heaven at the price of nothing but merely accepting Him believing, but they do not want to do that either and they wantonly give up all of it. Thus it is not His fault but theirs, and it is no wonder if He saves only His people, those who believe in Him, follow Him, and are willing to accept His grace.

In accordance with creation, everything is His, but here those are called His people who dedicate themselves to Him and through faith make Him their own so that they are His. So He chooses to save these people, that is, make them cleansed, free, rid, and void of their sins, which up to now have persisted with God's forbearance in order that He should administer in these times the justice that matters to God, namely, the forgiveness of sins. This is the greatest mystery in heaven and on earth that I herewith reveal to you. This is the decree with which God has been pregnant for all of eternity, the one that the person whom your pregnant spouse will bear will carry out. Therefore, consider yourself blessed to be the foster father of such a blessed son and father of salvation.

All this took place to fulfill what the Lord had spoken by the prophet.[188]

Eternal truth so rejoices in the fulfillment of its prophecies that the angel is permitted to say that it all took place to fulfill, etc. The highest good rejoices in itself when it does the good that it promised. God's fundamental goodness allows itself to enter into the sweetest promises so there is something to oblige it to show mercy, since it is otherwise completely free in all its operations. It is wont to make of its promises a spur for itself so that it has to fulfill these promises for the sake of honor. Although its honor is of an inviolable nature, it nevertheless makes of the pledge a point of honor that truth must fulfill.

The freedom to dispense grace, which is completely incapable of becoming ensnared, begins to cover itself with the net of truth so that the Almighty surrenders voluntarily: not only does He not desire to escape but He Himself weaves that to which truth pledged Him. Truth makes take place what has never taken place before and never will take place again so that the promise is fulfilled. It makes everything take place that the Sum of the Universe promised, even though it is more than all human thought and reflection can achieve, indeed, more than nature and reason in themselves can do and comprehend. Yes, the Almighty is so clear in the effect and truth, so certain in the fulfillment, that the angel says, "All this took place," before it

188. Mt 1: 22.

had even taken place, that is, at least in the view of the external world; for with God it had taken place with the promise; for when He speaks, it takes place. It is not merely that doing follows saying but that saying and doing are one and the same with Him.

God's words of promise are immediately and at once the most substantial works and substance, and an entire world filled with evidence is not as certain as a single syllable of promise. Thus the angel had full cause to speak of the past and perfect fulfillment, of things that to be sure had not yet been fulfilled or only halfway, for heaven is already filled with the fulfillment of the divine promises before they have commenced [their fulfillment] on earth. The omnipresence of the future and God's foreknowledge of everything leave nothing undone for heaven. When the angels peer into God they also see the doneness of all the undone things in Him and they speak according to their kind of comprehension, even if it seems incomprehensible to us.

God makes everything take place that His prophets proclaim; for it is not they who speak, but rather God speaks through them, as the angel spoke, "What the Lord had spoken by the prophet." They are the speaking tube or horn through which God speaks from heaven, the voice that speaks God's word, and the translator of His mysteries. In them the oracle that the Spirit speaks through them is presented as tableaux vivants.[189] Their tongues and lips are the instruments and musical tools with which the Spirit of God plays the most beautiful music. They must speak (as Balaam says) whatever the Spirit of God puts in their mouths.[190] They can speak in no other way than what the Lord puts in their mouths. The Lord, however, puts words, as with Balaam, in their mouths and says, "Go forth and speak!"[191] Even if it is deferred for many thousands of years, God is not like a human being that He would regret having said something. Should He say something and not do it? Should He make a promise and not keep it? For what they, the prophets, say is what God says. Thus infallibility is written in their speech.

189. Tableaux vivants (living pictures): as a form of entertainment, costumed actors, frozen in position, depict a scene or reproduce a painting.

190. The story of Balaam is recounted in Nm 22–24. Balaam is commanded by God to speak only as he instructs him, and Balaam repeats several times that he can speak only as God has him speak, as, for example, in Nm 24: 13. Here when Balaam's oracle does not please Balak, the king of the Moabites, Balaam replies, "If Balak should give me his house full of silver and gold, I would not be able to go beyond the word of the Lord, to do either good or bad of my own will; what the Lord speaks, that will I speak? [*sic*]"

191. Paraphrase of Nm 23: 5, Nm 23: 16: "Return to Balak, and thus you shall speak."

Who says, "Behold, a virgin shall be with child and bring forth a son."[192]

Over six and a half centuries have passed since this prophecy, yet God and the angels still remember it vividly as if it happened only yesterday; for no forgetting takes place in God except forgetting our sins. He is an eternal rememberer of the grace that He promised us. If six and a half *secula* or centuries can occasion no forgetting, then a single quarter of a year will not do so either![193] He knows when fulfillment can fill us with the most joy; He saves firing it off for that point.

However long it was deferred (the angel means to say), the divinely inspired promise that amazed angels and humankind and that came through Isaiah has to be fulfilled, since the angel says in the greatest rapture: "Behold!" Muster all your powers of amazement, all kinds of rapture, and all sorts of spontaneous transports.[194] You will need them all and still more in receiving this miraculous promise. Something that is divinely inspired will enter into human nature; it will be at once true and unbelievable. The matter will appear as impossible as it is impossible for it not to be done, since it was promised by God.

A virgin (meaning the most chaste of all) will be with child (the angel says), not conceive a child in the natural human manner, but be with child even as her virginity and unblemished chastity persist; indeed, she is with child from the Holy Spirit, says the prophet Isaiah chapter 7, verse 14, for the works of God are done before they appear, and they exist before the words of promise are uttered. Thus God said: "she is," because everything had already been done in His Providence.

192. Mt 1: 23. The German translation of the Bible reads a virgin "wird schwanger sein" (will *be* pregnant). To reproduce the sense of a state of being, which is important to the meditation that follows, I have here cited the King James Version rather than the RSV, which reads instead "shall conceive." Mt 1: 23 refers to Is 7: 14: "Therefore the Lord himself will give you a sign. Behold, a young woman shall conceive and bear a son, and shall call his name Immanuel." Greiffenberg writes "who says," and I have altered the verse accordingly.

193. Greiffenberg counts the centuries since the prophecy of Isaiah (Is 7: 14). When she refers to a quarter of a year, she is counting the months from quickening in the fifth month to birth in the ninth month.

194. The text reads "Ersetzungen," which as a rule means "replacements" or "compensations." These meanings do not fit the principal point of the exhortation, namely, that the news of Mary's pregnancy can be received by human beings only through strong emotional and spiritual responses. The verb from which "Ersetzungen" is derived can mean "to transfer," "to transplant," or even "to transport." Greiffenberg may thus intend "Ersetzungen" to mean something like English "transports." It is also possible that the text should read "Ergetzungen," which also can be translated as "transports."

Thus chastity is not perchance merely pregnant with holy thoughts, with beautiful conceits of divine praise, or with angelic purities and such things, but with a child that chastity will also bring into the world, for chastity will bear a son, a child that is at once divinely inspired and natural, such a son who has the very Almighty as His eternal father and weakness as His temporal mother, a son, I say, who takes upon himself both natures, a son of the wretched mother as well as of the omnipotent father, for whom the taking on of weakness serves as the guarantor of omnipotence's realizing therein the ardor of love.

She will bear Him too. He will not be an adoptive son, but He will take up human nature itself; not a chosen son, but a borne son, through whom we are chosen as God's children. His birth will happen both naturally and through divine inspiration so that natural humans may attain salvation beyond their natural powers.

"And they shall call his name Emmanuel, which being interpreted is, God with us."[195]

"They shall," says the angel, but the prophet says, "She shall."[196] Both can exist side by side, for first of all she, the holy mother, and then all Christians called Him this. God-with-us in our nature. God-with-us in our flesh and blood. God-with-us on earth. God-with-us in our weakness. God-with-us! Incarnate, corporeal, with body and soul, flesh and blood, skin and bones. God-with-us! Naturally, substantially with nature and being. God-with-us, really, truly in a conceivable form.

Although His divinity is inconceivable, He will nevertheless be conceived, He who is the true God. God, the unimaginable being, the inscrutable intelligence, the unfathomable chasm, the unimaginable miracle and inexhaustible mystery, the inconceivable sea, the unreachable majesty, the vertiginous depths, and the distance that is inconceivable to all things that can be conceived, is with us human beings, that is, with weakness, vanity, wretchedness, want, and the abyss of all misery, in short: the Sum of the Universe is with nothingness in order to make it into something for the purpose of praising His glorious grace.

All humankind is nothing, for what is not good is nothing. So if God is nothing but good, it follows that He alone is everything. In the beginning

195. Mt 1: 23. I have here cited the King James Version of the Bible rather than the RSV because the former contains rather than the passive "his name shall be called" the formulation "they called his name," which is necessary for the meditation that follows to make sense.

196. Greiffenberg compares the wording of the prophecy in Is 7: 14 with its restatement in Mt 1: 23.

He created humankind in His image in order to communicate this good to all people. When, however, that image was spoiled through the envy of the devil and they became nothing, He, as the sum of the universe, became the image of humanity or a human image so that we would become good again and become something.

God Himself became God-with-us so that we could be with God. To show the inconceivability of His divine being still more inconceivably in goodness, He made Himself conceivable in a human form. To make omnipotence more apparent, He became God-with-us in weakness. To surpass all the heavens with the unreachable good, He came from heaven to earth into our wretchedness. To exercise the greatest of all power against hell and its heavily armed minions, He relinquished His power and took on our weakness. The Omnipresent One became what He was not in order all the more to practice and to show what His being and life were, namely, goodness.

Becoming God-with-us made visible, as it were, the substance of the divinity, the substance that is otherwise hidden. As God-with-us, that is, as a human being, He demonstrates that He is infinitely higher than all humankind and, as God, He is that much more profound, having lowered Himself to humankind. His weakness is the proof of omnipotence. If He were less omnipotent, He would not have been able to take on weakness. He would have needed all of His divinity to become a child, for no one but God could voluntarily make himself into a child (if he had not been one previously) and suffer himself to be born. Thus His becoming a child is full proof of His divinity.

He is thereby a God-with-us. Not that God turned into humankind or humankind turned into God; rather, He was united with it. Also not that He devoured it like a consuming fire or that the light of His divinity was extinguished by it like a sea; rather God-with-us so that both natures persisted substantially in a unity and in an *unnatural nature* unique to Him alone. So they remained intact and unquenched—the water of humankind in the midst of the fire of divinity and the fire of divinity in the sea of humankind—and yet were not two separate entities. Rather it was the single champion with two origins and one person from the Holy Trinity, God-with-us, from eternity to eternity, as it was in the beginning and now and ever shall be: in the beginning in the deliberation and selection, now in the fulfillment of it, and ever more in the enjoyment of it, and thus blessed and praised God-with-us in angelic perpetuity from eternity to eternity too and especially now in time.

One can just as little leave off contemplating and admiring as leave off praising itself; for the fact that God-with-us is a sea [composed of] individual droplets merits the contemplation of all the grains of sand of time running through an eternally running hourglass. How can He whom we oppose with our sins be with us? For is it not written: These sins separate us and our God from one another?[197] But for precisely this reason God, who is good through and through, means to be with us in order to separate this separation from us, for He is and loves unity. In order, however, that what he cut in two may become one with Him again, the one from the one also becomes one with what has been cut in two and will nevertheless remain one in the one so that in Him both flow together and become one, because He is both in one.

However, because the consuming purifying fire of divinity tolerates nothing that is impure, He takes on the nature of humankind without the sin and with nothing of sin but the punishment! For He is only God-with-us, not with our sins, and He is God-with-us precisely because He can engulf them and preserve us. He became a God-human or the child of man to separate from human beings the sin that separates us from God so that we human beings become God's children.

O Divine Miracle! O heavenly God-with-us! Who shall be against us? Gracious God-with-us! Who shall damn us? Almighty God-with-us! Who shall overpower us? Most wise God-with-us! Who shall deceive or seduce us? Omnipresent God-with-us! Who shall insult us? God, the highest good, the totality with us! What more do we want, could we, should we ask for?

Desire has an aim, but an aim that is endless and boundless. An aim that exceeds all the world and all of nature, an aim that has no other place but the one that surpasses all places and destinations, an aim that is affixed in the one who is wider than eternity. So we have this aim in the desire we have attained. It is therefore the aim of our salvation. Who can think it, speak it, or describe it? It is greater than one can imagine, for having God-with-us is something that is inconceivable to the angels and above the angels, the next thing to God Himself, indeed, in a certain way a supradivine joy. For being God Himself is natural and thus an imperative and a necessity; this God-with-us is, however, a sign of grace and love of the highest perfection and thus even more gratifying.

God-with-us is like being united with the greatest conceivable good, like being melded at the point of all salvation, for God cannot exist except

197. The text probably alludes to Rom 8: 31–39, which preaches that the separation of God and humankind, which resulted from original sin (the fall from grace described in Genesis), has come to an end. These verses explain that God in sacrificing his own son has made certain that there will be no separation between God who loves humankind and those who love God. I thank the Rev. Paula V. Mehmel for identifying this allusion.

in most sublime happiness and bliss. If it is not according to the body, then it is certainly according to the spirit and virtue. If He is with us, then we dwell in the highest everlasting bliss of the soul even in the midst of sadness. This God-with-us ought to draw us to God to the extent that we perceive nothing but God. God ought thereby to be in all our faculties and thoughts, to prevail in all powers and capacities, to reign in all operations and practices, to appear in all desire and appetites. All stirrings ought thereby to be His impetus, and all movements His stimulation.

Because He gave us Himself, the Sum of the Universe, we ought to submit ourselves as nothingness to Him in everything, and even if it were but the smallest of the small, indeed, only a shadow of gratitude, give nothing for everything! What less can we do than nothing? And we do not even want to do that! Is it not lamentable that we are so thoroughly iniquitous? For that very reason, arise to gratitude, all you people, we who have God-with-us! Pour out floods of knowledge, rivers of exultation, streams of praising, and floodtides of glory! Let the wellsprings bubble with eternal thanksgiving and pour out great seas of God's glory! Exhale an entire airy element of praise and have no other breath than what can glorify God! May all the blood in you become the fire of love and send an offering of praise up to Him. May the body, as the earth of the microcosm, in all its undertakings shoot up growth of gratitude. Do nothing that you do not do to praise God! Cast off your selfness and let God be your self, God who Himself has become what you are! He took care of your redemption and salvation; thus you ought to take care of His praise and glory. Not that He needs your care, but because you no longer need to take care of yourselves, since this most faithful God-with-us has taken care of you in all things. Be concerned about serving Him, because He has so faithfully served you that you no longer need be concerned about anything.

O Thou omnipotent God-with-us! Be with us too in gratitude! Free those hearts that Thou redeemest from hell [and] from the hellish vice of ingratitude as well! Thou who hast gained heaven for us, give us the fruit of heaven too for which to be grateful to Thee! Thou hast already given me the will. Give me also the fulfillment! Since my misery pulled Thee from heaven, pull my weakness heavenward again with Thy fulfillment. When it is a matter of the will, there is none more ardent and eager in nature and among all living creatures than my will to thank and serve Thee. I feel more thoughts of thanks in me than I can utter, yet certainly even more cause [for giving thanks], which causes me to wish my soul out of my body and up to God in heaven to be able properly to praise the God-with-us on earth, indeed, in heaven and on earth.

O Thou God-with-us, the epitome of virtue, may it be thus with our life as well. As Thou art God-human, let then Thy life be our life! It is too little when nothing but the breath of words praises Thee, if our entire life and being do it not. For Thou didst not become an airy, transitory, and fleeting word but instead a living being and a substantial life. Thus let my life, too, praise Thee in uniformity and in emulation of Thy life, insofar as it is possible.

Since, however, I have as good as no power to live in such a holy fashion, live in me and be God-with-me in my sensing and commencing, speaking and writing, thought and poetry, intention and plans. Especially be God-with-us in humility, gentleness, forbearance, patience, and peacemaking! Animate these virtues in me according to the measure of Thy grace and drive out the repugnant ones that try to create confusion in me!

Douse with Thy sweetest cooling liquid all the ardor in my appetites that might resist them [these virtues] and let their lovely cool moisture run through my fiery soul so that all fury is extinguished and I receive the sweetest admixture of Thy gentle goodness. Let Thy forbearance bridle my rashness and give it the weight of decorum. May Thy patience melt and flow into my heart, which would melt from love, and let them thus unite with one another; in short, may Thy life live in my life, and whatever there is in me that does not want to live in this way, let it die.

When Joseph woke from sleep, he did as the angel of the Lord commanded him.[198]

Here it appears once again that this apparition occurred during sleep because Joseph awoke from sleep following it, and thus he proves that he who goes to sleep with virtue wakes up with the angels. This would be the place to say a lot about the sleep of the holy, about the nature of dreams and angelic inspiration. But since I am concerned not with curiosity and sophistry but with devotion and piety, I will pass over all this. Just consider on the other hand Joseph's quick pious obedience: no sooner did Joseph wake and have his senses and limbs ready to go than he did what had been bidden him. He thereby showed his glorious faith by not doubting divinely inspired matters one iota; [he showed] his fear of God by regretting that he had thought the holy bearer of God anything but holy; his humility by resolving henceforth to revere her as a living shrine through abstinence; his remorse for the unjust thoughts he had had, which he countered right away with his actions when he did what the angel had bidden with utmost speed.

198. Mt 1: 24.

He took his wife, but knew her not until she had borne a son.[199]

So he understood that through God's dispensation the presumed disgrace served to honor him and that his spouse's pregnancy was proof of her chastity, that his reason for wishing to leave her was a magnet to take her to him, and that the presumed sign of guilt was the clearest indication of her innocence—just as it still sometimes happens in the world that precisely that which causes people to believe a person guilty and criminal is the truest substance of that person's innocence, indeed, that which makes people slander and despise someone, were it to be revealed and known, would truly be cause for the reverse and the proper purpose of honor.

It sometimes happens that one is hated on account of a presumed vice, which thing would in fact be capable of placing one in the ranks of the saints, just as Mary was thought to be impure precisely on account of the guarantor of her holiness. And God imposes such strange crosses on his saints so that they have an all-the-sweeter friend in their good conscience and so that they one day serve as a source of ineffable astonishment when their miraculous innocence is discovered.

Joseph doubtless had this terrifying and reverential awe, because he not only took her to him but also had such a holy respect for her and especially her divine fruit that he spared them everything that his estate otherwise would have allowed him, not only as long as she was pregnant with this holiness, but her whole life long, because she (as all the holy patriarchs and church histories testify) remained a *semper Virgo* and an eternal virgin.[200]

Since there were and still are many holy women who forever remain chaste for love of devotion and virtue, we can be completely assured that the most holy mother of Jesus persisted in chastity all the more so. Since many men have likewise been celebrated on that account, that person, above all, whom the Most High Himself chose as the screen and shadow of chastity must have remained chaste. Indeed, because there have been and still are examples not only of individual chaste men and women but also of holy chaste marriages, it is all the more credible, indeed beyond doubt, that this most holy married couple had an angelic marriage until they came into an angelic life in eternity and became completely like the angels there.

The Evangelist did not actually say anything about this matter in order to obscure this holy mystery even more, honoring God but not claiming

199. Mt 1: 24–25.

200. The idea that Mary remained a virgin even after the birth of Jesus corresponds with both Lutheran and Catholic teaching.

to have fathomed Him.[201] Moreover, the little word "until" is often used in Holy Scripture for things that never ever come to pass, as can be proven from many authors. Thus it is intended here to mean never ever, since Joseph never ever lost his holy deference and thought of nothing but the fulfillment of the angelic words.

And he called his name Jesus.[202]

God's command through the angel occupied all his holy thoughts, and he yearned for the time of birth and circumcision so that he could soon give the holiest name in heaven and on earth. There was such sweetness in the name Jesus as well as in his own heart that his mouth yearned to overflow with it, and with ardent joy he called Him Jesus.[203]

All bliss that can be found in all the languages and in their books on the arts and sciences is gathered together in the single name Jesus. Just as Lord Jesus is the Eternal Word that created everything, all redemption that He gained for us also inheres in His name. The Incarnate Word in which all wisdom and all abundance reside chose such a word for His own name, with which all [our] salvation is expressed.

The name Jesus is a chasm filled with mystery, but not in itself, as in superstition, but in and through Him to whom it is given. It is the actual expression of His being and His operation: a picture in which all of His beneficence is painted; a book containing all of His miracles; a mirror showing His divine and human form; a seal that expresses His crest and shield, namely, the divine and human, invented by God, revealed by angels, named by Joseph, and received by the little child, through whom the world received not merely the name but its substance as well.

The holy name of Jesus is the name of all names, just as its lord is the Lord of all Lords. It is, however, not powerful in and of itself but only because in it He who is everything is named and noted. When the person is not included in the name, the name has no power in and of itself. It is only the little case holding the jewel. Thus all reverence shown the name of Jesus is to be understood as meant for the person himself; otherwise it would lead to superstition and idolatry. But no creature in heaven or on or beneath the earth can do Jesus so much honor that He would not be worthy of a mil-

201. Greiffenberg means Matthew here, but in fact none of the Gospels is specific on this point.

202. Mt 1: 25.

203. Paraphrase of Mt 13: 34, "For out of the abundance of the heart the mouth speaks," and Lk 6: 45, "for out of the abundance of the heart his mouth speaks."

lion times more [honor] and that He would not be owed still more, even if one poured out an entire heaven replete with gratitude, breezes replete with praise, seas replete with glory, fire replete with love, and earth replete with the fruits of knowledge, and even if one exalted His name above all the heavens.[204]

I thank Thee, my God, for filling the little child in the mother's womb with Thy Holy Spirit and thus making the yet unborn child of Elizabeth jump for joy. The Holy Spirit experienced no childhood, but He does not disdain children on this account. He wrought the childhood of Jesus so that He can also operate within children; for without Jesus, the Holy Spirit does not come to us.

Above all, I laud Thee for filling women too with the Holy Spirit, not just Elizabeth but also many others, indeed all who ask Thee for it, for Thou didst not except us from this promise.

O God! And won't we be filled with Thy praise, for Thou hast filled us with Thy Holy Spirit! And won't there be a river of benediction flowing from our mouths for the blessed fruit of the blessed fruit, for the gift of the Holy Spirit that the Incarnate Spirit, that is, God, Christ, gained for us!

Blessed be the fruit of the womb of Mary, Jesus Christ! Blessed be all the fluids and all the moisture! Blessed be its growth and formation from minute to minute, from moment to moment! Blessed be each hair's breadth of an increase of that flesh and blood that Divinity has as its twin and companion.

So that I can praise this blessed fruit from the top of His head to the soles of His feet, let the skull be blessed and praised, the skull that contains not only a common and single reason but also that intelligence from which all intelligence and reason originally sprang forth and which is a fount of reason and the source of all intelligence. Blessed be the three cells or little chambers of the brain, the apartments of the intelligence and the treasure chests of the three heavenly powers, in which the Holy Trinity not only painted its own likeness but whose image one member of the Trinity Himself chose in turn to assume.[205]

Blessed be the imagination taken on by Him, by the power of whose primal imagining all powers of imagination were created. Blessed be His little middle chamber, which contains reason or the power of understand-

204. Greiffenberg here enumerates the four elements of Aristotelian and Western alchemical cosmology—air, water, fire, and earth—as she imagines a cosmos resounding with hymns of thanksgiving.

205. Greiffenberg follows with a traditional description of the brain as portrayed in medieval anatomies, as containing, front to back, three cells: imagination, reason, and memory.

ing in it so that the center of the Trinity and all reason not only restores our reason, which was lost through sin, but sanctifies it, sharpens it, and makes it holy and wise.

Blessed be the third chamber as well, the one of memory that the Eternal Primal Memory first planted in us and then chose to assume to be able to remember us in all manner of remembering. In order to save and sanctify memory, it poured the sea of divine memory into this dimple of memory, or rather it chose to take on this little fount of memory along with the sea; for Divinity dwells in the entire body and not merely in the memory, and Divinity is also not in the brain as the memory but instead takes on the natural, human powers of imagination, reason, and memory, just as it does the other parts of the human body.

I also bless Thy *dura mater*, or hard mother, which divides and differentiates the small and large brain at the top of the head as well as lengthwise, but which also allows the veins, air, mucous, and nerves their egress;[206] it envelops the spinal cord and the nerves and provides multifarious services for the head and the entire body.

Blessed be Thou forever and eternally, O blessed fruit of the womb, that Thou didst suffer the picking of the fruit in paradise by our hard mother to move Thee to take on this hard mother as a piece of humanity, in which Thou wouldst have it so hard. Be praised still more that Thou didst put the good mother or *pia mater* into Thy holy head as well in order to be able to remember, as it were, that Thy love is our good mother; it sends itself like her into all the bends and corners of the brain and thus into all our troubles and affairs, however we might excogitate them with our brain and intelligence.[207]

This powerful preserver and provider of the brain, which also gives it sensitivity, be it eternally blessed in the one who in the beginning so miraculously created it and afterward, as the living miracle, still more miraculously took it on Himself so that He could suffer for us through the injury of it.

Blessed be once again, indeed, a thousand times over, the brain, which

206. I.e., the cerebellum and cerebrum.

207. "Pia mater" is a Latin translation from the Arabic, meaning "tender mother." Greiffenberg takes some liberties in translating "pia" into German as "good" in order to bring anatomy in line with her vision of salvation. We note here that the words "pia mater" appear in the well-known Catholic hymn Stabat Mater in reference to Mary. Even if Greiffenberg, the staunch Lutheran, was not familiar with the Stabat Mater (although she may well have been in Catholic Austria), it is surprising that she lets this opportunity for punning pass since she has just referred to Eve as the "hard mother," and thus the association of the "pia mater" with Mary seems obvious. Instead she here sees Christ's love as the "good mother."

is the seat of the image of God, a fortress of the rational soul, a throne of intelligence, and a source of all comprehension and invention, a gathering place of all rational and vital spirits, which on account of the amazing nest of nerves is, in a word, a nest and root of the entire body that originates in the head.

Blessed be every little morsel of the brain, every little coil of the blood vessels, every little spark of spirit, every little piece of the brain, from which the inner part of the head is composed!

Blessed be no less the noble tool of the spirit, the dear eyes, the mirror of the spirit, the translator of memory, and the revealer of the heart, the suns of the body, the stars of the microcosm, and the lights of nature, which thou, O Eternal Sun of Justice, O Morning Star of Redemption and Light of the World, also chose to receive in Thine incarnation. Blessed be the crystalline liquid that is united with the diamond of Divinity.

Blessed be the glassy moisture in the lovely little eyes that thereby makes the glass of our weakness [hard] like steel! Praised be its natural watery moistures that chose to make us like Him in all things; lauded and glorified be all the thin little membranes that separate off these ocular liquids and hold them together; praised be each little blood vessel, especially the nerves of sight that bring the power of seeing from the brain into the eyes. Blessed be the lovely eyebrows and the eye sockets that envelop not only the most beautiful little eyes in the world but Divinity itself, which is, as I said, in the entire body and thus in these heavenly little lights too.

Blessed be the charming little nose, the face's ornament, which commandeers the air and its vital spirits in and out by means of its air tubes and canals; the tool of smell, the watering can of the brain, and the one who ushers out all superfluity. Who, however, can venerate the Most High with sufficient laudation for the fact that the eternal Primal Being of all air and life, who blew the breath of life into the nose of the first person in the creation, now takes on a nose Himself so that He, as that very life, can communicate to us the scent of life.

Blessed be likewise the darling little temples, the alabaster embroidered with little veins of sapphire, and the lovely little cheeks next to them, on which in time the loveliest white and red little roses will bloom! Blessed be each droplet of blood that will paint this little Jesus-Paradise-Flower.

Above all, infinitely blessed, consecrated, and praised be the charming little mouth of Him whose word without a mouth created our mouths to praise Him, and when Eve was seduced through the mouth of the serpent and we through hers, He determined, as Heavenly Wisdom, to take on a human mouth from a woman to make us taste Him Himself as the eternal truth in our mouths.

Blessed be the lovely lips that will console poor sinners in the kindest manner and comfort all the downcast. The lips that otherwise serve as the tools of nourishment and the head cooks of the microcosm in Him (to be sure because they are like nature, but not from necessity) will preserve the micro- and macrocosm with words of life.

Blessed be as well the holy tongue, which in the form of a triangle is generally a sign of the Holy Trinity, but here indeed one of its three parts![208] Blessed be all the blood vessels, nerves, little joints, and cartilage of this miraculous tool that give it the power of moving and stirring and working and that bring all liquid and moisture that serve taste and speech to it from the brain. This member is sometimes judged to be the best one, even in imperfect humankind. How should it not be all the more the best of the best in the supremely perfect one united with God! The double-edged sword that conquers all, the banner of security, the flame of love, the column of truth, and the scepter of the kingdom of Christ! All the millions of tongues of the world (like the millions of grains of sand) cannot praise His most heavenly little tongue enough, even if they were to do nothing but go around praising. Mine would never cease doing so, if it did not need to bless the remaining parts of the body, namely, the two rows of marble and double strand of pearls, the teeth next to it, which to be sure had not yet emerged in the Jesus lying in His mother's womb, but the possibility of them lay already in the gums.

Blessed be therefore the lovely little milk teeth from which the sweet milk of the Gospel sprang forth for us. Blessed be their blood vessels and the little roots that made them sensitive and bound and held them in place. Blessed be these most lovely mouth-mills that grind the bread for the very bread of life, the living, sensitive, and ever-growing little bones, the newly shorn little sheep of the little lamb of God that has come from the watering place, the chosen arrows that shoot at the target of truth, the tools of speech of the words of the Eternal Word, the beauty of the mouth of Jesus that before He had a mouth expressed all beauty. Eternally extolled and praised be the heavenly teeth that will redeem us from the eternal clattering of teeth in hell through their chattering on the Mount of Olives.[209]

Be infinitely blessed as well the artful hourglass of the ears that the ur-ear planted in itself, the beautiful pair of virtue-shells that spiral in and go to the smith and workshop of hearing, which is enclosed between two walls

208. In other words, Christ is only one of the persons of the trinity.

209. Jesus foretold Peter's denial on the Mount of Olives (Mt 26: 30–35, Mk 14: 26–31, Lk 22: 31–34, Jn 13: 36–38).

or membranes.[210] Blessed be the most artful little hammer and the lovely anvil that beats on it and that forms the hearing that heard and will give a favorable hearing to poor sinners and wretched people.

You blessed portals of the soul that ever stand open to the downcast! Image of the Trinity reiterated by the aforementioned three little bones that are beneath the curtain of the little membrane and that lead sound through the artfully coiled maze to the secret little room of hearing! I would say that the Most High was to be praised most highly for it, if it did not require still greater praise than the greatest praise for His humbling Himself to come into such a workshop of hearing to unite it with His unheard-of hearing of everything.

In a word, blessed be the entire head of Him who is the head of all heads and who not only heads them all but also heads all of heaven! Blessed be each little hair that the most noble vapor and moisture will drive out of the brain and that will be true threads of bliss and just the right hair for winding our way out of the labyrinth of the world into the splendor of heaven.[211]

Blessed be the lower inward parts of the head, such as the gorge, by means of which we shall be torn from the jaws of hell; the noblest palate to which the most eloquent tongue will later cleave to provide us with eternal nectar and sweetness; the uvula or little grape, which later on will practically fall down into [the throat] with groaning; the throat that is the stairway of the voice, on whose steps it ascends and descends.[212] Praised and blessed be it in Him who with His voice will call to Him all those who labor and are heavy laden.[213]

Blessed be likewise the heavenly neck, the column of the supra-angelic and yet human head, the living alabaster tower that clothes and covers the windpipes, the veins, sinews, and nerves and that is a joining of the head and body through which the lungs send up the air and the heart and liver the vital spirits and the blood and that is, as it were, the highway of the air, blood, food, and spirits.[214]

210. Greiffenberg makes a pun here that is difficult to translate into English; she uses the words "Uhrwerk" (clockwork) and "Uhr-Ohr." "Uhr" can refer to what I have translated as hourglass, and thus the English can at least make a gesture toward the homonym. However, this "Uhr" also carries the meaning of English *ur* (primal) and of course sounds like the German word *Ohr* (ear). The virtue-shells are the auricles, i.e., the outer projecting portion of the ear.

211. The text again alludes to the Greek myth of Theseus and the Minotaur.

212. Small grape is a translation of Latin *uvula*.

213. Paraphrase of Mt 11: 28.

214. See above, note 118. The neck is referred to as a tower of ivory in the Song of Songs.

Blessed be each little piece of cartilage that in place of blocks built this God-human-tower that reaches to heaven and through which we shall emerge from the debtor's prison of hell and eternal captivity.

Blessed be in the same degree the holy shoulders, which are peculiar to humans alone above all creatures: the origins of the arms and hands, which are the source of all arts and works, especially of His, who, before He received human hands, formed the first human being with His hand, as Job says, "Thy hands fashioned and made me," etc.[215]

Blessed be the dear arms that later on will so wretchedly have to lift the cross and bear it and ultimately be stretched out on it.

Blessed and praised be all the veins that like strings of sapphire run through these heavenly hands and arms.[216] The median or middle vein, the pulmonary, cephalic, hepatic, and purple veins, and all the other veinlets and lesser little blood vessels, whatever they are called.[217] A thousand times blessed be each little droplet of blood that flows in these most noble veins and that later will flow from them on the cross for the sake of the forgiveness of our sins and finally [will flow] even in Holy Communion in our mouth for the purpose of sealing that forgiveness.

Lauded and honored be all sinews, nerves, spindle bones, limbs, pulses and bones, also all air and marrow in them, all flesh, fat, and skin, from which the most splendid construction of the arms and hands is composed by the hand of God.[218]

Blessed be the little muscles in the arms in which life resides; the noble elbows that give the entire arm agility and movement; above all the darling hands themselves, the tools of all art, the images of prayer, the suppliers of all beneficence, the givers of alms, the executors of redemption, and the means of all grace.

215. Jb 10: 8.

216. Greiffenberg employs the German word "Hände" here which can mean both "hands" and "hands and arms." The mention of the arteries that run though the arms suggests that "hands and arms" is a better translation.

217. Greiffenberg refers here to "Median=oder Mittel-Ader/ Lungen=Leber=Haupt=und Virtel- Ader." These are the five veins used in bloodletting in the early modern period. The cephalic vein, median or cardiac vein, and the basilica or hepatic vein are the three veins used in the Greco-Roman tradition. The other two, the *vena titillaris* or vein for the lungs, which I have translated as "pulmonary vein," and the *funis brachii* or purple vein belong to Arabic knowledge. See Linda E. Voigts and Michael R. McVaugh, "A Latin Technical Phlebotomy and Its Middle English Translation," *Transactions of the American Philosophical Society* 74, no. 2 (1984): esp. 4, 38, 39, and 56.

218. The German word that Greiffenberg uses here is "Spindeln," literally "spindles," which probably refers to the radius, the smaller bone of the lower arm.

Blessed be all the lines and streaks of chiromancy or palmistry, their seven planets or rather mountains of mercy, their lifeline that was cut through by the violent death on the cross.[219]

Blessed be the dear fingers, the styluses of the heart, the looseners of the tongue, the openers of the eyes and ears, the beckoners to salvation: the thumb that is good for everything; the indicator of heaven; the middle finger of the middlemost of the Trinity; the heart-and-gold finger of the Creator of all hearts and gold, to which not only a little vein runs from His heart but which can touch and guide all the veins of the heart, [the finger] that all the gold and jewels in the whole world ought to adorn as ring and ornament.

Be no less blessed the little fingers too of the Greatest of All who became small for us. Be praised and thanked for all the little members and joints that make them move and stir. Be likewise blessed the dear fingernails that are the horns, helmets, and little shields of the fingers. The blessed fingernails, on which our bliss blooms, that later on will turn pale from pain and that will be dead before the dying [is over].

Blessed be the holy shoulders that are the real Atlas of the world and our debts.[220] Blessed be the dear backbone that is composed of both virtues and bones in which the marrow of life resides.

Blessed be the dear, darling ribs that fit in the backbone so neatly and close up the most beautiful body and hold it together: the dear ribs, I say, of the second and true Adam, from which I am edified.[221] Blessed be the wisest and most miraculous dispensation of God: just as He formed a woman from the first man's rib, He now takes from a woman the ribs of the first or premier man in heaven and on earth.

Blessed and praised be the back that covers over this bridge, which is not ivory but heavenly and which will so willingly offer itself up to them who choose to beat it, indeed, which will carry the very cross to which they will nail Him.

219. In the art of reading palms, the eminences on the palm were coordinated with the so-called seven planets: Venus, Mars, Mercury, the sun, Saturn, Jupiter, and the moon, and thus chiromancy was connected to astrology.

220. In Greek mythology, Atlas is the giant who is forced by Zeus forever to carry the heavens on his shoulders as a punishment.

221. Jesus is sometimes referred to as the second Adam because he reversed the consequences of the banishment from the Garden of Eden and the fall from grace by redeeming the sins of humankind. Greiffenberg uses the term "erbaut," which here primarily means "edified," that is, built in a moral or spiritual sense (i.e., with reference to Christ and the redemption). "Erbaut" can also literally mean "built" and thus simultaneously recalls the creation of woman from the rib of the first Adam (Gn 2: 21–22).

No less, but instead equally, be praised to the heavens the divine shield of the heart, the holiest of the holy breast, in which no deceit was ever found and which covers over the purest and most innocent heart and, as it were, is the oyster shell of the most precious pearl in heaven and on earth, namely, Jesus' heart.

Praised be all its cartilage, little bones, and layers of fat, which constitute the roof of the most noble innermost part, the treasure chest of the spirit, the Ark of the Covenant, the jeweled casing of the soul, in sum, all of that which eternity will in future reveal to us.

Still higher, indeed, far above all the heavens be praised the holy sides that hold together the breast and back and round out this heavenly column of redemption. O Benediction! Pour out yourself into that side from which redemption and salvation will be poured out over us!

Oh, yes! Blessed over and over be the entire precious chest, the most beautiful body of Jesus that contains the most excellently noble inner parts. But where do I find praise and blessing for the heart of all hearts, the throne not merely of His body but of all our lives? Oh! Since words and utterances are lacking, I shall do what I can. I bless you, therefore, you sanctity entangled with many little veins and nerves! You incomparable pyramid of rubies! You triangle of the Trinity! Blessed be your two little treasure chests of redemption, the one filled with the gold of the blood, the other with the spirit of life.[222] Blessed be each rose noble drop in this little purple bag, which is much larger than that of the other part, because the lovesick blood could never satisfy its hunger to redeem us, to flow to us, and to well up in us.[223]

Blessed be the dear little ears of the heart that grant our prayers such a gracious hearing and take our need to heart.[224] Blessed be the vena cava, which is a container and, as it were, the pitcher of the heart through which this spring of redemption runs, which joins the right and larger part.[225]

222. Greiffenberg follows Galenic medicine here when she understands the heart to have two chambers (rather than four).

223. The rosenoble is a gold coin current in the fifteenth and sixteenth centuries. It is a variety of the coin termed a noble and has the figure of a rose stamped on it. Greiffenberg imagines the heart as a coin purse filled with coins that are at the same time drops of blood. The larger part that she mentions is the right side of the heart, namely, the right auricle and ventricle.

224. Auricles of the heart, i.e., ear-shaped appendages of the left and right atria of the heart. The word *auricle* derives from Latin *auris* (ear).

225. The German reads "Leber-Ader," literally "liver artery" or "liver vein." Greiffenberg refers here to the vena cava, the large blood vessel that delivers blood to the heart and that joins the right auricle. Her later use of the same word to refer to the aorta (see below, note 227) makes clear that she does not have our modern understanding of the anatomy of the heart.

Praised and lauded be you, pulmonary artery, as well, who are a chariot of the vital spirits and who play ball with the lungs and the heart.[226] Extolled be each little puff of an angel that flies into this heart-heaven and climbs back down on this angelic ladder and disperses throughout the entire body too.

I also glorify and infinitely bless those arteries that as it were like a crown from the aorta wrap around the heart; blessed be all the little nets and lattices that contain and enclose the heart.[227] Blessed be the most delicate blood of the heart on the left side that is refreshed by the pulmonary artery and that sends heat and along with it strength and refreshment to the entire body. I praise you, O you organ—the first to be animated and the last to die—of Him who is immortal.[228] I could never stop blessing you, if the other noble inward parts did not demand of me their praise too.

Oh! Let the holy lungs therefore be lauded and praised, the bellows of the heart, the fan of the human being, the angel wings of cooling, the west wind in the springtime of health. Blessed be you unceasingly, you glorious embracer of the heart, who as it were envelop [it], as does the curtain the Ark of the Covenant, so that no harm comes to it from the bones, ribs, and breast.[229] O you eternally blessed tool of the voice and thus of speech, from which the sweetest words in heaven and on earth are born for us, since the words, as it were, climb up your voice-stairs. Angelically blessed airy villa that opens one Zephyr chamber after another and is to be called a real fortress of refreshment! You blessed heart-restorer of the One who is a restorer of all our hearts! My lungs do not have enough air to extol the air of Thine.

226. The text reads "Ballon-Spielerin mit der Lunge und Herzen" (literally, female ball-player with the lung and heart). The feminine gender derives from the German word for artery, which is grammatically feminine. A *Ballon* is a ball filled with air. Presumably the image refers to a game of some kind in which an airy ball is struck since the aorta is understood to pulsate.

227. The German text reads "Leber-Ader," literally, "liver artery" or "liver vein." Greiffenberg refers here to the aorta, which arches above the heart with three ascending arterial branches with the effect of a three-pronged crown. The central trunk of the aorta descends from this arch as the abdominal artery and branches again into three parts in the abdomen, eventually branching again into, among others, the hepatic artery, which connects to the liver. The term "liver artery" derives from earlier ideas of circulation.

228. The text refers here to theories of fetal development current in the seventeenth century, according to which organs develop in sequence. These theories contrast with pre-formation theory, also current in the seventeenth century, according to which the adult human already exists in complete form and in miniature in the sperm and thus simply increases in size in the uterus. See Joseph Needham, *A History of Embryology* (Cambridge: Cambridge University Press, 1934), 96–157.

229. The ark of the covenant is to be kept in a tabernacle, which according to Ex 26: 1 is to be made of ten curtains: "Moreover you shall make the tabernacle with ten curtains of fine twined linen." The German word is "Teppich" more commonly translated as "carpet."

But I am unable to sate my desire to praise the stomach, which is the head cook of Him who feeds the entire world. It cooks the food in this body, whose mouth created all food. Blessed be therefore the holy fire or the natural heat of the stomach that serves digestion and cooks the happy liquid from which the entire body receives nourishment. Blessed be its points of exit, through which it sends it over to the liver.

But blessed still more extravagantly be the holy liver itself, which receives [the liquid] and turns it into blood. O you blessed and first-completed, noble part of the noblest of the noble and the most excellently perfect of the perfect. You [who are] one of the three most important columns and to be sure the first of those, on which the entire structure of the body rests, namely, the liver, heart, and brain. You blessed birth of blood and bearer of the blood that will bear us to heaven. Blessed seat of the growing soul! Praised be all your effects, namely, the drawing to yourself, the containing and cooking of the material of the blood! Blessed be your tools, that is, the life spirit and the natural warmth that help you to attract, retain, and produce what needs to be distributed throughout the entire body, for you are the blessed source from which all the limbs draw blood and nourishment. Praised be the net that embraces you, blessed be all the fats and fenestrae that appear to constitute [your] hypochondria.[230] In a word, blessed be the entire inward and noble viscera of that Compassion itself, which not only provided for and made innate in the viscera natural pity and ardor, but which also out of pity assumed viscera itself so that it could feel our misery in its viscera or inmost parts.

O you blessed machine of motion! Blessed be all your parts and pieces, including the main net that holds you together in all eternity, even if the fortress of the heavens and the borders of the sea break to pieces. Praised be also the dear loins, which, like buckles, hold the entire body together. Praised be all their sinews and veins, which they send into the legs and feet, and the noble blood that they pour into the thighs. Likewise be lauded the lovely hips, which are the mechanism of movement and the origin of motion, from which all tools of walking emerge. Blessed be the most worthy stout legs, all their nerves, sinews, and tendons, and the noblest flesh and

230. The "net" refers to the visceral peritoneum, the membrane encasing the liver. "Fenestrae," which can indicate depressions in organs, are literally "little windows" and stand in here for the original German "Fensterlein" (little windows). I have used the word "fenestrae" here, surmising that Greiffenberg means thereby to indicate the abdominal lines that are produced by the configuration of the abdominal muscles and that thus define the surface anatomy of the abdomen. The hypochondria is an area of the abdomen just under the ribs, held to be the seat of melancholy.

blood that clothe them. Oh! Blessed columns of redemption! Pillars of truth! Miraculous colossus of the miracle itself! All my joy and bliss subsists and rests on you!

I bless upon my knees the most holy knees too of this blessed fruit of the body, which often bent and kneeled down to plead for us. Blessed be the kneecaps, joints, and, so to speak, the locks that unlock and lock them and now and again make them turn![231] Praised be the holy thighs and legs, the lower parts of the column; blessed be the straight shinbones that externally are covered over with the round and delicate calves and appear, as it were, to be turned in alabaster and studded with sapphires. Blessed be all the turquoise veins that creep through this flesh marble! All the sinews that strengthen it, all the spindle bones that extend through it, indeed, above all, the marrow that gives the shinbone the power and capacity to carry and bear everything.[232]

From the very bottom of my heart be blessed as well the bottom support of this most holy edifice of the body, the dear feet, or trotters, as people tend to call them. Above and beyond everything in the world, the blessed heel of the blessed seed of woman, which the serpent will bite when you crush its head.[233] You eternally blessed tool for redeeming us from the eternal curse! Blessed toes, along with your nails and little members and joints, which will sometimes move to serve us, but especially will move from pain.

O you forefeet and soles, blessed by every drop of my blood, you who will feel and suffer the sharpest sting of nails! Extolled and praised be all the spindle bones, veins, cartilage, and little bones and joints that are in you, the thick skin of the sole, which is the cornerstone of the Christ-Temple![234] In short, with this one blessing standing in for a thousand words, blessed be the most heavenly holy body from the soles of the feet to the top of the head, with all the blessings that the fount of thought itself could think up and that eloquence itself could utter! Blessed fruit of the body! Let my entire life bring you fruits of blessing to and for all eternity!

231. The term that Greiffenberg uses here is "Schloss-Glieder," literally, "lock-joints or lock-members." She probably means the ligaments.

232. Greiffenberg again employs the word "Spindeln" (spindles), which can refer to the fibula, i.e., a bone shaped like a spindle.

233. Allusion to Gn 3: 15 and the fall from grace.

234. Greiffenberg here again employs the term "Spindeln" (spindles), which she used above to refer to the radius and the fibula. *Grimms Wörterbuch* does not record the use in anatomy of *Spindeln* to refer to bones in the feet; Greiffenberg, who of course did not study medicine formally, may simply call the metatarsus (part of the forefoot consisting of five slender bones) "Spindeln" by analogy.

I praise Thee too for the fact that Thy hidden presence made John, who likewise lay in his mother's womb, leap for joy to tell us in advance that we too would feel Thine impulses of joy in secret.

How infinitely laudable is also Thy divine good will, O Dispenser of Grace, Jesus, that through the utterance of Thy Holy Spirit Thou didst cause salvation to be attributed to faith.[235] This grace alone deserves an entire eternity filled with demonstrations of gratitude; for what is more comforting than the fact that faith redeems, faith that God will not fail to make active in us? What is more delightful than believing? What is easier when divine grace gives us the strength for it?

I praise Thee too for the gracious fulfillment of Thy promises, that Thou sufferest to be fulfilled what was told to us. Oh! Let it be fulfilled in me too, wretched one, what was particularly said to me by the Lord. Let the secret word of grace be realized, O self-sufficient Word of God and Life, so that Thy glory and splendor can be praised to the skies, since Thou knowest well that I have no more serious and zealous desires than these alone that aim at Thy glory and its exaltation.

But how can I sufficiently praise and extol Mary's song of praise, which was inspired by the Holy Spirit? My soul magnifies the Lord for the magnification of hers! My spirit rejoices with her over God, the Savior of us both! I praise Thee for regarding her with grace and making her worthy so that all the generations would glorify her. I glorify Thee, O magnificent God, for doing great things for her, from whom the greatest beneficence in the world sprang forth for us. I praise and honor Thee, indeed, thank Thee endlessly for the fact that Thy mercy endures forever and thus also [is extended to] me, unworthy one, who loving Thee fears Thee and fearing Thee honors Thee! I magnify Thee for the exalting of the wretched, and I fill heaven and earth with Thy praise for filling the hungry with goods. For the memory of

235. The text alludes here to a central tenet of the Lutheran faith as expressed in Luther's Small Catechism as the third article of the creed. Here Luther explains that by stating "I believe in the Holy Spirit, one holy Christian Church, the community of the saints, forgiveness of sins, resurrection of the flesh, and eternal life," one indicates that one believes that one cannot by one's own "understanding or strength . . . believe in Jesus Christ, my Lord, or come to Him; but the Holy Spirit has called me through the gospel, enlightened me with his gifts, made me holy and kept me in the true faith; just as he calls, gathers, enlightens, and makes holy the whole Christian Church on earth, and keeps it with Jesus Christ in the one common, true faith." Martin Luther, "The Small Catechism," in *The Book of Concord: The Confessions of the Evangelical Lutheran Church*, ed. Robert Kolb and Timothy J. Wengert (Minneapolis: Fortress Press, 2000), 355. In other words, as stated in Eph 2: 8, "For by grace you have been saved through faith; and this is not your own doing, it is the gift of God." Humankind has been given the gift of faith by God, the very faith that will provide salvation.

Thy mercy shall I be mindful of Thine immutable praise. For Thy succoring of Thy spiritual Israel, as Thou didst speak to Abraham and forever and ever to us, his faithful seed, I shall help with all my might, soul, honor and goods, life and limb to magnify and spread Thine honor, love, and laudation in time and eternity. Amen.

SERIES EDITORS' BIBLIOGRAPHY

PRIMARY SOURCES

Agnesi, Maria Gaetana, Giuseppa Eleonora Barbapiccola, Diamante Medaglia Faini, Aretafila Savini de' Rossi, and the Accademia de' Ricovrati. *The Contest for Knowledge*. Ed. and trans. Rebecca Messbarger and Paula Findlen. The Other Voice in Early Modern Europe. Chicago: University of Chicago Press, 2005.

Agrippa, Henricus Cornelius. *Declamation on the Nobility and Preeminence of the Female Sex*. Ed. and trans. Albert Rabil Jr. The Other Voice in Early Modern Europe. Chicago: University of Chicago Press, 1996.

Alberti, Leon Battista. *The Family in Renaissance Florence*. Trans. Renée Neu Watkins. Columbia, SC: University of South Carolina Press, 1969.

Aragona, Tullia d'. *Dialogue on the Infinity of Love*. Ed. and trans. Rinaldina Russell and Bruce Merry. The Other Voice in Early Modern Europe. Chicago: University of Chicago Press, 1997.

Arenal, Electa, and Stacey Schlau, eds. *Untold Sisters: Hispanic Nuns in Their Own Works*. Trans. Amanda Powell. Albuquerque: University of New Mexico Press, 1989.

Astell, Mary (1666–1731). *The First English Feminist: Reflections on Marriage and Other Writings*. Ed. Bridget Hill. New York: St. Martin's Press, 1986.

Astell, Mary, and John Norris. *Letters concerning the Love of God*. Ed. E. Derek Taylor and Melvyn New. The Early Modern Englishwoman, 1500–1750: Contemporary Editions. Aldershot: Ashgate, 2005.

Atherton, Margaret, ed. *Women Philosophers of the Early Modern Period*. Indianapolis, IN: Hackett, 1994.

Aughterson, Kate, ed. *Renaissance Woman: Constructions of Femininity in England: A Source Book*. London: Routledge, 1995.

Barbaro, Francesco. *On Wifely Duties*. Trans. Benjamin Kohl. In *The Earthly Republic*, ed. Kohl and R. G. Witt, 179–228. Philadelphia: University of Pennsylvania Press, 1978.

Battiferra degli Ammannati, Laura. *Laura Battiferra and her Literary Circle*. Ed. and trans. Victoria Kirkham. The Other Voice in Early Modern Europe. Chicago: University of Chicago Press, 2006.

Behn, Aphra. *The Works of Aphra Behn*. Ed. Janet Todd. 7 vols. Columbus: Ohio State University Press, 1992–96.

Bigolina, Giulia. *Urania: A Romance*. Ed. and trans. Valeria Finucci. The Other Voice in Early Modern Europe. Chicago: University of Chicago Press, 2005.

Bisha, Robin, Jehanne M. Gheith, Christine Holden, and William G. Wagner, eds. *Russian Women, 1698–1917: Experience* and *Expression: An Anthology of Sources*. Bloomington: Indiana University Press, 2002.

Blamires, Alcuin, ed. *Woman Defamed and Woman Defended: An Anthology of Medieval Texts*. Oxford: Clarendon Press, 1992.

Boccaccio, Giovanni. *Corbaccio or the Labyrinth of Love*. Trans. Anthony K. Cassell. 2nd rev. ed. Binghamton, NY: Medieval and Renaissance Texts and Studies, 1993.

———. *Famous Women*. Ed. and trans. Virginia Brown. I Tatti Renaissance Library. Cambridge: Harvard University Press, 2001.

Booy, David, ed. *Autobiographical Writings by Early Quaker Women*. Aldershot: Ashgate, 2004.

Brown, Judith. *Immodest Acts: The Life of a Lesbian Nun in Renaissance Italy*. New York: Oxford University Press, 1986.

Brown, Sylvia, ed. *Women's Writing in Stuart England: The Mother's Legacies of Dorothy Leigh, Elizabeth Joscelin and Elizabeth Richardson*. Thrupp, Stroud, Gloucester: Sutton, 1999.

Bruni, Leonardo. "On the Study of Literature (1405) to Lady Battista Malatesta of Moltefeltro." In *The Humanism of Leonardo Bruni: Selected Texts,* trans. and intro. by Gordon Griffiths, James Hankins, and David Thompson, 240–51. Binghamton, NY: Medieval and Renaissance Studies and Texts, 1987.

Caminer Turra, Elisabetta. *Selected Writings of an Eighteenth-Century Venetian Woman of Letters*. Ed. and trans. Catherine M. Sama. The Other Voice in Early Modern Europe. Chicago: University of Chicago Press, 2003.

Campiglia, Maddalena. *Flori: A Pastoral Drama: A Bilingual Edition*. Ed., intro., and notes by Virginia Cox and Lisa Sampson. Trans. Virginia Cox. The Other Voice in Early Modern Europe. Chicago: University of Chicago Press, 2004.

Castiglione, Baldassare. *The Book of the Courtier*. Trans. George Bull. New York: Penguin, 1967.

———. *The Book of the Courtier*. Ed. Daniel Javitch. New York: W. W. Norton, 2002.

Cereta, Laura. *Collected Letters of a Renaissance Feminist*. Ed. and trans. Diana Robin. The Other Voice in Early Modern Europe. Chicago: University of Chicago Press, 1997.

Christine de Pizan. *The Book of the City of Ladies*. Trans. Earl Jeffrey Richards. Foreword by Marina Warner. New York: Persea Books, 1982.

———. *Epistre au dieu d'Amours*. Ed. and trans. Thelma S. Fenster. In *Poems of Cupid, God of Love,* ed. Thelma S. Fenster and Mary Carpenter Erler. Leiden: E. J. Brill, 1990.

———. *A Medieval Woman's Mirror of Honor: The Treasury of the City of Ladies*. Trans. Charity Cannon Willard. Ed. Madeleine P. Cosman. New York: Persea Books, 1989.

———. *The Treasure of the City of Ladies*. Trans. Sarah Lawson. New York: Viking Penguin, 1985.

Clarke, Danielle, ed. *Isabella Whitney, Mary Sidney, and Aemilia Lanyer: Renaissance Women Poets*. New York: Penguin Books, 2000.

Coignard, Gabrielle de. *Spiritual Sonnets: A Bilingual Edition*. Ed. and trans. Melanie E. Gregg. The Other Voice in Early Modern Europe. Chicago: University of Chicago Press, 2004.

Colonna, Vittoria. *Sonnets for Michelangelo: A Bilingual Edition.* Ed. and trans. Abigail Brundin. The Other Voice in Early Modern Europe. Chicago: University of Chicago Press, 2005.

Couchman, Jane, and Ann Crabb, eds. *Women's Letters across Europe, 1400–1700.* Aldershot: Ashgate, 2005.

Crawford, Patricia, and Laura Gowing, eds. *Women's Worlds in Seventeenth-Century England: A Source Book.* London: Routledge, 2000.

Daybell, James, ed. *Early Modern Women's Letter Writing, 1450–1700.* Houndmills, England: Palgrave, 2001.

De Erauso, Catalina. *Lieutenant Nun: Memoir of a Basque Transvestite in the New World.* Trans. Michele Stepto and Gabriel Stepto. Foreword by Marjorie Garber. Boston: Beacon Press, 1995.

Dentière, Marie. *Epistle to Marguerite de Navarre and Preface to a Sermon by John Calvin.* Ed. and trans. Mary B. McKinley. The Other Voice in Early Modern Europe. Chicago: University of Chicago Press, 2004.

Elisabeth of Bohemia, Princess, and René Descartes. *The Correspondence between Princess Elisabeth of Bohemia and René Descartes.* Ed. and trans. Lisa Shapiro. The Other Voice in Early Modern Europe. Chicago: University of Chicago Press, 2007.

Elizabeth I. *Elizabeth I: Collected Works.* Ed. Leah S. Marcus, Janel Mueller, and Mary Beth Rose. Chicago: University of Chicago Press, 2000.

Elyot, Thomas. *Defence of Good Women: The Feminist Controversy of the Renaissance.* Ed. Diane Bornstein. New York: Delmar, 1980.

Erasmus, Desiderius. *Erasmus on Women.* Ed. Erika Rummel. Toronto: University of Toronto Press, 1996.

Fedele, Cassandra. *Letters and Orations.* Ed. and trans. Diana Robin. The Other Voice in Early Modern Europe. Chicago: University of Chicago Press, 2000.

Ferguson, Moira, ed. *First Feminists: British Women Writers, 1578–1799.* Bloomington: Indiana University Press, 1985.

Ferrazzi, Cecilia. *Autobiography of an Aspiring Saint.* Ed. and trans. Anne Jacobson Schutte. The Other Voice in Early Modern Europe. Chicago: University of Chicago Press, 1996.

The Fifteen Joys of Marriage. Trans. Elizabeth Abbott. New York: Orion Press, 1959.

Folger Collective on Early Women Critics. *Women Critics, 1660–1820: An Anthology.* Bloomington: Indiana University Press, 1995.

Fonte, Moderata (Modesta Pozzo). *Floridoro: A Chivalric Romance.* Ed. and intro. by Valeria Finucci. Trans. Julia Kisacky. The Other Voice in Early Modern Europe. Chicago: University of Chicago Press, 2006.

———. *The Worth of Women.* Ed. and trans. Virginia Cox. The Other Voice in Early Modern Europe. Chicago: University of Chicago Press, 1997.

Francisca de los Apóstoles. *The Inquisition of Francisca: A Sixteenth-Century Visionary on Trial.* Ed. and trans. Gillian T. W. Ahlgren. The Other Voice in Early Modern Europe. Chicago: University of Chicago Press, 2005.

Franco, Veronica. *Poems and Selected Letters.* Ed. and trans. Ann Rosalind Jones and Margaret F. Rosenthal. The Other Voice in Early Modern Europe. Chicago: University of Chicago Press, 1998.

Galilei, Maria Celeste. *Galileo's Daughter: A Historical Memoir of Science, Faith, and Love.* Trans. Dava Sobel. New York: Penguin Books, 1999.

———. *Sister Maria Celeste's Letters to Her Father, Galileo*. Ed. and trans. Rinaldina Russell. Lincoln, NE: Writers Club Press of Universe.com, 2000.

———. *To Father: The Letters of Sister Maria Celeste to Galileo, 1623–1633*. Trans. Dava Sobel. London: Fourth Estate, 2001.

Gethner, Perry, ed. *The Lunatic Lover and Other Plays by French Women of the Seventeenth and Eighteenth Centuries*. Portsmouth, NH: Heinemann, 1994.

Glückel of Hameln. *The Memoirs of Glückel of Hameln*. Trans. Marvin Lowenthal. New intro.by Robert Rosen. New York: Schocken Books, 1977.

Gournay, Marie le Jars de. *Apology for the Woman Writing and Other Works*. Ed. and trans. Richard Hillman and Colette Quesnel. The Other Voice in Early Modern Europe. Chicago: University of Chicago Press, 2002.

Grimmelshausen, Johann. *The Life of Courage: The Notorious Thief, Whore and Vagabond*. Trans. and intro. Mike Mitchell. Gardena, CA: SCB Distributors, 2001.

Grumbach, Argula von. *Argula von Grumbach: A Woman's Voice in the Reformation*. Ed. and trans. Peter Matheson. Edinburgh: T. & T. Clark, 1995.

Guasco, Annibal. *Discourse to Lady Lavinia His Daughter*. Ed. and trans. Peggy Osborn. The Other Voice in Early Modern Europe. Chicago: University of Chicago Press, 2003.

Guevara, María de. *Warnings to the Kings and Advice on Restoring Spain: A Bilingual Edition*. Ed. and trans. Nieves Romero-Díaz. The Other Voice in Early Modern Europe. Chicago: University of Chicago Press, 2007.

Harline, Craig, ed. *The Burdens of Sister Margaret: Inside a Seventeenth-Century Convent*. Abridged ed. New Haven: Yale University Press, 2000.

Haselkorn, Anne M., and Betty S. Travitsky, eds. *The Renaissance Englishwoman in Print: Counterbalancing the Canon*. Amherst: University of Massachusetts Press, 1990.

Henderson, Katherine Usher, and Barbara F. McManus, eds. *Half Humankind: Contexts and Texts of the Controversy about Women in England, 1540–1640*. Urbana: University of Illinois Press, 1985.

Hill, Bridget, ed. *Eighteenth-Century Women: An Anthology*. London: George Allen and Unwin, 1984.

Hobbins, Daniel, trans. *The Trial of Joan of Arc*. Cambridge: Harvard University Press, 2005.

Hoby, Margaret. *The Private Life of an Elizabethan Lady: The Diary of Lady Margaret Hoby, 1599–1605*. Thrupp, Stroud, Gloucestershire: Sutton, 1998.

Houlbrooke, Ralph, ed. *Family Life in Early Modern England: An Anthology of Contemporary Accounts, 1576–1716*. London: Blackwells, 1988.

Joscelin, Elizabeth. *The Mothers Legacy to Her Unborn Childe*. Ed. Jean leDrew Metcalfe. Toronto: University of Toronto Press, 2000.

Julian of Norwich. *Revelations of Divine Love*. Trans. Elizabeth Spearing. Introduction and notes by A. C. Spearing. New York: Penguin Books, 1998.

Jussie, Jeanne de. *The Short Chronicle*. Ed. and trans. Carrie F. Klaus. The Other Voice in Early Modern Europe. Chicago: University of Chicago Press, 2006.

Kallendorf, Craig W., ed. and trans. *Humanist Educational Treatises*. I Tatti Renaissance Library. Cambridge: Harvard University Press, 2002.

Kaminsky, Amy Katz, ed. *Water Lilies, Flores del agua: An Anthology of Spanish Women Writers from the Fifteenth through the Nineteenth Century*. Minneapolis: University of Minnesota Press, 1996.

Kempe, Margery. *The Book of Margery Kempe*. Trans. John Skinner. New York: Doubleday, 1998.

———. *The Book of Margery Kempe*. Ed. and trans. Lynn Staley. Norton Critical Edition. New York: W. W. Norton, 2001.

———. *The Book of Margery Kempe*. Trans. B. A. Windeatt. New York: Penguin Books, 1985.

King, Margaret L., and Albert Rabil Jr., eds. *Her Immaculate Hand: Selected Works by and about the Women Humanists of Quattrocento Italy*. Binghamton, NY: Medieval and Renaissance Texts and Studies, 1983; second revised paperback edition, 1991.

Klein, Joan Larsen, ed. *Daughters, Wives, and Widows: Writings by Men about Women and Marriage in England, 1500–1640*. Urbana: University of Illinois Press, 1992.

Knox, John. *The Political Writings of John Knox: The First Blast of the Trumpet against the Monstrous Regiment of Women and Other Selected Works*. Ed. Marvin A. Breslow. Washington, DC: Folger Shakespeare Library, 1985.

Kors, Alan C., and Edward Peters, eds. *Witchcraft in Europe, 400–1700: A Documentary History*. Philadelphia: University of Pennsylvania Press, 2000.

———. *Witchcraft in Europe, 1100–1700: A Documentary History*. Philadelphia: University of Pennsylvania Press, 1972.

Kottanner, Helene. *The Memoirs of Helene Kottanner, 1439–1440*. Trans. Maya B. Williamson. Library of Medieval Women. Rochester, NY: Boydell & Brewer, 1998.

Krämer, Heinrich, and Jacob Sprenger. *Malleus Maleficarum*. Trans. Montague Summers. London: Pushkin Press, 1928; reprint, New York: Dover, 1971.

Labé, Louise. *Complete Poetry and Prose: A Bilingual Edition*. Ed. and intro. by Deborah Lesko Baker. Trans. Annie Finch. The Other Voice in Early Modern Europe. Chicago: University of Chicago Press, 2006.

Lafayette, Marie-Madeleine Pioche de La Vergne, Comtesse de. *Zayde: A Spanish Romance*. Ed. and trans. Nicholas D. Paige. The Other Voice in Early Modern Europe. Chicago: University of Chicago Press, 2006.

Larsen, Anne R., and Colette H. Winn, eds. *Writings by Pre-Revolutionary French Women: From Marie de France to Elizabeth Vigée-Le Brun*. New York: Garland, 2000.

L'Aubespine, Madeleine de. *Selected Poems and Translations: A Bilingual Edition*. Ed. and trans. Anna Kłosowska. The Other Voice in Early Modern Europe. Chicago: University of Chicago Press, 2007.

Lock, Anne Vaughan. *The Collected Works of Anne Vaughan Lock*. Ed. Susan M. Felch. Medieval and Renaissance Texts and Studies, 185; English Text Society, 21. Tempe: Arizona Center for Medieval and Renaissance Studies, 1999.

Lorris, William de, and Jean de Meun. *The Romance of the Rose*. Trans. Charles Dahlbert. Princeton: Princeton University Press, 1971; reprint, University Press of New England, 1983.

Mahl, Mary R., and Helene Koon, eds. *The Female Spectator: English Women Writers before 1800*. Bloomington: Indiana University Press, 1977; Old Westbury, NY: Feminist Press, 1977.

Maintenon, Madame de. *Dialogues and Addresses*. Ed. and trans. John J. Conley, SJ. The Other Voice in Early Modern Europe. Chicago: University of Chicago Press, 2004.

Marguerite d'Angoulême, Queen of Navarre. *The Heptameron*. Trans. P. A. Chilton. New York: Viking Penguin, 1984.

Marinella, Lucrezia. *The Nobility and Excellence of Women and the Defects and Vices of Men*. Ed. and trans. Anne Dunhill. Introduction by Letizia Panizza. The Other Voice in Early Modern Europe. Chicago: University of Chicago Press, 1999.

Mary of Agreda. *The Divine Life of the Most Holy Virgin*. Abridgment of *The Mystical City of God*. Abridged by Fr. Bonaventure Amedeo de Caesarea, MC. Trans. from French by Abbé Joseph A. Boullan. Rockford, IL: Tan Books, 1997.

Matraini, Chiara. *Selected Poetry and Prose: A Bilingual Edition*. Ed. and trans. Elaine Maclachlan. Introduction by Giovanna Rabitti. The Other Voice in Early Modern Europe. Chicago: University of Chicago Press, 2007.

McWebb, Christine, ed. *Debating the "Roman de la rose": A Critical Anthology*. New York: Routledge, 2007.

Medici, Lucrezia Tornabuoni de'. *Sacred Narratives*. Ed. and trans. Jane Tylus. The Other Voice in Early Modern Europe. Chicago: University of Chicago Press, 2001.

Montpensier, Anne-Marie-Louise de, Duchesse d'Orléans. *Against Marriage: The Correspondence of La Grande Mademoiselle*. Ed. and trans. Joan DeJean. The Other Voice in Early Modern Europe. Chicago: University of Chicago Press, 2002.

Moore, Dorothy. *The Letters of Dorothy Moore, 1612–64: The Friendships, Marriage, and Intellectual Life of a Seventeenth-Century Woman*. Ed. Lynette Hunter. The Early Modern Englishwoman, 1500–1750: Contemporary Editions. Aldershot: Ashgate, 2004.

Morata, Olympia. *The Complete Writings of an Italian Heretic*. Ed. and trans. Holt N. Parker. The Other Voice in Early Modern Europe. Chicago: University of Chicago Press, 2003.

Mullan, David George. *Women's Life Writing in Early Modern Scotland: Writing the Evangelical Self, c. 1670–c. 1730*. Aldershot: Ashgate, 2003.

Myers, Kathleen A., and Amanda Powell, eds. *A Wild Country Out in the Garden: The Spiritual Journals of a Colonial Mexican Nun*. Bloomington: Indiana University Press, 1999.

Nogarola, Isotta. *Complete Writings: Letterbook, Dialogue on Adam and Eve, Orations*. Ed. and trans. Margaret L. King and Diana Robin. The Other Voice in Early Modern Europe. Chicago: University of Chicago Press, 2004.

O'Malley, Susan Gushee, ed. *"Custome Is an Idiot": Jacobean Pamphlet Literature on Women*. Afterword by Ann Rosalind Jones. Urbana: University of Illinois Press, 2004.

Ostovich, Helen, and Elizabeth Sauer, eds. *Reading Early Modern Women: An Anthology of Texts in Manuscript and Print, 1550–1700*. New York: Routledge, 2004.

Ozment, Steven. *Magdalena and Balthasar: An Intimate Portrait of Life in Sixteenth-Century Europe Revealed in the Letters of a Nuremberg Husband and Wife*. New York: Simon and Schuster, 1986; reprint, New Haven: Yale University Press, 1989.

Pascal, Jacqueline. *A Rule for Children and Other Writings*. Ed. and trans. John J. Conley, SJ. The Other Voice in Early Modern Europe. Chicago: University of Chicago Press, 2003.

Petersen, Johanna Eleonora. *The Life of Lady Johanna Eleonora Petersen, Written by Herself*. Ed. and trans. Barbara Becker-Cantarino. The Other Voice in Early Modern Europe. Chicago: University of Chicago Press, 2005.

Poullain de la Barre, François. *Three Cartesian Feminist Treatises*. Ed. Marcelle Maistre Welch. Trans. Vivien Bosley. The Other Voice in Early Modern Europe. Chicago: University of Chicago Press, 2002.

Pulci, Antonia. *Florentine Drama for Convent and Festival*. Ed. and trans. James Wyatt

Cook. The Other Voice in Early Modern Europe. Chicago: University of Chicago Press, 1996.

Riccoboni, Sister Bartolomea. *Life and Death in a Venetian Convent: The Chronicle and Necrology of Corpus Domini, 1395–1436*. Ed. and trans. Daniel Bornstein. The Other Voice in Early Modern Europe. Chicago: University of Chicago Press, 2000.

Roches, Madeleine and Catherine des. *From Mother and Daughter*. Ed. and trans. Anne R. Larsen. The Other Voice in Early Modern Europe. Chicago: University of Chicago Press, 2006.

Salazar, María de San José. *Book for the Hour of Recreation*. Ed. Alison Weber. Trans. Amanda Powell. The Other Voice in Early Modern Europe. Chicago: University of Chicago Press, 2002.

Sarrocchi, Margherita. *Scanderbeide: The Heroic Deeds of George Scanderbeg, King of Epirus*. Ed. and trans. Rinaldina Russell. The Other Voice in Early Modern Europe. Chicago: University of Chicago Press, 2006.

Schurman, Anna Maria van. *Whether a Christian Woman Should be Educated and Other Writings from Her Intellectual Circle*. Ed. and trans. Joyce L. Irwin. The Other Voice in Early Modern Europe. Chicago: University of Chicago Press, 1998.

Schütz Zell, Katharina. *Church Mother: The Writings of a Protestant Reformer in Sixteenth-Century Germany*. Ed. and trans. Elsie McKee. The Other Voice in Early Modern Europe. Chicago: University of Chicago Press, 2006.

Scudéry, Madeleine de. *Selected Letters, Orations, and Rhetorical Dialogues*. Ed. and trans. Jane Donawerth and Julie Strongson. The Other Voice in Early Modern Europe. Chicago: University of Chicago Press, 2004.

———. *The Story of Sappho*. Ed. and trans. Karen Newman. The Other Voice in Early Modern Europe. Chicago: University of Chicago Press, 2003.

Shepherd, Simon, ed. *The Woman's Sharp Revenge: Five Women's Pamphlets from the Renaissance*. New York: St. Martin's Press, 1985.

Sidney, Robert, and Barbara Gamage Sidney. *Domestic Politics and Family Absence: The Correspondence (1588–1621) of Robert Sidney, First Early of Leicester, and Barbara Gamage Sidney, Countess of Leicester*. Ed. Margaret P. Hannay, Nowl J. Kinnamon, and Michael G. Brennan. The Early Modern Englishwoman, 1500–1750: Contemporary Editions. Aldershot: Ashgate, 2005.

Siegemund, Justine. *The Court Midwife*. Ed. and trans. Lynne Tatlock. The Other Voice in Early Modern Europe. Chicago: University of Chicago Press, 2005.

Tarabotti, Arcangela. *Paternal Tyranny*. Ed. and trans. Letizia Panizza. The Other Voice in Early Modern Europe. Chicago: University of Chicago Press, 2004.

Teresa of Avila, Saint. *The Collected Letters of St. Teresa of Avila*, vol. 1: *1546–1577*. Trans. Kieran Kavanaugh. Washington, DC: Institute of Carmelite Studies, 2001. Volume 2 is forthcoming.

———. *The Life of Saint Teresa of Avila by Herself*. Trans. J. M. Cohen. New York: Viking Penguin, 1957.

Tilney, Edmund. *The Flower of Friendship: A Renaissance Dialogue Contesting Marriage*. Ed. Valerie Wayne. Ithaca: Cornell University Press, 1993.

Travitsky, Betty, ed. *The Paradise of Women: Writings by Englishwomen of the Renaissance*. Westport, CT: Greenwood Press, 1981.

Travitsky, Betty, and Anne Lake Prescott, eds. *Female and Male Voices in Early Modern England: An Anthology of Renaissance Writing*. New York: Columbia University Press, 2000.

Villedieu, Madame de. *Memoirs of the Life of Henriette-Sylvie de Molière: A Novel*. Ed. and trans. Donna Kuizenga. The Other Voice in Early Modern Europe. Chicago: University of Chicago Press, 2004.

Vives, Juan Luis. *The Education of a Christian Woman: A Sixteenth-Century Manual*. Ed. and trans. Charles Fantazzi. The Other Voice in Early Modern Europe. Chicago: University of Chicago Press, 2000.

Weyer, Johann. *Witches, Devils, and Doctors in the Renaissance: Johann Weyer, De praestigiis daemonum*. Ed. George Mora with Benjamin G. Kohl, Erik Midelfort, and Helen Bacon. Trans. John Shea. Binghamton, NY: Medieval and Renaissance Texts and Studies, 1991.

Wiesner-Hanks, Merry, ed. *Convents Confront the Reformation: Catholic and Protestant Nuns in Germany*. Trans. Joan Skocir and Merry Wiesner-Hanks. Women of the Reformation. Milwaukee: Marquette University Press, 1996.

Wilson, Katharina M., ed. *Medieval Women Writers*. Athens: University of Georgia Press, 1984.

———, ed. *Women Writers of the Renaissance and Reformation*. Athens: University of Georgia Press, 1987.

Wilson, Katharina M., and Frank J. Warnke, eds. *Women Writers of the Seventeenth Century*. Athens: University of Georgia Press, 1989.

Wollstonecraft, Mary. *A Vindication of the Rights of Men and a Vindication of the Rights of Women*. Ed. Sylvana Tomaselli. Cambridge: Cambridge University Press, 1995.

———. *The Vindications of the Rights of Men, The Rights of Women*. Ed. D. L. Macdonald and Kathleen Scherf. Peterborough, Ontario, Canada: Broadview Press, 1997.

Women Writers in English, 1350–1850. Projected 30-volume series suspended. 15 volumes published. Oxford: Oxford University Press.

Wroth, Lady Mary. *The Countess of Montgomery's Urania*. Ed. Josephine A. Roberts. 2 parts. Tempe, AZ: Medieval and Renaissance Texts and Studies, 1995, 1999.

———. *Lady Mary Wroth's "Love's Victory": The Penshurst Manuscript*. Ed. Michael G. Brennan. London: Roxburghe Club, 1988.

———. *The Poems of Lady Mary Wroth*. Ed. Josephine A. Roberts. Baton Rouge: Louisiana State University Press, 1983.

Zayas, Maria de. *The Disenchantments of Love*. Trans. H. Patsy Boyer. Albany: State University of New York Press, 1997.

———. *The Enchantments of Love: Amorous and Exemplary Novels*. Trans. by H. Patsy Boyer. Berkeley: University of California Press, 1990.

SECONDARY SOURCES

Abate, Corinne S., ed. *Privacy, Domesticity, and Women in Early Modern England*. Burlington, VT: Ashgate, 2003.

Ahlgren, Gillian. *Teresa of Avila and the Politics of Sanctity*. Ithaca: Cornell University Press, 1996.

Åkerman, Susanna. *Queen Christina of Sweden: The Transformation of a Seventeenth-Century Philosophical Libertine*. Leiden: E. J. Brill, 1991.

Akkerman, Tjitske, and Siep Sturman, eds. *Feminist Thought in European History, 1400–2000*. London: Routledge, 1997.

Allen, Sister Prudence, RSM. *The Concept of Woman: The Aristotelian Revolution, 750 B.C.–A.D. 1250*. Grand Rapids, MI: William B. Eerdmans, 1997.

———. *The Concept of Woman*, vol. 2: *The Early Humanist Reformation, 1250–1500*. Grand Rapids, MI: William B. Eerdmans, 2002.

Altmann, Barbara K., and Deborah L. McGrady, eds. *Christine de Pizan: A Casebook*. New York: Routledge, 2003.

Amussen, Susan D. *An Ordered Society: Gender and Class in Early Modern England*. Oxford: Basil Blackwell, 1988.

Amussen, Susan D., and Adele Seeff, eds. *Attending to Early Modern Women*. Newark: University of Delaware Press, 1998.

Anderson, Karen. *Chain Her by One Foot: The Subjugation of Women in Seventeenth-Century New France*. New York: Routledge, 1991.

Andreadis, Harriette. *Sappho in Early Modern England: Female Same-Sex Literary Erotics, 1550–1714*. Chicago: University of Chicago Press, 2001.

Arcangela Tarabotti: A Literary Nun in Baroque Venice. Ed. Elissa B. Weaver. Ravenna: Longo Editore, 2006.

Armon, Shifra. *Picking Wedlock: Women and the Courtship Novel in Spain*. New York: Rowman & Littlefield, 2002.

Atkinson, Clarissa W. *Mystic and Pilgrim: The Book and the World of Margery Kempe*. Ithaca: Cornell University Press, 1983.

Backer, Anne Liot. *Precious Women*. New York: Basic Books, 1974.

Bainton, Roland H. *Women of the Reformation in France and England*. Minneapolis: Augsburg, 1973.

———. *Women of the Reformation in Germany and Italy*. Minneapolis: Augsburg, 1971.

Ballaster, Ros. *Seductive Forms*. New York: Oxford University Press, 1992.

Barash, Carol. *English Women's Poetry, 1649–1714: Politics, Community, and Linguistic Authority*. New York: Oxford University Press, 1996.

Bardsley, Sandy. *Venomous Tongues: Speech and Gender in Late Medieval England*. Middle Ages Series. Philadelphia: University of Pennsylvania Press, 2006.

Barker, Alele Marie, and Jehanne M. Gheith, eds. *A History of Women's Writing in Russia*. Cambridge: Cambridge University Press, 2002.

Barstow, Anne L. *Joan of Arc: Heretic, Mystic, Shaman*. Lewiston, NY: Edwin Mellen Press, 1986.

Battigelli, Anna. *Margaret Cavendish and the Exiles of the Mind*. Lexington: University of Kentucky Press, 1998.

Beasley, Faith. *Revising Memory: Women's Fiction and Memoirs in Seventeenth-Century France*. New Brunswick: Rutgers University Press, 1990.

———. *Salons, History, and the Creation of Seventeenth-Century France*. Aldershot: Ashgate, 2006.

Becker, Lucinda M. *Death and the Early Modern Englishwoman*. Burlington, VT: Ashgate, 2003.

Beilin, Elaine V. *Redeeming Eve: Women Writers of the English Renaissance*. Princeton: Princeton University Press, 1987.

Bell, Rudolph M. *Holy Anorexia*. Chicago: University of Chicago Press, 1985.

Bennett, Lyn. *Women Writing of Divinest Things: Rhetoric and the Poetry of Pembroke, Wroth, and Lanyer*. Pittsburgh: Duquesne University Press, 2004.

Benson, Pamela Joseph. *The Invention of Renaissance Woman: The Challenge of Female Inde-*

pendence in the Literature and Thought of Italy and England. University Park: Pennsylvania State University Press, 1992.

Benson, Pamela Joseph, and Victoria Kirkham, eds. *Strong Voices, Weak History? Medieval and Renaissance Women in Their Literary Canons: England, France, Italy*. Ann Arbor: University of Michigan Press, 2003.

Berman, Constance H., ed. *Women and Monasticism in Medieval Europe: Sisters and Patrons of the Cistercian Reform*. Kalamazoo: Western Michigan University Press, 2002.

Berry, Helen. *Gender, Society and Print Culture in Late Stuart England*. Burlington, VT: Ashgate, 2003.

Berry, Philippa. *Of Chastity and Power: Elizabethan Literature and the Unmarried Queen*. New York: Routledge, 1989.

Bicks, Caroline. *Midwiving Subjects in Shakespeare's England*. Burlington, VT: Ashgate, 2003.

Bilinkoff, Jodi. *The Avila of Saint Teresa: Religious Reform in a Sixteenth-Century City*. Ithaca: Cornell University Press, 1989.

———. *Related Lives: Confessors and Their Female Penitents, 1450–1750*. Ithaca: Cornell University Press, 2005.

Bissell, R. Ward. *Artemisia Gentileschi and the Authority of Art*. University Park: Pennsylvania State University Press, 2000.

Blain, Virginia, Isobel Grundy, and Patricia Clements, eds. *The Feminist Companion to Literature in English: Women Writers from the Middle Ages to the Present*. New Haven: Yale University Press, 1990.

Blamires, Alcuin. *The Case for Women in Medieval Culture*. Oxford: Clarendon Press, 1997.

Bloch, R. Howard. *Medieval Misogyny and the Invention of Western Romantic Love*. Chicago: University of Chicago Press, 1991.

Blumenfeld-Kosinski, Renate. *Not of Woman Born: Representations of Caesarean Birth in Medieval and Renaissance Culture*. Ithaca: Cornell University Press, 1990.

Bogucka, Maria. *Women in Early Modern Polish Society, Against the European Background*. Burlington, VT: Ashgate, 2004.

Bornstein, Daniel, and Roberto Rusconi, eds. *Women and Religion in Medieval and Renaissance Italy*. Trans. Margery J. Schneider. Chicago: University of Chicago Press, 1996.

Brant, Clare, and Diane Purkiss, eds. *Women, Texts, and Histories, 1575–1760*. London: Routledge, 1992.

Breisach, Ernst. *Caterina Sforza: A Renaissance Virago*. Chicago: University of Chicago Press, 1967.

Bridenthal, Renate, Claudia Koonz, and Susan M. Stuard. *Becoming Visible: Women in European History*. 3d ed. Boston: Houghton Mifflin, 1998.

Briggs, Robin. *Witches and Neighbours: The Social and Cultural Context of European Witchcraft*. New York: HarperCollins, 1995; Viking Penguin, 1996.

Brink, Jean R., ed. *Female Scholars: A Tradition of Learned Women before 1800*. Montréal: Eden Press Women's Publications, 1980.

Brink, Jean R., Allison Coudert, and Maryanne Cline Horowitz. *The Politics of Gender in Early Modern Europe*. Sixteenth Century Essays and Studies, 12. Kirksville, MO: Sixteenth Century Journal Publishers, 1989.

Broad, Jacqueline S. *Women Philosophers of the Seventeenth Century*. Cambridge: Cambridge University Press, 2002; reprint, 2007.

Broad, Jacqueline S., and Karen Green. *A History of Women's Political Thought in Europe, 1400–1700*. Cambridge: Cambridge University Press, 2008.

———, eds. *Virtue, Liberty, and Toleration: Political Ideas of European Women, 1400–1700*. Dordrecht: Springer, 2007.

Brodsky, Vivien. *Mobility and Marriage: The Family and Kinship in Early Modern London*. London: Blackwells, 1988.

Broude, Norma, and Mary D. Garrard, eds. *The Expanding Discourse: Feminism and Art History*. New York: HarperCollins, 1992.

Brown, Judith C. *Immodest Acts: The Life of a Lesbian Nun in Renaissance Italy*. New York: Oxford University Press, 1986.

Brown, Judith C., and Robert C. Davis, eds. *Gender and Society in Renaissance Italy*. London: Addison Wesley Longman, 1998.

Brown, Pamela Allen, and Peter Parolin, eds. *Women Players in England, 1500–1660: Beyond the All-Male Stage*. Brookfield: Ashgate, 2005.

Brown-Grant, Rosalind. *Christine de Pizan and the Moral Defence of Women: Reading Beyond Gender*. Cambridge: Cambridge University Press, 1999.

Brucker, Gene. *Giovanni and Lusanna: Love and Marriage in Renaissance Florence*. Berkeley: University of California Press, 1986.

Burke, Victoria E., ed. *Early Modern Women's Manuscript Writing*. Burlington, VT: Ashgate, 2004.

Burns, Jane E., ed. *Medieval Fabrications: Dress, Textiles, Cloth Work, and Other Cultural Imaginings*. New York: Palgrave Macmillan, 2004.

Bynum, Carolyn Walker. *Fragmentation and Redemption: Essays on Gender and the Human Body in Medieval Religion*. New York: Zone Books, 1992.

———. *Holy Feast and Holy Fast: The Religious Significance of Food to Medieval Women*. Berkeley: University of California Press, 1987.

———. *Jesus as Mother: Studies in the Spirituality of the High Middle Ages*. Berkeley: University of California Press, 1982.

Cahn, Susan. *Industry of Devotion: The Transformation of Women's Work in England, 1500–1660*. New York: Columbia University Press, 1987.

Callaghan, Dympna, ed. *The Impact of Feminism in English Renaissance Studies*. New York: Palgrave Macmillan, 2007.

Campbell, Julie DeLynn. "Renaissance Women Writers: The Beloved Speaks Her Part." Ph.D diss., Texas A & M University, 1997.

Catling, Jo, ed. *A History of Women's Writing in Germany, Austria, and Switzerland*. Cambridge: Cambridge University Press, 2000.

Cavallo, Sandra, and Lyndan Warner, eds. *Widowhood in Medieval and Early Modern Europe*. New York: Longman, 1999.

Cavanagh, Sheila T. *Cherished Torment: The Emotional Geography of Lady Mary Wroth's Urania*. Pittsburgh: Duquesne University Press, 2001.

Cerasano, S. P., and Marion Wynne-Davies, eds. *Readings in Renaissance Women's Drama: Criticism, History, and Performance, 1594–1998*. London: Routledge, 1998.

Cervigni, Dino S., ed. *Women Mystic Writers*. *Annali d'Italianistica* 13 (1995).

Cervigni, Dino S., and Rebecca West, eds. *Women's Voices in Italian Literature*. *Annali d'Italianistica* 7 (1989).

Charlton, Kenneth. *Women, Religion, and Education in Early Modern England*. London: Routledge, 1999.

Chojnacka, Monica. *Working Women of Early Modern Venice.* Baltimore: Johns Hopkins University Press, 2001.

Chojnacki, Stanley. *Women and Men in Renaissance Venice: Twelve Essays on Patrician Society*. Baltimore: Johns Hopkins University Press, 2000.

Cholakian, Patricia Francis, and Rouben Charles Cholakian. *Marguerite de Navarre: Mother of the Renaissance*. New York: Columbia University Press, 2006.

Cholakian, Patricia Francis. *Rape and Writing in the Heptameron of Marguerite de Navarre*. Carbondale: Southern Illinois University Press, 1991.

———. *Women and the Politics of Self-Representation in Seventeenth-Century France*. Newark: University of Delaware Press, 2000.

Clogan, Paul Maruice, ed. *Medievali et Humanistica: Literacy and the Lay Reader*. Lanham, MD: Rowman & Littlefield, 2000.

Clubb, Louise George. *Italian Drama in Shakespeare's Time*. New Haven: Yale University Press, 1989.

Clucas, Stephen, ed. *A Princely Brave Woman: Essays on Margaret Cavendish, Duchess of Newcastle*. Burlington, VT: Ashgate, 2003.

Coakley, John W. *Women, Men, and Spiritual Power: Female Saints and Their Male Collaborators*. New York: Columbia University Press, 2006.

Conley, John J., SJ. *The Suspicion of Virtue: Women Philosophers in Neoclassical France*. Ithaca: Cornell University Press, 2002.

Cook, Ann Jennalie. *Making a Match: Courtship in Shakespeare and His Society*. Princeton: Princeton University Press, 1991.

Cox, Virginia. *Women's Writing in Italy, 1400–1650*. Baltimore: Johns Hopkins University Press, 2008.

Crabb, Ann. *The Strozzi of Florence: Widowhood and Family Solidarity in the Renaissance*. Ann Arbor: University of Michigan Press, 2000.

Crawford, Patricia. *Women and Religion in England, 1500–1750*. London: Routledge, 1993.

Crowston, Clare Haru. *Fabricating Women: The Seamstresses of Old Regime France, 1675–1791*. Durham: Duke University Press, 2001.

Cruz, Anne J., and Mary Elizabeth Perry, eds. *Culture and Control in Counter-Reformation Spain*. Minneapolis: University of Minnesota Press, 1992.

Datta, Satya. *Women and Men in Early Modern Venice*. Burlington, VT: Ashgate, 2003.

Davis, Natalie Zemon. *Society and Culture in Early Modern France*. Stanford: Stanford University Press, 1975.

———. *Women on the Margins: Three Seventeenth-Century Lives*. Cambridge: Harvard University Press, 1995.

Davis, Natalie Zemon, and Arlette Farge, eds. *Renaissance and Enlightenment Paradoxes*. Vol. 3 of *A History of Women in the West*. Cambridge: Harvard University Press, 1993.

Dean, Trevor, and K. J. P. Lowe, eds. *Marriage in Italy, 1300–1650*. Cambridge: Cambridge University Press, 1998.

DeJean, Joan. *Ancients against Moderns: Culture Wars and the Making of a Fin de Siècle*. Chicago: University of Chicago Press, 1997.

———. *Fictions of Sappho, 1546–1937*. Chicago: University of Chicago Press, 1989.

———. *The Reinvention of Obscenity: Sex, Lies, and Tabloids in Early Modern France*. Chicago: University of Chicago Press, 2002.

———. *Tender Geographies: Women and the Origins of the Novel in France*. New York: Columbia University Press, 1991.

D'Elia, Anthony F. *The Renaissance of Marriage in Fifteenth-Century Italy*. Cambridge: Harvard University Press, 2004.

Demers, Patricia. *Women's Writing in English: Early Modern England*. Toronto: University of Toronto Press, 2005.

Diefendorf, Barbara. *From Penitence to Charity: Pious Women and the Catholic Reformation in Paris*. New York: Oxford University Press, 2004.

Dinan, Susan E. *Women and Poor Relief in Seventeenth-Century France: The Early History of the Daughters of Charity*. Women and Gender in the Early Modern World. Burlington, VT: Ashgate, 2006.

Dixon, Laurinda S. *Perilous Chastity: Women and Illness in Pre-Enlightenment Art and Medicine*. Ithaca: Cornell University Press, 1995.

Dolan, Frances, E. *Whores of Babylon: Catholicism, Gender, and Seventeenth-Century Print Culture*. Ithaca: Cornell University Press, 1999.

Donovan, Josephine. *Women and the Rise of the Novel, 1405–1726*. New York: St. Martin's Press, 1999.

Dreher, Diane Elizabeth. *Domination and Defiance: Fathers and Daughters in Shakespeare*. Lexington: University Press of Kentucky, 1986.

Dyan, Elliott. *Proving Woman: Female Spirituality and Inquisitional Culture in the Later Middle Ages*. Princeton: Princeton University Press, 2004.

Eccles, Audrey. *Obstetrics and Gynaecology in Tudor and Stuart England*. Kent, OH: Kent State University Press, 1982.

Eigler, Friederike, and Susanne Kord, eds. *The Feminist Encyclopedia of German Literature*. Westport, CT: Greenwood Press, 1997.

Emerson, Kathy Lynn. *Wives and Daughters: The Women of Sixteenth-Century England*. Troy, NY: Whitson, 1984.

Erdmann, Axel. *My Gracious Silence: Women in the Mirror of Sixteenth-Century Printing in Western Europe*. Lucerne: Gilhofer and Rauschberg, 1999.

Erickson, Amy Louise. *Women and Property in Early Modern England*. London: Routledge, 1993.

Evangelisti, Silvia. *Nuns: A History of Convent Life, 1450–1700*. New York: Oxford University Press, 2007.

Ezell, Margaret J. M. *The Patriarch's Wife: Literary Evidence and the History of the Family*. Chapel Hill: University of North Carolina Press, 1987.

———. *Social Authorship and the Advent of Print*. Baltimore: Johns Hopkins University Press, 1999.

———. *Writing Women's Literary History*. Baltimore: Johns Hopkins University Press, 1993.

Farrell, Michèle Longino. *Performing Motherhood: The Sévigné Correspondence*. Hanover, NH: University Press of New England, 1991.

Ferguson, Margaret W. *Dido's Daughters: Literacy, Gender, and Empire in Early Modern England and France*. Chicago: University of Chicago Press, 2003.

Ferguson, Margaret W., Maureen Quilligan, and Nancy J. Vickers, eds. *Rewriting the Renaissance: The Discourses of Sexual Difference in Early Modern Europe*. Chicago: University of Chicago Press, 1987.

Feroli, Teresa. *Political Speaking Justified: Women Prophets and the English Revolution*. Newark: University of Delaware Press, 2006.

Ferraro, Joanne M. *Marriage Wars in Late Renaissance Venice*. Oxford: Oxford University Press, 2001.

Fisher, Will. *Materializing Gender in Early Modern English Literature and Culture*. Cambridge: Cambridge University Press, 2006.

Flandrin, Jean-Louis. *Families in Former Times: Kinship, Household, and Sexuality in Early Modern France*. Trans. Richard Southern. Cambridge: Cambridge University Press, 1979.

Fletcher, Anthony. *Gender, Sex, and Subordination in England, 1500–1800*. New Haven: Yale University Press, 1995.

———. *Growing Up in England: The Experience of Childhood, 1600–1914*. New Haven: Yale University Press, 2008.

Franklin, Margaret. *Boccaccio's Heroines: Power and Virtue in Renaissance Society*. Women and Gender in the Early Modern World. Burlington, VT: Ashgate, 2006.

Froide, Amy M. *Never Married: Singlewomen < in Early Modern England*. Oxford: Oxford University Press, 2005.

Frye, Susan, and Karen Robertson, eds. *Maids and Mistresses, Cousins and Queens: Women's Alliances in Early Modern England*. Oxford: Oxford University Press, 1999.

Gallagher, Catherine. *Nobody's Story: The Vanishing Acts of Women Writers in the Marketplace, 1670–1820*. Berkeley: University of California Press, 1994.

Garrard, Mary D. *Artemisia Gentileschi: The Image of the Female Hero in Italian Baroque Art*. Princeton: Princeton University Press, 1989.

Gelbart, Nina Rattner. *The King's Midwife: A History and Mystery of Madame du Coudray*. Berkeley: University of California Press, 1998.

George, Margaret. *Women in the First Capitalist Society: Experiences in Seventeenth-Century England*. Urbana: University of Illinois Press, 1988.

Gibson, Wendy. *Women in Seventeenth-Century France*. New York: St. Martin's Press, 1989.

Gies, Frances. *Joan of Arc: The Legend and the Reality*. New York: Harper & Row, 1981.

Giles, Mary E., ed. *Women in the Inquisition: Spain and the New World*. Baltimore: Johns Hopkins University Press, 1999.

Gill, Catie. *Women in the Seventeenth-Century Quaker Community*. Burlington, VT: Ashgate, 2005.

Glenn, Cheryl. *Rhetoric Retold: Regendering the Tradition from Antiquity through the Renaissance*. Carbondale: Southern Illinois University Press, 1997.

Goffen, Rona. *Titian's Women*. New Haven: Yale University Press, 1997.

Goldberg, Jonathan. *Desiring Women Writing: English Renaissance Examples*. Stanford: Stanford University Press, 1997.

Goldsmith, Elizabeth C. *Exclusive Conversations: The Art of Interaction in Seventeenth-Century France*. Philadelphia: University of Pennsylvania Press, 1988.

———, ed. *Writing the Female Voice*. Boston: Northeastern University Press, 1989.

Goldsmith, Elizabeth C., and Dena Goodman, eds. *Going Public: Women and Publishing in Early Modern France*. Ithaca: Cornell University Press, 1995.

Grafton, Anthony, and Lisa Jardine. *From Humanism to the Humanities: Education and the Liberal Arts in Fifteenth- and Sixteenth-Century Europe*. London: Duckworth, 1986.

Grassby, Richard. *Kinship and Capitalism: Marriage, Family, and Business in the English-Speaking World, 1580–1740*. Cambridge: Cambridge University Press, 2001.

Greer, Margaret Rich. *Maria de Zayas Tells Baroque Tales of Love and the Cruelty of Men*. University Park: Pennsylvania State University Press, 2000.

Grossman, Avraham. *Pious and Rebellious: Jewish Women in Medieval Europe*. Trans. Jonathan Chipman. Waltham: Brandeis/University Press of New England, 2004.

Gutierrez, Nancy A. *"Shall She Famish Then?" Female Food Refusal in Early Modern England*. Burlington, VT: Ashgate, 2003.

Habermann, Ina. *Staging Slander and Gender in Early Modern England*. Burlington, VT: Ashgate, 2003.

Hacke, Daniela. *Women, Sex, and Marriage in Early Modern Venice*. Burlington, VT: Ashgate, 2004.

Hackel, Heidi Brayman. *Reading Material in Early Modern England: Print, Gender, Literacy*. Cambridge: Cambridge University Press, 2005.

Hackett, Helen. *Women and Romance Fiction in the English Renaissance*. Cambridge: Cambridge University Press, 2000.

Haigh, Christopher. *Elizabeth I*. London: Longman, 1988.

Hall, Kim F. *Things of Darkness: Economies of Race and Gender in Early Modern England*. Ithaca: Cornell University Press, 1995.

Hamburger, Jeffrey. *The Visual and the Visionary: Art and Female Spirituality in Late Medieval Germany*. New York: Zone Books, 1998.

Hampton, Timothy. *Literature and the Nation in the Sixteenth Century: Inventing Renaissance France*. Ithaca: Cornell University Press, 2001.

Hanawalt, Barbara A. *Women and Work in Pre-Industrial Europe*. Bloomington: Indiana University Press, 1986.

Hannay, Margaret, ed. *Silent but for the Word*. Kent, OH: Kent State University Press, 1985.

Hardwick, Julie. *The Practice of Patriarchy: Gender and the Politics of Household Authority in Early Modern France*. University Park: Pennsylvania State University Press, 1998.

Harness, Kelley Ann. *Echoes of Women's Voices: Music, Art, and Female Patronage in Early Modern Florence*. Chicago: University of Chicago Press, 2006.

Harris, Barbara J. *English Aristocratic Women, 1450–1550: Marriage and Family, Property and Careers*. New York: Oxford University Press, 2002.

Harth, Erica. *Cartesian Women. Versions and Subversions of Rational Discourse in the Old Regime*. Ithaca: Cornell University Press, 1992.

———. *Ideology and Culture in Seventeenth-Century France*. Ithaca: Cornell University Press, 1983.

Harvey, Elizabeth D. *Ventriloquized Voices: Feminist Theory and English Renaissance Texts*. London: Routledge, 1992.

Hawkesworth, Celia, ed. *A History of Central European Women's Writing*. New York: Palgrave Press, 2001.

Hegstrom, Valerie, and Amy R. Williamsen, eds. *Engendering the Early Modern Stage: Women Playwrights in the Spanish Empire*. New Orleans: University Press of the South, 1999.

Heller, Wendy. *Emblems of Eloquence: Opera and Women's Voices in Seventeenth-Century Venice*. Berkeley: University of California Press, 2004.

Hendricks, Margo, and Patricia Parker, eds. *Women, "Race," and Writing in the Early Modern Period*. London: Routledge, 1994.

Herlihy, David. "Did Women Have a Renaissance? A Reconsideration." *Medievalia et Humanistica*, n.s., 13 (1985): 1–22.

Hibbert, Christopher. *The Virgin Queen: Elizabeth I, Genius of the Golden Age*. Reading, MA: Addison-Wesley, 1991.

Hill, Bridget. *The Republican Virago: The Life and Times of Catharine Macaulay, Historian.* New York: Oxford University Press, 1992.

Hills, Helen, ed. *Architecture and the Politics of Gender in Early Modern Europe.* Burlington, VT: Ashgate, 2003.

Hirst, Jilie. *Jane Leade: Biography of a Seventeenth-Century Mystic.* Burlington, VT: Ashgate, 2006.

Hobby, Elaine. *Virtue of Necessity: English Women's Writing, 1646–1688.* London: Virago Press, 1988.

Hogrefe, Pearl. *Women of Action in Tudor England: Nine Biographical Sketches.* Ames: Iowa State University Press, 1977.

Hopkins, Lisa. *Women Who Would Be Kings: Female Rulers of the Sixteenth Century.* New York: St. Martin's Press, 1991.

Horowitz, Maryanne Cline. "Aristotle and Women." *Journal of the History of Biology* 9 (1976): 183–213.

Houlbrooke, Ralph A. *Death, Religion, and the Family in England, 1480–1760.* Oxford Studies in Social History. New York: Oxford University Press, 1998.

Howe, Elizabeth. *The First English Actresses: Women and Drama, 1660–1700.* Cambridge: Cambridge University Press, 1992.

Howell, Martha C. *The Marriage Exchange: Property, Social Place, and Gender in Cities of the Low Countries, 1300–1550.* Chicago: University of Chicago Press, 1998.

———. *Women, Production, and Patriarchy in Late Medieval Cities.* Chicago: University of Chicago Press, 1986.

Hufton, Olwen H. *The Prospect before Her: A History of Women in Western Europe,* vol. 1: *1500–1800.* New York: HarperCollins, 1996.

Hull, Suzanne W. *Chaste, Silent, and Obedient: English Books for Women, 1475–1640.* San Marino, CA: Huntington Library, 1982.

Hunt, Lynn, ed. *The Invention of Pornography: Obscenity and the Origins of Modernity, 1500–1800.* New York: Zone Books, 1996.

Hurlburt, Holly S. *The Dogaressa of Venice, 1200–1500: Wife and Icon.* New Middle Ages. New York: Palgrave Macmillan, 2006.

Hutner, Heidi, ed. *Rereading Aphra Behn: History, Theory, and Criticism.* Charlottesville: University Press of Virginia, 1993.

Hutson, Lorna, ed. *Feminism and Renaissance Studies.* New York: Oxford University Press, 1999.

Ingram, Martin. *Church Courts, Sex and Marriage in England, 1570–1640.* Cambridge: Cambridge University Press, 1987.

Ives, E. W. *Anne Boleyn.* London: Blackwells, 1988.

Jaffe, Irma B., with Gernando Colombardo. *Shining Eyes, Cruel Fortune: The Lives and Loves of Italian Renaissance Women Poets.* New York: Fordham University Press, 2002.

James, Susan E. *Kateryn Parr: The Making of a Queen.* Burlington, VT: Ashgate, 1999.

Jankowski, Theodora A. *Women in Power in the Early Modern Drama.* Urbana: University of Illinois Press, 1992.

Jansen, Katherine Ludwig. *The Making of the Magdalen: Preaching and Popular Devotion in the Later Middle Ages.* Princeton: Princeton University Press, 2000.

Jardine, Lisa. *Still Harping on Daughters: Women and Drama in the Age of Shakespeare.* Totowa, NJ: Barnes and Noble, 1983.

Jed, Stephanie H. *Chaste Thinking: The Rape of Lucretia and the Birth of Humanism.* Bloomington: Indiana University Press, 1989.

Jones, Ann Rosalind. *The Currency of Eros: Women's Love Lyric in Europe, 1540–1620*. Bloomington: Indiana University Press, 1990.

Jones, Ann Rosalind, and Peter Stallybrass. *Renaissance Clothing and the Materials of Memory*. Cambridge: Cambridge University Press, 2000.

Jones, Michael K., and Malcolm G. Underwood. *The King's Mother: Lady Margaret Beaufort, Countess of Richymond and Derby*. Cambridge: Cambridge University Press, 1992.

Jordan, Constance. *Renaissance Feminism: Literary Texts and Political Models*. Ithaca: Cornell University Press, 1990.

Kagan, Richard L. *Lucrecia's Dreams: Politics and Prophecy in Sixteenth-Century Spain*. Berkeley: University of California Press, 1990.

Karant-Nunn, Susan C., and Merry E. Wiesner-Hanks, eds. *Luther on Women: A Sourcebook*. Cambridge: Cambridge University Press, 2003.

Kehler, Dorothea, and Laurel Amtower, eds. *The Single Woman in Medieval and Early Modern England: Her Life and Representation*. Tempe, AZ: Medieval and Renaissance Texts and Studies, 2002.

Kelly, Joan. "Did Women Have a Renaissance?" In *Women, History, and Theory: The Essays of Joan Kelly*. Chicago: University of Chicago Press, 1984. Also in *Becoming Visible: Women in European History*, ed. Renate Bridenthal, Claudia Koonz, and Susan M. Stuard. 3rd ed. Boston: Houghton Mifflin, 1998.

———. "Early Feminist Theory and the *Querelle des Femmes*." In *Women, History, and Theory: The Essays of Joan Kelly*. Chicago: University of Chicago Press, 1984.

———. *Women, History, and Theory: The Essays of Joan Kelly*. Women in Culture and Society. Chicago: University of Chicago Press, 1984.

Kelso, Ruth. *Doctrine for the Lady of the Renaissance*. Foreword by Katharine M. Rogers. Urbana: University of Illinois Press, 1956, 1978.

Kendrick, Robert L. *Celestical Sirens: Nuns and Their Music in Early Modern Milan*. New York: Oxford University Press, 1996.

Kermode, Jenny, and Garthine Walker, eds. *Women, Crime, and the Courts in Early Modern England*. Chapel Hill: University of North Carolina Press, 1994.

King, Catherine E. *Renaissance Women Patrons: Wives and Widows in Italy, c. 1300–1550*. Manchester: Manchester University Press, 1998.

King, Margaret L. *Women of the Renaissance*. Foreword by Catharine R. Stimpson. Chicago: University of Chicago Press, 1991.

King, Thomas A. *The Gendering of Men, 1600–1700: The English Phallus*. Vol. 1. Madison: University of Wisconsin Press, 2004.

Klapisch-Zuber, Christiane. *Women, Family, and Ritual in Renaissance Italy*. Trans. Lydia G. Cochrane. Chicago: University of Chicago Press, 1985.

———, ed. *Silences of the Middle Ages*. Vol. 2 of *A History of Women in the West*. Cambridge: Harvard University Press, 1992.

Kleiman, Ruth. *Anne of Austria, Queen of France*. Columbus: Ohio State University Press, 1985.

Knott, Sarah, and Barbara Taylor. *Women, Gender, and Enlightenment*. New York: Palgrave Macmillan, 2005.

Kolsky, Stephen. *The Ghost of Boccaccio: Writings on Famous Women in Renaissance Italy*. Late Medieval and Early Modern Studies 7. Turnhout: Brepols, 2005.

Krontiris, Tina. *Oppositional Voices: Women as Writers and Translators of Literature in the English Renaissance*. London: Routledge, 1992.

Kuehn, Thomas. *Law, Family, and Women: Toward a Legal Anthropology of Renaissance Italy*. Chicago: University of Chicago Press, 1991.

Kunze, Bonnelyn Young. *Margaret Fell and the Rise of Quakerism*. Stanford: Stanford University Press, 1994.

Labalme, Patricia A., ed. *Beyond Their Sex: Learned Women of the European Past*. New York: New York University Press, 1980.

Lalande, Roxanne Decker, ed. *A Labor of Love: Critical Reflections on the Writings of Marie-Catherine Desjardins (Mme de Villedieu)*. Madison, NJ: Fairleigh Dickinson University Press, 2000.

Lamb, Mary Ellen. *Gender and Authorship in the Sidney Circle*. Madison: University of Wisconsin Press, 1990.

Laqueur, Thomas. *Making Sex: Body and Gender from the Greeks to Freud*. Cambridge: Harvard University Press, 1990.

Larsen, Anne R., and Colette H. Winn, eds. *Renaissance Women Writers: French Texts/American Contexts*. Detroit: Wayne State University Press, 1994.

Laven, Mary. *Virgins of Venice: Broken Vows and Cloistered Lives in the Renaissance Convent*. New York: Viking, 2003.

Ledkovsky, Marina, Charlotte Rosenthal, and Mary Zirin, eds. *Dictionary of Russian Women Writers*. Westport, CT: Greenwood Press, 1994.

Lehfeldt, Elizabeth A. *Religious Women in Golden Age Spain: The Permeable Cloister*. Burlington, VT: Ashgate, 2005.

Leonard, Amy. *Nails in the Wall: Catholic Nuns in Reformation Germany*. Women in Culture and Society. Chicago: University of Chicago Press, 2005.

Lerner, Gerda. *The Creation of Feminist Consciousness, 1000–1870*. New York: Oxford University Press, 1994.

———. *The Creation of Patriarchy* New York: Oxford University Press, 1986.

Levack. Brian P. *The Witch Hunt in Early Modern Europe*. London: Longman, 1987.

Levin, Carole, and Jeanie Watson, eds. *Ambiguous Realities: Women in the Middle Ages and Renaissance*. Detroit: Wayne State University Press, 1987.

Levin, Carole, Jo Eldridge Carney, and Debra Barrett-Graves. *Elizabeth I: Always Her Own Free Woman*. Burlington, VT: Ashgate, 2003.

Levin, Carole, et al. *Extraordinary Women of the Medieval and Renaissance World: A Biographical Dictionary*. Westport, CT: Greenwood Press, 2000.

Levy, Allison, ed. *Widowhood and Visual Culture in Early Modern Europe*. Burlington, VT: Ashgate, 2003.

Lewalski, Barbara Kiefer. *Writing Women in Jacobean England*. Cambridge: Harvard University Press, 1993.

Lewis, Gertrud Jaron. *By Women for Women about Women: The Sister-Books of Fourteenth-Century Germany*. Toronto: University of Toronto Press, 1996.

Lewis, Jayne Elizabeth. *Mary Queen of Scots: Romance and Nation*. London: Routledge, 1998.

Lindenauer, Leslie J. *Piety and Power: Gender and Religious Culture in the American Colonies, 1630–1700*. London: Routledge, 2002.

Lindsey, Karen. *Divorced Beheaded Survived: A Feminist Reinterpretation of the Wives of Henry VIII*. Reading, MA: Addison-Wesley, 1995.

Liss, Peggy K. *Isabel the Queen: Life and Times*. Rev. ed. Philadelphia: University of Pennsylvania Press, 2004.

Loades, David. *Mary Tudor: A Life*. Cambridge: Basil Blackwell, 1989.

Lochrie, Karma. *Margery Kempe and Translations of the Flesh*. Philadelphia: University of Pennsylvania Press, 1992.

Longfellow, Ewrica. *Women and Religious Writing in Early Modern England*. Cambridge: Cambridge University Press, 2004.

Lougee, Carolyn C. *Le Paradis des Femmes: Women, Salons, and Social Stratification in Seventeenth-Century France*. Princeton: Princeton University Press, 1976.

Love, Harold. *The Culture and Commerce of Texts: Scribal Publication in Seventeenth-Century England*. Amherst: University of Massachusetts Press, 1993.

Lowe, K. J. P. *Nuns' Chronicles and Convent Culture in Renaissance and Counter-Reformation Italy*. Cambridge: Cambridge University Press, 2003.

Lux-Sterritt, Laurence. *Redefining Female Religious Life: French Ursulines and English Ladies in Seventeenth-Century Catholicism*. Burlington, VT: Ashgate, 2005.

MacCarthy, Bridget G. *The Female Pen: Women Writers and Novelists, 1621–1818*. Preface by Janet Todd. New York: New York University Press, 1994. Originally published by Cork University Press, 1946–47.

Macfarlane, Alan. *Marriage and Love in England: Modes of Reproduction, 1300–1840*. New York: Basil Blackwell, 1986.

Mack, Phyllis. *Visionary Women: Ecstatic Prophecy in Seventeenth-Century England*. Berkeley: University of California Pres, 1992.

Maclean, Ian. *The Renaissance Notion of Woman: A Study of the Fortunes of Scholasticism and Medical Science in European Intellectual Life*. Cambridge: Cambridge University Press, 1980.

———. *Woman Triumphant: Feminism in French Literature, 1610–1652*. Oxford: Clarendon Press, 1977.

MacNeil, Anne. *Music and Women of the Commedia dell'Arte in the Late Sixteenth Century*. New York: Oxford University Press, 2003.

Maggi, Armando. *Uttering the Word: The Mystical Performances of Maria Maddalena de' Pazzi, a Renaissance Visionary*. Albany: State University of New York Press, 1998

Marshall, Sherrin, ed. *Women in Reformation and Counter-Reformation Europe: Public and Private Worlds*. Bloomington: Indiana University Press, 1989.

Masten, Jeffrey. *Textual Intercourse: Collaboration, Authorship, and Sexualities in Renaissance Drama*. Cambridge: Cambridge University Press, 1997.

Matter, E. Ann, and John Coakley, eds. *Creative Women in Medieval and Early Modern Italy*. Philadelphia: University of Pennsylvania Press, 1994.

McGrath, Lynette. *Subjectivity and Women's Poetry in Early Modern England*. Burlington, VT: Ashgate, 2002.

McIver, Katherine A. *Women, Art, and Architecture in Northern Italy, 1520–1580: Negotiating Power*. Women and Gender in the Early Modern World. Burlington, VT: Ashgate, 2006.

McLeod, Glenda. *Virtue and Venom: Catalogs of Women from Antiquity to the Renaissance*. Ann Arbor: University of Michigan Press, 1991.

McSheffrey, Shannon. *Gender and Heresy: Women and Men in Lollard Communities, 1420–1530*. Philadelphia: University of Pennsylvania Press, 1995.

McTavish, Lianne. *Childbirth and the Display of Authority in Early Modern France*. Burlington, VT: Ashgate, 2005.

Medwick, Cathleen. *Teresa of Avila: The Progress of a Soul*. New York: Doubleday, 1999.

Meek, Christine, ed. *Women in Renaissance and Early Modern Europe.* Dublin, Ireland: Four Courts Press, 2000.

Mendelson, Sara, and Patricia Crawford. *Women in Early Modern England, 1550–1720.* Oxford: Clarendon Press, 1998.

Merchant, Carolyn. *The Death of Nature: Women, Ecology, and the Scientific Revolution.* New York: HarperCollins, 1980.

Merrim, Stephanie. *Early Modern Women's Writing and Sor Juana Inés de la Cruz.* Nashville: Vanderbilt University Press, 1999.

Messbarger, Rebecca. *The Century of Women: The Representations of Women in Eighteenth-Century Italian Public Discourse.* Toronto: University of Toronto Press, 2002.

Midelfort, Erik H. C. *Witchhunting in Southwestern Germany, 1562–1684: The Social and Intellectual Foundations.* Stanford: Stanford University Press, 1972.

Migiel, Marilyn, and Juliana Schiesari. *Refiguring Woman: Perspectives on Gender and the Italian Renaissance.* Ithaca: Cornell University Press, 1991.

Miller, Nancy K. *The Heroine's Text: Readings in the French and English Novel, 1722–1782.* New York: Columbia University Press, 1980.

Miller, Naomi J. *Changing the Subject: Mary Wroth and Figurations of Gender in Early Modern England.* Lexington: University Press of Kentucky, 1996.

Miller, Naomi J., and Gary Waller, eds. *Reading Mary Wroth: Representing Alternatives in Early Modern England.* Knoxville: University of Tennessee Press, 1991.

Miller, Naomi J., and Naomi Yavneh. *Sibling Relations and Gender in the Early Modern World: Sisters, Brothers and Others.* Burlington, VT: Ashgate, 2006.

Monson, Craig A., ed. *The Crannied Wall: Women, Religion, and the Arts in Early Modern Europe.* Ann Arbor: University of Michigan Press, 1992.

Monson, Craig A. *Disembodied Voices: Music and Culture in an Early Modern Italian Convent.* Berkeley: University of California Press, 1995.

Monter, E. William. *Witchcraft in France and Switzerland: The Borderlands during the Reformation.* Ithaca: Cornell University Press, 1976.

Montrose, Louis Adrian. *The Subject of Elizabeth: Authority, Gender, and Representation.* Chicago: University of Chicago Press, 2006.

Mooney, Catherine M. *Gendered Voices: Medieval Saints and Their Interpreters.* Philadelphia: University of Pennsylvania Press, 1999.

Moore, Cornelia Niekus. *The Maiden's Mirror: Reading Material for German Girls in the Sixteenth and Seventeenth Centuries.* Wiesbaden: Otto Harrassowitz, 1987.

Moore, Mary B. *Desiring Voices: Women Sonneteers and Petrarchism.* Carbondale: Southern Illinois University Press, 2000.

Mujica, Bárbara. *Women Writers of Early Modern Spain.* New Haven: Yale University Press, 2004.

Murphy, Caroline. *The Pope's Daughter: The Extraordinary Life of Felice Della Rovere.* New York: Oxford University Press, 2005.

Musacchio, Jacqueline Marie. *The Art and Ritual of Childbirth in Renaissance Italy.* New Haven: Yale University Press, 1999.

Nader, Helen, ed. *Power and Gender in Renaissance Spain: Eight Women of the Mendoza Family, 1450–1650.* Urbana: University of Illinois Press, 2004.

Nevitt, Marcus. *Women and the Pamphlet Culture of Revolutionary England, 1640–1660.* Women and Gender in the Early Modern World. Burlington, VT: Ashgate, 2006.

Newman, Barbara. *God and the Goddesses: Vision, Poetry, and Belief in the Middle Ages.* Philadelphia: University of Pennsylvania Press, 2003.

Newman, Karen. *Fashioning Femininity and English Renaissance Drama*. Chicago: University of Chicago Press, 1991.

Novy, Marianne. *Love's Argument: Gender Relations in Shakespeare*. Chapel Hill: University of North Carolina Press, 1984.

O'Donnell, Mary Ann. *Aphra Behn: An Annotated Bibliography of Primary and Secondary Sources*. 2nd ed. Brookfield: Ashgate, 2004.

Okin, Susan Moller. *Women in Western Political Thought*. Princeton: Princeton University Press, 1979.

Ozment, Steven. *The Bürgermeister's Daughter: Scandal in a Sixteenth-Century German Town*. New York: St. Martin's Press, 1995.

———. *Flesh and Spirit: Private Life in Early Modern Germany*. New York: Penguin Putnam, 1999.

———. *When Fathers Ruled: Family Life in Reformation Europe*. Cambridge: Harvard University Press, 1983.

Pacheco, Anita, ed. *Early [English] Women Writers: 1600–1720*. New York: Longman, 1998.

Pagels, Elaine. *Adam, Eve, and the Serpent*. New York: Harper Collins, 1988.

Panizza, Letizia, ed. *Women in Italian Renaissance Culture and Society*. Oxford: European Humanities Research Centre, 2000.

Panizza, Letizia, and Sharon Wood, eds. *A History of Women's Writing in Italy*. Cambridge: University Press, 2000.

Pantel, Pauline Schmitt. *From Ancient Goddesses to Christian Saints*. Vol. 1 of *A History of Women in the West*. Cambridge: Harvard University Press, 1992.

Pardailhé-Galabrun, Annik. *The Birth of Intimacy: Privacy and Domestic Life in Early Modern Paris*. Philadelphia: University of Pennsylvania Press, 1992.

Park, Katharine. *The Secrets of Women: Gender, Generation, and the Origins of Human Dissection*. New York: Zone Books, 2006.

Parker, Patricia. *Literary Fat Ladies: Rhetoric, Gender, and Property*. London: Methuen, 1987.

Perlingieri, Ilya Sandra. *Sofonisba Anguissola: The First Great Woman Artist of the Renaissance*. New York: Rizzoli, 1992.

Pernoud, Regine, and Marie-Veronique Clin. *Joan of Arc: Her Story*. Rev. and trans. Jeremy DuQuesnay Adams. New York: St. Martin's Press, 1998. French original, 1986.

Perry, Mary Elizabeth. *Crime and Society in Early Modern Seville*. Hanover, NH: University Press of New England, 1980.

———. *Gender and Disorder in Early Modern Seville*. Princeton: Princeton University Press, 1990.

———. *The Handless Maiden: Moriscos and the Politics of Religion in Early Modern Spain*. Princeton: Princeton University Press, 2005.

Perry, Ruth. *The Celebrated Mary Astell: An Early English Feminist*. Chicago: University of Chicago Press, 1986.

Peters, Christine. *Patterns of Piety: Women, Gender and Religion in Late Medieval and Reformation England*. Cambridge: Cambridge University Press, 2003.

Petroff, Elizabeth A., ed. *Medieval Women's Visionary Literature*. New York: Oxford University Press, 1986.

Phillippy, Patricia Berrahou. *Painting Women: Cosmetics, Canvases, and Early Modern Culture*. Baltimore: Johns Hopkins University Press, 2006.

Plowden, Alison. *Tudor Women: Queens and Commoners*. Rev. ed. Thrupp, Stroud, Gloucestershire: Sutton, 1998.

Poor, Sara S., and Jana K. Schulman. *Women and Medieval Epic: Gender, Genre, and the Limits of Epic Masculinity*. New York: Palgrave Macmillan, 2007.

Price, Paola Malpezzi, and Christine Ristaino. *Lucrezia Marinella and the "Querelle des femmes" in Seventeenth-Century Italy*. Madison, NJ: Fairleigh Dickinson University Press, 2008.

Prior, Mary, ed. *Women in English Society, 1500–1800*. London: Methuen, 1985.

Quilligan, Maureen. *The Allegory of Female Authority: Christine de Pizan's "Cité des Dames."* Ithaca: Cornell University Press, 1991.

———. *Incest and Agency in Elizabeth's England*. Philadelphia: University of Pennsylvania Press, 2005.

Rabil, Albert. *Laura Cereta: Quattrocento Humanist*. Binghamton, NY: Medieval and Renaissance Texts and Studies, 1981.

Ranft, Patricia. *Women in Western Intellectual Culture, 600–1500*. New York: Palgrave, 2002.

Rapley, Elizabeth. *The Devotés: Women and Church in Seventeenth-Century France*. Kingston, Ontario: McGill-Queen's University Press, 1989.

———. *A Social History of the Cloister: Daily Life in the Teaching Monasteries of the Old Regime*. Montreal: McGill-Queen's University Press, 2001.

Raven, James, Helen Small, and Naomi Tadmor, eds. *The Practice and Representation of Reading in England*. Cambridge: Cambridge University Press, 1996.

Reardon, Colleen. *Holy Concord within Sacred Walls: Nuns and Music in Siena, 1575–1700*. Oxford: Oxford University Press, 2001.

Reid, Jonathan Andrew. "King's Sister—Queen of Dissent: Marguerite of Navarre (1492–1549) and Her Evangelical Network." Ph.D diss., University of Arizona, 2001.

Reiss, Sheryl E., and David G. Wilkins, eds. *Beyond Isabella: Secular Women Patrons of Art in Renaissance Italy*. Kirksville, MO: Turman State University Press, 2001.

Rheubottom, David. *Age, Marriage, and Politics in Fifteenth-Century Ragusa*. Oxford: Oxford University Press, 2000.

Richards, Earl Jeffrey, ed., with Joan Williamson, Nadia Margolis, and Christine Reno. *Reinterpreting Christine de Pizan*. Athens: University of Georgia Press, 1992.

Richardson, Brian. *Printing, Writers, and Readers in Renaissance Italy*. Cambridge: Cambridge University Press, 1999.

Riddle, John M. *Contraception and Abortion from the Ancient World to the Renaissance*. Cambridge: Harvard University Press, 1992.

———. *Eve's Herbs: A History of Contraception and Abortion in the West*. Cambridge: Harvard University Press, 1997.

Robin, Diana. *Publishing Women: Salons, the Presses, and the Counter-Reformation in Sixteenth-Century Italy*. Chicago: University of Chicago Press, 2007.

Robin, Diana, Anne R. Larsen, and Carole Levin, eds. *Encyclopedia of Women in the Renaissance: Italy, France, and England*. Santa Barbara, CA: ABC Clio, 2007.

Roelker, Nancy L. *Queen of Navarre, Jeanne d'Albret, 1528–1572*. Cambridge: Harvard University Press, 1968.

Roper, Lyndal. *The Holy Household: Women and Morals in Reformation Augsburg*. New York: Oxford University Press, 1989.

Rose, Mary Beth. *The Expense of Spirit: Love and Sexuality in English Renaissance Drama.* Ithaca: Cornell University Press, 1988.

———. *Gender and Heroism in Early Modern English Literature*. Chicago: University of Chicago Press, 2002.

———, ed. *Women in the Middle Ages and the Renaissance: Literary and Historical Perspectives*. Syracuse: Syracuse University Press, 1986.

Rosenthal, Margaret F. *The Honest Courtesan: Veronica Franco, Citizen and Writer in Sixteenth-Century Venice*. Foreword by Catharine R. Stimpson. Chicago: University of Chicago Press, 1992.

Rublack, Ulinka, ed. *Gender in Early Modern German History*. Cambridge: Cambridge University Press, 2002.

Ruggiero, Guido. *Binding Passions: Tales of Magic, Marriage, and Power at the End of the Renaissance*. Oxford: Oxford University Press, 1993.

———. *The Boundaries of Eros: Sex Crime and Sexuality in Renaissance Venice*. New York: Oxford University Press, 1985.

Russell, Rinaldina, ed. *Feminist Encyclopedia of Italian Literature*. Westport, CT: Greenwood Press, 1997.

———. *Italian Women Writers: A Bio-bibliographical Sourcebook*. Westport, CT: Greenwood Press, 1994.

Sackville-West, Vita. *Daughter of France: The Life of La Grande Mademoiselle*. Garden City, NY: Doubleday, 1959.

Safley, Thomas Max. *Let No Man Put Asunder: The Control of Marriage in the German Southwest: A Comparative Study, 1550–1600*. Kirksville, MO: Sixteenth Century Journal Publishers, 1984.

Sage, Lorna, ed. *Cambridge Guide to Women's Writing in English*. Cambridge: University Press, 1999.

Sánchez, Magdalena S. *The Empress, the Queen, and the Nun: Women and Power at the Court of Philip III of Spain*. Baltimore: Johns Hopkins University Press, 1998.

Sankovitch, Tilde A. *French Women Writers and the Book: Myths of Access and Desire*. Syracuse: Syracuse University Press, 1988.

Sartori, Eva Martin, and Dorothy Wynne Zimmerman, eds. *French Women Writers: A Bio-bibliographical Source Book*. Westport, CT: Greenwood Press, 1991.

Scaraffia, Lucetta, and Gabriella Zarri. *Women and Faith: Catholic Religious Life in Italy from Late Antiquity to the Present*. Cambridge: Harvard University Press, 1999.

Scheepsma, Wybren. *Medieval Religious Women in the Low Countries: The "Modern Devotion'," the Canonesses of Windesheim, and Their Writings*. Rochester, NY: Boydell Press, 2004.

Schiebinger, Londa. *The Mind Has No Sex? Women in the Origins of Modern Science*. Cambridge: Harvard University Press, 1991.

———. *Nature's Body: Gender in the Making of Modern Science*. Boston: Beacon Press, 1993.

Schofield, Mary Anne, and Cecilia Macheski, eds. *Fetter'd or Free? British Women Novelists, 1670–1815*. Athens: Ohio University Press, 1986.

Schroeder, Joy A. *Dinah's Lament: The Biblical Legacy of Sexual Violence in Christian Interpretation*. Philadelphia: Fortress Press, 2007.

Schutte, Anne Jacobson. *Aspiring Saints: Pretense of Holiness, Inquisition, and Gender in the Republic of Venice, 1618–1750*. Baltimore: Johns Hopkins University Press, 2001.

———, Thomas Kuehn, and Silvana Seidel Menchi, eds. *Time, Space, and Women's Lives in Early Modern Europe*. Kirksville, MO: Truman State University Press, 2001.

Seelig, Sharon Cadman. *Autobiography and Gender in Early Modern Literature: Reading Women's Lives, 1600–1680*. Cambridge: Cambridge University Press, 2006.

Seifert, Lewis C. *Fairy Tales, Sexuality, and Gender in France, 1690–1715: Nostalgic Utopias*. Cambridge: Cambridge University Press, 1996.

Shannon, Laurie. *Sovereign Amity: Figures of Friendship in Shakespearean Contexts*. Chicago: University of Chicago Press, 2002.

Shemek, Deanna. *Ladies Errant: Wayward Women and Social Order in Early Modern Italy*. Durham: Duke University Press, 1998.

Shepherd, Simon. *Amazons and Warrior Women: Varieties of Feminism in Seventeenth-Century Drama*. New York: St. Martin's Press, 1981.

Slater, Miriam. *Family Life in the Seventeenth Century: The Verneys of Claydon House*. London: Routledge and Kegan Paul, 1984.

Smarr, Janet L. *Joining the Conversation: Dialogues by Renaissance Women*. Ann Arbor: University of Michigan Press, 2005.

Smith, Hilda L. *Reason's Disciples: Seventeenth-Century English Feminists*. Urbana: University of Illinois Press, 1982.

———. *Women Writers and the Early Modern British Political Tradition*. Cambridge: Cambridge University Press, 1998.

Snook, Edith. *Women, Reading, and the Cultural Politics of Early Modern England*. Brookfield: Ashgate, 2005.

Sobel, Dava. *Galileo's Daughter: A Historical Memoir of Science, Faith, and Love*. New York: Penguin Books, 2000.

Sommerville, Margaret R. *Sex and Subjection: Attitudes to Women in Early-Modern Society*. London: Arnold, 1995.

Soufas, Teresa Scott. *Dramas of Distinction: A Study of Plays by Golden Age Women*. Lexington: University Press of Kentucky, 1997.

Spencer, Jane. *The Rise of the Woman Novelist: From Aphra Behn to Jane Austen*. Oxford: Basil Blackwell, 1986.

Spender, Dale. *Mothers of the Novel: One Hundred Good Women Writers before Jane Austen*. London: Routledge, 1986.

Sperling, Jutta Gisela. *Convents and the Body Politic in Late Renaissance Venice*. Foreword by Catharine R. Stimpson. Chicago: University of Chicago Press, 1999.

Staley, Lynn. *Margery Kempe's Dissenting Fictions*. University Park: Pennsylvania State University Press, 1994.

Steinbrügge, Lieselotte. *The Moral Sex: Woman's Nature in the French Enlightenment*. Trans. Pamela E. Selwyn. New York: Oxford University Press, 1995.

Stephens, Sonya, ed. *A History of Women's Writing in France*. Cambridge: Cambridge University Press, 2000.

Stephenson, Barbara. *The Power and Patronage of Marguerite de Navarre*. Burlington, VT: Ashgate, 2004.

Stevenson, Jane. *Women Latin Poets: Language, Gender, and Authority, from Antiquity to the Eighteenth Century*. New York: Oxford University Press, 2005.

Stocker, Margarita. *Judith, Sexual Warrior: Women and Power in Western Culture*. New Haven: Yale University Press, 1998.

Stone, Lawrence. *Family, Marriage, and Sex in England, 1500–1800*. New York: Weidenfeld & Nicolson, 1977; abridged edition, New York: Harper & Row, 1979.

Straznacky, Marta. *Privacy, Playreading, and Women's Closet Drama, 1550–1700*. Cambridge: Cambridge University Press, 2004.

Stretton, Timothy. *Women Waging Law in Elizabethan England*. Cambridge: Cambridge University Press, 1998.

Strinati, Claudio M., Carole Collier Frick, Elizabeth S. G. Nicholson, Vera Fortunati Pietrantonio, and Jordana Pomeroy. *Italian Women Artists: From Renaissance to Baroque*. Ed. National Museum of Women in the Arts, Sylvestre Verger Art Organization. New York: Skira, 2007.

Stuard, Susan Mosher. *Gilding the Market: Luxury and Fashion in Fourteenth-Century Italy*. Middle Ages Series. Philadelphia: University of Pennsylvania Press, 2006.

Summit, Jennifer. *Lost Property: The Woman Writer and English Literary History, 1380–1589*. Chicago: University of Chicago Press, 2000.

Surtz, Ronald E. *The Guitar of God: Gender, Power, and Authority in the Visionary World of Mother Juana de la Cruz (1481–1534)*. Philadelphia: University of Pennsylvania Press, 1991.

———. *Writing Women in Late Medieval and Early Modern Spain: The Mothers of Saint Teresa of Avila*. Philadelphia: University of Pennsylvania Press, 1995.

Suzuki, Mihoko. *Subordinate Subjects: Gender, the Political Nation, and Literary Form in England, 1588–1688*. Brookfield: Ashgate, 2003.

Tatlock, Lynne, and Christiane Bohnert, eds. *The Graph of Sex and the German Text: Gendered Culture in Early Modern Germany, 1500–1700*. Amsterdam: Rodopi, 1994.

Teague, Frances. *Bathsua Makin, Woman of Learning*. Lewisburg, PA: Bucknell University Press, 1999.

Thomas, Anabel. *Art and Piety in the Female Religious Communities of Renaissance Italy: Iconography, Space, and the Religious Woman's Perspective*. New York: Cambridge University Press, 2003.

Thompson, John Lee. *John Calvin and the Daughters of Sarah: Women in Regular and Exceptional Roles in the Exegesis of Calvin, His Predecessors, and His Contemporaries*. Travaux d'Humanisme et Renaissance 259. Geneva: Librairie Droz, 1992.

Tinagli, Paola. *Women in Italian Renaissance Art: Gender, Representation, Identity*. Manchester: Manchester University Press, 1997.

Todd, Janet. *The Secret Life of Aphra Behn*. London: Pandora, 2000.

———. *The Sign of Angelica: Women, Writing, and Fiction, 1660–1800*. New York: Columbia University Press, 1989.

Tomas, Natalie R. *The Medici Women: Gender and Power in Renaissance Florence*. Burlington, VT: Ashgate, 2004.

Traub, Valerie. *The Renaissance of Lesbianism in Early Modern England*. Cambridge: Cambridge University Press, 2002.

Valenze, Deborah. *The First Industrial Woman*. New York: Oxford University Press, 1995.

Van Dijk, Susan, Lia van Gemert, and Sheila Ottway, eds. *Writing the History of Women's Writing: Toward an International Approach*. Proceedings of the Colloquium, Amsterdam, 9–11 September. Amsterdam: Royal Netherlands Academy of Arts and Sciences, 2001.

Vickery, Amanda. *The Gentleman's Daughter: Women's Lives in Georgian England*. New Haven: Yale University Press, 1998.

Vollendorf, Lisa. *The Lives of Women: A New History of Inquisitional Spain*. Nashville: Vanderbilt University Press, 2005.

———, ed. *Recovering Spain's Feminist Tradition*. New York: MLA, 2001.

Waithe, Mary Ellen, ed. *A History of Women Philosophers*. 3 vols. Dordrecht: Martinus Nijhoff, 1987.

Walker, Claire. *Gender and Politics in Early Modern Europe: English Convents in France and the Low Countries*. New York: Palgrave, 2003.

Wall, Wendy. *The Imprint of Gender: Authorship and Publication in the English Renaissance*. Ithaca: Cornell University Press, 1993.

Walsh, William T. *St. Teresa of Avila: A Biography*. Rockford, IL: TAN Books, 1987.

Warner, Marina. *Alone of All Her Sex: The Myth and Cult of the Virgin Mary*. New York: Knopf, 1976.

———. *Joan of Arc: The Image of Female Heroism*. Berkeley: University of California Press, 1981.

Warnicke, Retha M. *The Marrying of Anne of Cleves: Royal Protocol in Tudor England*. Cambridge: Cambridge University Press, 2000.

———. *Mary Queen of Scots*. Routledge Historical Biographies. New York: Routledge, 2006.

———. *The Rise and Fall of Anne Boleyn: Family Politics at the Court of Henry VIII*. Cambridge: Cambridge University Press, 1989.

———. *Women of the English Renaissance and Reformation*. Westport, CT: Greenwood Press, 1983.

Warren, Nancy Bradley. *Women of God and Arms: Female Spirituality and Political Conflict, 1380–1600*. Philadelphia: University of Pennsylvania Press, 2005.

Watt, Diane. *Secretaries of God: Women Prophets in Late Medieval and Early Modern England*. Cambridge, England: D. S. Brewer, 1997.

Weaver, Elissa B. *Convent Theatre in Early Modern Italy: Spiritual Fun and Learning for Women*. New York: Cambridge University Press, 2002.

Weber, Alison. *Teresa of Avila and the Rhetoric of Femininity*. Princeton: Princeton University Press, 1990.

Weinstein, Donald, and Rudolph M. Bell. *Saints and Society: The Two Worlds of Western Christendom, 1000–1700*. Chicago: University of Chicago Press, 1982.

Welles, Marcia L. *Persephone's Girdle: Narratives of Rape in Seventeenth-Century Spanish Literature*. Nashville: Vanderbilt University Press, 2000.

Whitehead, Barbara J., ed. *Women's Education in Early Modern Europe: A History, 1500–1800*. New York: Garland, 1999.

Wiesner-Hanks, Merry E. *Christianity and Sexuality in the Early Modern World: Regulating Desire, Reforming Practice*. New York: Routledge, 2000.

———. *Gender, Church, and State in Early Modern Germany: Essays*. New York: Longman, 1998.

———. *Gender in History*. Malden, MA: Blackwell, 2001.

———. *Women and Gender in Early Modern Europe*. Cambridge, UK: Cambridge University Press, 1993.

———. *Working Women in Renaissance Germany*. New Brunswick, NJ: Rutgers University Press, 1986.

Willard, Charity Cannon. *Christine de Pizan: Her Life and Works*. New York: Persea Books, 1984.

Wilson, Katharina, ed. *Encyclopedia of Continental Women Writers*. 2 vols. New York: Garland, 1991.

Wiltenburg, Joy. *Disorderly Women and Female Power in the Street Literature of Early Modern England and Germany*. Charlottesville: University Press of Virginia, 1992.

Winn, Colette, and Donna Kuizenga, eds. *Women Writers in Pre-Revolutionary France*. New York: Garland, 1997.

Winston-Allen, Anne. *Convent Chronicles: Women Writing about Women and Reform in the Late Middle Ages*. University Park: Pennsylvania State University Press, 2004.

Woodbridge, Linda. *Women and the English Renaissance: Literature and the Nature of Womankind, 1540–1620*. Urbana: University of Illinois Press, 1984.

Woodford, Charlotte. *Nuns as Historians in Early Modern Germany*. Oxford: Clarendon Press, 2002.

Woods, Susanne. *Lanyer: A Renaissance Woman Poet*. New York: Oxford University Press, 1999.

Woods, Susanne, and Margaret P. Hannay, eds. *Teaching Tudor and Stuart Women Writers*. New York: MLA, 2000.

Wormald, Jenny. *Mary Queen of Scots: A Study in Failure*. London: George Philip Press, 1988.

Zinsser, Judith P. *Men, Women, and the Birthing of Modern Science*. DeKalb: Northern Illinois University Press, 2005.

INDEX